MORE FOR TIMOTHY

The first instalment of this letter,
already published, is called
MY DEAR TIMOTHY
★
Compiled by the writer
A YEAR OF GRACE:
*Passages chosen and arranged to
express a mood about God and man*
8th impression

MORE FOR TIMOTHY

being

the second instalment of an

Autobiographical Letter to his Grandson

by

VICTOR GOLLANCZ

LONDON
14 HENRIETTA STREET COVENT GARDEN
1953

For David Somervell
as well as for Timothy

But if there had been a circumcision of such natures in the days of their youth . . . the very same faculty in them would have seen the truth as keenly as they see what their eyes are turned to now.

PLATO (*The Republic*)

CONTENTS

"IN FRONT OF US a curious figure was standing, a little crouched, legs straddled, arms held out from his sides. He had no eyes, and the whole of his body, nearly all of which was visible through tatters of burnt rags, was covered with a hard black crust speckled with yellow pus. A Korean woman by his side began to speak, and the interpreter said: 'He has to stand, sir, cannot sit or lie.'

"He had to stand because he was no longer covered with a skin, but with a crust like crackling which broke easily."

The orchard is very peaceful this morning. Freshness seems everywhere. The grass sways gently, mottled with shadow and sun. A little hay is still lying about: it makes the air smell sweet. The apples are just beginning.

God forgive us all.

The napalm bomb, which turns a man into the creature just described, was first used in Korea—used by us, the United Nations—after I'd finished the draft of *Tim I* (that's how I think now of "My Dear Timothy"). When I read that account in the *Manchester Guardian* just as I was embarking on revision I longed to introduce it somewhere, because silence, I felt, would be shameful; but this was impossible—I had dated the writing throughout, and couldn't pretend things had occurred when they hadn't. So I decided to wait till I was ready for this second instalment, but for not a single moment longer.

What am I to say, Timothy? I don't think I've ever felt so poignantly how inadequate words are, and how feeble, even when working at its hardest, is the power of imagination. I sit here in this paradise, and try to experience in my own person what it must feel like to stand—never to lie, never to sit, never to lean—till the moment of death; and I find I cannot do it. Oh but we must somehow *learn* to do it if we are ever to stop betraying so dreadfully our common human nature; for we shall go on devising new torments, and increasingly horrible ones, for the enemy Christ told us to love, until we know—not postulate intellectually but spiritually know—that what we are doing to the other we are doing to ourselves: and we cannot know it, know it immediately in this spiritual sense, until we have really become that *one* with the other it is our human destiny to be.

I did succeed, many years ago, in identifying myself, all but fully, with the suffering of others. This was early in 1943, when we were trying to rescue a few victims of Hitlerite terror. My job was to address meetings and raise money; but I found that I quickly grew stale, and could no longer make people realise what such agony must be like. So I thought, Very well then, begin at home: realise it yourself. After that, I would arrive at the hall about half an hour early, and spend it feeling myself, with all the wholeness I could manage, into the situation of people at Dachau or Buchenwald. One night I was being gassed in a gas-chamber: the next, I was helping others dig our own mass grave, and then waiting for the splutter of a machine-gun. The physical results were a bit disastrous, as you'll learn; but—well, the audience responded. And now, ten years older, I find, to my sorrow and remorse, that I can no longer do it: can no longer do what a man should be able to do, and do with increasing wholeness, till the day of his death. A doctor of the early Greek Church, or Angelus Silesius, I forget which, said that we must all be Christs: so we must, if we are to be men.

And yet if few, even of those who may feel the necessity, have the power to live in others, and if centuries perhaps must go by before we all have it, we can at least, if we pause for a moment, understand at the level of intellect what we are doing to these Koreans; and I for my part will do it, or acquiesce in the doing of it, no longer. There was a lot about pacifism in *Timothy*, and one outburst in particular; but I was hanging in stays all that time, unwilling, in view of counterbalancing considerations, to take the plunge. I hesitate no further: I now declare myself a pacifist. I do so very diffidently, because at the moment I see no useful procedures for implementing my pacifism, and it is easy to say you are something and have done with it: easy, too, to be a pacifist in a negative sort of way—simply to abjure war as such, however "righteous", however

self-defensive, however genuinely undertaken from altruistic
motives—whereas the one thing required is an active pacifism
of help and love. On top of that, pacifism is particularly easy,
and in a sense you will appreciate particularly uncomfortable,
for a person no longer of military age. And yet—having arrived
at a certain position, one dare not be silent.

That "I declare myself" rings unpleasantly for another
reason too. Aren't you saying in effect, one is bound to ask
oneself, I at least will keep my hands clean? And isn't any such
personal consideration extremely dislikeable? It is, if it is there.
But I honestly don't think it *is* there. One isn't thinking of
oneself: one is acting with spontaneity as a man, a human
being, an indistinguishable bit of the universal humanity. The
temptation is no doubt immense to slide into personal involve-
ment or even into a deplorable self-satisfaction; and it cannot
be denied that pacifists are specially prone to these vices.
Nothing could be more important than to guard against them.
A pacifist ought to leave the "I" out of it altogether: his reaction
should be, "That particular expression of humanity just has to
act like this". But because a position one believes to be right
involves great spiritual perils that is no reason for refusing to
adopt it. Refusal for such a reason is indeed a mark of the
very egoism in question.

The napalm bomb—it is composed, I understand, of jellied
petrol, which unites stickily with a man's skin as it blazes and
cannot be detached, so that the man and the petrol burn as one
indivisible unit—has horrified me more than any single piece
of devilry, other than the murder camps, I've heard tell of or
personally witnessed since my boyhood: since the day, half a
century ago, when I saw that gravure of a decapitated infantry-
man on our table at Elgin Avenue. It has horrified me more
than what my friends used to tell me about no-man's-land in
Flanders, and about the creatures that lay about there with
their guts out until an ambulance or death brought release;
more than the photographs I suddenly noticed in a Paris shop-
window on my way to a good lunch, of obliterated features and
limbless trunks (but the remnants were alive); more than a
skeleton I saw die of starvation in a Düsseldorf hospital some
six years ago; more than a body I photographed near Hamburg,
so swollen with hunger oedema that its testicles reached the
ground; and more even than the account, in *We of Nagasaki*, of

what the atomising we debate with such dispassion had actually
meant:

"As I watched, two things that looked like great big hideous
lizards crawled in slowly, making croaking, groaning sounds.
Others followed. I was paralysed with horror for minutes.
Then the light got a little stronger and I could see they were
human beings—skinned alive by fire or heat, their bodies all
smashed where they had been thrown against something hard."

"After a few minutes I saw something coming up the road
along the river that looked like a parade of roast chickens. Some
of them kept asking for 'Water! Water!'
"They were all naked and they were skinned. The skin of
their hands had been torn away at the wrists. It was hanging
from their fingertips just behind the nails, turned inside-out
like a glove. In the dim light I thought I saw many other
children lying all about the yard."

Why the napalm bomb has had this effect on me I cannot
say. Perhaps, in a sense, it hasn't: perhaps any new instrument
of torture would have affected me similarly, and all this particular one did, when I was ready for the lesson, was to make
me realise at long last that men will go on for ever devising
subtler innovations of wickedness until enough of us have the
strength to say finally, "We will have done with this meeting of
evil by evil: to whatever evil, we will oppose only good."
Perhaps enough of us will never say it: perhaps a crescendo of
cruelty will continue till the end of time. That cannot matter:
or rather, for of course it can matter, that cannot affect how we
are to declare ourselves when we have at last achieved certainty; and cannot affect, which is far more important, what
we are to feel, what we are to do. Somehow we must become
pacifists in our whole inner being, so that our light may shine
forth with the activity of love even when, in the sense in which
we ordinarily understand the expression "doing", we can do
nothing. By our answering of evil with good at some moment
of time the more goodness there eternally *is* in the time process;
and that is sufficient.

Understand me, please, about Korea. I am not one of those
who would pretend that "the enemy" is guiltless, the more to
emphasise, as though this were necessary, the guilt we bear,

each of us, ourselves. They have done, I daresay, most of the things that we charge them with; and, yes, to make that awful rejoinder with which time after time we have sought to excuse our own villainies—I mean we of every nation at every period of history—"they started it": started it, of course this is, in the context of the last few years, though not of that secular process which produces one oppression out of another, one injustice out of another, one hatred out of another, and will continue to do so until we learn to cut in, with the rapier of living spirit, on the dead, brute cycle of cause and effect. And what if "the enemy" did start it? What if they also have committed outrages? Our business is not with them, but with ourselves.

And never fall, Timothy, as so many people fall in their spiritual carelessness, for the lying mental jargon of professional soldiers. They think of targets and scores (as in a game) and objectives: they fail to think of human beings. But a target doesn't *mean* anything, in the way in which a man means something. Humanity—such and such a human being, concrete, individual: unique in a self-consciousness that trembles and suffers, however many times you may multiply it—this is the sole reality in war. Cling to that truth, live with it: and you may be able, when your time comes, to be sure and direct where I have merely fumbled.

Brimpton, July 15th

What a lot people miss who lie asleep till all hours! I was writing in bed before daybreak this morning, at the little low window looking East; and as I put my nose out to smell the air, such a landscape met my eyes as you might come upon somewhere far North, or in a country of Poesque imagination. The crescent moon shone piercing cold, Venus still colder: the pines might have been soaring in an earlier, glacial epoch: and the heavens were white, behind thin bars of bluish cloud, "with the whiteness of driven snow". *Tekeli-li, tekeli-li.*

I went in at half past six to see Ruth, who has herpes on the face. It is extremely painful. What a horrible paradox is here! We do everything we can to ease the pain of a single human being: we would ask nothing better than to bear it ourselves, if only we could: and yet we are willing to inflict it, with napalm and atom bombs—inflict it deliberately—on millions. I felt again, as I stood by Ruth's bedside, that we shall never stop war, whatever machinery we may devise, until we have learned to think always, with a sort of desperate urgency and an utter self-identification, of single human beings.

Brimpton, July 17th

I want to add a footnote to these remarks about pacifism—or, better call it, non-retaliation. Lord Goddard has just been making a plea for the revival of flogging; and not only for its revival, but for its extension. He had previously, as you may remember from *Tim I*, merely advocated "a good hiding for young scamps".

For flogging, as ordinarily understood, read a whipping with the cat o' nine tails. The effect of it is to tear the flesh off a man's back, whereupon a hurricane of strokes is rained down on the raw and bleeding surface. (That the flesh is torn off is denied, but I do not believe the denial. Have a look at your own back in the glass, read a description of the cat, and visualise the result.) Lord Goddard, however, prefers the birch—as making the recipient "look ridiculous". The point is: you administer the whip to a man's back, but the birch to his bottom.

I say nothing of the mess that statistics could make of Lord Goddard, seeing that crimes formerly punishable by the lash have decreased since the lash was abolished: for statistics, I agree, can be jockeyed into proving anything—except, for the present example, what amateurs of lashing would like them to prove. But they are irrelevant anyhow. It isn't a question of mathematics, it's a question of right and wrong. The only real point is this. Lord Goddard believes, explicitly, in hurting and humiliating people; and Lord Goddard is the highest legal functionary in an England nominally Christian.

I am beginning to see this whole matter of crime and punishment as symbolic of the evil at the heart of our civilisation. On a single day, and in no more than two newspapers, I recently happened on the following:

(1) A woman with eight children was sentenced to five years' prison for blackmail. It is an awful sin: the more reason for being less than awful in the treatment of it. I am not referring to the length of the sentence: I am referring to the Judge's comment as he imposed it. "You are now asking for

mercy," he said. "How much mercy did you extend to him?" Tit for tat. "But I say unto you . . ."

(2) "Perhaps our prisons are too comfortable," another Judge, a Recorder, suggested. He had no use, he proceeded, for "sentimentality"—you could hear the word coming, it was inevitable—in the treatment of crime. "It raises a pleasant lump in the throat of a sentimentalist, but it makes a large hole in the pockets of the rest of us." Opportunities for reform, he agreed—I must add this in fairness—"should not be neglected".

(3) A Member of Parliament wrote as follows in a letter to the *Times*: "The fact remains that public opinion as expressed in the Press and the pulpit seems to be fairly unanimous. The growth of cruelty, the disregard of suffering, the greed of taking, even at the expense of life itself, have become so widespread that the national conscience has become gravely disturbed. Therefore, Sir, it seems to me, and to many others, that after a trial of three full years it is time that the abolition of corporal punishment should be reviewed by Parliament." In other words: There is an awful lot of cruelty about; be cruel, then, yourself, and so add to it.

What seems so odd in these people is that they should fail to put the blame for this violence where it clearly belongs. Have they ever, I wonder, read an account of how commandos were trained for the war recently ended? Of the bestialities deliberately induced in them? In case they haven't I append one—a very mild one indeed, with some of the foulest inhumanities no more than suggested:

"For nearly a year I ran a crime school. My pupils came to me from respectable homes. The Army paid me £15 a week and first-class travel to teach these boys how to pick locks and blow safes, how to kill with their bare hands or do scientific murder with a light walking-cane.

"They were young, special-service commandos—green-bonnets. Healthy, respectful, eagerly anxious to learn.

"We taught them how to make skeleton keys . . . how to hold a woman so that she could not scream while her hands were tied. And rough-house fighting that went even further than the vile stuff taught to infantrymen as 'unarmed combat'.

"They spent long summer afternoons in the English sunshine,

playing with slender, wicked killing-knives. Fresh young faces bent over a text-book illustration that showed exactly where to stick a knife-blade into a man from any angle, how far to push the blade into the flesh, and precisely how long—in calculated seconds—before he (a) lost consciousness; (b) died.

"Teaching a quiet polite lad to be ruthless is an art in itself. Expert psychologists hired by the War Office gave a lot of thought to it. We finally worked out a system.

"For instance, one morning they wouldn't get much break-fast. Then there would be long hours of exertion in the fresh air and sunlight. And the corporal would keep repeating: 'It's a smashing good dinner to-day, lads,' and detail a luscious menu of what was for lunch.

"Mouths watering, the students would finally trot to the dining-huts . . . where they found the orderly officer waiting.

" 'Sorry, men—but there's been an accident with the rations. One in four of you will have to go without food. So we've put portions out on plates in there'—indicating the interior of the mess hut. 'The first men to get to the plates, get the dinners!'

"Then the riot started. Scores of hungry, over-healthy youngsters who had spent all morning studying the arts of violence would rend, rip and scrimmage at the dining-hut doorway, clamber over each other, roll on the floor.

"No, it was not good manners. But it was never meant to be. Next time it would just be a blunt announcement: 'First fifty in get fed!'

"It was the same with week-end passes. 'Ten applicants—seven passes.' Seven specially marked identity discs were laid on the wooden table. 'Any man who produces one of those discs to the orderly-room sergeant gets a week-end pass.' Then they would be left alone with each other and with the passes for half an hour, with the door locked, after a significant wink from the departing sergeant.

"It was not just a question of snatching a lucky disc; you had to keep possession for thirty minutes. The three losers got fatigues and a universal shoving around for being unable to look after themselves.

"The essential spirit of the training was that every com-mando should be an independent unit, trained to live, think and kill as a man alone, with no aid and no advice from any-body.

"Sometimes, dismissing a parade at evening, the commanding officer would say: 'Next parade is ten o'clock tomorrow morning at Blackpool North Pier.' Nothing else. Men had to find their own way there. Perhaps it meant stealing a bicycle, filching some other unit's transport, dodging a ticketless ride on the railway. But by ten o'clock next day they had to be at the appointed place of parade—or in hospital or the police station. There was no other excuse taken.

"So, of course, they found it valuable knowledge to know how to steal a car, which is of course dead easy for the expert. The central pin of the door-handle on nearly every car is of cast-iron. Slip a hollow steel tube (or sparking-plug spanner) over the door-handle for extra leverage, give one sharp wrench, and the door opens . . .

"We had to teach how to overcome a man or woman quickly and silently. These men were being trained for stealthy work in enemy territory. There were several ways of doing it. How to tie their hands? Simply slip both wrists through the leather loop of a pocket truncheon, and twist the truncheon quickly until the thing is tight. A blow on the throat will prevent them uttering a sound for quite a while (if you administer it too hard it may prevent the victim from ever calling out again).

"One lad of nineteen earned a smile of praise for disarming a sentry, with deadly science, from behind. He is in Strangeways, Manchester, now. He robbed a man of his wallet by the same technique as we taught him.

"Knock a man out from behind? A child could do it. Give him a properly administered 'commando ear-box'. You will k.o. him, may give him concussion, may burst his ear-drums, may burst his brain. It will put him at your mercy. It may cripple him for life.

"You have to learn how to jump on a man when he is down, so you can be sure of killing him in one kick.

"As for the more thoughtful lectures, well, there are four ways to open somebody else's safe. You either (a) blow, (b) punch, (c) cut, (d) rip. We taught all methods.

"We taught them the whole filthy business. It didn't seem wrong, then. There was a kind of dedicated sincerity about it.

"And of course everybody praised us, told us we were doing a fine job. Very Important Persons inspected us, nodded encouragement.

"Well, the war is over now. We remembered to take the rifles from these lads—but we did nothing to take away those remembered months of satanic schooling."

Or do you want something shorter? The late Hilary St George Saunders, librarian at the time to the House of Commons, wrote a book, *The Green Beret,* in praise of these men's exploits. This, from Hobbes' *Leviathan,* is what he inscribed on the title page, as though glorying in it: "Force and Fraud are in war the two Cardinal Virtues."

I am making no attack on commandos as such, who I am sure showed exemplary courage: nor suggesting—I honestly haven't an idea, one way or the other—that the knifers and sluggers and cosh-boys are conspicuously drawn from their ranks. But their training was typical of the cruelty we not only licensed, but did our utmost to encourage, for six long years; and with human nature so malleable, and cruelty being cruelty whether licensed or not, did anybody really imagine that hey presto, when the fighting was over, you could call off the aftermath? There is only one remedy: not indulgence in still more cruelty, but a refusal to have truck any longer with any sort of cruelty at all.

CHAPTER II

THE COMMUNIST MENTALITY,
CONSCIENCE, AND TREASON

AFTER A GOOD DEAL of fumbling at the outbreak of the
1914 war (the point at which, a year ago, I came to a pause
in this letter), I joined up—with the Inns of Court O.T.C.:
formed fours on a parade ground in London: proceeded to
Berkhampstead: was among the first of my lot to become a lance-
corporal: enjoyed night ops, for their freshness and romance
and the smell of the country: learned the know-how of cleaning
a rifle, but not of shooting with it: got floored in map-reading:
was thought fit, after a month or so of this, to lead men into
battle, or at any rate home battle: got a commission, that first
winter, in a battalion (home service) of the Northumberland
Fusiliers: proceeded to Cambois (pronounced Cammus) near
Blyth: patrolled the coast of Northumberland: got involved
with the barbed-wire entanglements, or fell into the trenches,
when inspecting them by night: rather enjoyed this: enjoyed,
very much more, popping in from the darkness at intervals and
going to sleep on a moth-eaten sofa a couple of inches from an
anthracite furnace in a diminutive log-cabin: had little in
common with my associates: was extremely and deservedly
unpopular: borrowed a horse without asking permission in a
moment of enthusiasm, never having been on one before:
coaxed it down an incline to the ferry you took for Newcastle:
didn't know that I had to dismount before the diesel began
gasping: was immediately thrown, and brought the horse down
on top of me: faced a subalterns' court-martial, the horse being
the Colonel's: was found guilty, but can't remember the punishment: once awarded a few days' C.B. to a tomato-faced stam-
merer, who stared dumbly awhile and pumped away at his arm,
rather like Arnold Bennett, and then articulated, with quiet
force and extreme clarity, "booger, booger, booger": got intol-
erably bored: heard they wanted a master at Repton to lend a
hand, however flabby, with the school O.T.C.: applied, in the
jargon, to be "seconded": had my eyes tested: was judged unfit
for foreign service: proceeded to Repton in the March of that

year, which was nineteen-sixteen: and almost immediately found myself launched, along with David Somervell, on the experiment in "political education" that was to make me a publisher. It will be the heart, that experiment, of this volume; and should make a good story.

But it's jam, my dear Timothy, and you must wait for it. If only this were a diary! It's not merely that I'm always wanting to describe for you the sights and sounds, the events, odd or beautiful, that crop up every day of one's life with such charming prodigality. I should like to tell you, for instance, about the tiniest of episodes that I witnessed last week. I was standing, one of the stationary row, on an escalator at Paddington. Just behind me a little girl of six or seven was looking round us and up; and such an eagerness for life was on her face, such a glow of enchantment at the wonder of things (and of escalators in particular), that I went on my way as if from watching the dawn, or looking at crocuses in grass, or hearing a melody by Haydn.

And I should like to tell you, apropos of dawns, about the feel of the dew on my toes as I walk in the garden these mornings, at about half past four or five; with such a peace from head to foot of me afterwards as nothing else in all my life has ever given me, apart from sexual intercourse (the aftermath of sexual intercourse is identical). And I should like to tell you about last night. The great drought was still unbroken; every flower had lost its sweetness; then a few raindrops fell, and the whole garden, incontinently, was a counterpoint of fragrances. A little later we heard *Parsifal* from Bayreuth. What a mixture the man is! The bogus sensuality! Compare his flower-maiden claptrap with *Voici des roses*. And the bogus religion, you are inclined to add: then Good Friday is about you, borne in gently on the flute, and you stop criticising, and go to bed in peace.

(I can never mention Wagner without celebrating Verdi. What is it that makes one love Maestro Verdi with such a tender and smiling affection—love the man and not merely his music, and I mean really love and not worship him as one worships Beethoven? I was listening the other evening to *I Due Foscari* on the wireless. This is the rarest of incunables, antedating the canonical *Rigoletto* by a solid nine years; and I had thought of it as crude and even grotesque to the point of laughability. I began by tinkering away at some sentences I'd been writing before dinner and that you'll read in due course: but on a sudden—there it came, the great melody, sweet and easy and rounded and strong ("out of the strong came forth sweetness"); and then another and another and another—pouring out, flowing on, with a sort of inevitable prodigality like nature's in spring. So what could one do but just sit there and listen, and beam happily, and bless the old man? He is all heart, and will forever have mine.

There are two Foscari, as it happens, today. We drank cocktails with both of them at a party in Venice five or six years ago. Verdi, for me, was in the midst of us.

Better than any Verdi—but I insist one can speak of them in the same breath—was Beethoven's last quartet, opus 135, a few nights earlier. In what other piece of music, in what poem, in what painting, is heaven brought to earth with such an utter annihilation of distance as in the movement, solemn, slow, that all but ends it? And yet the dialogue that follows, THE VERY DIFFICULT RESOLUTION—isn't it even a little closer, in its spiritual gaiety, to ultimate faith? Don't believe all that nonsense about a reference in those words to Frau Schnaps or von Dembscher. The dying Beethoven is contemplating death: broodingly he asks, with terrible stridencies every time he breaks off, "Must it *be*?": there is one of those pauses that seem expectant on the peak of eternity: and then—oh, words cannot say it, it's no good talking of confident rapture, or even of a child's spontaneity as it begins to welcome life—the cry "It *must* be! It *must* be!" I know nothing so moving in the whole realm of art.)

Still, I can manage to keep my mouth shut, more or less, about such privacies as these—not that I've just been doing so: but about public affairs—I'm so made that I *cannot* keep silent. And I've been reading some paragraphs by Edward Crankshaw, in the current "Observer", that almost physically compel me to comment. Here they are:

"The continued failure of the Kremlin to wipe out large-scale corruption in industry . . . and the growing menace of widespread embezzlement and appropriation of communal property, is confirmed by a constant flow of reports through underground channels, which indicate a remarkable degree of demoralisation.

"Corruption is not limited to local managers and party officials, but extends to officials of the Republican Governments and even to visiting inspectors from Moscow, who put in favourable reports in return for appropriate bribes. . . .

"Many people in the West find it difficult to believe in this state of affairs . . . because they do not realise the extent to which the Russian heart has been reconquered by petty bourgeois ideals.

"Foreign visitors know what the glitter and splendour of the new officialdom looks like from the outside. One of the most praised plays of recent years, *Beketov's Career* by Sofronov, gives glimpses of what it looks like from the inside.

"The play deals with a wicked engineer who is trying to sabotage the production effort of his factory in order to get the factory director ruined so that he may step into his shoes.

"In one of the scenes, in order to explain the motives of his careerist villain, Sofronov gives a picture of the prizes open to the most able . . .

" 'Think!' exclaims the wicked engineer to his wife Masha, 'in a year or two, if all goes well, we shall get to Moscow! Moscow, Masha. Moscow! Because it is to Moscow that the best, the tested, the really capable, are always called.

" 'I might, who knows, become a departmental head. . . . Not so bad, Masha. Not so bad! And then, why not, a deputy Minister! . . . Think, Masha. . . . A flat on the Gorky street! A private villa on the outskirts, somewhere out by the reservoir!

" 'Oh, Moscow—city of cities. . . . And you, Masha—with your beauty you will dazzle the world. . . .

" 'I can see us together at a great reception. I stand a little apart and feast my eyes on you, surrounded by Ministers and Vice-admirals. If I close my eyes I can see you now. . . . You are wearing a long velvet dress the colour of a ripe cherry. You have golden bracelets glittering on your wrists. . . . And here, Masha, just a little above your heart, my heart, Masha, in the little groove, burns a diamond rose.'

"Beketov is a villain. He is a villain, however, not because he

wants to get to Moscow with a flat and a summer villa and
jewellery for his wife. These are legitimate prizes. He is a
villain because of the way he sets about it.

"It is hard to remember that he is not a provincial snob in a
short story by Chekhov, but a citizen of the first socialist
country in the world who has known only the Soviet way of
life."

Now I'm one of those people, as you know, who are always
pretty certain about the things they are certain about, but are
childishly delighted when a bit of evidence comes along to
confirm them; and I have the emotion of being helplessly in
prison, and yet of wilfully—in spite of my helplessness—
betraying the truth, until I've seen to it, somehow or other,
that anyone I can in any way get hold of learns what I have
just learned, and has had his last hesitation removed. I have
even rung up the printer, in the hope of inserting Crankshaw's
article as a sort of appendix to *Tim I*; but I'm too late—the
book's already on the machine.

You have probably guessed what I want to say. At the very
heart of *Tim I* was an enormously long chapter about socialism.
The burden of it was simple, and as follows: (1) Capitalism,
which consecrates the profit-motive, tends to make a man think,
in the context of earning his livelihood, first and mainly of himself, and so produces an atmosphere unfriendly to goodness—to
the going out of his self into a union that realises selfhood. The
capitalist way of living encourages greed: discourages altruism: makes gentleness, tolerance, mercy, fellow-feeling very
much harder than they might have been. (2) The machinery of
socialism—nationalisation and the rest—can make it easier for
men to be good, if certain conditions are fulfilled: and can do so
positively as well as negatively, because the right kind of socialism (a) has abolished the climate of pushfulness in workaday
life (this is its negative contribution) and (b) has replaced it by
a climate of altruism (this is its positive one): and altruism, co-
operation—in an activity so ubiquitous as earning our livelihood
—must encourage our other-regarding impulses over our whole
way of thinking and feeling. (3) But economic and political systems, capitalism and socialism and whatnot, can act *only* as

encouragers or discouragers: they cannot *make* us, fundamentally, good or bad. Goodness is something that happens in the
depths of our being, and happens by our co-operation with
grace; and badness is its failure to happen, through misunderstanding. (4) So the individual is everything—the single, the
unique human being, the heart and mind in every localised expression of the universal personality. Religion, therefore—I use
the word, I need not say, in no credal definition—has an absolute priority over economics; and the function of economics (a
function so important that one must be ever on one's guard, in
such a summary as this, against appearing to undervalue it) is
to be the handmaid of religion.

Call it, if you like, what I've been saying, the ethical approach
to socialism. No other could be mine. Even the abolition of
world hunger and of the beastly degradation to which millions
are doomed—even or especially this—is strictly ethical in aim.
How can anybody live like a son of God—or maybe saints can,
but they're rare—if he hasn't enough to eat? If his body is
wasted by hunger and corrupted by disease, not for a day or a
month or a year, but for ever and ever? And yet—here is the
crux—it doesn't follow at all that if a man has enough to eat
he must live like a son of God.

Now consider Crankshaw's article. Private capitalism has
been abolished in Russia; everything has been nationalised. But
are the *people*—and only *people* are real, only people, and other
forms of life, and the life hidden in matter, and God: only
spirit, never systems—are the *people* any better? What atom of
difference emerges between the vulgarest go-getter in America,
in America at its worst, and the villain of that play? To qualify
for Moscow: to become a departmental head: to have a flat in
Gorky Street, and a pretty villa on the outskirts: to feast his eyes
on his Masha, glittering with gold bangles and in a long velvet
dress—this, and this only, is his bourn. He wants, in other
words, to "get on". But "getting-on" is the popular morality
of capitalist America.

And the dreadful thing is this: to judge from *Beketov's Career*,
"getting-on" is endemic in the Soviet atmosphere. For Beketov
is a villain, it seems, "not because he wants to get to Moscow
with a flat and a summer villa and jewellery for his wife.
These are legitimate prizes. He is a villain because of the
way he sets about it." In other words: the old Russia was

abolished for the purpose of establishing fraternity; and the new Russia applauds, not fraternity, but the meanest sort of pushfulness.

It's not a bit of use Appleby-Smythe telling me—you'll remember him from *Tim I*—that things have gone wrong in the Soviet Union. Of course they have; but the point is, why? "I still consider," said Appleby-Smythe when attacking my economic equalitarianism, "that Marx and Engels thought most clearly about this, and accept their position, namely that we should aim at abolishing inequality only in the form of *class privilege*. Then, when we've got a classless society—in their definition, not Stalin's—let's see whither humanity will go." One of the clues to the trouble is here—not in the issue of equal incomes, but in the class-struggle mania. The impulse behind Marxism, and therefore behind the Leninist revolution, was an ethical or broadly religious one—you can't insist on it too often. Why did Marx slave away at the British Museum? Because he was dyspeptic, and hated society, as a lot of clever stupids would make out? Nonsense. He hated, that is true: not society, however, but an order of society that corrupted human nature and robbed people of their birthright. Atheist though he was (with a religious sort of atheism), it was the glorious liberty of the children of God that he wanted for all mankind; and he thought they could get it in one way only—by abolishing destitution. But destitution was a function of wage-slavery, and wage-slavery was a function of a class-ridden order: so abolish classes, and all would be well. Marx was dyspeptic, and had a beard: Isaiah may have been dyspeptic, and almost certainly had a beard: but Isaiah wasn't excluded by these (conjectural) accidentia from the role of Hebrew prophet: and Marx wasn't either. He was a lot of other things too, I daresay—not only bearded and dyspeptic; but when psychology has done its worst with him, and the mess it can make is considerable, moral passion remains, no matter what its origin, as his leading characteristic. It was his passion, not his bile, that rocked the world. I ought to add, to avoid misunderstanding, that I find him, from a purely personal point of view, almost uniquely repulsive.

Marx's trouble was this: that he was hypnotised by systems, and, wanting to serve spirit, forgot it, so to speak, in the meantime. He was right about the need for a classless society. He was right in believing that freedom, spiritual freedom, would be impossible for men in the mass until poverty had been abolished. He was half-right, too, about the class struggle: but half-right only, for he forgot, or never knew, that hatred and violence can by no means usher in the millennium. Where he was wholly wrong was in imagining that if you could only get a decent kind of system, and no matter how you got it, everything else would take care of itself: meaning by a decent kind of system one that provided, by the character of its mechanism, for just relations, in the economic sphere, between man and man. "Then when we've got a classless society," as Appleby-Smythe puts it, "let's see whither humanity will go." Well, he sees now, or ought to. He sees now, or ought to, that the Soviet man is nothing other than the oldest sort of Adam in a slightly different form: whereas what the world is crying out for is a new sort of Adam —the new sort of Adam guaranteed us by Christ. And no system can ever produce him: he is spirit, and it is only through the operation of spirit that he can blessedly come. What systems can do, and they can do nothing else, is to help or hinder that spiritual process. And beware always—for this is the crux—lest by an obsessive concentration on systems you hinder the very process you are anxious to help.

That is what has happened in the Soviet Union. They have been so anxious to achieve the millennium—mechanically— that they have overlooked what a millennium means: namely a society of millenarian men and women. But millenarian men and women don't come into existence as a result of unregenerate living: they come into existence, in whatever remote future or in whatever dimension of reality, as a result of innumerable little efforts here and now—in the every here and now of the whole human race—to be more merciful, more tolerant, more kindly, more forgiving, more selfless, more gentle, in a word more Christian. Marxism, starting with the impulse to create a more Christian society (and never let us forget it, despite our disillusionment), but obsessed by the need for a new system, and by the indispensability of class-struggle as the way to achieve it, has been making its devotees, in the meantime, certainly not more Christian than the rest of us, and probably less so: but if people are less Christian they cannot be midwives of a more Christian society. And that is not all. There is a certain moment by moment continuity, revolutions or no revolutions, in the life of all human associations: if the climate is pagan today it will tend to be pagan tomorrow: so a paganism of today may prevent, not only the emergence of a more Christian society in the foreseeable future, but its emergence altogether. That is why, as I suggested before, each one of us must break in, so far as he is able, on the vicious circle of unregeneracy.

And now I find, as I read back, that I have been understating. For things have arrived at this pass in the Soviet Union: to stabilise an order whose whole purpose, as envisaged by those who once dreamed of it, was to embody ethical principles in economic life, an unethical or anti-ethical sort of man and woman is being deliberately "engineered". There is a terrible warning in this paradox: and not only against specifically Soviet methods, but, more generally, against concentrating on the creation of machinery, and then "seeing whither humanity will go".

For we run similar dangers here, if perhaps in a more English form, unless we see to it that the building of a spiritual socialism keeps pace with the building of a political and economic one. The very need for distinguishing between the two kinds of socialism shows at once how unsocialist we are, and how irreligious; for they ought to coincide. In terms of leadership, that of politicians ought to be spiritual in the very act of being political, and that of churchmen ought to be political in the very act of being spiritual. But as I see little sign of any such leadership in either Church or State, I look for it, very urgently, to informal groupings of such ordinary men and women as may be spiritually and politically realistic: groupings from which, naturally, neither churchmen nor politicians would be excluded.

§ 2

But I dare not proceed without developing a little what I said in the last paragraph but one about the Soviet Union deliberately engineering an unethical or anti-ethical type of human being; for to leave it at that would be to give a dangerously and even wickedly misleading impression. So I must speak rather more fully about communist mentality, in the context of right and wrong as I see them.

If we omit all those countries, other than Russia, in which

communism has already come to power, or in which the movement towards it is (a) largely associated with the struggle for
national emancipation, or (b) so determined and widespread
that its victory in the foreseeable future is a matter of practical
politics—for in cases such as these there are complicating factors
—and if we confine ourselves to Russia on the one hand and to
countries like our own on the other, we can safely say this: The
communist movement, indifferently everywhere, aims at producing human instruments for the utmost consolidation and
expansion of Soviet power.

But there must clearly be a considerable variation within
this unity of aim: for the sort of service required of a Soviet
citizen will not be the same as that required of an Englishman.
The Soviet citizen will be required, simply and directly, to
build a Soviet economy of maximum strength. And because,
for reasons already explained in this volume and at greater
length in my earlier one, public service has been spat upon,
despite a hang-over of lip-service to it, as the sort of incentive
that no one but a fool could take seriously—and spat upon,
Timothy, by inheritors of the socialist dream—the powers that
be in the Soviet Union have encouraged selfishness to the
uttermost, just as capitalism encourages it: for thus, and thus
only, they think, will they be able—who knows?—to surpass,
in material prosperity, even capitalist America itself. Hence
the "Soviet man" depicted, or rather implied, in that play:
hence Stakhanovism, and everything it presupposes and
involves: hence those incomes so appallingly disparate, and
the whole unregenerate system of economic bribery and punishment.

But that is not all. Because nothing can matter but the
interests of "the socialist fatherland" (and never mind what
sort of "socialist fatherland"—or what sort of "socialists"—
may be in question) men and women must be conditioned,
not only to seek the best for themselves and so increase the
general body of Soviet wealth (what was the old Manchester
phrase? enlightened self-interest?), but also to ignore, if Soviet
safety or Soviet power or Soviet prestige would appear to
demand it, all those promptings to decent living in our personal,
moment-by-moment relations which are what make us truly
human. Their ideal must be contrary to the Christian one:
they must spy on one another, denounce one another, be

"tough", be unforgiving. It is sad to be writing all this, for I remember the generous hopes of 1918. It is specially sad at this moment. I listened last night to a broadcast performance of *The Magic Flute*: greatest of operas, if *Fidelio*, its more flesh-and-blood counterpart, had not been destined to come after it. Its burden is purity of heart. As I lay through the night by my window, a wet breeze on my face and the water and fire of my spirit giving passage to the flute's serenity, I reflected, for the thousandth time, that what finally matters is not the preservation or power of any State, but the answer each one of us makes to the Dorian voice that is in him.

So the dominant characteristic of Soviet humanity, in the economic field, is tending more and more to show as pushfulness and self-seeking. I say only "dominant", and even with that qualification there must be a high percentage of exceptions—a much higher one, perhaps, than in the majority of capitalist countries: but that the sentence as I have written it is in accordance with the facts appears quite beyond question. And the dominant characteristic of Soviet humanity, in the social sphere, is tending more and more to show as ruthlessness. Here the percentage of exceptions, I am afraid, is very much lower than in any capitalist country—or in any that has not abandoned, of set purpose, the traditions of Christianity.

But a dominant characteristic of the communists in a country like England is not self-seeking but self-sacrifice: or of some such communists, rather: I mean of those whom a certain clear urge, not at work in them all, has impelled to their communism. *Distinguo*: otherwise I shall get into a mess.

"Beginning" communists in England seem divisible into three major classes, with a lot of overlapping between them and plenty of mixed types in each:

(1) There are those, mainly of the working class, whose motive is selfish: and I say it, sitting in my comfortable library, with no accent of condemnation or disrespect. They see communism as the one potent instrument for extracting more human conditions from employer or State: or feel sure that they will never live decently until capitalism has been abolished, and that only communist internationalism can be relied upon to see the job through. Mixed up with all this may be thirst for revenge—against an order that has treated them so cruelly, and their fathers even worse: I know a labour leader, a

prominent and rather savage one, who saw his mother done to death in his boyhood by the dirt, semi-starvation and lack of medical facilities endemic at that time. No, I do not condemn: I merely categorise.

(2) There are those, largely of the middle class, who are neurotic or psychotic, and bare their teeth at the existing order. They may hate the father and see Stalin as a surrogate, or something of the kind: they may be too short: they may be too tall: they may be Jews who have paid for their Jewishness: they may have had a younger brother, and felt displaced, or an older one, and felt anticipated: they may have developed masochistically or sadistically, as a result of outrages suffered in childhood: they may simply, through a combination of circumstances outside their control, be sexually unsatisfied. You know the kind of stuff—or you will, Timothy: the trouble is that it's true. Take an aristocrat, a brilliant writer, now dead, who adopted communism in his twenties. Any tyro could have analysed him. His communism was partly attributable to generous emotions and sense of justice: that you would have had to describe him as the worst sort of communist was almost wholly attributable to something else—to the fact that he was impotent. God forbid, once again, that I should think of condemning: I condemn, if anybody, myself—for having sprinkled tepid water on psychoanalysis, somewhere or other in *Tim I*.

(3) There are those, not exclusively of the middle class but predominantly so, who may be categorised, in a convenient catchword, as idealists. And there are not just a few of them: most middle-class communists belong to this category or belonged to it once. It's not a bit of use denying it: I worked with them month after month in the Popular Front, and know what I'm talking about. Psychoanalysis is all very well, as I've just been at pains to make clear: but I'm sick and tired of the owlish tendency to make a set at all nobility of motive and muckrake it away. The heavens above are as real as whatever it may be that lies hid in our unconscious, and if we are plagued by the one we receive light from the other.

Idealists, when they turn towards communism, do it neither in selfishness nor in morbidity, but from concern for the good of mankind. And they become, not the Christian type of communist they might have been, but instruments of Soviet expansion, because they "fall" for an argument which, as put by a more seasoned comrade who is such an instrument already, appears eminently valid to them. As follows. There will never be plenty or peace until communism rules the earth: Russia is the spearhead of communism: so if plenty and peace are your aim (for mankind, and not just for yourself) you must be spiritually a Russian—must give yourself body and soul to the cause of Russian aggrandisement, as the instrument chosen by God (or by history, or fate, or dialectics, or whatever you will) for making human existence what it ought to be. And this implies, in its turn, doing everything that Russia demands, for the socialist fatherland knows best: or if occasionally it doesn't, but grotesquely miscalculates (as when the comrades, under Stalinist instruction, were comforting Hitler a split second before, and in the case of remoter dependencies a lot of full seconds after, his onslaught on Stalin), well, no matter: your officer is your officer, and you don't stab him in the back when he blunders.

Now the rights or wrongs of this whole argument are for the moment irrelevant. The only point I want to make here is this: be the argument faulty or otherwise, and it's as faulty as could be, you find two elements of paramount goodness in beginners of the sort just described. One of them is commonly permanent, or permanent, rather, for so long as party membership persists: the other is inevitably transformed into its opposite, but into an opposite that may nevertheless harbour a dark trace of what it was. I must make this as clear as I can, for my reference to the engineering in Russia of "unethical or anti-ethical types of humanity" might otherwise involve a grave injustice.

The first of these goodnesses, the more or less permanent one, is that readiness for self-sacrifice already alluded to.

Now this goodness isn't engineered away by the communist movement in a country like Britain: on the contrary, it is tremendously reinforced. For what Russia requires of a British communist is not at all, as I have said, what she requires of her domestic citizenry. The entire raison d'être of the latter is to build the Soviet economy: and a strengthening of their self-regarding instincts is thought the only sure way of getting them to do it. But a British communist can nohow build the Soviet economy, or not directly: his job is the less direct one of converting people to communism, or propagandising for Russia, or intervening, over an appropriate area of the political

B

or industrial field, in the Russian interest. One or other of these activities, or a mixture of them, is allotted to every comrade as his "party work", over and above a more general obligation to work for Russia and communism: and this daily routine, combined with pressure from public opinion, is so powerful in its effect on people's lives that what might otherwise have been a transitory impulse becomes second nature. A "good" communist literally lives for his communism; and a "bad" communist, or an inactive one, is a contradiction in terms.

The selfless lives led by thousands of communists should fill the rest of us with shame. A double first, or a talented composer, or a leading scientist in his field, will get up before dawn (but not because he likes it, as I do), take up his stand at an Underground, and sell his quota of *Daily Workers* in the pouring rain: and will do it, not as an occasional bit of freakish-ness that anyone could enjoy, but morning after morning and month after month. A girl will put off having children, the children she wants, until the party can spare her the time. I speak in both cases of what I know, and could multiply these instances indefinitely. And what applies to the rank and file applies to leaders. I think of one in particular. He is a long, dark, sheer sort of a man, with a quiet saturninity about him often relieved by a smile—how shall I describe Sakki's smile? —in which charity for the world's eccentricities is barely separable from a cynical delight in them, or in their trans-parency to his own intelligence. I used to have some acquaint-ance with Sakki, though I never knew him well. His ability is of the first order, and his culture exceptional: I always rather liked him, but when I heard that he had been a Balliol Scholar, a Craven and Ireland Scholar, and a Hertford Scholar (whereas I, who had gone in for the lot of them, had failed to get even a mention) I somehow liked him still more. There must have been many positions, big with money and repute, that he would have occupied with distinction. But he has preferred to slave away among the pass-men of King Street, and lives, I am told, on an occasional sardine.

There is no limit in self-dedication to which communists will not go. I recall an episode from the late thirties. One night, before a meeting at Swindon (the Popular Front was in spate), I was dining, or having dinner, with a communist very top-notch indeed, whom I shall call Tudie Mimmickin. His

COMMUNIST MENTALITY, CONSCIENCE, TREASON 35

talk was of a certain Willie Munzenberg. This man, a rich communist tycoon formerly in charge of German youth work, had more recently, as an emigré, been conducting operations from the Paris *apparat*: but, suspected of diversionary activities, had been summoned to Moscow a week or so before my encounter with Tudie. Fearing the event, he had proceeded, not to Moscow, but to a pleasantly remote village in the South of France (not that this was to save him: he was subsequently found hung near Grenoble, some said by fascists, others said by communist sectaries). That is what Mimmickin told me, across the greens, the fish and chips, the dirty table-cloth and the tomato-ketchup bottles of a very English Swindon; and added: "The booger! I can't understand it. If *I* were sent for in similar circumstances I shouldn't hesitate a second, even if I knew they were going to shoot me the very moment I got in." You couldn't possibly doubt his sincerity: such a mixture of emotions was on his face—of disgust, of incredulity, of grim determination—as even a Kemble, or a Dean of Canterbury, couldn't have simulated. And if there was something very dirty about him at that moment, for masochism of a certain kind is always dirty, there was something rather noble as well.

Quite apart from an instance like this, there is doubtless a pathology of communist self-sacrifice, just as there is a pathology, if different in kind, of the ordinary patriotic self-sacrifice and the ordinary religious self-sacrifice. In addition to masochism, death-wishes, hatred, and all the rest of it, an inverted sort of power-mongering is often present; and, on top of this, self-sacrifice that has become a habit, something almost mechanical, has already lost a good deal of its Holy Ghost: for to be utterly itself it must rise from a man's deepest cavern, in spontaneous reply to a given situation. But when all has been said, and whatever its origin—and however many, and however unpleasant, may be the other elements that shade off into it—communist self-sacrifice remains admirable: or I, at any rate, admire it enormously. For these communists, by and large, are altruistic (I am speaking only, you will remember, of "idealist" ones) in a world in which altruism is rare: and that is something to be grateful for. I have been interested to note what Laurence Thompson has had to say about this in his "Portrait of England". Mr Thompson, an heir to the religious or nonconformist tradition of our truly native socialism, is very far from being either a communist or a fellow-traveller: even a Church paper I might name could hardly think it—or perhaps it could: for its pharisaical myopia is of a sort to delight any amateur of rarities. Now Mr Thompson did a big tour of England on behalf of my firm, for the purpose of writing the study I've mentioned. I haven't read it, I am sorry to say—I've been too busy with this letter: but I've read the review in the *Times Literary Supplement*. Here is an extract: "The danger, as Mr Thompson sees it, is in the apathy of the multitude, to which is added the even more disquieting symptom of industrial neurosis [yes, there is neurosis everywhere, not only among communists]. He finds certain earnest minorities: therapeutists, city-planning officers, communist cells, bands of Friends living in slums like Franciscans. These are the altruists: all in their diverse ways are moved by a spirit. The future may depend on them." This conjunction of communists with Quakers is of a significance that will not escape you.

A continual readiness for self-sacrifice, therefore, is the first element of great goodness to be discovered in idealist "party members": the element I characterised as more or less permanent. The second element—the one I characterised as "inevitably transformed into its opposite, but into an opposite that may nevertheless harbour a dark trace of what it was"— is their attention to conscience.

§ 3

How delighted I am that I've got on to conscience! I shall have a lot of things to say about it, and shall enjoy saying them. For a lot of other things have been said about it, these last few months, that seem to me so blasphemous, such a stab in the back at religious decency and spiritual honour, that I am as anxious to refute their perpetrators as I have ever been to refute anybody, and this is saying a good deal. They are committing the identical *trahison des clercs* that I attacked in Mr C. S. Lewis (whether self-righteously or not—and be hanged, for the nonce, to self-righteousness) in my earlier volume.

Most communists of the type in question, the idealist type, join the movement, primarily at least—and never mind about the mixture of motives, never mind what I've called their pathology—because their conscience has so instructed them, and they listen to it. They nohow fail to face what is in store for them, and what they are giving up. They realise that they will be required to do anything—and much they recoil from in contemplation—for communism and Russia. And they take the step, they commit themselves, because they believe, as they listen to the argument I set out in an earlier passage, that the good of humanity demands it. Gravely mistaken though I judge their decision, and fraught with consequences potentially disastrous to themselves and the world, I refuse to attack as Satanic what they do in the name of God—however little religious they may be in any ordinary fashion: or to withhold my humble tribute of respect from them. For I refuse, once again, to psychoanalyse away something decent—this time conscience.

And don't imagine, my dear Timothy, that their decision is always easy. I think, though this isn't her real name, of Mary Joyce. She was a lovely young creature, slender as a tall sapling, with a blessed and blessing radiance about her that lit up a room as she entered, and the sort of whiteness—not negative, but passionate—that is better than any other colour in the world. She reminded me of my Oxford girl Joy: "beautiful she looked, like a tall garden lily." She loved literature and music (especially music) and people and dancing and gaiety: and as her parents were distinguished figures in the literary London of that time, and did a lot of entertaining, this world was open to her. Her intelligence darted and glanced with an Irish kind of wit, and her spirit glowed with a spontaneity of affection such as I was to remember, years afterwards, when Franci, the youngest of my daughters, was developing into the gracious thing she is. I loved her very much: I still love her (as perhaps you have gathered) though she began hating me years ago for what I was writing and saying about Russia and communism. I see her as of a piece with the sunlit landscape in front of me, and bless her.

Her temperament had always been religious. With a mother militantly rationalist, she had got herself baptised, at about sixteen, into one of the larger nonconformist communions. She was then an eager Liberal, as her father was, and remained one till her early twenties. I would talk to her now and again about socialism, but she always repelled me: "If all employers were like you," she would say, "socialism would be unnecessary."

But she hated war and poverty, and had a conscience: and one day, coming up from Oxford, she was to share her compartment with someone who could talk her own language, and was to prove as effective in an hour or so's argument for communism as I had shown myself feeble in all my lengthier ones for socialism. Not that arguments alone were in question: the call to self-dedication, I am sure, was as potent as logic, and it was self-dedication to righteousness that her conscience demanded—and should demand of us all. The tragedy of democratic socialism is this: that it has largely lost the power of appealing to an instinct for religion in the depths of young people. Unless this power is recovered, our road to salvation will be a bloody and tearful one.

I know something of Mary Joyce's Gethsemane. She did not *want* to join the party. She struggled a good deal to keep her young road still open—for gaiety, and a justifiable measure of ease, and agreeable work, and a pleasant environment. But conscience won. She became a communist. More: she developed—to be as frank at this point as I have been heretofore—into a particularly hard, bitter, narrow, censorious, I can only say unchristian, type of communist: which means, I suppose, that the original sin in her corresponding to these adjectives—it had occasionally peeped out in the old days—was being strengthened by her communism. She does a great deal of harm, I am sure, and must be opposed, albeit in a Christian way, with a self-dedication as large as her own. And yet:

> "But lives and spreads aloft by those pure eyes
> And perfect witness of all-judging Jove:
> As he pronounces lastly on each deed,
> Of so much fame in Heaven expect thy meed."

All-judging, but all-understanding, too: and I cannot escape the conviction that Jove regards her, in his wisdom, as not only, *malgré tout*, a good woman, but even, for all the temporal misunderstanding that has so tragically spoiled her, as one of his rather special children. Few of us can have the hope that he may think of us likewise.

Now listen to this passage in a book by Alan Moorehead, called "The Traitors", that was published a few months ago by my friend Jimmy Hamilton, and seems to be enjoying a great vogue: though I understand as well as anybody that you can never really say. The subject is Emil Klaus Fuchs, a British citizen of German origin (with a Quaker background) who communicated atomic secrets to Russia during the nineteen forties; and Mr Moorehead concludes as follows:

"The real charge against Fuchs is that of impudence. He rushed in and took the whole problem on his own shoulders. He knew less than most men about human nature, he had never been to Russia, he had no experience of diplomacy or political administration, he was an atheist, but he still judged himself competent to put the world to rights. Mr Alan Barth makes a point about the Fuchses of this world. Describing another traitor, an American, in his book, he says he had 'a kind of idealism, however mistaken and misplaced. The sense that because "something drastic had to be done" he, personally, had to do it, is a sense out of which saints, as well as sinners, great patriots as well as base traitors, are made.'

"Possibly, as Mr Barth suggests when he quotes the letters of the younger Pliny to the Emperor Trajan about A.D. 112, you have to go back to the Early Christians to find any sort of parallel for the atomic traitors. [Describing his method of dealing with the Christians, Pliny says that he gives them a chance of recanting—some of them even curse Christ—and punishes only the ones that refuse: adding that anonymous letters often put him on the track of secret Christians.]

"Trajan approved these practices but he warned Pliny that he should have nothing to do with anonymous accusations; they were thoroughly bad and out of keeping with the spirit of the age. This was a humane and statesmanlike approach but the end result of it was that the Roman gods vanished and the Christians survived and multiplied. . . . *The seat of treason in each case is the same—the inner conviction of the accused that what he is doing is right.* The Christians were moved by their faith in God while Fuchs acted upon his megalomaniac confidence in his own brain, but both were so convinced of their rightness that they were prepared to destroy the State in order to have their way.

"Perhaps Fuchs was telling the truth when he claimed after his arrest that his loyalties were now fixed on England, and his public cursing of Russian Marxism was sincere. *But he was basically a man who would always refer to his own conscience first and society afterwards. There is no place for such men in an ordered community.*

They belong where Fuchs now is, sewing mailbags in Stafford Gaol."

It would be difficult to find a passage, on any subject, in which more blindnesses and paganisms were concentrated. I wonder only in passing whether that parallelism with primitive Christianity may not have flushed Moorehead's face as he wrote, and, if so, why he went on: and whether he thinks the "end result" undesirable—whether he would prefer the Roman gods to have survived and the Christians to have vanished. Nor am I overmuch concerned, in this context, with the fatal lack of sympathetic charity displayed in those awful last words. There is indeed no vestige of spiritual good sense to be anywhere discerned: but note particularly the passage italicised and even more so the one underlined—for they strike at the heart of religion. Not but that an instinct for decency, coming through all muddied up, makes him write as he does.

I should take all this a good deal less seriously if Mr Moorehead stood alone. But Rebecca West had already published her "Meaning of Treason", and I had read it uneasily. Now Rebecca, of course, is a very different cup of tea from Mr Moorehead; and many of the qualities that give her such stature, and make her so lovable, are apparent in this study of Klaus Fuchs, William Joyce and the rest. The incisiveness of her mind, the grip and range of her knowledge, the power and brilliance of her style, her ability to open up vistas with no more than a phrase—these are as evident as might have been expected, and to make a fuss of them would be impertinent. More important, perhaps, is her pity, her kindness, her sense of the *lacrimae rerum* and of the mortality that touches human minds. When it is there—when it shines from the print with a radiance that blesses the reader—one takes it almost for granted. But—it is not always there. And one discerns a tension in these pages. One might almost suspect—she must forgive me for saying it—that, giving up the struggle a little, she is trying to make a case, now and then, for a secure and rather spiritless respectability: and yet on a sudden, as I catch myself thinking it, spirit floods in again at the turn of a page. Occasionally, as I re-read her, a wicked memory came to me: how someone had remarked, of a certain highbrow, that his brow had grown so monstrously high as to look even lower than average. Occasionally, too, I thought this: we must beware lest our liberalism, appalled by illiberalisms committed in the name of that liberalism, become illiberalism itself. "The devil of nationalism," writes Rebecca, "had been driven out of man, but he had not become the headquarters of the dove. Instead there had entered into him the seven devils of internationalism, and he was torn by their frenzies." Again she must forgive me, but there is something of the lost leader in that sentence, and something also a little too easy. There may be, there are, seven devils in a perverted internationalism, and only one in a decent nationalism; but the best internationalism is far better, for all that, than the best nationalism. Love of country is another matter: it is always, when pure enough, internationalist.

But that was not the passage I had in mind when I began talking about Rebecca. It was this: "The Lutheran right to private judgment in spiritual matters had been magnified to the right of private judgment in all fields, and it was claimed with a confidence which has only been equalled in those devotees who believe that divinity enters into them and illuminates them."

Let us look at this matter in the simplest or if you will the most childlike of terms. That is usually the best way of stripping off inessentials and getting to the heart of a thing. Subtleties and qualifications can be introduced later.

What is conscience? God speaking to a man. That basic assumption I must make. If you do not make it with me: if conscience, you think, is a fear of cosmic processes and powers surviving in racial memory from a day when the world was still young; or fear, a more recent survival, of your own human father; or fear of society; or anything else you can think up for yourself or read about in books—then everything that follows will be meaningless to you. I do not deny that such interpretations can be put upon conscience by a good and honest man— even by a specially good and honest man, who is determined, in conscience, to avoid easy answers. I do not deny, either, that conscience may often be somehow mixed up with such fears— which are distorted intimations, themselves, of a divinity misunderstood. And I should respect, finally, without agreeing with him, anyone who might say that what speaks to a man in his conscience is not God actual but God potential: God not yet fully realised, but on the road to fuller realisation through the response that each one of us makes to the conscience within him. So Samuel Alexander:

"Accordingly, in its relation to conduct, religion does not so much command us to perform our duties with the consciousness that they are the commands of God, as rather it is religion to do our duty with the consciousness of helping to create his deity."

Or

"The temper of acquiescence [in the existence of evil] is at the same time the temper which impels us to amelioration without the fond expectation that the springs of pain will ever be sealed; and when it takes in the relation of God to the world, it prompts the recognition that this same attempt at betterment is at once implanted in us by the Space-Time out of which we are precipitated, and secures the divinity to which the world is tending."

What Alexander is trying to express here is the mystery of the magnet. There is fulfilment when the iron and magnet are united. The magnet is not fully itself—it hungers and thirsts for a realisation of its potentialities—until the iron is united with it. But the potentiality of the iron to unite with the magnet is also given, and given by the hunger of the magnet. The unfulfilled magnet is alpha, the fulfilled one omega. There are difficulties in this conception, and I cannot, as I have said, quite agree with it: but whether you hold it or not—whether you hold this view of conscience, or my own more naïf one—the difference for conduct is non-existent.

We must beware of confusing the issue by mere verbalisms. "He was an atheist," says Mr Moorehead of Fuchs. (I have formed no impression, from reading his book, of what his own convictions are about God and religion.) No: *in so far as he really listened to conscience* (which is the crux, and I shall come to it later), Klaus Fuchs was the contrary of an atheist, however he may have classed himself: just as, if I may so far presume, you cannot imagine that God denies sonship to a rationalist Gilbert Murray who has spent a whole life in his service. "Not every one that saith unto me, Lord, Lord, shall enter into the kingdom of heaven; but he that doeth the will of my Father which is in heaven." Words on the one hand, spirit and truth on the other: there is no distinction more important.

But if conscience is God speaking to us, what is he saying? He is asking us to co-operate: he is asking us to help him do his work. This is the central fact of religion, and the religious literature of all peoples is instinct with a sense of it. "God can no more do without us," said Meister Eckhart, "than we can do without him." When Moses excused himself from the Lord's service because he was slow of speech and of a slow tongue, the Lord said unto him "Now therefore go, and I will be with thy mouth, and teach thee what thou shalt say." (The special genius of the Hebrew religion resides largely in this: that it sees God as friendly with man—as walking and talking by his side in Brimpton gardens at the cool of the day.) "For it is not ye that speak," said Christ, "but the Spirit of your Father which speaketh in you." "God himself," writes Nicolas Berdyaev, "awaits man's help and contribution towards Creation." William James, whom I quoted in *Tim I*, closely resembles Alexander: "I confess that I do not see why the very existence of an invisible world may not in part depend on the personal response which any one of us may make to the religious appeal. God himself, in short, may draw vital strength and increase of very being from our fidelity." But it is in a legend from the Midrash, with its flavour of man-to-man familiarity of the sort just described, that this truth is most clearly expressed:

"And Isaac asked the Eternal: 'King of the World, when Thou didst make the light, Thou didst say in Thy Torah that the light was good; when Thou didst make the extent of the firmament and the extent of the earth, Thou didst say in Thy Torah that they were good; and every herb Thou hast made, and every beast, Thou hast said that they were good; but when Thou hast made man in Thine image, Thou didst not say in Thy Torah that man was good. Wherefore, Lord?' And God answered him: 'Because man I have not yet perfected, and because man is to perfect himself, and to perfect the world.' "

As it is through conscience that God asks us to co-operate, so it is through conscience, and through conscience alone, that he intimates, in each given instance, the sort of co-operation he requires. Mr Moorehead attacks Fuchs for his "impudence". No:

in so far as he really listened to conscience—I must add that
again—he was as far from being impudent as a child at the
throne of God's glory. The real impudence, the final impudence, the impudence against God, would have been not to listen.
Rebecca speaks of a confidence "that has only been equalled in
those devotees who believe that divinity enters into them and
illuminates them." But it is of the essence of divinity to enter
into people and illuminate them: and man impudently rebels
against divinity if he bars his humanity to it. Alan Moorehead
half answers Rebecca without knowing it: "Still, the seat of
treason," he writes, "in each case is the same—the inner conviction of the accused that what he is doing is right." And the
"each case"? The treason of Fuchs against Great Britain: and
the treason of the Christians against Rome—against a State—
in the service of Christ. Rebecca is wrong, too, in the distinction she draws between "spiritual matters" and "all fields".
There is no such distinction. All matters are spiritual matters,
and the whole field is divine.

Awful perils, to be sure, are involved for a man and the world
when he relies on his conscience. We are pitiably fallible. We
may mistake the voice of Satan for the voice of God: and I
intend by Satan that part of our nature that is not yet re-
deemed—our pride, our fear, our faithlessness. Pride operates
in another way too: it may indeed be God's voice that we hear,
but as we hear it we may forget we are God's children, and
imagine we are God himself. Our brains, too, may be weak,
and our spiritual hearing defective: so that the message may come
through all muddied up, very confused and misleading. And
if things fall out thus, we may be stumbling-blocks, not only to
ourselves, but to others also. "Beware of false prophets, which
come to you in sheep's clothing, but inwardly they are ravening
wolves. Ye shall know them by their fruits. Do men gather
grapes of thorns, or figs of thistles? Even so every good tree
bringeth forth good fruit; but a corrupt tree bringeth forth evil
fruit. A good tree cannot bring forth evil fruit, neither can a
corrupt tree bring forth good fruit. Wherefore by their fruits ye
shall know them." By their fruits ye shall know, not merely the
false prophet in others, but the same in yourself. A man has
only to look back with remorse over the days of his life to realise
the truth of this. The evil fruit is recognisable (Fuchs recognised
it): we understand that we heard wrong: and at the last, if by

grace it has happened so, the mirror of our conscience has become a little less speckled and dusty, a little more capable of receiving the divine radiance unobscured (or obscured, let me say, not too dreadfully) and giving it out again. But "inwardly they are ravening wolves"—pay attention to that. The mirror will shine as it ought only if the whole man is cleansed: only if, as I said in *Tim I*, he has put himself, moment by moment, in a posture for the receipt of grace.

Yes, awful perils are involved in relying on conscience. But a soldier does not fly from the battle for fear of injury or death, or even because, by committing some blunder, he may injure or kill his own comrades. One might say that worse perils are involved in not relying on conscience, if this were the right way of putting it. But it is not. Listen for a moment to some more from that essay—*The Will to Believe*—by William James:

"If this life be not a real fight, in which something is eternally gained for the universe by success, it is no better than a game of private theatricals from which one may withdraw at will. But it *feels* like a real fight—as if there were something really wild in the universe which we, with all our idealities and faithfulnesses, are needed to redeem; and first of all to redeem our own hearts from atheisms and fears. For such a half-wild half-saved universe our nature is adapted. The deepest thing in our nature is this dumb region of the heart in which we dwell alone with our willingnesses and our unwillingnesses, our faiths and our fears. As through the cracks and crannies of caverns those waters exude from the earth's bosom which then form the fountain-heads of springs, so in these crepuscular depths of personality the sources of all our outer deeds and decisions take their rise. Here is our deepest organ of communication with the nature of things; and compared with these concrete movements of our soul all abstract statements and scientific arguments—the veto, for example, which the strict positivist pronounces upon our faith—sound to us like mere chatterings of the teeth. . . .

"These then are my last words to you: Be not afraid of life. Believe that life *is* worth living, and your belief will help create the fact. The 'scientific' proof that you are right may not be clear before the day of judgement (or some stage of being which that expression may serve to symbolise) is reached. But the faithful fighters of this hour, or the beings that then and there

will represent them, may turn to the faint-hearted, who here
decline to go on, with words like those with which Henry IV
greeted the tardy Crillon after a great battle had been gained:
'Hang yourself, brave Crillon! We fought at Arques, and you
were not there!' "

A superb passage! Didn't I do well, my dear Timothy, to
repeat it in full?
It is not a question, in this battle, of smaller perils or greater
perils: if we are to fight at all, conscience—"our deepest organ
of communication with the nature of things"—is our only real
weapon. Tradition, public opinion, authority in all its forms,
the fiat of organised society—to obey these, when our conscience
tells us not to, is a way of declining to go on; and such faint-
heartedness merits the rebuke in eternity, "You were not there."
What, after all, is the fiat of organised society? At its very best it
is the fossilised residue of other people's consciences. (Not but
that a wise man will test his conscience by tradition. For God
has spoken to men in the past as surely as he is speaking to us
now: and we may discover, when we listen to what they heard,
that they heard better than we are hearing. But we must assure
ourselves of this: we must use tradition only as a guide.) Does a
man serve God better by gazing throughout a lifetime at the
shadows in Plato's cave, or instead—given the capacity—
by turning about and getting a glimpse of the figures that
cast them, and even maybe of the sun? By remaining Donizetti,
when a Verdi is in him? By being polished and unobjectionable,
but second-hand, instead of first-hand, though covered with
blemishes? About my own answer I could never be in doubt.
Only, it must always be a question of service: only, there must
always be the humble achievement, realised as identical with
self-expression itself, of self-forgetfulness.
"But he was basically a man," says Mr Moorehead, "who
would always refer to his own conscience first and society afterwards. There is no place for such men in an ordered community.
They belong where Fuchs now is, sewing mailbags in Stafford
Gaol." If Mr Moorehead is not declaring that the safety of the
State is the highest law, then he is talking in the spirit of that
dictum. It was not a Christian dictum. It was a Roman dictum,
it was a Nazi dictum, it is a Stalinist dictum.
Now let there be no misunderstanding. If Mr Moorehead were

face to face with me he would be tempted, I feel sure, to make an obvious retort. "If everyone follows his conscience," he would ask, "how can organised society be possible?" A debating point, and a wretched one; for it exhibits a total misunderstanding of the way conscience works. Conscience is a high thing, and deals only with high things: it comes flashing its imperative message only when supreme right and wrong appear at stake. To compromise in everything else is a matter of very conscience itself, which instructs us, when we have reached a certain stage of politico-moral development, to live in amity with our neighbour: and we cannot do that unless, as a general rule of social intercourse, we abide by majority decisions. Conscience doesn't bid me withhold my taxes when the Tories are in power, or wangle myself lire in Italy because the limitation of foreign currency to a few pounds a year is in my view not only unpleasant but idiotic. Quite the reverse; it bids me honour the law. But conscience impelled Mahatma Gandhi to civil disobedience, because the right to self-government, it told him, was a divine right: and conscience forbids a pacifist to bear arms, because murder, it tells him, is an outrage against God. Then must everyone decide for himself? Certainly: this is highly inconvenient, but cannot be helped, for that is the way conscience works.

Thus society proceeds on its more or less ordinary way, and is given a jolt, every now and again, by people's consciences. Any particular jolt may be dangerous, for conscience isn't infallible: yet it is only by people listening to their consciences, however imperfect may be their hearing, that providence can do its work. And your and my purpose in being here is to help providence.

So, returning to the communists, I repeat what I said at the beginning: that their readiness, in conscience, to embark on the communist road—for the good of mankind as they see it—argues virtue in them.

Then is all well? No, all's as bad as it could be. The fact is that Mr Moorehead, and people like him, are barking up a ludicrously wrong tree. They attack communists for listening to conscience: they ought to attack them, if anyone ought to attack

anyone, for exactly the opposite—for *refusing* to listen. For here's
the rub: the original decision—a genuine decision of conscience,
though a wildly mistaken one—involves, *ipso facto*, a decision to
abrogate conscience; and deliberate abrogation of conscience is
about as bad a variety of the sin against the Holy Ghost as a
man can commit. What they say to themselves, Fuchs and the
rest of them, is this: "Conscience tells me I must work for the
good of mankind. Reason tells me that the spread of communism, under the leadership of the Soviet Union, is necessary
for the good of mankind. So I must enrol in the army of communism, officered by the Soviet Union. But as a soldier in that
army I must not only do what my officers instruct me to do, but
must learn to think, automatically, as they think and to feel,
automatically, as they feel—otherwise victory will be impossible.
So decisions, from this moment, are out of my hands. Not for
me to reason why: my conscience is in the keeping of Comrade
Stalin."

(It may be noted, in passing, that this same abrogation of
conscience, if a more temporary one, was assumed to be binding
on the rank and file of all national armies until recent events in
Germany made it convenient to pretend otherwise. But the
point, though I enjoy glancing at it, is irrelevant.)

So the decision they take, from high motives but with appalling blindness, is a decision to do away with the very conscience
that has led them to take it. What they fail to understand, if
they have thought about the matter at all, as I am sure some of
them have—or perhaps what, if they do understand it, they reject as outbalanced by more weighty considerations—is that the
Lord our God, though by no means the jealous God my remote
forebears imagined, is a living one: not dead power, but a vital,
a second-by-second, a to-all-eternity spirit: and one who speaks
to us second by second, not once and for all. This is his essence:
or, to look at it from our side, the essence of conscience, in which
he speaks to us, is that it is a second-by-second affair. And God is
not mocked: reality may not be tampered with. The man who
decides, by an act of conscience, to do anything that Stalin may
bid him, however repugnant it might otherwise have been (and
may still blessedly be, on occasion) to the very conscience in
question, is perpetrating a blasphemous and literally fatal self-
contradiction. He is turning himself into something unreal: he
is cutting himself off from reality, from God.

Unreality—that is what, as one gets to know them, one discovers in communists. They are shut up: they live behind a veil: they have lost their antennae. And unless you're shut up yourself in their bethel you can't really get in touch with them, can't meet them: your relation to them is a shadow one. I remember very vividly how I felt when I was discussing Russia's onslaught on Finland, one day at the Ivy, with a decent party member. He is in many ways—in his self-dedication, for instance —a far better person than I am. But (I'm going to say something pretty desperate) he no longer seemed fully human. I got the appalling impression, once or twice, that he wasn't there.

A footnote before I pass on. You will remember that, speaking about two elements of great goodness in communists, I described one of them as "inevitably transformed into its opposite, but into an opposite that may nevertheless harbour a dark trace of what it was": this one of them being their primal attention to conscience. And what I meant by so describing it was this: Commonly, a second-hand kind of conscience takes the place of its first-hand original, and compels them to do things its original would forbid. A second-hand conscience is what demands their utter loyalty to the party and the Soviet Union; and there may be something of the original sort in it, because (a) loyalty of any kind, the thing in itself, may represent a response, in however partial a measure, to a conscience direct and naïf, and (b) the goal—peace and happiness for everyone—may remain vividly present to them. Sometimes the two sorts of conscience, the new one and a relic of the old, are at war with one another. If you look up the documents reproduced by Mr Moorehead—the only valuable part of his book—you will see this happening in the case of Fuchs. I was greatly moved as I read them. Words echoed in my ears from a birthplace of religion, with an accent more than usually imperative: "Judge not, that ye be not judged". And, though I can imagine few things bigger with evil for the world than the things done by Fuchs, I had a curious impulse to act as Bernard Shaw and Robbie Ross acted when Oscar Wilde left his dock for Reading Gaol— to raise my hat in respect.

And this also must be said—that a second-hand conscience, in spite of everything, is better, a lot better than no conscience at all.

§ 4

Once a man is in the party, the conditioning process begins. The difference between a Soviet citizen and a British party member, in their approaches to the business of earning their living, has already been noted; but what otherwise happens is identical (except that an ordinary citizen in the Soviet Union is not affected to quite the same degree as a party member either there or elsewhere). To invalidate the appeal of first-hand conscience, and atrophy the tyro's response to it, this is the aim; and it is achieved, in a measure by the party's deliberate attempt to achieve it (for the sake of second-hand conscience), and in a measure automatically—as a result of what a man must consent to for the sake of discipline and security. He must lie about himself and others—must pretend, for example, that he's not a communist at all, but uninterested in politics, or a Liberal, or at the very worst a Labour Party man, which he often is, additionally: and must invent subtle alibis and specious verbalisms to make the lie pass muster. He must denounce "weaker elements" to the appropriate organ—a weaker element being a comrade who persists in retaining some vestige of original conscience or bourgeois morality. He must be, not only "tough" in his own person, but ever on the alert to detect lack of toughness in others. To put it shortly, he must deceive and betray. And his business is not confined to the party: he must creep and intrude and climb into other people's folds. As a result, he may become unable—and I mean literally unable, I mean the machinery wouldn't work however eagerly he might wish it to—he may become literally unable to distinguish between right and wrong as first-hand conscience would present them. The reasoning faculty meanwhile decays, and to such an extent, on occasion, that he may honestly believe himself thinking when he's merely recording: and spiritually he becomes an automaton, moved from without. This is the "new type of human being" that communism engineers.

Of course I cannot say too soon—I have written the last paragraph very hurriedly in order to say it as soon as possible —that this is a black-and-white sort of picture, whereas in the real one there are many different greys. Some idealists, retaining first-hand conscience, sooner or later leave the party —though if it's later rather than sooner they rarely escape undamaged, as you may discover by reading the books that they afterwards publish. A few, while remaining in the party, still suffer surprisingly little. A few, a very few, suffer not at all. They possess a certain innocence that carries them undefiled through a contamination they have deliberately incurred. I have known one or two such: and happily salute them.

Henrietta Street, August 28th

Driving down to the office this morning and passing Kensington Town Hall, where the red and yellow flowers in the window-boxes were set off by falling tendrils of green, I momentarily longed, not only to be back in the childhood when I first fell in love with such things, but back or forward in a dimension of existence where I and the boxes were one. The sunlight, not yet through the mist, had wholly enveloped it; and the trees in Kensington Gardens, on our left as we went towards Knightsbridge, were fuzzy and massive and rounded—everything lost but their treeness. A minute later, down the Mall, the double avenue of planes, with their leaves topping stems scarred and crinkly, brought flashing into my mind an optique, *tuppenny-coloured, of Versailles; and I was everywhere.*

I have been having a curious and beautiful experience these last few days. I have been seeing London, and more than London the world, almost literally "with new eyes". For many years, out of laziness, I had kept on my reading-glasses pretty nearly the whole time, and used my ordinary ones for nothing except the opera and cinemas and theatres and concerts and, occasionally, drives in the car. But two or three nights ago I changed over to my ordinary ones as I left the office at half past six, and since then have been using them regularly. And it is as if I had been seeing the world, up to then, through a veil—a very light sort of veil but still a veil: instead of face to face. Everything, suddenly, looked sharp and clean and brilliant, and yet softer (not in outline but in essence) at the same time—the group of buildings and trees down at Westminster as I came out from a Piccadilly cinema at half past eight; the National Gallery, seen alongwise from a window in Suffolk Street; and a bit of red, a woman's dress, showing up—like the flag on a boat going to paradise in a painting by Stanley Spencer—against the long and far expanse of August green as I drove through Hyde Park on my way back to supper this evening. Delightful to think I have such daily experiences in store. And, to moralise about it

—if a little change in two bits of glass can so enhance what was beautiful already, how transformed everything will be, into a beauty and rightness how inexpressible, when the thick veil of temporality is removed from us!

§ 5

I come finally to a characteristic, bound up with their attitude to conscience, typical of Stalinists everywhere, except in (more or less) Stalinist countries: namely their readiness to commit treason. I want to ask, what is wrong about treason? This may seem an odd sort of question, but the answer is by no means as simple as you might think.

First of all, what is treason?

Here are definitions of the word, and of four others, from the Oxford English Dictionary:

Treason. (1) The action of betraying; betrayal of the trust undertaken by or *reposed in* anyone; breach of faith, treachery. (2) Violation by a subject of his allegiance to his sovereign or to the State.

Traitor. (1) One who betrays any person that trusts him or any duty entrusted to him; a betrayer. (2) *spec.* One who is false to his allegiance to his sovereign or to the government of his country; one adjudged guilty of treason or any crime so regarded.

Treachery. (1) Deceit, cheating, perfidy: violation of faith or betrayal of trust; perfidious conduct. (2) *esp.* The deception or perfidy of a traitor; treason against a sovereign, lord or master.

Allegiance. The relation or duties of a liegeman to his lord; the tie of a subject to his sovereign or government.

Liege-man. (*Feudal law*). A vassal sworn to the service and support of his superior lord. *Trans. & fig.* A faithful follower or subject.

Now I know nothing whatever about comparative law or many of its associated topics: but perhaps the concept of treason, though far older than feudalism, can be best understood in the light of it. The notion is of a contract, explicit or implicit— the words "reposed in", italicised above, are as important as the words "undertaken by": and communal life is conducted on the assumption that the contract will be honoured. On the one side is sovereign, lord, master, government or State: on the other, liege-man or citizen. The former undertakes to bestow certain benefits, of which a chief is security: the latter, to serve and obey. All this is as true of a modern democracy (so long as it remains a democracy, and has neither been replaced by, nor developed into, a tyranny) as of feudalism: people assume the reciprocity, perhaps with qualifications—a conscientious objector, for instance, may be excused from bearing arms. In a dictatorship, on the other hand, no such contract is implied, at any rate to begin with: though acquiescence in the dictatorship by the general body of citizens, if sufficiently prolonged, may produce an assumption, and even a reasonable one, that the contract exists.

But not every possible breach of the contract is considered treason: nor every "perfidious" one, either. A man who cheats the Inland Revenue by faking his books is a criminal to be sure, but not a traitor either legally or in public opinion. For the idea of a contract is emotionally coloured by an overwhelming actuality never far from men's minds, that of "one against another" —of lord against lord, sovereign against sovereign, State against State; and by a second actuality bound up with the first and no less vivid or persistent—that of war. If these actualities, from time to time, are, so to put it, but potential actualities, that makes no difference. A traitor, in fine, means a person who commits a breach of the contract in one clearly understood particular: who so behaves during a war that the actual enemy, or during peace that the possible or probable one, may find it easier to win: behaves deliberately with that intent, no matter what his motive. People who cheat the Inland Revenue in wartime, or operate black markets, are helping the enemy: but they cannot be called traitors, except by a loose extension, unless helping the enemy is their object.

Now consider two concrete examples. Take Fuchs, who communicated atomic secrets to Russia because, in the event of a war between Russia and Great Britain, he wanted Russia to win. And take the Freiherr von ——, who communicated Hitler's blueprints to the Allies because, in a war actually proceeding between Hitler and the Allies, he wanted Hitler to lose. Fuchs had originally taken the plunge into communism which was to determine all his future actions because he believed that, if it came to a conflict, a Russian victory would be better for mankind than a Russian defeat: and the Freiherr plotted against the Germany of Hitler because he believed that, in the war then proceeding, a German defeat would be better for mankind than a German victory. But their motives, for our present purpose, are irrelevant.

The first question is, were they traitors?

Fuchs was, trebly so: because (1) he belonged to a democratic community in which the contract of reciprocity was assumed; (2) he belonged to it, not by birth, but by choice; and (3) he divulged secrets obtainable only as a result of work for its defence, so that he broke a specific and overt contract as well as the general and implied one. As for the Freiherr, your answer must depend on your estimate of the situation in Germany—on whether you consider that a contract existed or not.

And the second question is this. Did Fuchs, who is a traitor, commit a sin? Did the Freiherr, who may or may not have been a traitor, commit one? I said a sin: we are not discussing crimes, which are often sins, but not always.

I am bound to believe that they did; that they both did, and equally. If I would have wished, given their actions, that the Freiherr should succeed and Fuchs shouldn't, this is not in point; nor is my humble gratitude to the Freiherr, or the devotion that I cannot but feel at the memory of his martyrdom.

To begin with, they were helping one or other of the two sides to win a victory of force; and as a pacifist, however tardily, I must think that always wrong—I must want, first and last, reconciliation. That, however, is by the way. But secondly:

(1) As an "absolutist", I cannot but regard certain spiritual attitudes (and any actions that may flow from them) as absolutely wrong, irrespective either of circumstances or of temporal results. I do not mean, when I call them absolutely wrong, that they have no place in the divine purpose: everything has such a place: I mean that, in any conceivable circumstance and whatever the counterbalancing considerations, it is our human obligation, or the proper human part of an inclusive divine-human activity, not merely to overcome them but to convert them into their opposites. Such convertibility, which always resides in them, is perhaps their purpose or essence: consider St Paul before and after his vision, or St Francis before and after his unconsciousness: and just as "it is the proper human part of an inclusive divine-human activity" to effect this conversion, so we

effect it, not by unilateral human struggle, but by co-operation
with grace.

(2) Let me repeat here the theological myth I propounded
in *Timothy*. God was (or should we say, in the more appropriate
language of eternity, is?) undifferentiated. But he perceives
differentiation, concreteness, Blake's "minute particulars", as
supreme value. He therefore creates (splits himself up into,
produces as emanations?) these concrete particulars. But, by
a law of reality, multiplicity involves relation, and a concrete
particular, if it is to be a concrete particular, must have being
and the potentiality for growth within itself. Each particular,
therefore, being and growing, must be in relation with every
other particular, also being and growing. Now the particulars,
not being God (though being of or from God), cannot feel or
know perfectly meanwhile—though they can and do have
intimations about it—how the value of individual being and
growth, and the value of relation, may be realised not as two
conflicting values but as the one value which in fact they are:
for individual being can be perfect only when there is perfect
relation, and relation can be perfect only when there is perfection of individual being. The particulars cannot feel or know
perfectly how to manage this, I said, "meanwhile": during the
intermediate stage, that is—to use again the perhaps inapplic-
able language of temporality—between the undifferentiated
God and the God become a unity of innumerable rejoicing
particulars. The goal, if the word can be used when eternity is
in question, is beautifully illuminated by a sentence from the
Zohar: "When mankind is at one, God is One."

God, desiring this consummation (which may or may not be
involved in the historical process), can help men understand
how to live by the intimations he gives them; but he cannot do
more than help; for if he did more he would be derogating from
the value of individual being, which is the point, as it were, of
the whole business.

(3) The goal is unity: and all spiritual attitudes that we must
classify as absolutely wrong—all sins, let me say—are but
variants of a single, of the only sin: the sin against unity. This
is the sin of a cancerous cell-group in the spiritual body:
the sin of striving to save one's life (and thereby of losing it)
at the expense of Life as a whole.

(4) To achieve a perfect relation with our neighbour, or to

attempt its achievement, is our own human share in the divine-human task of establishing, or re-establishing, unity. Our neighbour, naïvely, is the man we live with, the one more or less vivid to our consciousness, the fellow-member of our homestead or nation: but he is also, by imaginative insight, every single man and woman in the whole human race. It may be that a perfect relation between one human being and another, even between the closest friends and the most passionate lovers and the most faithfully married, is impossible on this side of eternity, and that the total unity in which this relation consists has to wait, despite our longing, for a "restoration of all things" that must inevitably include it: but just as to fight against unity, or to hinder it, is the ultimate sin, so an effort to achieve it, however limited by human weakness or the nature of things, is of heavenly repute. We might say, with William James, that God lives by this effort; or, with Samuel Alexander, that it makes God.

(5) In what does it consist, this perfect human relationship? In something very simple indeed: in a genuine meeting between two individuals.

(6) There is but one fatal impediment to the achievement of such a meeting, namely deceit (not a temporary or unsuccessful deceit, which the other's abundant truth may still convert into its opposite, but a permanent and successful one): for utter openness on both sides is the very condition for establishing contact, at however long last. Even the exercise of gross physical power, though always abominable, can be less obstructive than deceit. That it tends to obstruct needs no argument: a true meeting is for the most part of equals, and to control a man's body is for the most part to make him a slave. And yet a man and his executioner may meet: such an outflow of compassion and forgiveness may proceed from the tormented—at the very moment of execution—as will break down all barriers and bring the other to his side. But how can there be a meeting between two persons when one of them isn't there? When one of them, still locked up in his prison-house, has despatched to the rendezvous but a meaningless simulacrum?

(7) So it was by no means in their repudiation of a contract, a contract explicit as well as implicit, that the sin of Fuchs and those others resided: for to repudiate a contract, whether explicit or implicit, may be demanded, on occasion, by con-

science and honour. No, their sin resided rather in this: that the repudiation was clandestine. They lied and deceived: by acting falsely towards their neighbour, by being unreal before their neighbour, by shutting themselves off from their neighbour, they obstructed, to that extent, the large work of divine-human integration. They adventured for the good of mankind—by an outrage against spirit: by diminishing the possible number of those faithfulnesses which are already, at the instant they happen, eternal buildings for mankind as a whole in the Kingdom of Heaven. Could self-negation go further?

As for the Freiherr, his sin was identical with that of Fuchs, whether there was a contract in his case or not, and for all the nobility of his motive. It is quite impossible, without the grossest intellectual dishonesty, to vilify the one and glorify the other. That Fuchs' conscience had become second-hand is irrelevant for the point I am now making: so is the fact—and I have no doubt it is a fact—that both were doing what they thought best for humanity. My point at the moment is simply this: Both deceived. Their sin was the sin of clandestinity.

Just as now I utterly rule out war, which is physically violent, so as utterly I rule out all secret plotting, which is spiritually violent. "If my body is not my own," wrote Chuang Tzǔ, "pray then whose is it? It is the delegated image of God. Your life is not your own; it is the delegated harmony of God. Your individuality is not your own; it is the delegated adaptability of God." As delegates we have to do God's work: we have to help him in redeeming the world and establishing the Kingdom of Heaven. And what is the Kingdom of Heaven? The Kingdom where men love one another: no longer by a desperate effort, no longer as a matter of duty, but because the divinity within them can at last find its natural expression:

"Serene will be our days and bright,
And happy will our nature be,
When love is an unerring light,
And joy its own security."

But if we love one another—if we really love our neighbours as we ought to love ourselves—then our respect for their freedom is absolute. Love and freedom—they are correlatives. And I ask you, Timothy: Do you respect a man's freedom if you shackle him by power? By your power over his body, when you kill him or wound him or imprison him, and by your power over his intellect, when you keep back the truth? No, you are not respecting his freedom: you are outraging it. And the spiritual or intellectual outrage is worse than the physical one: it makes a man more helpless.

The Kingdom of Heaven cometh not by a nice calculation of advantages and disadvantages in the earthly order: the Kingdom of Heaven cometh by living it. In no other way can it come: or let me say, with greater humility and reverence, that in no other way can we help it to come. For the Kingdom of Heaven is not like unto temporal governments that replace one another: nothing sudden, nothing mechanical or en-gineered, can ever bring it to pass. No, the Kingdom of Heaven is life—life abundant, the life of freedom and love: and how can humanity have a life it refuses to live?

So all clandestine plots, conspiracies and revolutions—what the Freiherr thought it proper to do, no less than what Fuchs thought it proper to do—must be thought of as sinful: or, better, as based on incomplete understanding. Conspirators, even in the best of causes, have their eyes fixed, not on goodness itself, but on the shadow of goodness. Nor can the nature of the regime that they are anxious to overthrow be in any way relevant: to conspire against a tyrannous and deceitful regime is no better than to conspire against a model one. Indeed, in one sense, it is worse—just as I suggested, in *Timothy*, that to hate a man full of hate is more lamentable than to hate a man full of love. Power and deceit must be met, not by power and deceit, but by openness and goodwill. Of course the phrases "is worse" and "is more lamentable" don't really mean anything: what is right is right and what is wrong is wrong: and if I use inappropriate relatives, I do so merely to ram home my point.

(8) Then should the Freiherr have done nothing? If you expect me to say yes you will have totally misunderstood my position. The Kingdom of Heaven cometh by living it: but an essential element in this living is ceaseless opposition to the cruelty, violence, deceit, power-mongering, race-discrimina-tion, materialism and aggressiveness that make living it more difficult. Only, there must be no self-contradiction: only, the opposition must be void alike of deceit and of ill-will. Socrates, second only to Christ in the order of human merit, is our

safest model here. He spent a lifetime in attack. He attacked governmental wickedness: he attacked current morality: he attacked false religion. But his attacks were always open: and as for any trace of ill-will in his make-up—even Xantippe merely bored him. He is one of the world's supreme examples of a candid oppositionist.

The Freiherr should have acted likewise. When, already in 1933, the concentration camps were established, he should have called upon the gaolers to walk out. When first Austria, then Czechoslovakia, and finally Poland were invaded, he should have called upon the soldiers to lay down their arms. He should have appealed to Hitler, and to his friend General so and so, and to guests at great functions: he should have spoken in theatres and streets. Always, publicly, he should have proclaimed the right and denounced the wrong. But how could he have done it, you may ask, under a totalitarian dictatorship? Well, he could have done it at least once, and perhaps three times or four times or five times: then, probably, he would have been killed. This would not have worried him, for he was the bravest of men, and was anyhow horribly martyred. What would have worried him was something quite different: the fear, perhaps the certainty, that aggression, after his death, would go on as before, whereas a plot might have ended it. But he oughtn't to have calculated like that— oughtn't to have calculated, even, that by frank opposition, with death as the result, he might be helping, positively helping, the worse side to win. There is no pietistic sentimentalism, but a recognition of stark reality, in the belief that men must do what is right, and leave the issue to God. But to assassinate, to throw bombs, to deceive—these can never be right. If I believe, also, that by the earthly calculation aforesaid—in the perspective of decades or a century—greater temporal success is to be expected from a candid opposition than from a secret conspiracy, that is not here the point. But I do believe it: for the one, strong in its purity, lives to influence men and women yet unborn, while the other, fighting evil by evil, can have no positive spiritual aftermath.

There is a sentence of Chuang Tzŭ, whom I quoted just now, which expresses the truth about activity and calculation in a beautiful image: "It is easy enough to stand still; the difficulty is to walk without touching the ground." The Bhagavad-Gita speaks similarly: "He who acts without attachment, dedicating all to the Supreme Spirit, is not touched by sin, as the lotus leaf is not wetted by water." The attachment here in mind is no doubt attachment to the personal fruits of action—to their fruits for a man's self: but the same might be said about attachment to its fruits for mankind.

I have been writing, this last half-hour, with quiet sadness: with the brooding remorse that always lives with a man when, remembering his own weakness, he appears to sit in judgment on his fellows. That I should have done no better than the Freiherr is almost certain: that I should have done worse is most probable. By any showing, this was a man. Could I have drunk the cup that he drank—could I have waited for the knock on my door, with the torture and shame that must follow? I do not think so. I cannot even be at all sure about something far less heroic: I cannot even say for certain, as I wrote at the time in my horror of "denazification", whether, if instructed to join the Party or face the consequences—to my children and my wife and myself—I should have been able to refuse. But what is one to do? If the truth, as one thinks it, cries within one, should a consideration of one's own weakness keep one silent?

As I sit here and work things out in my mind, a man as ugly as Socrates, and perhaps as pregnant of salvation, fills the room for a moment with such undying *ahimsa* as few bodily presences could radiate. (Is there any significance, I wonder, in the con-trast or contradiction, as between body and spirit, in some of the world's towering men? Moses, a great prophet, was defective in the organ of speech: Beethoven, a great musician, was defec-tive in the organ of hearing: Socrates, a great adept of spiritual and intellectual beauty, was displeasing to look at. Was Christ, I wonder, ugly? I rather hope so.)

Mahatma Gandhi knew the way. He spiritualised action, and made a weapon of spirit. People have called him half-saint and half-fox. Well, he doubtless had faults, and may have been contaminated, on occasion, by the men and systems he opposed; but even half-saints are rare, and we ought to be grateful when they come to us. His life was one continuous protest against tyranny and oppression as he saw them; but he eschewed, if not completely then to the very limit of his power, any violence or deceit or ill-will. When civil disobedience, as a mass-movement, appeared to be developing these vices, he righted the balance by fasting, in token of repentance. A man of far smaller stature has attacked him as a muddle-head or worse: civil disobedience, he complains, is the exercise of a power no less real than its physical counterpart, and always works, however specious your denials, for loss or damage to your opponent. He is wholly wrong: and his error resides in this, that he fails to understand either the virtue of unattached activity or, to put it from the other angle, the sin of calculation. It was by no means the Mahatma's business to calculate whether his opponents might "lose" by his activity (not that anybody can ever really lose by abandoning oppression): his business was non-cooperation with evil—coupled with utmost goodwill to the doers of it. I am far from pretending that no element of calculation was present: Gandhi doubtless believed, and believed honestly, that the right way, the way of non-cooperation, was also the *best* way of liberating his countrymen. But if he hadn't: if he had believed that an armed and clandestine revolt, with assassinations and bomb-throwing as part of it, would be far more effective—he would still have eschewed it utterly.

(9) I asked, at the beginning of paragraph 8, "Then should the Freiherr have done nothing?", but not, as might also have been expected, "Then should Fuchs have done nothing?" The reason is this. I can make the Freiherr's initial assumption, namely that Hitler had to be opposed: more, that wickedness must always be opposed is one of the bases of my thinking. I complain only of the Freiherr's method. But I cannot make the initial Stalinist assumption—namely that communism, under Russian leadership, must be established by all conceivable methods over the entire surface of the globe: because method ("all conceivable methods") is already involved in that assumption. So the question would have been meaningless.

(10) In conclusion: what I want above all to make clear is that the sin of a traitor (and it is possibly the gravest of sins) by no means consists, as is commonly supposed, in "lining up" against "one's own" with "the others". To "line up", truly, is always heinous—except against evil, wherever it may occur: "one's own" or "the others" can never be in point. For there is a sin of patriotism also—also and especially: and we sin it

from our failure to realise, first, that everything living is our neighbour, and, secondly, that the only reputable alliance is an alliance for good against evil. Christ was very clear on these points. "For I am come to set a man at variance against his father, and the daughter against her mother, and the daughter in law against her mother in law. And a man's foes shall be they of his own household. And he that taketh not his cross, and followeth after me, is not worthy of me." Or again: "Then one said unto him, Behold, thy mother and thy brethren stand without, desiring to speak with thee. But he answered and said unto him that told him, Who is my mother? and who are my brethren? And he stretched forth his hand toward his disciples, and said, Behold my mother and my brethren! For whosoever shall do the will of my Father which is in heaven, the same is my brother, and sister, and mother."

Over against these hard sayings—and the yoke of Christian ethics is indeed very hard, for all except saints—we may put Rebecca's statement, on the very first page of her book, about William Joyce: "He sinned that sin which is the dark travesty of legitimate hatred because it is felt for kindred, just as incest is the dark travesty of legitimate love." There are two errors here. There is no legitimate hatred—of persons—only a legitimised one: and true kinship is not necessarily kinship after the flesh.

CHAPTER III

WAITING ON GOD

AND STILL I'M NOT ready for "political education" at
Repton. We've just returned, Ruth and I, from a few days'
holiday at Edinburgh, where there's been a festival of music
and plays; and I want to tell you about it immediately, and
above all about a book, very germane to the real subject of
this volume (and the one already published, and any others
still to come), that I read there.

"He giveth his beloved sleep." Morning after morning as I
woke up in Edinburgh the lovely cadence of those words rose
from somewhere within me and came silently to my lips.
How different had been 1943!—my year of hell, and the only
other time I've ever gone to Scotland for anything lengthier
than a conference. Now, I could accept sleep from God:
then, I begged and begged it of myself, and myself, being
guilty, couldn't give it. Very different had been the music I had
heard on that previous occasion: the music of a voice that
cried forever through the watches of the night

> "Glamis hath murder'd sleep, and therefore Cawdor
> Shall sleep no more: Macbeth shall sleep no more."

On and on it went, as though fastened, in the company of my
whole being, to an Ixion's wheel: on and on, as I lay paralysed
by drugs but with the clock of my brain ticking thunderously:
on and on, in a rhythm slow and majestic with the awful
majesty of doom—"and therefore—shall sleep no more:
Macbeth shall sleep no more."
"He giveth his beloved sleep." Always, these last ten days
or so in Edinburgh, this was the sentence that rose first to my
consciousness; but other gracious familiarities would soon enter
in canon. By a beautiful compensation, Macbeth himself
would voice my thankfulness:

"The innocent sleep,
Sleep that knits up the ravell'd sleave of care,
The death of each day's life, sore labour's bath,
Balm of hurt minds, great nature's second course,
Chief nourisher in life's feast."

John Keats would come in too, with the sonnet I had loved
as a child:

"O soft embalmer of the still midnight!
Shutting, with careful fingers and benign,
Our gloom-pleased eyes, embower'd from the light,
Enshaded in forgetfulness divine;
O soothest Sleep! if so it please thee, close,
In midst of this thine hymn, my willing eyes,
Or wait the amen, ere thy poppy throws
Around my bed its lulling charities;
Then save me, or the passed day will shine
Upon my pillow, breeding many woes;
Save me from curious conscience, that still hoards
Its strength, for darkness burrowing like a mole;
Turn the key softly in the oiled wards,
And seal the hushed casket of my soul."

And often God the Father's own gloria, his own hymn to sleep
as overheard by Charles Péguy, would try to enter and praise
him, but could never, except for a word or so, get beyond my
forgetfulness.

I have it before me now; and surely even that God-drunken
poet can have written nothing more tender. Shall I quote a
few lines? Or, better still, a few adequate extracts? Friends
have told me that I quoted too much in my earlier pages: you
should say it in your own words, they objected, and not borrow
from others. This I consider, with respect, rather stupid.
Why on earth should I do, all over again, what my betters have
done before me? And can you hear a perfect melody too often?
(Some say yes, I say no.) I am writing, moreover, for myself,
quite as much as for you—or for anybody else who may read
me: and nothing pleases me more than to rehearse, in the
intervals of composition, a great utterance from the past. I even
enjoy, and you may consider this curious, the very copying

of such things out with my pencil. So I shall follow my inclination:

Je n'aime pas celui qui ne dort pas, dit Dieu.
Le sommeil est l'ami de l'homme.
Le sommeil est l'ami de Dieu.
Le sommeil est peut-être ma plus belle création.
Et moi-même je me suis reposé le septième jour.
Celui qui a le coeur pur, dort. El celui qui dort a le coeur pur.
C'est le grand secret d'être infatigable comme un enfant.
D'avoir comme un enfant cette force dans les jarrets.
Ces jarrets neufs, ces âmes neuves
Et de recommencer tous les matins, toujours neuf,
Comme la jeune, comme la neuve
Espérance . . .
Celui qui ne dort pas est infidèle à L'Espérance.
Et c'est la plus grande infidélité.
Parce que c'est l'infidélité à la plus grande Foi.
Pauvres enfants ils administrent dans la journée leurs affaires avec sagesse.
Mais le soir venu ils ne se résolvent point,
Ils ne se résignent point à en confier le gouvernement à ma sagesse . . .
Et l'administration et tout le gouvernement.
Comme si je n'étais pas capable, peut-être, de m'en occuper un peu.
D'y veiller.
De gouverner et d'administrer et tout le tremblement.
J'en administre bien d'autres, pauvres gens, je gouverne la création, c'est peut-être plus difficile.
Vous pourriez peut-être sans grand dommage me laisser vos affaires en mains, hommes sages.
Je suis peut-être aussi sage que vous.
Vour pourriez peut-être me les remettre l'espace d'une nuit.
L'espace que vous dormiez
Enfin
Et le lendemain matin vous les retrouveriez peut-être pas trop abîmées . . .
Remettez à demain ces larmes qui vous emplissent les yeux et la tête.

c

Qui vous inondent. Qui vous tombent. Ces larmes qui vous
  coulent.
Parce que d'ici demain, moi, Dieu, j'aurai peut-être passé.
La sagesse humaine dit: Malheureux qui remet à demain.
Et moi je dis Heureux, heureux qui remet à demain.
Heureux qui remet. C'est-à-dire Heureux qu espère. Et qui
  dort.

Wasn't I right to copy it out for you, Timothy? I hope you
can read it in French, which is the language of clean integrity:
but if you can't you'll find a good translation (by Ann and
Julian Green) in the Appendix.

I can never have slept so many hours, or with such regularity,
since earliest childhood. I slept often from midnight to seven,
and then, after lunch, from two to three: eight hours in all,
against my ordinary five. Only once, on most nights, was there
a break—at about four in the morning; and then I would creep
into our bathroom—a monstrous large one, with Doulton tiles
and all amenities—and throw up the window high, and look
out over Princes Street. This was always good, but best of all
twenty-four hours after we'd got there. I had been very tired,
and hadn't managed to rest much on the train, though our
sleepers were comfortable: and *Acis and Galatea* (at eleven in
the morning: can there be anything in this world more like
heaven than music at eleven in the morning? Your proper
business, all at once, is to be a cherub, and hear the angels
quiring: and at the very moment, if you please, when at
ordinary seasons the muddy vesture of decay—office ledgers—
doth most grossly close you in. For now "love's a duty")
Acis and Galatea, I was saying, had been spoiled just a little,
that morning, by the strain in my body and the stuffiness of
Freemasons' Hall: so that ever and anon I was carried to Lethe
by the ripple and flow of the music. But now as I stood at my
window in the small hours of Sunday, such a languor was in
me, a sort of conscious and deliberate languor, as is always the
first intimation that a long spell of weariness has at last run its
course. The cool of the night was very grateful after the stuffiness of Freemasons' Hall: a wet breeze was on my face, with a
smell, very faint, of the sea in it: and the long row of lights
down on Princes Street made the darkness more palpable.

I first opened, and then took off, my pyjama top: I leaned full out, to feel the cold on my chest. They were very good substitutes, the salty breeze and cool rain on my body, for the dew against my feet, early mornings, on the grass here at Brimpton.

In such a moment of tranquil communion only one prayer was possible: that the communion, then and there, should be utter, or, if this should be forbidden, that one should lose oneself as wholly as one could, and so gain what one might. For the opportunity was here, and one dare not forego it. But the prayer was peaceful: and that the prayer should be peaceful was part of the prayer. Anxiety—that the communion might not be perfect, that the prayer might not be peaceful, that the opportunity might not be taken: an anxiety felt so often in the past—this had vanished: something else was in its place—a sense of waiting on God. I have used those last words quite deliberately, because I was to read, during the following few days, a book by Simone Weil with that title; and I shall have something to say about it presently.

How holy, in very truth, is the night! I love it more and more as I grow older. It is a sort of mirror, or not a mirror but a living example, of the primal unity: and a foreshadowing of the ultimate one: and an intimation that both are eternally there. The fretful stir of separate strivings is stilled: men and animals sleep: God sleeps: all, all are in the bosom of the ineffable *Ain Souf*.

The power to be unanxious, even about anxiety itself: the power to wait on God, and accept: the power to live in charity with all the evil or all the error that mars one—this power, or this negation of power, or this grace, has been coming to me lately in a measure more abundant than before, if only by a little (and anxiety about measure, of this as of everything, must also be rejected). I was telling you, half an hour ago, about my beautiful sleep: but twice, in those few days, I had a nightmare—I have them often: a nightmare, very gross and very terrible, that revealed something straitly involved with me I had rather be without. And I dealt with it better than with the one here at Brimpton, when I made, as I told you, the sign of the Cross. (No, I find, on revision, that I cut it out: never mind.) Terror lasted only an instant: I was able to say, and to say with goodwill, "If I am like that, I am like that": and when Satan came to show me a vision of horror eternal (... *but in that sleep of death what dreams may come*) I cast him off with a reply that had no remnant of doubt in it: Though he slay me, yet will I trust in him. I added, however, what is sometimes forgotten, namely the conclusion of that verse: But I will maintain mine own ways before him. For I abominate enslavement, and above all enslavement to God.

Something else was to happen on our holiday that may argue a little progress in my ability to accept my own evil. Thirty-three years ago, or thirty-three years and eight months to be precise, I did a wrong—by omission—that I have always been specially ashamed of (I shan't tell you what it was, for such things can mean little to others, and you might wrongly think it trivial). I had lived with my guilt all those years, lived with it continuously; every few months or so the thought of its presence would leap up and stab me. And I had lived with it alone—had not talked of it even to Ruth, who is spirit of my spirit. Why? Because until we can accept our own sins, once they have been committed, as also part of reality: until remorse for them, that must ever remain, has been purged of all egoism and rebelliousness—we can be free neither with ourselves nor with others. And perhaps I had been unable to feel, really to feel in my own case though I had believed it theoretically, that repentance and forgiveness are one. How can we tell, asked a Hasid, Rabbi Bunam of Pzhysha, when a sin we have committed has been pardoned? And replied: By the fact that we no longer commit it.

We had driven out to Peebles over the moorland, and before us, as we sat resting in the hydro, were the immortal hills. My sin was very close to me again, perhaps because, only a few days earlier, I had been writing of treason. And suddenly, for the first time in all our married life, I knew that I could tell Ruth about it. Thrice on our way back I tried to, and thrice I failed: the fourth time, with a sob that broke the ice up and set me free, I succeeded.

So that now is that.

§ 2

But to wait on God, and accept, is only half the story: it must be coupled with that desire, or intention, or direction of

the heart towards God, which the mystics of our race called
Kavvanah.

We had given ourselves a send-off from London, the
evening we left for Edinburgh, by inviting the David Lows
and John Collins's to dine with us. Now David and I make
a very odd couple. Close friends for a quarter of a century,
we spar at one another whenever we meet: but as if spar-
ring at ourselves—for we are halves, you might think, of one
person. I serve the relative, to the degree that my weakness
permits, by fixing my eyes on the absolute: he serves the absolute (for he recognises, or so I fancy, its existence) by exclusive
attention to the relative. My concern for the good of humanity
makes me dubious about trimmers: his equal concern makes
him dubious about fanatics. Something passionless and calcu-
lating in him, a sort of positive liking for compromise, for the
thing in itself, is the product of a moral passion as spontaneous
and uncompromising as my own. Religion plainly bewilders
him, and you can see him throw up his hands (in the spirit) at
any talk of it: but his politics are as essentially religious as my
religion is political—as my religion, I mean, takes on body in
political action. I love God, consciously: he, without knowing
it. He is a moderate, I an extremist. If, which is not improbable,
he were made a peer, *Festina lente* or μηδὲν ἄγαν might be the
motto inscribed on his scutcheon: if, which is impossible, I
were, *de l'audace, encore de l'audace, toujours de l'audace* might be
the motto inscribed on mine. His benevolence, which is exceptional, is unqualified by personal considerations but flavoured
with irony: mine, which is warmer and less detached, has to
fight its way up, more often than I like, through resentments
egoistic in origin. He will play the Devil's advocate when it
suits him, partly to tease and partly to arrive at the truth—but
is always, in his heart, on the side of the angels: I sympathise
with the Devil and even love him (which David would think
nonsense), but to be his advocate—oh never!

We are both liberals, and both socialists.

Well: we had been astonishingly unanimous, that evening,
for more than a solid hour, when we fell to discussing Malaya,
and the destruction, or threatened destruction, of a village there
by way of reprisal. Somebody asked David whether he was
going to do a cartoon about it, and suggested as the underline
"Lidice". Immediately a whole battery of signals came glittering

into David's eye—and if you object that a man's eye can't exhibit all this much I assure you that it did, at least to anyone who knew him as I do. A sense of responsibility; a dread of haste and over-simplification; a distrust of emotionalism; a vigilance in face of it, of his own and other people's; a determination, self-conscious and almost professional, to weigh up pros and cons and not be rushed, by himself or whomever; a gentle wryness, a charitable irony; and a modicum of affectionate malice—impossible, Timothy, to imagine a more beautiful counterpoint. "It's a terrible thing, isn't it?" he asked; and answered "yes" as we nodded, in a tone which simultaneously suggested that (a) he had assumed our agreement, (b) he was gratified by it, and (c) he had the ace up his sleeve. And what was this ace when he played it? Hitler's ace, Stalin's ace, the Devil's ace. Namely: means, however appalling, may possibly—he didn't go further than that, but may possibly —be justified by the end, if the end is important enough. And David Low isn't Hitler or Stalin, nor yet the Devil: David Low is as just, in the Biblical sense, as anyone now living.

Diana Collins was sitting by me: a lovely young woman, all spiritual eagerness, and very near to the Kingdom of Heaven. I let the general conversation run its course, and began talking to her softly, as if we were alone. Doesn't all this show, I asked her, what a terrible muddle a man gets into, even a man as good as David Low: how (but not really, of course, if he's as good as David Low) he finds himself driven from a first acquiescence in a minor form of wickedness to a second acquiescence in a major one, and so progressively on towards a final abandonment of every standard he once cherished, if, deliberately and human weakness apart, and from whatever motive, he strays an inch, whether privately or publicly, from the firm, sure ground of Christian ethics—in respect, I mean by publicly, of the attitudes and activities he will support as a citizen and the attitudes and activities he will not?

Diana agreed with me—of course she agreed with me, for we had discussed the matter dozens of times, and always found ourselves unanimous. "But what are we going to do about it?" she asked—reminding me of my outburst in *Timothy*, with its description of the torment I was feeling, during the summer of 1951, at the gulf between my theory and my practice. Let me

copy out that passage for you, Timothy; let me quote what I
said two years ago:

"I don't know for how many years now I have been struggling
against the conviction that my whole spiritual and intellectual
position is false, and I have been growingly aware of this falseness whenever I have called to mind, for the purpose of this
letter, my ideas at various periods of my life. I feel this falseness,
for some reason or another, more acutely than ever tonight.
Can I correct it before I shall have finished? When I come to the
final page, shall I find that I have at last been able to conquer
whatever it may be in me, 'wretched man that I am', that prevents me from accepting intellectually, and living spiritually,
the truths which, deep down in me, I believe I have always
known, known since early childhood, to be truths that conscience, or apprehension of reality, or whatever you may like to
call it, demands that I should accept and live?

"What I am trying to say is this. I look at the world around
me, and at my own life. At the world of atom bombs; at the
hatred between East and West; at the vileness of the press; at
the sadism of films; at the murder of children and old women;
at murderers hung by the neck until they are dead; at millions
and millions starving miserably, and no one caring anything
about it; at my own wretched efforts to make profits for my
firm and provide for my own present comfort and my future
old age. And I know, with every atom of my being, that there
is only one answer: absolute pacifism, absolute communism
(not in the Stalinist sense, but in the early religious sense of
holding all things in common), an absolute living of the
Christian ethic. I not only know it: I knew it when the positions I honestly held, and shall honestly describe in later chapters—positions that I still largely hold—were the positions
neither of absolute pacifism nor of absolute communism.

"There may appear to be a startling paradox in all this: I
use the word 'false' one moment and 'honestly' the next. But
the paradox is the point: both 'false' and 'honestly' are exact.

"Take, for purposes of clarification, my present position on
pacifism and Christian communism. I am not—not yet—a pacifist. Why, if I know it is right? Because, fighting with this deeper
knowledge, is another kind of knowledge that I cannot deny—a
δόξα, as Bernard Strauss might have called it, in contrast with

γνῶσις. I know, with this other kind of knowledge, that but for armed resistance to Hitler fascism might have conquered the world; that freedom might have vanished everywhere; and that, worst of all, generation after generation might so have been conditioned that freedom might have vanished not only everywhere but for ever. And this knowledge, the knowledge of a possibility so horrible that I am unable to face it, is like a great lump of lead shutting down what is both deeper and more real in me, and preventing it from occupying my whole being. (But isn't all this utterly faithless? Isn't such a fear nonsensical, seeing that (a) the eternal God is freedom, and (b) there cannot be anything 'wrong' with the totality of things?)

"It is the same with Christian communism—which, for individuals in our present society, would mean following the spirit of Eckhart's words.* I run a business for profit; and though I give away a good deal of money, I am careful to keep enough of it to ensure that I shall live very comfortably both now and in the future. Why do I do it, knowing deep down what I know? Not only from selfishness and greed, though those of course come in. But also because I know, honestly with the other kind of knowledge, that to publish the sort of books I specialise in is a valuable service to the community: that power in this way to advocate a better society is more likely to assist in achieving it than the abandonment of such power: that no business can survive, in present conditions, except on the basis of profitmaking: that, family considerations apart, if I give my last penny away I may make myself a burden to the community: and that I am the sort of human being whose personality would shrivel up, be robbed of any value it may have, not only in conditions of penury but even if deprived of the country and travel and books. (And in the very act of writing these words I half know that I'm making excuses, and then again I half know that I'm not.)

"Well, there is the dilemma, and it agonises me. . . ."

That is what I wrote two years ago, Timothy, and that is what Diana rehearsed to me when, on the eve of our holiday in Edinburgh, I talked about the need for not departing a millimetre from the firm, sure ground of Christian ethics.

* "He who withholds but a pennyworth of worldly goods from his neighbour, knowing him in need of it, is a robber in the sight of God. Further I declare, who spares a penny for himself to put it by for a rainy day, is a murderer before God."

"Well," I replied, "part of that's behind me: I've finally become a pacifist." "I know," she said, "but isn't that a bit easy? Isn't it Christian communism—living moment by moment in the spirit of Eckhart, giving everything we have to the poor: isn't it *this* that we ought to think of as the crux—or the Cross? And what do we do? We go away sorrowful, because we have (relatively) great possessions."

Ah, she spoke with my own voice. But I had my answer ready, for I had been trying to face things anew—month by month, week by week—since that outburst in *Timothy*. Or rather had been letting them face me: for that, more and more, had been becoming the heart of the matter.

This, in effect, is what I said in reply to her:

"We may not storm the ramparts of heaven. We must enter, if at all—for God may not wish us to enter, and that also must be accepted—by the gate of our own heart. We must become as one of Christ's little children. [And my heart sings within me, dear Timothy, as I put down these words: for I am become at this instant, if only by a passing favour, as one of Christ's little children myself—consoled, calm of mind, all passion spent.] We must long much and wait much: long much—this is the point I want to make here—as well as wait much: and if we long enough and wait enough, then a moment may come when, please God, we are suddenly there. All else is Satanic presumption.

"We must purify our hearts. We must strengthen the longing within us for the good or the more good, and let it annihilate, or rather absorb, all contentment with the bad or the less good. And to long for the good is a grace that is freely vouchsafed us: we are able, without qualification, to long for the good. (Or say, if you prefer, 'some of us are able': no point in being delayed here by sidetracking objections.) We live always with a sense of this grace: and this freedom—to long for the good—is the only freedom, I think, we possess. But this freedom, if our only freedom, is also a freedom to unlock the last door that would otherwise bar us from heaven. It is a freedom to enter at the end—and any moment may be the end, a split second may be our millennium—into life more abundant, life eternal: so that all other freedoms, all limited freedoms, are included in it. Let me put it like this: The longing, to the extent of the longing, is already the goal. 'Blessed are the righteous'—is this what Christ said? No, but 'Blessed are they which do hunger and thirst after righteousness; for they shall be filled.' Namely: filled with righteousness. Knock, and it shall be answered unto you: seek, and ye shall find.

"We may know beyond argument, you and I, that it is right to live with all things in common, and that this is our goal: we do know it. But a struggle to live with all things in common is by no means the road to that goal: the road to that goal is such a longing to live with all things in common—an ever intensified longing, however poignant we may think it already—that sooner or later, when our longing, if ever, is great enough, we find ourselves compelled to live thus and not otherwise.

"There are some things we *cannot* do—I cannot do this, you cannot do that, hardly anyone can do the other—unless armed with a sword of such metal as can annihilate impossibility. This is the sword of our desire—of our desire to do the impossible thing in question, or of our desire to become a person who will do it automatically. St Francis of Assisi was so armed, and, terrified of leprosy, kissed the leper. But the sword is not a sword of unchangeable condition: we can sharpen it, or let it rust. We sharpen it by co-operation with grace. And this co-operation, I think, must always be a lengthy one. Sudden grace, unless I am mistaken, is as a flame leaping up from a smouldering fire.

"There are things, on the other hand, that we can do without wanting to do them, very much or at all: we can do them from a sense of duty. Now I am not one of those who regard the Stoic ideal as altogether worthless, even when of the type that rejects *agape*: or think that actions performed from a mere sense of duty are devoid of all value. To act dutifully, and either without inclination or against it, may be useful as a piece of self-discipline, and thereby, or additionally, may evoke inclination itself. And that is not all. The result of such action, the result for another, may be of a kind that will hallow it—I mean objectively: hallow it as a dead instrument of beneficence. Whatever the motive, for instance, to save a man's life is clearly better than to let him die, and to feed him clearly better than to let him starve. But a sense of duty, for all that, and even when it shines at its brightest, is but as a candle to the sun of desire. You don't *meet* what you do, when you do it because you ought to and not because you want to: there is a chasm between you and what you do, so that the potentiality of full being for both (for you in this complex, for the deed altogether) is never realised. The deed is a ghost, and so, in your relation to it, are you. A new element of externality, of the bogus and dissociated, of merely mechanical relationship, has entered into existence. And further: if inclination is absent, less staying-power is probable; for a man does not pant after duty as the hart panteth after the water-brooks, but so panteth—cannot help himself panting—after the object of his desire. Further again: do a thing from sense of duty, and you may do it wrong. I mean worse than imperfectly, worse than with all the glory of life and all the holiness of spirit gone out of it and leaving it bare: I mean that the very propriety of your action, its mechanical and externalised propriety, may be pregnant of evil. Help a man because you ought, without desire or *Kavvanah*, and you commonly injure him. Benefactors are often hated, as we know: but never when the benefit has been prompted by love.

"And if a deed done from duty leaves the world still as cold as before, or at worst makes it colder, what a new warmth and radiance has been added to the whole sum of things by every deed done from love! Works and faith—it is a stupid contrast, when unregenerately understood. But a terrible and lovely truth lies embodied at the heart of it.

"As for my own present attitude to Christian communism: it differs greatly, and in two respects, from what I felt on that other occasion. My objections, whether genuine or otherwise, have gone by the board: here also, as in the case of pacifism, worry about relativities is over. I accept, without reservation, the duty of living with all things in common; and my inclination to do so, already strong, has become even stronger. Then do I feel still more agonised by a position still more false than it was? By the contrast in my manner of living, become more blatant, between what is, and what ought to be? No, I am agonised less, if at all.

"To strengthen my desire—both for living with all things in common, and for goodness in general; to purify my heart; to hope and wait; not to struggle or rebel: this is now my endeavour.

"Let me say more precisely what I mean by living with all things in common. I do not mean dropping my publishing business and becoming a monk. Given the circumstances of my personal life and of modern life generally, that wouldn't at all be the way to convert Christian-communist ideas into contemporary practice. My business, despite all the bric-à-brac, attractive bric-à-brac some of it, mixed up with the gold, is of value to the community, and ought to be preserved; moreover, it must be run at a profit, for much of its capital is controlled by outsiders. But two procedures are open to anyone who professes what I profess, both of them sharp as a razor's edge, and neither of them lacking in feasibility. I could pay equal salaries, and (after satisfying my shareholders with the minimum they would put up with) an equal share of profits, to every member of the staff—from packers and porters to heads of departments—myself included: and if even so I got more than I needed for a minimum standard of decency—a genuinely minimum standard, that is: not my own minimum standard, but anyone's—I could dedicate the balance to people with less than they needed, or to broad human purposes: keeping no sixpence for foul weather. (Even the minimum of decency is questionable, so long as need still exists.) Alternatively, for some of the staff mightn't play, I could take what I do, and then give as I've mentioned. By either of these methods I could achieve a rough equivalent, and given the will not at all an unworkable one, of Christian communism. I ought to do so, and not only with a very large part of me, but essentially, have a longing to do so. What prevents me is partly inertia (so easy, moment by moment, to slither along the path of routine, so hard to make a stand and turn aside towards a *vita nuova!*—I used to write those very words in my diary, at the top of every page, with red pencil, for weeks ahead, as a sort of childish admonition) what prevents me is partly inertia, but also love of comfort and luxury: a moderate and occasional luxury, yet still luxury.

"Now I'm not going to pretend for a moment that I haven't got, or don't still get, a great deal of joy from my manner of living. And I'm using the word joy exactly. Naturally, I've got pleasure as well: but even what, in ordinary judgment, would be considered mere purveyors of pleasure have been instruments, throughout the whole of my life, for awakening or intensifying in me the joy in communion, or communion in joy, that I made an effort to describe in *Tim I*: the communion being a communion with everything. But no: I doubt, on reflection, if I've ever got joy from my 'manner of living': I am sure that I haven't. The awareness, indeed, never absent and sometimes obtrusive, that I was living like this has caused me frequent distresses. What has given me joy (but with the qualification I'm coming to) has been each separate occasion in this manner of living, every pearl that has made up the chain. The distinction is important: indeed, if not the essence of the matter, it makes that essence clearer.

"Listen. For a full quarter of a century—ever since, in the late nineteen-twenties, a relative prosperity began coming to me—I have felt an undercurrent of discomfort, of personal unworthiness, even of treachery, at or after almost every new instance of luxurious living: not only, I mean, after indulgence in a new kind of luxury, but after repetitions of an old one as well. Or, to put it better, I have felt rather soiled. And I understand perfectly why. The reason is twofold. First, to live 'well' in a world marred by misery and starvation is irreligious and unchristian; and I have been a Christian at heart, in my own understanding of the term, for close on thirty years. It is unchristian, obviously, as disobeying Meister Eckhart's injunction, but in another way as well: for it cuts a man off from the overwhelming mass of his neighbours, and so sins against fellowship. You will understand, better than most people, what I mean. Think of the *poverello*, and of someone dining—where we are dining. Think of Society, and society. There is something vile in the capital.

"The second reason—why I have so often felt soiled—is like unto the first: only the setting, as it were, is far wider. In the one case, it is a question of cutting oneself off from humanity: in the other, of cutting oneself off from everything, or God. For luxurious living—even in a life like my own, which has been one, on the whole, of hard work, with the luxury incidental or sporadic—may even all but rule out, and always tends to make harder or less integral, communion with the totality of things.

"What I'm struggling to express is this. Joy can come through luxury, yes: it has often come so to me. You may think me grotesque, but I tell you that I have felt joy, joy in the true sense, joy in the sense of communion with everything, at the smell of a cigar in my nostrils, and the bouquet of a wine on my palate, and the jollity and ease and good fellowship of a dinner like this: at the coincidence of all these, as well as at all these individually. I feel it now! But one knows, afterwards if not at the moment, that the joy, the communion—with everything, with God—has not been complete. The note has been too personal: one has lost oneself, but not enough. You understand the difference next morning, as you watch the sun rise through the haze, or feel the dew on your toes. Before, there was as much enjoyment as joy: now, you are lost—with the Other who is also the you.

"Do I sound heavy? Am I making an ado about trivialities? Really, I'm not. By some law of spiritual energy (identical with that of physical energy? Perhaps, for all things are one: but I know nothing of science, and may be talking like a fool) the more enjoyment, the less joy: the more energy you direct to 'your' person, the less you direct to the Person beyond personality. You cannot help yourself: by the very act of directing more to the one, at the very moment of doing so, you direct less to the other. But this is treachery.

"And, apart from what you do at that moment, the spirit has a way of forming habits, even as the body has.

"There is something else, or perhaps it's only another way of looking at the same thing. In any act of luxury, as in any piece of work done for personal ends, there is a *double* attachment—attachment, of course I mean, in the sense defined by the Bhagavad-Gita. There is not only an element of attachment, greater or smaller, to the enjoying self, like the attachment in the other case, in the case of work done for personal ends, to the working self: there is also an element of attachment, greater or smaller, to the particular thing being enjoyed, like the attachment, in the other case, to the particular piece of work being done. And this attachment to particular things inhibits, to the degree of it, communion with the totality of things. Enjoy an exquisite wine, and *you* are attached to the *wine*: watch a sunrise, and there's no attachment to the sunrise any more than to you. Similarly: when I publish a book to make money, there's a sort of feverish attachment to the publishing; but when I publish a book to save souls there's—I've felt the contrast so often!—as it were a merging, not only of me the doer but also of the thing being done, in a totality of . . . let me put it like this: no longer am *I* rowing a *boat* down a *stream*, but the three of us, stream, boat and I, are gliding peacefully

together, or not together but as one. And the stream is the
stream of reality, or of God.

"Good, common living doesn't attach us to any element in
that living. Bread, if we are hungry enough but not too hungry,
peacefully and happily satisfies us, but no more. When we eat
it we are at one, in a natural kind of way—not taking thought
—with the fields. But when we drink a vin extraordinaire *as* a
vin extraordinaire, not, if you will forgive the refinement, as a
vin ordinaire of happily exceptional flavour—we are not
really at one with the vineyards: the wine sticks out too much,
we stick out too much, and the relation between us sticks out
too much, from the general scheme of things. And the scheme
of things is hurt when things stick out. Even a lump or two can
spoil porridge: and if there are too many of them it's no
longer porridge but lumps.

"You may see all this as contradicting what I've said so often
in the past, namely that we must meet the universal by
way of the particulars. So we must: but we can hope to find
the fair guerdon only if we are unattached to the particulars,
only if, in and through them, we merge with the Whole.

"So that's the second reason why luxury makes me feel
rather soiled. It imperils the joy of communion; and to rejoice
in communion is a duty, the sum of duties, imposed by religion.
But 'imposed' is wrong; for if in all other cases love and duty
are antithetical, in this case they are not so—the duty, in this
case, is the duty of allowing oneself to love.

*   *   *

"I can tell you more precisely, after that, what I meant by
my remark a bit earlier—that nowadays I try to purify my
heart and strengthen my desire. A conflict, as I said, has been
there for a quarter of a century; the conflict between a liking
for luxury and a disgust at it, and, beyond and above that, the
conflict between a wish to live 'normally' (or call it, in the
economic sense, unchristianly) and a wish to live with all
things in common. It has been an odd sort of conflict. The
victory, so far, has gone to the worse side, but the weight,
the real weight, has always been with the better. For I have felt,
from the beginning, that the wish to live 'normally' was being
fought against by something essential in me, but that the wish

to live with all things in common was being fought against by something incidental.

"Now how have I dealt with this conflict? Until recently, by two methods, which have alternated. Coming away from an extravagant lunch-party or dinner-party with a sense of discomfort, of having committed some treachery, of being soiled, I have quickly, in a minute or two—before reaching my office, let us say, from the Savoy—got rid of the sensation, suppressed it, 'forgotten about it'——

Oh but that is the one thing we mustn't do with the promptings of conscience. I have just been interrupted by the nine o'clock news on the wireless, for I'm writing this downstairs instead of up in the library: perhaps impelled by a dim ancestral instinct to be with Ruth on the eve of the Sabbath. The first all-British atomic bomb has been exploded, in a test known as Operation Havoc; and the announcer has been telling us, in his high neutral voice, that Mr Churchill has sent congratulations to Professor Penney, and all the others concerned, for bringing "this great enterprise" to "fruition". Just "this great enterprise": not, even, as Mr Churchill, who has a sense of values, might well have described it, "this dreadful but necessary enterprise". The room, as I listened, became dark, dead, icy, Roman, another Place of a Skull: mirror for the moment of the world to me, I saw it as spiritless—as inertia, as gross stuff, knowing nothing of right and wrong, and nothing, or less than nothing in its brutishness, of the love that shines on both. We were vaunting our ability to blast and destroy with greater "brilliance" than the rest: we were congratulating ourselves on the "devotion" with which we had "achieved" this result. And not even, this is the point, with the tiniest indication that we were ashamed of being involved in this wickedness. Look at the word "devotion". Devotion to what? Devotion to atomising our neighbours, or to work that has this as its end. I confess I cannot look at a photograph of Dr Penney in the newspapers, all smiles and his children beside him, without a feeling of horror. Oh, I know all about the necessities of defence, irrelevant though I consider them—all about the aim of this devilishness being to prevent war, not make it. Let the thing, then, be done with contrition, and the news of it whispered as we whisper a confession of sin, and not shouted at the top of our voices as we shout when our

*side scores a century at cricket or a goal at a football match. But
the fact is we feel no contrition, or rather our statesmen don't:
or if they do they conceal it. They have been caught up and rushed
forward, it would seem—moment by moment, on and on—by
what they regard, to say the very best for them, as their professional duty: and if conscience still speaks, as it may, they haven't
the leisure to listen. As for the religion that should help them to
listen, should keep conscience alive—how many sermons, I wonder,
will even so much as mention this broadcast when exhorting the
faithful to love their neighbour as themselves? How many preachers
of Christ's word, who go about in special livery to give notice of
the fact, will I do not say denounce, but even make an effort to
justify, Operation Havoc itself? And yet they were quick to
denounce something else: when Lady Megan preached the gospel
at St Paul's—on the text 'feed the hungry'—they protested in
their thousands, because she is a nonconformist.*

*So let those of us who do feel contrition at any rate keep it alive.
When Peter Ustinov comes on, as he came on just now after the
News, to delight us with his comicalities, do not let us brush off
our contrition, do not let us suppress it, 'forget about it'——*

'Forget about it'—this is the point. "Yes," I continued in my
talk with Diana, "coming away from an extravagant lunch-
party or dinner-party with a sense of discomfort, of having
committed some treachery, of being soiled, I have quickly got rid
of the sensation—by suppressing it or 'forgetting about it'. I
have hidden myself from my conscience, and my conscience
from me: or better, for 'conscience' might be misinterpreted, I
have sought to bury my desire—the real desire of my heart, the
Kavvanah within me—below the surface of my itch. I have
hurriedly gone on my way.

"But that hasn't always worked, even superficially. There
have been times—my other method, this has been, of dealing with my conflict—when for hours or days or weeks or
months I have fiercely rebelled against my whole way of life:
partly as jeopardising the joy of communion, partly as cutting
me off from humanity, but most of all as disobeying Meister
Eckhart's injunction. I remember a period—the better part of
a year, it must have been—when day after day I could hardly
bear to sit in my office: I was always wanting to rush off and

do something—devote the whole of my time to prison or hospital visiting or the like. And I recollect another and longer one: after the months, from '45 to '47, when I really *had* 'given up' everything—but spontaneously, unquestioningly, happily, tranquilly, not from rebellion, wanting to—for the work of German relief. But these fevers came to nothing, and suppression, sooner or later, succeeded them. Forgetting about it, rebellion, forgetting about it—this was the pattern.

"Nowadays, my method is different. I neither forget about it, nor rebel. When I have that aftermath of spiritual discomfort—I may have it tonight, when we've gone—I use it, use it consciously and peacefully, to nourish my essential desire: my desire to live with men as Christ told us to, my desire, which is an identical desire, to live with God. I let it sink into me, this desire, for as long as I can, sink into me and spread through me; not only on the occasions in question, when the clash of what I do with what I want to do seems specially vivid, but, after summoning it, at as many moments as I may. And to change my whole way of life, as it were, prematurely, before my wish, my *Kavvanah*, is integral—before I can no longer help myself, but must—this would be, I think nowadays, artificial and even impious.

"Well, Diana, there it is. Desire . . . or direction of the heart towards God: waiting . . . for the issue: acceptance . . . of that issue when it comes—this is the chord I try to sound (oh, but feebly—who could know it better than I?) in my effort to live as decently as I can. And a conviction is growing that one day my desire will be great enough, and I shall have it.

"But I mustn't leave you with a sentence like that, for I've been carried away by a wish, such as often beguiles me, to present things as a good deal less qualified than I know them to be, and so have painted, in the spiritual sense, too rosy a picture. I said, 'a conviction is growing': I ought to have said, perhaps, 'I play with the idea that a conviction is growing'. And as to this whole new effort of mine, I doubt whether it's more than a mere tendency, fumbling and fitful."

That's what I said to Diana, though of course not at such length, nor so formally (I've expanded and polished a bit, put in a quip or two, elaborated some similes, and explained for your enlightenment, Timothy, things Diana knew already): but substantially that. An odd kind of discourse, you may think, over the brandy and cigars at a *restaurant de grand luxe* on the eve of a rather extravagant holiday.

One mustn't rebel, I thought just now as I came in from the garden, even against an inability to praise enough. (The dawn was —but I cannot say what the dawn was: that is the essence of the matter.) One can only put a check on one's impatience: one can only quietly wait—perhaps for a morning next week, perhaps for the moment of one's death, perhaps for ever. But waiting doesn't mean doing nothing about it. One must long more (to praise) as well as wait more (for praising to come): and then maybe . . . Or, if it's a question of waiting "for ever", then perhaps, if one really is longing enough, the bewildered dumbness which is all one seems capable of sounds as good to divinity as music sounds to us.

§ 3

I brooded a good deal on our way up to Scotland over my talk with Diana, and particularly over the words "to change my whole way of life prematurely would be artificial and even impious". I had thought at the time that my answer to this whole problem was the right one: I thought so in the sleeper: I think so now. But had I thought so, did I think so, do I think so, quite honestly? That's the doubt, the drip drip on the stone, that will rarely let me be. The old way, the comfortable way, the unregenerate way—can anything be easier than to justify it? To invent reasons, good reasons, for believing it the right way? "Good" reasons: the Tempter is subtle, and his surest hope of success, in dealing with the less ingenuous, is to present wickedness as spirituality.

But I'm not saying quite what I mean. I have the utter conviction, with no reservation at all about its honesty, that my answer is the right one—that it reveals, let me say, an element wholly indispensable for any proper relation between the human and divine. What I am doubtful about is my personal use of this answer. Being impure of heart—wanting, simultaneously, to live the old way and the new, though wanting to do so, in the two cases, at different levels (wanting *essentially*, as I have said, to

live the new way), am I using this answer, which as applied by
the purer in heart has no flaw in it, to postpone in my own case,
for as long as I can, the foregoing of impurity? Well, truly I don't
know. If you turn out to be a writer, Timothy, you will discover
at first hand a very curious phenomenon. You will put down a
sentence: you will read it over, and be certain it rings wrong—
I mean that its rhythm is faulty: you will substitute another:
and you will be equally certain that the second rings wrong and
the first rang right. You don't know definitely, one way or the
other, till next morning. So I think myself a humbug: and immediately I think myself honest. I shan't know definitely, perhaps, till eternity. I hope you won't think me pilpulistic: if you
do, you must remember that I derive from generations of
Rabbonim.

So, I suppose, did Simone Weil: so do all Jews, or say they
do—and indeed, until recently (recently, that is, on the Jewish
time-scale: the boast is idiotic, but I can rarely resist it), every
Jew, even a butcher or rag-and-bone man, was in some sense a
Rabbi. Simone, anyhow, writes like a Rabbi, even more than
I do. I began reading her—between *Acis* and *Rosenkavalier*—
within hours of our arrival in Scotland, and found her, turn by
turn, almost uniquely sympathetic and almost uniquely repellent. So repellent, indeed, that I am all eagerness, not to argue
with her, for she is dead before her time, but to contradict her:
and, using her as a text, to attack certain tendencies in current
religious thinking that seem to me disastrous.

But now that I am actually on the point of doing it (a night
has intervened, during which I have re-read a good deal of her)
all my eagerness has vanished. To begin with, I find I love her,
in a way and for a reason that you'll soon understand. Secondly,
her spiritual depth, acuteness of intellect and power of expression are all so much greater than mine—she is a religious genius,
without question, of the first order—that I feel like a man who
can just play a five-finger exercise but dares to criticise Beethoven. And I am reluctant for another reason too, which is
this: I write a good deal myself—and often find, to my amaze-
ment, that I'm supposed to have written something utterly
different from what I meant to write. Now my own thought is
simple and plain, like the tune of a ballad, but Simone's rich
and deep, all aglimmer with fugitive intimations, like the
quartet in C sharp minor, opus 131; and I dread the more to

misinterpret her (whether from ignorance, or hasty reading, or inability to understand) because she is no longer here to correct me. Again, one constantly comes across passages—in *Waiting on God*, even, itself—which illumine, and so justify, other passages that at first seemed repellent: but this is not the only book she wrote, or left material for: so that one ought to be silent, or at least very cautious, till one has studied her a good deal more fully. Take what follows, then, as a desire to explain my own thinking, rather than as a refutation of hers.

But I must first express my gratitude: the gratitude a man always feels when he hears his own thoughts and emotions voiced in words he has looked for in vain. As I read her at the North British Hotel, there were passages in which she seemed to be saying, but with greater force and precision, exactly what I had been saying to Diana only a few hours before:

"God rewards the soul which thinks of him with attention and love, and he rewards it by exercising a compulsion upon it which is strictly and mathematically in proportion to this attention and love. We have to abandon ourselves to the pressure, to run to the exact spot whither it impels us and not go one step further, even in the direction of what is good. At the same time we must go on thinking about God with ever increasing love and attentiveness, in this way gaining the favour of being impelled ever further and becoming the object of a pressure which possesses itself of an ever growing proportion of the whole soul. When the pressure has taken possession of the whole soul, we have attained the state of perfection. But whatever stage we may have reached, we must do nothing more than we are irresistibly impelled to do, not even in the way of goodness."

Every word here seems right. We travel the same road, she and I: but I am a dilettante, and she is a devout.

I wrote in the margin against that passage—delighted, no doubt, by the chance of justifying, if only for a moment, my perhaps dubious position—the following note: "Just so am I ready, and have been ready for almost as long as I can remember, to work and fight for the establishment of a society in which everyone, including myself, will have to live, so far as material circumstances are concerned, like a Christian communist; but am not ready to live like one—yet—in our present society. It is as if a man spent all his time in an effort to get taxes increased against people at his own level of income, but wasn't ready meanwhile to make a voluntary gift of his equivalent surplus to the State. Rather like G.B.S.—not a bad model."

Simone has other fine passages on the same theme:

"I cannot get rid of my inhibition by direct means but only indirectly, by becoming less imperfect, if I am helped by grace."

"I think that with very important things we do not overcome our obstacles. We look at them fixedly for as long as is necessary until, if they are due to the powers of illusion, they disappear. What I call an obstacle is quite a different thing from the kind of inertia which we have to overcome at every step we take in the direction of what is good. I have experience of this inertia. Obstacles are quite another matter. If we want to get over them before they have disappeared, we are in danger of those phenomena of compensation, referred to I think by the Gospel passage about the man from whom one devil had gone out and into whom seven others entered forthwith."

"It is the part played by joy in our studies that makes of them a preparation for spiritual life, for desire directed towards God is the only power capable of raising the soul. Or rather, it is God alone who comes down and possesses the soul, but desire alone draws God down. He only comes to those who ask him to come; and he cannot refuse to come to those who implore him long, often and ardently."

"Above all our thought should be empty, waiting, not seeking anything, but ready to receive in its naked truth the object which is to penetrate it . . . We do not obtain the most precious gifts by going in search of them but by waiting for them. Man cannot discover them by his own powers and if he sets out to seek for them he will find in their place counterfeits of which he will be unable to discern the falsity . . . There is a way of waiting, when we are writing, for the right word to come of itself at the end of our pen, while we merely reject all inadequate words."

There are perils in all this, to my way of thinking, if one stresses the elements of compulsion and obedience rather than the element of co-operation, or if, what comes to the same thing,

one's view of God is—but I shall come to that presently. Apart
from this, these passages seem perfect.

I find my own voice, again, in what she has to say about
acceptance of ourselves:

"I have germs of all possible crimes, or nearly all, within me.
I became aware of this in the course of a journey, in circumstances which I have described to you. The crimes horrified me,
but they did not surprise me; I felt the possibility of them within
myself; it was actually because I felt this possibility in myself
that they filled me with such horror. This natural disposition is
dangerous and very painful, but, like every variety of natural
disposition, it can be put to good purpose if one knows how to
make the right use of it with the help of grace."

And there is a passage on her very first page that Spinoza
might have written. How like they are, she and Spinoza, and
how unlike! Both of them were Jews, and both of them partially
Jewish in thought; though Simone, who every now and again
exhibits a Jewish self-hatred of the most tragic ferocity, would
have repudiated the suggestion:

"We have to distinguish between three domains. First that
which is absolutely independent of us; it includes all the accomplished facts in the whole universe at the moment, and everything which is happening or going to happen later beyond our
reach. In this domain everything which comes about is in
accordance with the will of God, without any exception. Here
then we must love absolutely everything, as a whole and in each
detail, including evil in all its forms; notably our own past sins,
in so far as they are past (for we must hate them in so far as
their root is still present), our own sufferings, past, present and
to come . . . In other words, we must feel the reality and presence of God through all external things, without exception, as
clearly as our hands feel the substance of paper through the
pen-holder and the nib."

She writes beautifully, too, about truth, and the categorical
imperative of intellectual honesty:

"Yet I still half refused, not my love but my intelligence.
For it seemed to me certain, and I still think so today, that one

can never wrestle enough with God, if one does so out of pure regard for the truth. Christ likes us to prefer truth to him because, before being Christ, he is truth. If one turns aside from him to go towards the truth, one will not go far before falling into his arms."

Or again:

"The degree of intellectual honesty which is obligatory for me . . . demands that my thought should be indifferent to all ideas without exception, including for instance materialism and atheism; it must be equally welcoming and equally reserved with regard to every one of them . . . This indifference of thought on the level of the intelligence is in no way incompatible with the love of God, or even with a vow of love inwardly renewed each second of each day, each time eternal and each time wholly complete and new. I should be like this if I were what I ought to be."

And still I have said nothing about her universalism; or her love of the world, of its order and beauty; or her understanding that there is no contradiction between this love of them and a very agony of compassion for the suffering to be found "here below", as she puts it (I had wondered, you may remember, how it could have been possible that 1916 and 1942 were times of such joy to me, and yet times when I felt so acutely the affliction of others: and had concluded, more or less like her, that the two experiences, though within a unity, were on different planes or in different dimensions); or her clarity about the utter absorption of evil by good—a clarity that helped me to sharpen my own vaguer thinking, and made me see, or see with greater precision, why, after that Satanic nightmare, I had signed myself with the Cross:

"Perfect purity alone cannot be defiled. If at the moment when the soul is invaded by evil the attention can be turned towards a thing of perfect purity, so that a part of the evil is transferred to it, this thing will be in no way tarnished by it, nor will it send it back. Thus each minute of such attention really destroys a part of the evil."

And though I cannot agree with her at all in her attitude to affliction—to the metaphysics of it, I mean, though I doubt whether that is the word—I nevertheless found myself, as I read her, with a sharpened understanding of why Ruth will hardly ever take drugs, even to stop a pain of some violence (so long as she can endure it without), and why my own state of mind about the use of narcotics to stop a bout of insomnia is invariably ambivalent. These are comparatively trivial examples, but the truth they illustrate is important. Let me explain what I mean.

I must first summarise her chapter entitled "The Love of God and Affliction", as nearly in her own words as possible. I have read it five times, and for the fifth only two hours ago; for her thought, although very precise—I think in a sense too precise—is also very difficult, and the logical progression of it, though always there, sometimes hard to discover. So I have endeavoured to give myself to it in the way she would herself have desired—to be attentive, time after time, as I sat receiving it into my mind. I hope and believe that I have largely succeeded. And I must say this: "The Love of God and Affliction" is the most remarkable essay in a very remarkable book; it stamps her unquestionably as a religious genius; it makes her infinitely lovable; it contains vital clues to the truth; its sincerity is beyond question; but for all that I cannot help thinking it to a high degree perverse, or rather, if the use of that word should seem to imply conscious wilfulness, pathological: and to represent a current trend in religious thought which, arising out of the impact on the most highly religious minds of contemporary abominations, seems to me essentially irreligious. I mean, her thought is conditioned, in part by her own agonising frustrations, and in part by a truly religious compulsion to justify the awful cruelties of today, and to see them as bound up with God's love: the result being—I must say it in terms—that God himself becomes a monster of cruelty.

Affliction (*malheur* in the original) is defined by Simone as physical pain, distress of soul and social degradation, all at the same time. It takes possession of the soul and marks it through and through with its own particular mark, the mark of slavery. It is an uprooting of life, a more or less attenuated equivalent of death, made irresistibly present to the soul by the attack or immediate apprehension of physical pain. If there is complete absence of physical pain there is no affliction for the soul, because our thoughts can in that event turn to no matter

what object, whereas physical pain has the power (and alone
has the power) to chain down our thoughts. Passing pain, on
the other hand, if not combined with the other elements which
go to make up affliction (toothache, for example), leaves no
trace on the soul; though prolonged or frequent physical
suffering, simply as such, is often an affliction. But (here
Simone's thought is not quite consistent) there is no real
affliction unless the event which has seized and uprooted a life
attacks it, directly or indirectly, in all its parts, social, psychological and physical. The social factor is essential. There is
not really affliction where there is not social degradation or
fear of it in some form or another.

Affliction, which leaves a being struggling on the ground like
a half-crushed worm, makes God appear to be absent for a
time, more absent than a dead man, more absent than light
in the utter darkness of a cell. A kind of horror submerges the
whole soul. During this absence there is nothing to love.
What is terrible is that if, in this darkness where there is nothing
to love, the soul ceases to love God, or at least to go on wanting
to love him though it may be only with an infinitesimal part
of itself, God's absence becomes final.

As for the human aspect, men have the same carnal nature
as animals. If a hen is hurt the others rush upon it, attacking
it with their beaks. This phenomenon is as automatic as
gravitation. Our senses attach all the scorn, all the revulsion,
all the hatred which our reason attaches to crime, to affliction.
Except for those whose whole soul is inhabited by Christ,
everybody despises the afflicted to some extent, though practically no one is conscious of it. This law of sensibility, moreover,
holds good with regard to ourselves also. In the case of someone
in affliction, all the scorn, revulsion and hatred are turned
inwards. They penetrate to the centre of the soul, and from
there colour the whole universe with their poisoned light.
Supernatural love, if it has survived, can prevent this second
result, namely the hatred of oneself, from coming about, but not
the first, namely the hatred of one by others. The first is of the
very essence of affliction; there is no affliction without it. (There
seems to be some contradiction between this statement and
"except for those whose whole soul is inhabited by Christ")

There is another reason why the afflicted are utterly isolated
in the world of men. They have no words to express what is

happening to them. Among the people they meet, those who
have never had contact with affliction in its true sense can have
no idea of what it is, even though they may have suffered a
great deal. Affliction is something specific and impossible to
describe in any other term, like the sounds of which nothing
can convey the slightest idea to anyone who is deaf and dumb.
And as for those who have themselves been mutilated by
affliction, they are in no state to help anyone at all, and they
are almost incapable of even wishing to do so. Thus compassion
for the afflicted is an impossibility. When it is really found we
have a more astounding miracle than walking on water, healing
the sick, or even raising the dead.

Affliction may be such that, even when it has been ended,
some poison remains within. The grace of God himself may be
unable to cure the wound "here below". The glorified body of
Christ bore the marks of the nail and the spear.

Now let me break in here for a moment on my summary of
Simone's thought, and say, before proceeding, that I understand what she means by affliction. I was afflicted myself, during most of 1943 and part of 1944, in a sense sufficiently close to
the one indicated by her for me to appreciate every term of her
description. There was not, it is true, acute physical pain. But a
dirty sort of pain, low, vague and indiscriminate, possessed the
whole of my body, and made me abominable to my consciousness; and a more specialised phenomenon not only almost physically annihilated me whenever it appeared—and it appeared
many times every day—but lived momently with my being as a
foe that was lying in ambush and would duly attack at the foreseeable moment. For the instant I sat down, whether to eat or
read or talk or rest or attempt a sort of stupefied doze, my
member would disappear: I would feel it retiring into my body,
and would know myself, with a catch of the breath and a stab
at the stomach, as not only unmanned but dehumanised. The
reason for this phenomenon is obvious: just as the *membrum
erectum* gives a confident greeting to the life in another, and
would be one with it, so if a man is in terror of life, is in terror
of it perpetually and as such, his member has the impulse, a
kind of negative impulse, to shrivel and vanish; and the movement of muscles that sitting involves gives this impulse its

chance. The result is common, I understand, in single instances
of particularised terror, unless an unusually intense sado-
masochism predominates in the individual's temperament,
when the opposite may happen; but my own case, that of an
extreme hyperaesthetic whose fear was unspecific and continuous, is probably rarer. The loathsome horror of the
sensation is of course indescribable. I would avoid sitting down
when I could; would make far-fetched excuses; would eat
standing if alone or with Ruth; and would sit on the edge of the
chair when I simply had to sit, for this slightly reduced the
sensation.

As to social degradation, in a sense it was never absent.
Truly, I was not outlawed by society: but I felt that I ought to
be and perpetually feared that I should be, and knew that when
the moment arrived reinstatement would be impossible. As I
sat over coffee at Craigellachie or the Nethy Bridge Hotel,
talking to an eminent biologist, Sir D'Arcy Thompson, about
a gentle wild flower called pyrola that grows in these parts—
you would think it a lily of the valley but for the little green
patches that speckle it and its lack of all fragrance—or
listening, other nights, to Willie Walton at the piano as he
played, in his courtesy, a few passages from Berlioz' *Faust*, I
was subjectively a pariah: my intercourse with Sir D'Arcy and
Willie Walton was like the gaiety of a man who goes about on
his lawful occasions after committing a murder, and the music
and small flowers were but reminders of a paradise lost. The
subjectivity of my pariahdom, and the absence of all basis for
my terror that decent people would outlaw me, cannot affect
my understanding of what, in the heart of a pariah, pariahdom
must mean.

For the rest, I was utterly derelict. I felt myself banished from
life and from God. And I was quite hopeless: not approxi-
mately, not in the sense people often intend when they play
with this terrible word, but in the sense that to have had the
very tiniest of hopes, for the very briefest of instants, would
have been wholly inconceivable. The doom that I lived with
in eternity was the doom that I must live in eternity with a self
I detested, and must live with it alone.

So my state of being, though not identical with affliction as
described by Simone, was certainly analogous to it: and I am
persuaded, as I have said, that I can realise to the full what it

must mean to be afflicted as she was (for that she wrote of what she knew cannot surely be questioned), or what it must mean, let us say, to live for years without hope in a Dachau or Buchenwald—forgotten utterly to all seeming of God and man, weak and weary from hunger and sickness, and tormented or mocked at by gaolers. You must bear this in mind when you come to my criticisms, for it is by no means irrelevant to at least one of them. Not that I would equate for a moment, or even remotely compare as objective realities, my own suffering of a decade ago with the fate of those desperate victims; though subjectively despair is despair, and any case of it is identical with any other, whatever their difference in origin, if both are absolute.

One can accept the existence of affliction, Simone continues, only by considering it at a distance.

God created through love and for love. God did not create anything except love itself, and the means to love. He created beings capable of love from all possible distances. Because no other could do it, he himself went to the greatest possible distance, the infinite distance. This infinite distance between God and God, this supreme tearing apart, this agony beyond all others, this marvel of love, is the crucifixion. Nothing can be further from God than that which has been accursed.

Men struck down by affliction are at the foot of the Cross, almost at the greatest possible distance from God. A blind mechanism, heedless of degrees of spiritual perfection, continually tosses and throws some of them at the very foot of the Cross. It rests with them to keep or not to keep their eyes turned towards God through all the jolting: for we are nailed down, only free to choose which way we look, ruled by necessity. (This was not always so: before the original sin humanity could walk, but turned its gaze away from God and walked in the wrong direction as far as it could go.) It does not mean that God's Providence is lacking. It is in his Providence that God has willed that necessity should be like a blind mechanism.

If the mechanism were not blind there would not be any affliction. Affliction is anonymous before all things, it deprives its victims of their personality and makes them into things. It is indifferent; and it is the coldness of this indifference—a metallic coldness—which freezes all those it touches to the depths of their souls. They will never find warmth again. They will never believe any more that they are anyone.

Only blind necessity can throw men to the extreme point of distance, right next to the Cross.

There are two forms of friendship: meeting and separation. They are indissoluble. Both of them contain some good, and this good of friendship is unique, for when two beings who are not friends are near each other there is no meeting, and when friends are far apart there is no separation. As both forms contain the same good, they are both equally good.

Before all things God loves himself. This love, this friendship of God, is the Trinity. Between the terms united by this relation of divine love there is more than nearness; there is infinite nearness or identity. But, resulting from the Creation, the Incarnation and the Passion, there is also infinite distance. The totality of space and the totality of time, interposing their immensity, put an infinite distance between God and God.

Lovers and friends desire two things. The one is to love each other so much that they enter into each other and only make one being. The other is to love each other so much that, having half the globe between them, their union will not be diminished in the slightest degree. All that man vainly desires here below is perfectly realised in God.

The love between God and God, which in itself *is* God, is the bond which unites two beings so closely that they are no longer distinguishable and really form a single unity, and the bond which stretches across distance and triumphs over infinite separation. The unity of God, wherein all plurality disappears, and the abandonment, wherein Christ believes he is left while never ceasing to love his Father perfectly, these are two forms expressing the divine virtue of the same Love, the Love which is God himself. The infinite separation over which God's love triumphs is the whole creation spread through the totality of space and time, made of mechanically harsh matter and interposed between Christ and his Father.

As for us men, our misery gives us the infinitely precious privilege of sharing in this distance placed between the Son and his Father. This distance is only separation, however, for those who love. For those who love, separation, although painful, is a good, because it is love. Even the distress of the abandoned Christ is a good. There cannot be a greater good for us on earth than to share in it. God can never be perfectly present to us here below on account of our flesh. But he can be almost perfectly absent from us in extreme affliction. This is the only possibility of perfection for us on earth.

This universe where we are living, and of which we form a tiny particle, is the distance put by Love between God and God. We are a point in this distance. Space, time and the mechanism that governs matter are the distance. Everything that we call evil is only this mechanism. Matter is entirely passive and in consequence entirely obedient to God's will. It is a perfect model for us. There cannot be any being other than God and that which obeys God.

The infinity of space and time separates us from God. How are we to seek for him? How are we to go towards him? Even if we were to walk for hundreds of years, we should do no more than go round and round the world. Even in an aeroplane we could do nothing else. We are incapable of progressing vertically. We cannot take a step towards the heavens. God crosses the universe and comes to us.

Over the infinity of space and time, the infinitely more infinite love of God comes to possess us. He comes at his own time. We have the power to consent to receive him or refuse. If we remain deaf, he comes back again and again like a beggar, but also, like a beggar, one day he stops coming. If we consent, God puts a little seed in us and he goes away again. The seed grows. A day comes when the soul belongs to God, when it not only consents to love but when truly and effectively it loves. Then in its turn it must cross the universe to go to God. The soul does not love like a creature with created love. The love within it is divine, uncreated; for it is the love of God for God which is passing through it. God alone is capable of loving God. We can only consent to give up our own feelings so as to allow free passage in one soul for this love. We are created for this consent, and for this alone.

Divine Love crossed the infinity of space and time to come from God to us. But how can it repeat the journey in the opposite direction, starting from a finite creature? When the seed of divine love placed in us has grown and become a tree, how can we, we who bear it, take it back to its origin? How can we make the journey which God made when he came to us, in the opposite direction? How can we cross infinite distance?

It seems impossible, but there is a way—a way with which we are familiar. We know quite well in what likeness this tree is made, this tree which has grown within us. Something still a little more frightful than the gibbet—that is the most beautiful of all trees. It was the seed of this tree that God placed within us, without our knowing what seed it was. If we had known, we should not have said yes at the first moment. It is this tree which has grown within us and which has become ineradicable. Only a betrayal could uproot it.

When we hit a nail with a hammer, the whole of the shock received by the large head of the nail passes into the point without any of it being lost, although it is only a point. If the hammer and the head of the nail were infinitely big it would be just the same. The point of the nail would transmit this infinite shock at the point to which it was applied.

Extreme affliction, which means physical pain, distress of soul and social degradation, all at the same time, constitutes the nail. The point is applied at the very centre of the soul. The head of the nail is all the necessity which spreads throughout the totality of space and time.

Affliction is a marvel of divine technique. It is a simple and ingenious device which introduces into the soul of a finite creature the immensity of force, blind, brutal and cold. The infinite distance which separates God from the creature is entirely concentrated into one point to pierce the soul in its centre.

The man to whom such a thing happens has no part in the operation. He struggles like a butterfly which is pinned alive into an album. But through all the horror he can continue to want to love. There is nothing impossible in that, no obstacle, one might almost say no difficulty. For the greatest suffering, so long as it does not cause fainting, does not touch the part of the soul which consents to a right direction.

It is only necessary to know that love is a direction and not a state of the soul. If one is unaware of this, one falls into despair at the first onslaught of affliction.

He whose soul remains ever turned in the direction of God while the nail pierces it, finds himself nailed on to the very centre of the universe. It is the true centre, it is not in the middle, it is beyond space and time, it is God. In a dimension which does not belong to space, which is not time, which is indeed quite a different dimension, this nail has pierced a hole through all creation, through the thickness of the screen which separates the soul from God.

In this marvellous dimension, the soul, without leaving the place and the instant where the body to which it is united is situated, can cross the totality of space and time and come into the very presence of God.

§ 4

That is a summary description, in her own superb language, of affliction and its metaphysics or meaning as Simone understands them. No one could read it, as I have said, or no one of any sensitiveness or insight, without saluting her genius. And yet I find it quite dreadful: shocking to such religious instincts as I have, shocking to my conception of God, shocking to my conception of man. But before giving my reasons I must return to my point of departure: for I said, you may remember, taking two comparatively trivial examples, that I found myself, as I read her, with a sharpened understanding of why Ruth will hardly ever take drugs, even to stop a pain of some violence (so long as she can endure it without), and why my own state of mind about the use of narcotics to end a bout of insomnia is invariably ambivalent. Passing pain of the sort I had in view is by no means affliction as defined by Simone, and she herself makes this clear: nor is insomnia, though it can become very much like an affliction, if sufficiently prolonged and combined with other distresses: but there are analogies between suffering and affliction, and it was when reflecting on affliction that what I had been feeling for many years about suffering became sharper to my consciousness.

Whatever the reason—and one of Simone's troubles, an element of irreligion, as I cannot help thinking it, in her make-up, is her determination to find a reason for every ultimate mystery, and her certainty, when she has found it, that she is right: this is what I meant when I said that her thought is in one way too precise—but whatever the reason, the existence of pain and suffering is an indisputable fact. That pain will one day be eliminated altogether is undoubtedly possible: we have come a long way since a man had to have his leg sawn off while fully conscious. But that suffering will be eliminated altogether—that is another matter. Suffering, it seems, some degree of suffering, and suffering whether in everyone or some, is inseparable from finite existence: inseparable, no doubt, because the existence *is* finite, and finitude, in the setting of infinity, implies a lack, a homesickness, a sense of exile. That is why an acute awareness of beauty, whether in nature or art or maybe (I am not sure about this) in the human soul, always brings a longing in its train with which suffering is intermingled. As for pain, it is a sort of sacrament of suffering.

Or, to use Simone's language, suffering is a necessity "here below"—namely at any time before, or in any dimension other than, "the restoration of all things": and pain, in whatever degree and however distributed, is also a necessity, at any rate for the time being, at any rate here and now.

Now we ought to accept necessity so far as we are able, and to accept it, so far as we are able, with love. If we refuse to do so—if we "get out of" what we *could*, according to our capacity, have endured—we become to that extent unreal. When we use a drug to still a pain, the pain, one might say, is still there, but we do not meet it or feel it. There is a disassociation. We are cut off from some of our own roots. We are deliberately forgoing part of our existence, and of existence as such. Provided we could have borne the pain, we are less than we might have been; and that is a sin.

When I say that the pain is still there, I am not of course speaking scientifically, for science would no doubt put it that the sensitivity of a nerve is what causes the pain, and that if we deaden the nerve (deaden is a good word for my purpose) the pain becomes non-existent. I am speaking—I don't know what the word is, but I suppose ontologically, or say religiously. I mean that the pain has happened, is a *fact* that has entered into us. Never mind how or why it has happened. It may have happened, immediately, as a result of our own or other people's folly, or any number of circumstances out of our own or anybody else's control, or the immaturity of medical science, etcetera: but the moment it has happened as a link in the inexorable process of cause and effect, it has become, as having happened, necessity. And we get rid of it by a sleight of hand.

Instead of getting rid of it like this, which isn't really getting rid of it at all—instead, that is, of getting rid of it by calling in matter—we should meet it (always provided we are able to) with spirit, absorb it in spirit, become one with it as spirit: and when we have done so we have to that extent spiritualised matter, and made of blind and mechanical necessity the very stuff of intentional love—of *Kavvanah*, of direction of the heart towards God. Even a desire, though unsuccessful, to meet pain in this way has a similar, and perhaps identical, result.

That a simple device could have prevented the pain from occurring is irrelevant. The device has not been used, so the pain has become a fact, and must be dealt with as such.

To take the matter a stage further back, it is the part of wisdom, even, on occasion and under certain conditions, to forgo such a device—to forgo an expedient which, if grasped at betimes, would prevent the otherwise all but inevitable occurrence of the pain in question. Every individual must decide for himself whether the occasion is there and whether the conditions have been fulfilled. There are women who very strongly object, for what must be called spiritual reasons, to the idea of bearing children in a state of semi-consciousness; and many insomniacs, I daresay, act as I do in the matter of narcotics. I never swallow one till I feel that I must, or, when I have decided to, without a sense of repugnance. I am always worried on such occasions by the idea that I shall somehow be cheating, taking the easy way out, handing myself over to dead, external matter: almost that, as I lie unconscious under the influence of the thing, I shall be a myth. I feel, even, that I am about to commit blasphemy. So I always try, for as long as I can when insomnia becomes persistent, to beat the enemy on common ground: by remembering that he is in fact not an enemy but a friend if I treat him as such—a friend who has given me an opportunity I must hasten to take. I get into a mood of calm acceptance—usually of accepting something painful that has happened to me during the day: and quite often this works. But when I do take a drug I feel differently next morning: the having taken it is now necessity, and I thank God for its beneficent result. For it happens that those two little seconals have a delightful effect on me: I open my eyes with what Meredith called "a waking-infant stare", see everything in the room as more *there* and more alive than before, and afterwards write, for at any rate a few hours, with an ease and a flow rarely otherwise granted me.

But to shirk pain—bearable pain—altogether is not only to be less real than one might have been: it is to isolate oneself from the common lot of pain, from the pain of humanity and the world. It is to blunt or cut off or withdraw one's antennae: it is to play only such notes as one chooses in the universal symphony, which is a symphony of suffering as well as of joy. And to do so is to dishonour the music. Unless every player duly plays every note on his score-sheet, the whole symphony is damaged: it does not "come out" as the composer, who is also the conductor, has planned it.

Do I deprecate, then, all the skill and devotion that have been lavished on the conquest of pain? God forbid: God a thousand times forbid. I see the hand of a surgeon in its beauty and strength as an instrument of God like few others: I see Lister in the company of Socrates and Beethoven on the right hand of the Father. And if before the event I had been compelled to make a choice and say which of them alone might exist, I should have chosen Lister, and let the other two go.

I sat for a few minutes, the night before last, at the bedside of an old Oxford friend. He is dying terribly. He looked gentle and calm as he lay on his side, and I couldn't have suspected, until he told me, what might soon be in store for him; what pain might be racking his body as I sat happily at dinner with John Collins in the shadow of St Paul's. For what he told me the other evening—what a man told another—was this: that presently he would know it was coming: that a few minutes later he would find himself screaming in agony: that the screaming would continue for hour after hour: that delirium would develop: that the nurse would give him two injections, three injections, four injections: that they would fail even slightly to diminish the pain, since his body had become inured to them: that the nurse would ring up his doctor, and ask "Shall I give him a fifth?": and that the doctor—not from callousness, but because there are limits to what medicine can do—would metaphorically shrug his shoulders. And this would go on to the day of his death.

(There is something I cannot help adding: this is the sort of thing we deliberately inflict on our neighbours when we go to war with them.)

So do not imagine for a moment that I deprecate scientific

devotion to the conquest of pain. If anyone could sit by that
bedside and not long for the day when such suffering would be
impossible, it could only be someone whom a corrupt religiosity,
or his own suffering, had made less than human.

The conclusion is this. There is nothing good about pain
in itself, even about the mildest of pains for the shortest of
durations; and pain of sufficient intensity, or of any intensity
if sufficiently prolonged, may damage or destroy personality,
except in a saint. The crucial points, of degree and of time,
differ in different people. Now we may know that in our own
case—while there is still nothing good about pain, about the
thing in itself—to bear certain degrees or amounts of it may
be good nonetheless, and for all that we might have avoided
them: for to do so may make us more real and more at one with
the pain of the world. But we can know nothing about others:
we cannot know whether a given degree of it, or a given amount
of whatever degree, will make them more real or less real,
though we do know that certain intensities, or certain durations,
would probably destroy them. Moreover: the value of accepting
an avoidable pain derives solely from the fact that the pain of
the world is in the order of necessities: the pain of the world
and not any particular pain, not the pain we might ourselves
have avoided. When pain is no longer a necessity the value has
gone. So, on all counts, we should strive to abolish it.

Christ is the supreme example of a saintliness that accepts
ultimate pain, and accepts it voluntarily. He faced, not a
headache, but crucifixion: and refused the anodyne which
charity provided for the easement of malefactors. For we read:
"And when they were come unto a place called Golgotha,
that is to say, a place of a skull, they gave him vinegar to
drink, mingled with gall: and when he had tasted thereof, he
would not drink. And they crucified him."

I must return, after that, to Simone, and explain why I find
her, in the essay I have summarised, so shocking: shocking to
my conception of God, shocking to my conception of man.
God first: though God and man cannot really be separated—
that is one of the points.

I said that her God was a monster of cruelty. Could anyone
deny it, after reading my summary? And not only a monster

of cruelty: a monster of self-love, in the bad not the good sense, and a tyrant of tyrants.

(Let me add something before proceeding. I thought at first that original sin, whether "in his Providence" or not (and whatever my view of that doctrine), might explain how a good God could or had to be Simone's God. But I am persuaded that this is not so.)

What is the starting-point? A God whose obsession is love of himself. He creates: but with only one object, that this love of himself may be expressed, not by but through, the created. That he may love himself better, love himself by means of infinite separation as well as of infinite nearness, he interposes between himself and himself an immensity of time, space and matter: harsh, blind, brute, dead, insensate matter: necessity. There is no question of this dreadful necessity being necessitous for God: he could have willed otherwise, but in the interest of love of himself he deliberately willed thus. "It does not mean that God's Providence is lacking. It is in his Providence that God has willed that necessity should be like a blind mechanism."

Now he cannot love himself perfectly, in terms of nearness, through the created—"on account of our flesh": but in terms of separation he can. So he "accurses" his chosen ones: he flings them away to the greatest possible distance: he afflicts them with the terrible affliction that Simone has described. This "marvel of divine technique", this "simple and ingenious device", permits God, through his creatures, to love God, the creator: and alone so permits him. The man to whom such a thing happens "has no part in the operation". But if when "struggling like a butterfly pinned alive in an album": if when "marked through and through with the mark of slavery": if when wriggling on the ground "like a half-crushed worm": if when suffering like that friend of mine, and from social degradation as well, and from spiritual dereliction on top of it—ah, if then "through all the horror he can continue to want to love God", God has found his opportunity: he can come to himself through the creature from an infinite distance. But only if, and only when.

If you think I must have parodied Simone look again at her own exposition in my scrupulous summary: then remember my friend: and bear in mind that his agony is only one of three elements in affliction as Simone understands it. Recall, in particular, "When we hit a nail with a hammer, the whole of the shock received by the large head of the nail passes into the point without any of it being lost, although it is only a point. If the hammer and the head of the nail were infinitely big it would be just the same. The point of the nail would transmit this infinite shock at the point to which it was applied. Extreme affliction, which means physical pain, distress of soul and social degradation, all at the same time, constitutes the nail. The point is applied at the very centre of the soul. The head of the nail is all the necessity which spreads throughout the totality of space and time." And when you have pondered this passage, when you have mentally visualised what it means, confess that I haven't exaggerated.

Simone herself is always explicitly using the words master and slave. I have already quoted one passage—"marked through and through with the mark of slavery." Here is another. "May each loving adolescent, as he works at his Latin prose, hope through this prose to come a little nearer to the instant when he will really be the slave—faithfully waiting while the master is absent, watching and listening—ready to open the door to him as soon as he knocks. The master will then make his slave sit down and himself serve him with meat. Only this waiting, this attention, can move the master to treat his slave with such amazing tenderness." Tenderness: worms wriggling on the ground, butterflies pinned in an album!

I say that this God is a terrible and odious God: and I say that he isn't God. And how do I know that he isn't? Because I am told so by the Voice that talked with Adam in the cool of the day: I am told so by every intimation within me of the beautiful, the true and the good. Tyranny, the Voice tells me, is vile: love of self, the Voice tells me, is vile: cruelty, the Voice tells me, is vile: and vilest of all, the Voice tells me, is love of self served by cruelty. And how can the Voice that has told me all this since the days of my youth be the Voice of a tyrant of tyrants? I will rescue the name of God from dishonour, for I love him, too, in my fashion.

Of course I do not know Who He Is. Nobody does. Nobody has seen God, and lived. Nor do I know the ultimate meaning of affliction: I know only that it must have a meaning, that this meaning cannot be Simone's, that we must accept it, and that simultaneously we must do all we can both to make it less likely and to relieve it in others. One of Simone's troubles, it seems to me, is that she is so anxious to be definite about God; that is what I meant when I said that her thought is in some ways too precise. She must construct a complete, watertight system: she must explain, to herself and others, everything about divine and human existence, down to the last detail. For all the saintliness that I should be the last to deny in her, there is something impious in the attempt. A wiser course is to pick up the hint or two that God's wisdom vouchsafes us, and be content. "Wherefore at certain times," writes St John of the Cross, "when the soul is least thinking of it and least desiring it, God is wont to give it these Divine touches, by causing it certain recollections of Himself." And "Suppose a man in hiding," says Meister Eckhart, "and he stirs, he shows his whereabouts thereby; and God does the same. No one could ever have found God; he gave himself away." This is the road of humility: all else is presumption. One of the odd things, indeed, about Simone is her attitude to dogma. She refused to join the Catholic Church, if I understand her aright, in the main for the following reasons: because all spiritual institutions become worldly, because *anathema sit* is profane, and because she was reluctant to bind herself down by a series of dogmas. And yet "Waiting on God" is more dogmatic in its way than almost any other book I have read. She might reply that the dogmas are her own and not those of a Church, and the reply would be a good one. Not that, in any case, I would wish to make much of such an oddity, or of the numerous inconsistencies you will have observed for yourself in the passages quoted: for a man who isn't full of contradictions is most probably a fool, and a man who's afraid of expressing them is almost certainly a knave. When people blandly complain of inconsistencies and contradictions in others, invoking logic as their yardstick, I sometimes wonder what response has been aroused in them (on the assumption that they've read it) by the Epistle of St Paul to the Romans, chapter 7, verses 14 to 20.

Simone's determination to be precise, or something deeper perhaps, something in truth pathological, has led her into what I cannot but see as the gravest of errors: she personalises God. In one passage, it is true, she insists on his impersonality: but otherwise—and the exception makes her normal mode of thought the more vivid—she invariably describes him as master (of beloved slaves) or as husband or lover (in the last analysis, of himself) and never as spirit that informs and interpenetrates all things. But it is as spirit, interpenetrating spirit, that he comes to me, and he comes to me only like that. Otherwise, I know nothing of him whatever. I feel him, panentheistically, in music and poetry and people and the countryside and my garden and my home and—on occasion—my office: in my body and soul: and in matter, which for me isn't "dead". I do not of course imply that I imagine him devoid of personality: for, as personality is the highest of all things we know, we must believe it subsumed into a reality still higher. All I mean is, we may not think of him as we think of a particularised person, and this is what Simone does. Unknown, universal, indeterminate, and yet intensely realised—that is how he lives in my consciousness; and those adjectives of description, if I may put it so, are the whole point of Christ. We cannot know the Father as a person, but only the Son.

Having personalised God, Simone places him, as a distinct and separate person, over against the creatures he has brought into being, and the space, time and matter which, whatever their origin, are at any rate "in his Providence". This brings me at once to the second feature in her thinking that I find so repellent—her concept of man. But before dealing with it there is something I wish to make clear.

If I repudiate her doctrine of affliction—if I refuse to regard it as a "marvel of divine technique", a "simple and ingenious device" through which God loves himself, and through which he gives creatures, as facilitating this love, "the only possibility of perfection on earth"—I by no means imply that affliction, extreme affliction, affliction as Simone would describe it, can never be the occasion for a man going out and loving God with a fulness of love he might otherwise have found impossible. To suppose that affliction must always produce this result, or produces it often, would be nonsensical: not many of the six million victims in Dachau and the rest loved God better, I dare swear, for the experience, or gave, to use her own terminology, a clearer passage to God's love of God—nor of course has Simone either made such a claim or suggested it (she suggests the opposite). But good *can* be occasioned by anything, by evil as well as by good, even in time as distinct from eternity: and an extremity of good by an extremity of evil. This is altogether different from saying, however, that affliction is a technique God

deliberately devises to make a saint here or there a better channel
for God's love of God—and never mind about the millions who
fall by the way. *This* is what seems to me so loathsome and
blasphemous in Simone's way of thinking. That all tends to
good in eternity I am persuaded: even hydrogen bombs cannot
shake my belief: there is a meaning in affliction: but it isn't
Simone's.

As to man, what does she make of him? A slave, as we have
seen already. But worse than a slave: non-existent. "At each
moment we only exist because God consents to think us into
being . . . really we have no existence." Though she adds,
as if shocked by herself: "At any rate that is how we represent
creation to ourselves, humanly and hence inadequately of
course, but this imagery contains an element of truth". Or
again: "We are created for this consent [namely, for consenting
to God loving himself] and for this alone." It follows that all
her emphasis is on human contemptibility, and none of it on
human splendour. There is a terrible passage in the essay,
Reflections on the Right Use of School Studies, which reads as
follows: "Above all it is thus that we can acquire the virtue of
humility, and that is a far more precious treasure than all
academic progress. From this point of view it is perhaps even
more useful to contemplate our stupidity than our sin. Consciousness of sin gives us the feeling that we are evil, and a kind
of pride sometimes finds a place in it. When we force ourselves
to fix the gaze, not only of our eyes but of our souls, upon a short
exercise in which we have failed through sheer stupidity, a
sense of our mediocrity is borne in upon us with irresistible
evidence. No knowledge is more to be desired. If we can arrive
at knowing the truth with all our souls we shall be established
on the right foundation." I have rarely read a passage that
inspired me with such horror. If I must choose between this
and the narrowest humanism, give me humanism first, last
and always. And if anybody points to the state of the world,
and attributes it to humanism without religion, I retort that,
while bound to agree, I attribute it equally to religion without
humanism.

To get the nasty taste out of my mouth, let me quote from
two others, both of them Jews like Simone. Here is what Martin
Buber has to say about humility: "If anyone abases himself too
much and forgets that a man through his works and behaviour

can call down an overflowing blessing on all the world, this is
not humility. It is called impure humility: 'The greatest evil is
if thou dost forget that thou art a son of the king'. Humility is
never forced, never a self-abasement, self-command, or self-
determination. It is as without discord as a child's glance, and
as simple as a child's speech. The humble man lives in every
being, and he knows the nature and the virtue of each. Because
to him no one is 'the other', he knows from within that no one
is wanting in some hidden value; he knows that no man exists
who does not have his hour. The colours of the world do not
merge for him in one another, but each soul stands in the
splendour of its own existence. In each man there is something
precious that is in no other man. Therefore one should honour
each man for that which is hidden within him, which only he
and no one of his companions possesses." And here is Baruch
Spinoza: "A man who desires to help others by counsel or deed
will refrain from dwelling on men's faults, and will speak but
sparingly of human weaknesses. But he will speak at large of
man's virtue and power, and the means of perfecting the same,
that thus men may endeavour joyously to live, so far as in them
lies, after the commandment of reason." And Spinoza, "blessed"
Spinoza, was rightly called a God-drunken man. There is all
the difference in the world between religious humility (which
honours mankind, oneself included, as God's creation) and a
pseudo-religious masochism.

As might have been expected, Simone draws a rigid distinction between the natural and the supernatural, in respect
above all of humanity. She sees us as objects of God, capable
of nothing good by our own human nature, capable of something good only when visited, or as she might put it when
kissed, by supernatural grace: when visited specially or kissed
specially. My thought is quite different. I feel God about
everywhere: and I feel him as far more *naturally* and regularly
mixed up with us, and us with him and his goodness, than
Simone does. Which is not at all to imply that I think grace
a myth.

Her dichotomy of natural and supernatural, and her
depreciation of human nature as such (the human nature that
God has created), is most startlingly displayed when she speaks
of the way people react to the affliction of others. Let me repeat
a passage already quoted: "Men have the same carnal nature

as animals. If a hen is hurt, the others rush upon it, attacking
it with their beaks. This phenomenon is as automatic as
gravitation. Our senses attach all the scorn, all the revulsion, all
the hatred which our reason attaches to crime, to affliction.
*Except for those whose whole soul is inhabited by Christ, everybody
despises the afflicted to some extent.*" Again: "The sympathy of the
weak for the strong is natural, for the weak in putting himself
into the place of the other acquires an imaginary strength. The
sympathy of the strong for the weak, being in the opposite
direction, is *against nature*." And again: "The sufferer and the
other . . . love each other for the love of the one for the other.
This is an impossibility. That is why it only comes about through
the agency of God." In other words: there is no difference at
all between animal nature and human nature ("for thou hast
made him a little lower than the angels") except that God,
every now and again, performs the impossible miracle of
making a particular little bit of human nature, or a particular
example of it, partially, or even wholly, human. He never
presumably does likewise to animals (*mutatis mutandis*), whom
he has also created: not to mention that the very animals themselves may not, even on their regular occasions, be as black as
Simone paints them.

*Apropos of animal nature, I was dining last night with Maurice
Browne, who was famous, a quarter of a century ago, as the pro-
ducer of Journey's End, my house's first publication; and
he told me the following story:*

"*In Lahore Marjorie and I stayed at a hotel three miles outside
the town; across the road lay the city zoo. The zoo's inhabitants
included an ancient and mangy tiger, of ill repute: a man-eater, it
was said; his character was so savage that the public were separated from his cage by two separate steel barriers, the first some four
feet back from the cage, the second a similar distance from the first;
even the keepers did not venture between the cage and the first barrier.
I used to rise before dawn and stroll round the hotel gardens in the
early coolness: one morning I crossed the road into the zoo; it was
still twilight: no one was about. Wandering at random, I turned
a corner, found myself about ten yards from the tiger's cage, and
saw to my horror that a little middle-aged Indian was leaning
against the bars, had his arm through them, and was scratching*

the tiger behind the ears; the tiger was purring. The man sensed my eyes upon him, looked up, hastily withdrew his arm and salaamed in terror: not of the tiger, of me; I felt an intruder. The tiger snarled viciously; I hurriedly withdrew, wondering. The next morning again the man was scratching the tiger's head, the tiger purring; again the man salaamed: I returned his greeting; both he and the tiger, perceiving that I intended no harm to either, resumed their avocation: I watched. On the third morning I spoke to the man: very timidly he replied; by the fifth I had his story.

"*He was a singularly ugly little man, of Dravidian stock, wretchedly clad, badly pock-marked; nor had he a pleasing personality. He knew these things; no one, he told me, could ever love him: he used to feel very sorry for himself; but, when he had seen that self-pity was eating into him, he was shamed and tried to think of someone unhappier and lonelier than he: he could think of no one. Then he tried to think of an unhappier four-legged animal, but again could think of none: even the pariah dogs of the city had their mates. And then suddenly one day he had thought of the tiger in the zoo, whom everyone hated. 'I shall love that tiger,' he said to himself, 'and the tiger will love me.' Every morning he walked those three miles from the city to the zoo, talked to the tiger till the keepers were stirring, walked back; and little by little the tiger had learned to know and trust him. 'And now, as the Excellency has seen with his eyes, the tiger loves me and I love him, and we are both happy. For, as the Excellency knows far better than I, what every living creature needs most—more than money, more than shelter, more than food, more even than life itself—is love.'* "

Simone's doctrine—about the way people react to affliction in others—is false. I know it to be false. My experience tells me it's false. When I was afflicted at Craigellachie and Nethy Bridge Ruth didn't attack me with her beak. She quietly loved me: so that nowadays, when I try to realise in recollection the terror and despair that engulfed me, everything seems to vanish in the reality of her love. Her whole soul, then, Simone would have to say, was inhabited by Christ. Perhaps it was: though Ruth, as a good Jewess, wouldn't like the suggestion. But *my* whole soul, I'm quite certain, isn't inhabited by Christ. There's some Christ in me, as in everybody—that's the point of Him, or another point, for I've already mentioned one:

Christ is every man's Tree, and He couldn't be every man's
Tree unless He were every man's seed. And yet I, who am very
like millions and millions, better than some, worse than others,
don't attack the afflicted with my beak: I love them—don't
merely want to help them, but love them. I could give you
dozens of examples. In the autumn of 1946 I visited Germany
on the work of Save Europe Now, and came to a little place
called Jülich, which, so terribly destroyed in an air raid that
hardly a house was left standing, will always live in my mind
side by side with Merano and Bibury, such is the affection I
bear it. In an underground cellar—everyone was underground
—I found a man of about seventy, alone. His wife was dead, and
he had heard nothing of his sons for two years: they might be
prisoners, he thought, in Russia. There was no artificial light
in his cell, and for natural light only a hole—a foot or so across,
covered with paper. The ceiling was wet. As I flashed my torch
about in this burrow I noticed the filthy bandage on the man's
neck, and saw that his hands, which he was trying to conceal,
were tuberous with those corrupt-looking spots—carbuncles,
impetigo, or something midway between—that I had noticed
so often during the previous few days, particularly among the
children. They never left people, it appeared: they looked like
clearing up, and then new ones would break out on the scars.
Well, if you want to know what I felt about him, and what
you would have felt about him, and what innumerable others
would have felt about him, read a thing called "The Beggar"
written by Turgenev seventy-five years ago:

"I was walking along the street . . . I was stopped by a
decrepit old beggar.

"Bloodshot, tearful eyes, blue lips, coarse rags, festering
wounds. . . . Oh, how hideously poverty had eaten into this
miserable creature!

"He held out to me a red, swollen, filthy hand. He groaned,
he mumbled of help.

"I began feeling in all my pockets. . . . No purse, no watch,
not even a handkerchief. . . . I had taken nothing with me. And
the beggar was still waiting . . . and his outstretched hand
feebly shook and trembled.

"Confused, abashed, I warmly clasped the filthy, shaking
hand . . . 'Don't be angry, brother; I have nothing, brother.'

"The beggar stared at me with his bloodshot eyes; his blue lips smiled; and he in his turn gripped my chilly fingers.

" 'What of it, brother?' he mumbled; 'thanks for this, too. That is a gift too, brother.'

"I knew that I too had received a gift from my brother."

There is something else. Simone, dishonouring the average man who comes in contact with the afflicted, dishonours also the afflicted themselves. She tells the story of the Samaritan, for the purpose of asserting that his act was "supernatural". And this is how she describes the one who had been set upon by thieves: "a little piece of flesh, naked, inert and bleeding beside a ditch: anonymous: humanity does not exist in it." There is disrespect in that description. Do you see the afflicted like that, average Timothy, or as Turgenev saw them: as brothers—who can give, as well as receive?

That nobody reacts to the afflicted with revulsion and contempt—I wouldn't wish to pretend it. I was walking on the Embankment one night, decades ago, with a prosperous business man (I knew him well, was quite closely involved with him) when we passed some down-and-outs on a bench. "Your fellow-men!" he said sneeringly. And I imagine that a number of gaolers in Soviet or Nazi concentration camps, and even in British prisons, have reacted similarly to their victims. What I deny about such a reaction is, first, that it is common, and, second, that (for human beings) there is anything "natural" about it. The victory of Augustine over Pelagius was the greatest disaster, I sometimes think, of all the many disasters in the history of religion. I am a Pelagian, or say a semi-Pelagian, and believe that everyone (by and large—there are pathological exceptions) has freedom of will, by God's grace, to choose good and reject evil: Simone is an extreme Augustinian, and believes, not only that an additional grace must be granted us if we are to utilize the freedom so available and choose good, but that very few of us are granted it. So love, for me, is as natural as hatred: more natural, for we are made in God's image. As to why, nevertheless, there is so much evil about in the world—I tried to deal with this issue in *Tim I*, when I hazarded the theological myth I have repeated in these pages.*

* See page 55.

When people do exhibit, in some degree or another, the reaction that Simone describes as natural, they usually turn out, on examination, to be people who have been specially warped by the unnaturalness of society. I say usually: for matter being the framework of spirit in us, and creation so prodigal, it is by no means remarkable that the mixture should sometimes go wrong *ab initio*; and I talk of society as unnatural because that's what it is when it ends, as it so far has ended, in atom bombs and Nazi gaolers. But aren't I begging the question, you may ask? Aren't I arbitrarily defining unnatural in a way that will suit my polemics? I think not. A thing that develops naturally is a thing that so develops as to fulfil its own nature: then how can a society be natural that is working tooth and nail to destroy itself? The atom bomb is only climax or nadir: everything in society that tends to split or antagonise is unnatural—every hatred, every greed, every selfishness—because humanity is social, we are all, whether we like it or not, members one of another, and a house divided against itself cannot stand. But never mind logical proof: ask your conscience, or your mere common sense, whether atomising babies is natural, and I haven't much doubt of your answer. And if you ask me in your turn why the world has developed unnaturally, I must refer you again to my myth.

You never find the reaction to suffering that Simone considers typical in people who, despite the unnaturalness of society, have found a way to express themselves freely and sweetly without detriment to communion, or, rather, with advantage to it: and rarely even in those who have been warped, but not outrageously. The great value of modern psychology, which I have criticised on occasion for what I think its excesses, is that it teaches us to set humanity, from those precious first months, on the road to harmonious living. It is a light, a new light, a contemporary light, shining in much darkness; and when I think of it and a great many other things, such as the growth, steady for all its imperfections, of socialist endeavour, I am not ashamed, *malgré tout*, to be an optimist. But everything depends on the extent to which we are willing, every one of us, to play a part in the conquest of darkness.

And when people do react to the afflicted without love or compassion, they react commonly, not with hatred and contempt, but with indifference. This latter is due for the most part

to feebleness of imagination, and that is why the majority react
so to affliction in the distant or dead. Very few, I imagine, sit
and watch through the night, trying moment by moment to get
across with a love that recks nothing of barriers, as a man they
don't know, far away in his cell, awaits death the next morning at dawn; and even fewer think often, if at all, of those
myriads through the ages who have gasped out their life on
some battlefield, or entered a gas-room to the tune of a Viennese
waltz, or been crucified like Christ. Simone herself, whose own
love for the afflicted was like that of few others, has some
words on the distant and dead that came ever and again to
my mind as I sat listening to *Mathis der Mahler*, which is full of
affliction; for I found in them the echo of an emotion that had
held me repeatedly, but with a strength so much feebler than
hers that a comparison seems out of place: "There is only one
time when I really know nothing of this certitude any longer. It
is when I am in contact with the affliction of other people, those
who are indifferent or unknown to me as much as the others,
perhaps even more, including those of the most remote ages of
antiquity. This contact causes me such atrocious pain and so
utterly rends my soul, that as a result the love of God becomes
almost impossible for me for a while. It would take very little
more to make me say impossible. So much so that I am uneasy
about myself. I reassure myself a little by remarking that Christ
wept on foreseeing the horrors of the destruction of Jerusalem.
I hope he will forgive me my compassion." When I thought
of that passage at *Mathis der Mahler* this question occurred
to me: are we doing any positive good to the afflicted of past
ages when we remember their agony and desire to assuage
it? I mean, do we succeed in assuaging it? I am persuaded that
somehow we do. We know little of time and still less of eternity,
of their nature and significance: but what was and will be, surely
is: and I grasp elusively, without the power to explain myself, a
coincidence (in some dimension of reality outside our ken, as
Simone would say, "here below") of affliction at whatever time
it may have occurred, of our love at whatever time we may
give it, and of the sufferer's response.

However that may be, some goodness accrues to the sum of
things when we love the afflicted who are distant or dead, for the
more love the more goodness: and we cannot in any case help
ourselves loving them, if we have been granted imagination.

But what we *can* control is our degree of attention: we can be lazy or otherwise. There have been nights when I have sat up on the eve of an execution, and made the effort I have described. But usually I have desired to avoid it; and so when my eye has caught a paragraph with the dreadful announcement I have hurriedly passed on and forgotten. This isn't the way. If, as I put it before, we are to help deity help us, we must do our utmost, our little utmost, to heal the wounds of existence, by intention, with *Kavvanah*, as much as in deed: we must send out our love through the universe, irrespective of time or distance, and so contribute, if only as with a grain of sand, to restoration and unity.

And thinking of the afflicted who are dead, I find myself at this moment, as I have found myself from the beginning for all the criticisms I have indulged in, greatly loving Simone herself. That she suffered affliction, extreme affliction of the sort she describes, is unquestionable; and this alone should win our love and compassion. But she was lovable in other ways too. Though I find her sexual imagery, as with some of the mystics, repellent, her devotion to God and her service to man were of a kind that has always been rare; and humble devotion to God is humble devotion to God, whether or not we misinterpret his meaning, and a life of service to man is a life of service to man, whether or not we undervalue his nature. And of course it may be I who am mistaken.

It would be easy to argue, rightly or wrongly, that her estimate of God and man, and her metaphysics, were largely conditioned by her affliction; and as easy to see sexual repression, and an awareness of inferiority, as responsible for much in her thought and emotion. Her ugliness was extreme, or became so —a friend of mine, who saw her often, has described her as *affreuse*: she was uncouth in social intercourse: and she experienced great cruelty, or thought she did, from her friends and acquaintances. In her testament to Father Perrin the farm-yard analogy is repeated: "Even if we only consider the plane of purely human relations," she writes, "the gratitude I owe you is infinite. I think that except you, all those human beings for whom I have made it easy to hurt me through my friendship, have amused themselves by doing so, frequently or occasionally, consciously or unconsciously, but all of them at some time or another. Where I recognised it to be conscious, I took a knife and cut out the friendship, without however warning the person in question. They did not behave like this from malice, but as a result of the well-known phenomenon which makes hens rush upon one of their number if it is wounded, attacking and pecking it . . . It is only with you that I have never felt the backlash of this mechanism." Now that she is dead things are different.

§ 5

I have used up a great deal of space in describing and criticising Simone's doctrine. To good purpose, I think: because the relation between God and man, good and evil, politics and religion, is the essential subject of my letter—the whole letter, that is, and not merely this second instalment—and Simone is an exponent, far more powerful than any other, of certain trends in contemporary thinking I regard as deplorable. Let me summarise these trends. They are not all to be found in Simone—I want to make that clear, beyond the possibility of a doubt, before proceeding: and the practical results that so often derive from them were absent in her case, for she was an unusually good woman, loved her neighbours "more than the publicans do", and not only desired, throughout the whole of her brief life, to serve them practically, but so indeed served them. Nevertheless she does represent—side by side with a very great deal that is exceptionally sympathetic in her thought and emotion, and for all her uniqueness—a general movement of ideas, rapidly growing in influence, which take their rise, beyond question, from our recent and present disasters, and from the effect that those disasters have produced on some of the most religiously sensitive minds: and are likely, in my opinion, not to mitigate any of the dangers, whether spiritual or political, that confront us, but to intensify most of them. If the ideas in question were true there would be nothing to be done about them, for truth cannot be tampered with, whatever the results of expressing it: but I do not believe them to be true, I believe them to be false. And Simone is of special importance because of her stature: she will carry far more weight, as time goes on, than the much smaller men who are at the moment more famous. That is why as soon as I read her I desired to have my say in rebuttal.

These are some of the trends I have in mind:

(1) A growing movement is to be observed throughout the West towards a sort of Manichaeism, or towards one of the beliefs, rather, that are basic to that system: a belief, whether explicit or not, whether recognised for what it is (by the one who believes it) or not, in the existence of two absolute principles, good and evil, that confront one another and do battle for the soul of the world. It is an attractive theory, as it has always been, for those who combine a passionate impulse towards goodness with a strongly militant nature; but the central body of Christian doctrine, springing from a Judaism that could say of Divinity "Shall there be evil in a city and the Lord hath not done it?", has always fought it tooth and nail. And with wisdom: for it is a faithless doctrine, and its contemporary prevalence arises, not from any enlargement of faith under the impact of an intensified wickedness and the resulting disillusionment, but from a failure to preserve it in spite of them. Our era has many affinities with the second and third centuries, when Manichaeism spread so rapidly: and did so, as an authority on the subject has written, because it offered a simple, apparently profound, yet convenient solution of the problem of good and evil, a problem which, in those centuries, had become peculiarly oppressive.

"These philosophical commonplaces of half a century ago," wrote a Christian last month, "namely that the universe is one stuff and good stuff, and that evil is relatively unreal, a kind of nothingness, have received a devastating retort from history —for the one thing which has emerged in the modern world is a sense of the reality of evil: we feel that evil is not simply misplaced good but an awful, *living principle* exhibited in concentration camps, gas chambers and slave settlements." Really, one hardly knows where to begin in refutation of such heresy. "Philosophical commonplaces of half a century ago"! No, not of half a century ago: of Christian thought throughout the ages. "Evil hath no substantial being," wrote Dionysius the Areopagite, "but only a shadow thereof." "God's mind," wrote Meister Eckhart, "perceives all sin and evil in the idea of the corresponding good, not in the form of sin; for instance, he knows lying in the form of truth." "If God exists," to summarise the doctrine of Erigena, "there is nothing absolutely evil." "Even the Devil is capable of goodness," wrote Origen. "It is, in fact, not possible," wrote Gregory of Nyssa, "to form any other notion of the origin of vice than as the absence of virtue." Or, if you think these minor men, here is something from Aquinas: "The will would never tend to evil, unless there were ignorance or error in the reason. Hence it is written: They err that work evil." Or here is something more explicit still: "Sin is nothingness, and when men sin they do nothingness." It was said by Augustine.

The plain truth is this: they lack, these neo-Manichaeans, all historical perspective. They make much play with concentration-camps and gas-chambers. There is really no need for them to do so: these are things that we shall none of us forget for the rest of our lives. But I would ask—what of the Roman Republic and Empire? Of slaves and gladiators crucified, to the number of 6,000 after a single revolt, as Jesus was crucified? Or of the Middle Ages, and its tortures so horrible that one sickens and faints to recall them? Or of Genghiz Khan, and the million and a half that he massacred within the walls of Herat? Or of someone or other—I forget his name, and have no wish to remember it—who built a wall from his enemies' skulls? Or of pogroms in Poland and Russia a good century before Hitler was born? Or of the Thirty Years' War? Do they know, these discoverers of evil in "the modern world", about the Thirty Years' War, and about how people ate the young and the sick, yes and even the dead? I commend to them Mr Huxley's description of the Callot engravings, called *Les Misères et les Malheurs de la Guerre*, which were published in the middle of it. From etching to etching, Mr Huxley tells us, we follow the artist's record of pillage, murder, arson, rape, torture and execution. "To the punishments meted out to disobedient soldiers, Callot devotes five of his best plates. In the first they are merely being tortured, before a large crowd of interested spectators. But this is only a beginning. Turning to the second, we see at the centre of the plate a noble oak tree, from whose boughs twenty-one corpses are already limply dangling. On a ladder a twenty-second victim is about to be turned off by the hangman, while, three or four rungs below, a friar holds up the crucifix before his eyes. A second friar gives his benediction to a twenty-third at the foot of the ladder; a twenty-fourth is playing dice on a drum-head against a group of halberdiers, and in the foreground yet another friar is busy with the twenty-fifth. After which we pass on to the most elaborate and the most impassively frightful of all the executions—that of a *voleur inhumain*, who, on a high scaffold, is being broken on the wheel. The executioner stands over him, his crowbar raised above his head, ready to shatter one of the victim's shins; and at the other end of the wheel's diameter an ecclesiastic in a biretta bends over the naked man, holding a little crucifix close to the up-turned face and praying inaudibly through the reiterated screams. At one corner of the scaffold, in a neat little heap, as though left there by a man who has gone for a swim and will be back in a moment, lie the victim's clothes and broad-brimmed hat . . . [Then there is the etching of a pillaged convent.] About twenty of the nuns are being marched off to be raped at leisure round the camp-fire, in the evening. . . . A year or two from now, these nuns—such of them as have survived—will have joined the hordes of male and female camp-followers, who followed the armies hither and thither across the face of Germany. Half starved, covered only with a few stinking rags, verminous and syphilitic, with burdens on their backs and naked pot-bellied children trailing after them, they will march all summer long behind their masters, they will cower in the rains and frosts of interminable winters, until finally, long before the war is over, the God who has forsaken them once more takes pity and they die, to be eaten by dogs or perhaps by their famished companions." Do people really imagine that because I talk, and shall continue to talk, about the relative unreality of evil—its unreality in a final analysis— I'm so stupid, or innocent, or myopically benevolent, as to know nothing of such wickedness—whereas the thought of it so appals me at times, for all its temporal distance, that I feel filthy in the flesh of my own body and in the spirit of my own soul? And this is the affliction, let me add (I mean the affliction described by Huxley), which God has devised, according to Simone, as a marvellous "divine technique" for allowing God to love God.

There is nothing new about evil, as there is nothing new about good. There is nothing new, either, about the way we should deal with it. Christ told us, nineteen hundred odd years ago, to meet it with good and not to meet it with evil. But we have refused to attend.

Like a blessing on what I have just written, there rises to meet me, as I go down to lunch, a voice so ultimate in goodness and purity that to talk of evil as an absolute in its presence seems nonsensical. Play it on the piano if you can:

The Manichaean attitude, whether consciously adopted or
not, has an inevitable result: it issues in physical militancy. The
hosts of light and the hosts of darkness, there they stand—two
utterly distinct forces, poised over against one another, arrayed
for battle; and you long to rush bravely across and smite
Dagon on the hip, crying: "In the name of Jehovah!" And
not merely smite him on the hip, annihilate him with the
sword: for he is the only true God's irredeemable enemy, and
there is no health in him. But Christianity, as I understand
it, does not see hosts of darkness at all, in any absolute sense,
and therefore never thinks of annihilation. It sees everywhere
children of God: erring children, as we all are, and erring in
some cases, we may judge, a little more than ourselves (or a
very great deal more? And yet, given a combination of circum-

stances, how might we not ourselves have behaved?), but children of God none the less, invariably made in his image, and never in the image of a non-existent Antigod. Everyone is therefore redeemable; and our share in the redemption, of others as well as of ourselves, is to be a channel, however petty, shallow, and obstructed by gigantic boulders, for God's love.

I would add, by way of footnote, that I have myself been accused of Manichaeism, because I hold that the profit motive is absolutely wrong. This criticism seems to rest on a confusion. To deny the absoluteness of evil in the whole scheme of things —in the vision of God, *sub specie aeternitatis*—is one thing: to deny its absoluteness for us "here below", if we see it, with the conscience God has given us, as evil, is quite another. I tried to make this distinction clear in *Tim I*: and to mark it I have invariably used the phrase "the relative unreality of evil". You may remember some lines that I quoted from Blake. The roaring of lions, he says, the howling of wolves, the raging of the stormy sea, and the destructive sword, are portions of eternity too great for the eye of man. That is one of the greatest anti-manichaean affirmations ever written. But Blake would have been the first to insist—open him anywhere, read on a bit, and see—that never to use the destructive sword, never to roar like a lion or howl like a wolf, is imperative for every one of us. Or forget Blake, and think of it like this. If God exists, if God is good, and if God is all—and that is the basis of my faith, a hypothesis which, of its nature, can in no way be a matter for argument—then there *must* be some ultimate goodness even in the existence of cruelty, little though I may understand what that goodness can be (though in fact, as I tried to show in my myth, I do vaguely understand it): but how can that, pray, affect the imperative, an imperative imposed by my conscience, first, to do no cruelty myself, and, second, to fight against systems that embody or facilitate it? For all I know, the very meaning of cruelty, of its existence in the world or the universe, may precisely be this: that it is there to be avoided or fought against. Think of Keats, and his "vale of soul-making". But your methods of fighting it will vary according to your basic assumptions about evil. If you are a Manichaean, you will fight it with the destructive sword (and therefore, by your own cruelty, will make nonsense of your claim that you are fighting in the name of the Lord): if you are a Christian you will fight it

like a Christian. As to the profit-motive, I see it as the con-
secration of greed; and I see greed, not to be sure as I see
cruelty, but as likewise, and absolutely, forbidden us.

(2) Apart from Manichaeism proper, there has been a
growing tendency, for a long time now, to concentrate the
attention on evil, on darkness and on horror, and to ignore
goodness and light: to be pessimist, and regard optimism as
moronic: to play the cynic, and sneer: to impale our mediocrity
and our wickedness, and say nothing of our sublimities: and
even to revel in a sort of grovelling misanthropy. The doctrine
of total depravity has renewed its appeal in our time; and
people have not only achieved a great following, but won
high official honours, for spurning humanity as contemptible.
And all this, again, is a token of faithlessness: forced into an
uncomfortable realisation that progress isn't as easy as we
thought (which isn't equivalent, by any means, to imagining it
a myth), we have simply been unable to confront the dark
knowledge without forgetting that we are sons of a king.

Yes, sons of a king: for the fashionable view of human nature
is grotesquely untrue. If a tithe of the publicity that is given to
evil were given to good, how startlingly different the picture
would look! As touching war, for example, I have had two remarkable experiences. Shortly after starting my business, I
wanted to prove that, when there was every temptation to be
brutal and merciless, gentleness and mercy could survive: not
only in exceptional characters, but in average human nature.
So we sent a letter to the press, and asked for documents that
might bear on the subject, in respect of the first world war; and
we received such a flood of replies that it took an editor a whole
year to get them sorted and grouped and to make a selection.
War Letters of Fallen Englishmen was the result; and masses of
material had to be jettisoned, as the book would otherwise have
been too long and expensive. Then, in the middle of the second
world war, Vera Brittain, Sheila Hodges and George Catlin
had a similar impulse. Things were not so easy then, for bitter-
ness was extreme, and a general letter to the press seemed
undesirable; but even so a little volume, called *Above All Nations*,
was got together in a matter of weeks, mainly from obscure
newspaper cuttings.

I am going to reproduce just four examples from these books,
because it gives me great pleasure to make hay of all this non-

sense about total depravity, and about people being unable to
act decently unless their "whole soul" is inhabited by Christ.
I have purposely chosen average examples, which could be
multiplied indefinitely; and have omitted such a story as that of
Elizabeth Pilenko, who took the place of a Jewess in the gas-
chamber (I told you about her in *Tim I*), and whose whole soul
may truly have been inhabited by Christ. But these others were
ordinary people, like you and me: even the Rabbi, who was
able, for love of his neighbour, to overcome the instincts of a
lifetime:

(a) The Grand Rabbin of Lyons was a Jewish chaplain to the
French forces in the 1914–1918 war. One day a wounded man
staggered into a trench and told the Rabbi that a Roman
Catholic was on the point of death in no-man's-land, and was
begging that his padre should come to him with a crucifix. The
padre could not be found. The Jew rapidly improvised a cross
from sticks of wood, ran out with it into no-man's-land, and was
seen to hold it before the dying man's eyes. He was almost immediately shot by a sniper; the bodies of the Catholic and the
Jew were found together.

(b) A private and a bugler, both stretcher-bearers in the
second world war, were returning to their lines on the Arakan
front when they heard a rustling in the bushes and the click of
a rifle-bolt. Out into their path stepped a six-foot Japanese with
his rifle at the ready. He looked at the two men and the third
man they carried on the stretcher, and then without a word or
a gesture dropped the muzzle of his rifle and stepped back into
the jungle.

(c) When a Yorkshireman was wounded during the invasion
of Normandy, a German prisoner succoured him as he fell.
"He carried me seventy yards to the beach, then looked down
at me, smiled, put a cigarette in my mouth, lit it, and put the
lighter in my pocket. Then he took off his white shirt, tore it
into shreds and dressed my wounds. Having done this, he kissed
me with tears in his eyes, and walked away to attend to other
wounded."

(d) Here is an extract from a letter I got myself, during the
autumn of 1944, from an Austrian Jew who was then in the
British pioneer corps at the front, attached to a hospital receiving German wounded. He had been for nine months in the concentration camps of Dachau and Buchenwald: he had been

hung by the wrists to a tree and had once nearly died of gangrene, Jews at that time not being allowed medical attention in concentration camps. He also had reason to believe that his old mother had been taken to Poland two years before:

"This is being written in the solitude of a ward in which I am guarding wrecked members of the Herrenvolk. It is so strange a situation that I can hardly describe what I am feeling. Loneliness is perhaps the only word for it. These are men who set out to conquer the world, and they and their kind have done unspeakable things to me and my kind, and I am supposed to hate them with all my strength, and would be right to do so according to recognised standards of human behaviour. But I cannot hate, or is it that in the face of suffering hatred is silent? So it happens that the guard is turned into a nurse, and if a man, from losing too much blood, goes out of his mind and stammers incoherently, I have to talk him to sleep again. And it sometimes happens that men try to hold my hand when I have helped them. That makes me feel lonely . . .

"Only a few lines. It is midnight, and I am going off duty after having had a busy time with that man who lost so much blood that he went crackers. He had an operation and blood transfusion, and I was the only one able to talk to him. In the end he obeyed my orders instantly with *Jawohl, Herr Doktor!** Once he said *Sie sind so ein feiner Mensch,*† and then *Sie sind zu mir wie ein Vater.*‡ What shall I make of that? I can only draw one conclusion, which is that I am a terribly bad soldier, and I am somehow glad about it.

"Later: The man I wrote about has died. The doctors fought for his life as if he were a celebrity."

Excessive concentration on evil and darkness and horror, and on human wickedness or infirmity—at the expense of attention to good, and to human worthiness—has results as inevitable as those of Manichaeism itself.

First, we positively add to the evil that's about in the world by becoming obsessed with it. I have already quoted Huxley's *Grey Eminence*: let me quote now his *Devils of Loudun*, for he makes my

* "Certainly, doctor."
† "You are a good man!"
‡ "You are like a father to me."

point, or rather half of it, better than I could: "No man can concentrate his attention upon evil, or even upon the idea of evil, and remain unaffected . . . Every crusader is apt to go mad. He is haunted by the wickedness which he attributes to his enemies: it becomes in some sort a part of him." But I would go further than Mr Huxley. Not only is the man affected himself: not only, by being affected, does he affect others: but, over and above himself and those others, a new evil has happened, really *happened*, in the sum of things by his attachment to evil and the idea of it.

The word attachment is important, for the following reason:

You may think it very odd that I should deprecate so strongly what I have called excessive concentration on evil, and on human wickedness and folly and so on, when this very letter, which is a reflection of my life, is so packed with an awareness of them, and so instinct with a desire to see them vanish, that you might wonder, at first blush, whether I am not suddenly going back, carried away by the argument, on everything I have previously written. But the first blush, I hope, would be the last. Anyhow, let me explain what I think *ought* to be our relation to evil and stupidity and wickedness, and after that we can briefly examine whether my own practice has measured up to the "ought" in question.

You will remember the sentence of Eckhart: "God's mind perceives all sin and evil in the idea of the corresponding good, not in the form of sin; for instance, he knows lying in the form of truth." Now it's not at all a bad idea to look at the world as we may imagine that God must look at it: though of course it's a very bad idea indeed if we begin equating ourselves with God and forgetting that we are fallible and finite creatures. So we ought, I think, when contemplating evil and folly, to be passionate (and it is right to be passionate), not about destroying them, for all destruction is itself so much evil and folly, but about doing what we can to release the goodness and wisdom that lie hidden in them, so that the goodness and wisdom may absorb the evil and folly. I think you will understand what I mean if you have read *Timothy* with care. The key passage is this, from Dionysius the Areopagite:

"The depraved sinner hath a share in the Good in so far as there is in him a distorted reflection of true love and communion. And anger hath a share in the Good, in so far as it is a movement which seeks to remedy apparent evils, converting them to that which appears to be fair. And even he that desires the basest life, yet in so far as he feels desire at all and feels desire for life, and intends what he thinks the best kind of life, so far participates in the Good. The Good must be the beginning and end even of all evil things. For the Good is the final purpose of all things, good and bad alike. Even when we act amiss we do so from a longing for the Good; for no one makes evil his definite object when performing any action. And if no thing in the world is without a share in the Good, and evil is the deficiency of Good and no thing in the world is utterly destitute of Good, then the Divine Providence is in all things, and nothing that exists can be without it."

So, insistently aware of evil and passionately desiring to see it vanish, we should try to fix our gaze, in the very midst of our awareness and passion—which we should in no wise damp down, but should keep ever burning within us—on the good rather than on the evil: not merely in a general sense, but in respect of the very evil that we feel a concern about. And above all we must not get *attached* to the evil in question: we must not even get attached to any particular good, but try to merge ourselves in goodness.

As to my own practice, that is another matter. Every crusader, says Mr Huxley, is apt to go mad. I am apt to go mad when I am up against an event that appals me, such as the announcement of our atom explosion or Lord Goddard's propaganda for birching; and I have thought it right, indeed essential for my whole purpose, to express what I feel at the moment of feeling it. But I don't, if I may say so, remain mad very long: and this cessation of madness I have also felt it right to express. You may remember that, within minutes of my outburst against Lord Goddard in *Timothy*, I wrote somewhat as follows: that until one could stand in his shoes, see the good in him that prompted his evil, and have as much charity for him as for criminals, one wasn't an inch on the road to the Kingdom of Heaven. One therefore tries: and practice, if it will never make perfect, may make, at perhaps very long last, just a little less imperfect than before.

*   *   *

If excessive concentration on evil, and on human wickedness
and infirmity, doesn't make people physically militant, it tends
to produce a result almost equally lamentable, but in an opposite direction. It makes them throw up their hands. If men and
the world are like this, they reflect, why bother about it all? So,
in cynicism or despair, they retire from the fray: cease to be
citizens of their country, let alone of the world: develop into
what Schweitzer would call world-denyers: and, if they have
strong religious impulses, cultivate their own religious garden,
and let mundanities go hang. I prefer this reaction to that of
physical militancy, but I don't like this either. They should
read, people who react so, a Catholic thinker of the type of
Péguy: who will tell them that it isn't enough to be a Catholic
(or Christian or mystic or Jew or whatever you please), but that
one must work in the temporal if one wishes to tear the future
from temporal tyrannies; that the Church will not reopen the
door of the workroom and will not be open once more to the
people, unless she too, like the rest of the world, pays the price
of an economic revolution—a social revolution, an industrial
revolution, in short a temporal revolution for eternal salvation;
that such is properly the inscription of the eternal itself in the
temporal; that economic expenses, social expenses, industrial
expenses, temporal expenses must be met; and that nothing can
evade it, not even the spiritual, not even the inner life. Or let
them read another Catholic, Maritain, who will tell them this:
Political society—if it by no means has the task (which is
vested in a higher jurisdiction) of guiding human beings to
their spiritual perfection, to utmost freedom of autonomy, to
Eternal Life—is none the less entrusted, by very reason of
its temporal character, with an essentially, albeit indirectly,
religious office: that of facilitating, through the standard it
secures for every one of its members in the material as well
as in the moral and intellectual domains, their spiritual endeavours. This is what Maritain writes: and I commend it to
people who stay shut up in an ivory tower of religious communion, instead of playing their part—a part arising spontaneously from that communion, if communion it be with the
Father of all—in producing such social conditions as will help
others to achieve it.

(3) Shading off into the tendency last described is one
directly concerned with the relation of God and man. God is

envisaged, at worst, as a despotic tyrant, over against a cower-
ing slave: in the middle, as a benevolent master, over against
a ready servant: and at best, as an insistent bridegroom, over
against a submissive bride. I have no liking for any of these
similes. If we are to have sexual imagery at all, I prefer, from
the Song of Songs, "I am my beloved's and my beloved is
mine"—which Ruth said to me, by the way, as she put a ring
on my finger at our wedding after I had put mine on hers, for
we were both ardent feminists, and didn't at all like the one-
sided nature of the ordinary ring business. But I think of God
and man, for my own part, in quite other terms: as fellow-
workers, as co-operators.

Now of course I don't mean by this that I think of them as
equals—how could anybody equate the finite with the infinite,
perfect goodness and mercy and love with our human imperfections? Let me put it like this. I have talked about the need,
with its tranquillity and blessedness, of waiting on God: and I
vividly feel that need. I have talked about the need, with the
freedom it brings us, of doing God's will: and I vividly feel that
need. And I have talked about man, in a sort of enthusiasm for
him (despite an awareness of his folly), as magnificent in his
power of initiative and in his ability to redeem if he uses his
power aright: and I feel that vividly too. And not only do I feel
all three vividly: the vividness with which I feel them is an
equal, an identical vividness. Can the third, then, be harmonised with the other two? I am sure that it can; but you can't
really write about *how*, you can only *live* how. Any logical or
dogmatic formulation would seem to me meaningless: like an
attempt to express the beauty of lilies in algebra or mathematics. There is a mystery here, and mysteries are better left
alone—better accepted as such. All sorts of images come into
the mind—that of a junior partnership, for instance. And all
sorts of hints from the sages. Bossuet wrote that we are, in
God's hands, our own masters; Buber wrote that man's action
is enclosed in God's action, but is still real action. Let me leave
it at that: adding only that human effort is immobilised just as
surely by a slave-despot concept, however disguised, as by
that excessive concentration on our wretchedness which is
merely another aspect of it.

(4) The fourth and final tendency that I notice and deplore
follows naturally after the third. It is a tendency to schematise

—to reduce to a formula what simply *cannot* be reduced to a formula. Clear-cut systems are the rage; and in certain circles only describable as highbrow-religious ones any manner of thinking or feeling that eschews a dogmatic precision is patronisingly shrugged out of court. You notice a positive horror in such people for what they call pantheism or immanentism. Yet why should it be more religious to believe in the Thirty-nine Articles —which proclaim, among other things, that concupiscence, namely sex, "hath the nature of sin": that "in every person born into this world, it deserveth God's wrath and damnation": and that "works done before the grace of Christ and the Inspiration of his spirit [for example, by Socrates] are not pleasant to God" —than to believe in, or rather feel and know, the presence of God everywhere: at the heart of every man and every beast and every flower, of every stick and every stone throughout the universe? There is danger in panentheism (which is what people usually mean when they talk about pantheism, for there are very few pantheists nowadays)* and the worshipper should beware of it: but not, I consider, as much of danger as of value: and isn't there danger too, and something worse than danger, in the worship, however covert or disguised, of a godhead wholly transcendent—a worship masquerading as the Christianity to which it is alien? The one thing, anyhow, that "pantheism" oughtn't to be criticised for is "vagueness": how can an emotion be vague if a man lives the whole of his life by it, little willing though he may be to splinter up into various factors the reality it responds to, and make a system of them?

Schematisers and dogmaticians adore the word "vague". An eminent religious critic had the hardihood the other day, apropos of Mr Hugh I'A. Fausset's *Towards Fidelity*, to castigate the "vague sublimities" of Eastern religions, by which he meant Buddhism and the like. What would have been his reaction, I wonder, if a Buddhist had thought it seemly to point a finger of fun at him and arraign his "arrogant certainties"—about the Person of God, and the relation between the Persons of God, and the intentions of God for the universe, etcetera? And so I come to the last of my points. We are shutting ourselves off from one another within the walls of our own dogmatisms: we are much farther off than we were from that harmonising of

* Pantheism equates God and the universe; panentheism sees God *in* everything.

E

faiths and religions which might do much to heal the wounds
of the world. Why, Christ's very own church is in fragments,
and its reunion seems more of a lost hope now than when I
was a boy.

Simone Weil, for whatever else I may criticise her, at least
never made that sort of error. She felt, she lived, and she
expresses in her writings, a religious universalism of singular
integrity. And I am glad to be ending, as I began, on a note of
agreement with her: for she was a great if (in some respects)
a rather twisted woman, and wrote a great if (in some respects)
a rather twisted book. And withal she is lovable: although
given little love in her lifetime.

INTERLUDE ABOUT CRITICS

"My Dear Timothy" has been out a month, and I want to clarify a few points that arise from the critical reaction to it. Apart for a couple of notices clearly intended, for some reason or other, to be offensive—one of them by a rather charming man, a Papageno however, on a London evening journal—the reviewers as a whole have been generous, not to mention a big batch of letters, some of them very moving, from the general public. But in a minority of cases there has been, I must not say a misunderstanding of what I produced, but certainly a misunderstanding of what I tried to produce. So let me tell you what I *did* try to produce, what I am trying to produce in this second instalment, and what I shall try to produce in any more volumes that may come.

As you know, when I started writing I had no clear intention in mind. I was sitting in my library, by the fire, and idly thinking of the pleasure your visit had given me two or three weeks before: and suddenly I was writing to you. You were very young, with a lifetime before you; I was getting old, three quarters of the way towards death. And I had a really passionate desire, little Timothy, that your life should be a good and happy one; for not only do I love you exceedingly, having longed since the first days of marriage for a son of my own, but I saw in you as in a mirror all the young and gentle creatures that were being born into a world so surpassingly beautiful and yet threatened by so awful a fate. It was the beauty and wonder of the world that I wanted at first to describe, for I had always been filled with an awareness of them, and I wanted to share it with you: I wanted, if you like, to sing a song of thanksgiving to you and to God. But then, as I went on, other elements began to creep in, and the thing was soon growing in a way that I hadn't intended. Why not, I asked myself—not often consciously, but increasingly at the back of my mind— why not use the opportunity for a larger and double purpose: to unfold my own life, with all its sorrows and joys, just as truthfully as I could, and, as an inextricable part of this, to explain the ideas that, for a period of more than fifty years, had been slowly developing in my mind about the way in which our beautiful world could be saved from degradation? It was always you, Timothy, that I was thinking of as I wrote, and it is you that I am thinking of at this moment; but more and more, simultaneously, I began to feel that what I had to say might be of value to the world, and more and more, while thinking of you, it has been the world I have been speaking to.

I know, I always knew, that I am poorly equipped for the task. My brain is not Einstein's: St Francis is my superior in virtue. There is no mock-modesty about that, and no inferiority complex either. But I didn't think it right that these inadequacies should deter me. I am, by and large, an average man, with a greater power of expression than the average man's, and with perhaps acuter sensibilities. Might I not act, then, as a sort of spokesman for the average man? Show him a little more clearly to himself? Bring into the forefront of his consciousness the hopes and aspirations, the fears and distresses, that lay partly concealed at the back of it, and so help him to play, play with purpose, that part in the salvation of the world which every one of us must play if the world is to be saved? I answered my own question in the affirmative, and, with doubts and hesitations on the way, went ahead.

I had to be as frank as I could: what sort of value could the thing otherwise have possessed? X talks of moral strip-tease. Does he really think I revelled in exposing some of the things I felt bound to expose? Does he really think, for instance, that I found it agreeable to dilate on my boyhood sexualities? He would no doubt reply that this is just what he does think: that, in his opinion, I get a kick out of self-revelation, and that it's the very pith and marrow of my egoism. I believe him to be wrong: indeed I cannot help saying that I know him to be wrong, for I tried desperately hard to wriggle out of that particular bit of self-revelation, until I knew that I mustn't and couldn't. But suppose—for self-deception is always possible, even at times of unusual groping for integrity— suppose he's right: isn't it valuable, then, to expose a delight in self-exposure? If indeed I feel such a delight, it's most improbable that I'm unique in that respect: and by being, as it were, franker than I know, I may be helping other people to understand themselves better, and avoid my errors. I could reply the same to Papageno. He says I am arrogant, and never more so than when I am being humble. Knowing, as I think, my own heart, I must say, as with X, that I believe him wrong:

but supposing he is right, then once again there may be value in my unconscious self-exposure, for bogus humility is something everyone should guard against.

There has been a certain amount of criticism about my setting myself up as a prophet. In heaven's name, don't we want prophets? The world is going to the devil: Hitler recently burnt up millions, and people are everywhere working overtime to produce atom bombs, napalm bombs, hydrogen bombs, and all the other obscenities whose whole raison d'être is to torture our fellows or stop them torturing us. We live in an enveloping atmosphere of hatred and fear. I detest these things, everyone detests them: they are a blasphemy against the creator, they make a mock of our humanity. Then, if I think that I know the way out—if I think I can put my finger on what's wrong, and can help others do the same, dare I be silent? I know, quite as well as Papageno and X, that I am a poor thing (and I also know, if they will excuse me for saying so, that they are poor things themselves, as we all are): I know that I may have been led into dangerous errors by my imperfect acquaintance with many of the subjects I've been speaking of, and by intellectual and spiritual shortcomings: but I also know that I am a human being, with all the duties and responsibilities and yes, the splendour of a human being, and that I must do the best I can with such equipment as I have, and that this is what God, through my conscience, has called me to do. Critics say I'm very Jewish in my penchant for prophecy. Well, of course I'm a Jew, but what of that? God may specially have created Jews to be prophets, indeed this seems very probable: anyhow, the live coal touched my lips, or so I thought, and what could I answer but "here am I"? Perhaps I was self-deluded; if so, there was a purpose in my self-delusion; for we are all God's instruments, and he has a habit of choosing, for some object of his own, the most improbable ones.

I know all about the dangers of prophecy. I wrote some paragraphs on the subject at a time I was feeling "blocked", but cut them out. I'll restore them:

"I think I really know what's wrong with me. I am 'dry'. I don't mean in the literary sense: I mean in the spiritual sense. I've lost the sense of communion: I really don't meet things, or the Thing behind them and in them. I can't pray; I can only pretend to. My apprehension of the world is an apprehension from the outside, an intellectual, almost an artistic, apprehension, not a mingling of myself in joy with the creation. And I feel desperately lonely. It is a loneliness that nothing human (or so I think at this moment) can assuage. I love Ruth: I love my friends, and one especially: and they love me. And yet—there's something above and beyond them that I can't get at (or that isn't getting at me): though I long to, perhaps because of the deprivation, more than at any other time in my life. I want, so terribly, to lose myself in the ultimate peace where self-consciousness ceases. I have done so, or done so nearly enough to know what it's like and to be satisfied with the knowledge, so often in the past: why can't I do so now?

"Do you understand what I mean, Timothy, when I say that this dryness, this deprivation, explains (as I suspect) the clash of wanting to write and not wanting to write that I have tried to describe for you? I've wanted to write because of my desire to speak what I see as the truth, to put people on the right path—you must forgive the egoism, I'm saying what I feel—to be, if you like, a prophet. But what restrains me is this lack of communion. It comes back, so very soon after I've used the word, to a question of egoism. When you're in communion you don't speak as yourself, you're just a bit of something bigger that's speaking: and so no clash between wanting and not wanting can possibly arise. The matter is out of your hands: you are serene. But when the communion's gone you are suddenly you; and then you are sickened by your pride, your presumption, your endlessly telling people what *you* think, what *you* feel, what *you* once accomplished.

"But there's something else. Isn't it perhaps, as I asked once before, that this writing itself—all this looking into one's own personality, this absorbing concentration on one's own, on V.G.'s set of emotions and ideas—isn't it perhaps precisely this that inhibits communion, makes one isolated and derelict? But if so, what is the answer? To be silent, because to talk means losing heaven? No: that is the way of quietism, and no way is more egoistical. Ansky said, in his play *The Dybbuk*, that everyone who speaks from his heart is the High Priest. Can you refuse to be a momentary High Priest, merely because (a) you're a wretched sinner anyhow, and (b) your acceptance of priesthood involves the loss of something infinitely precious? Yes, but what if

your loss of it robs the priesthood of its value? Or of most of it, or
of some of it? There is a whole series of paradoxes here, which I at
least cannot harmonise. All one can say to oneself, I suppose, is
this: Be still; get on with it; and perhaps grace will come."

There is something else I want to say—about the shape, or if
you prefer the shapelessness, of this letter. One or two critics
have objected that it's undisciplined and unplanned. Of course
it is: I said so myself. One of the few things I could have done
rather well, if I had wanted to, was to produce something good
in proportion, for my sense of form is well developed. But I
didn't want to. I gave a clue to what I was after (or not really to
what I was after, but to what was happening) when I said, in
Tim I, that this was not so much a piece of writing as a piece
of living. Here I am in the world of today, with the world of
today pressing dreadfully on me, and yet, except in moments of
dereliction, with my joy in the beauty and wonder of it undimmed; and I live it, and as I live it I write it, never knowing
what will be round the corner, but taking it as it comes. And
mixed up with the present me is the past me, and mixed up with
the present world is the past world: they break in on one another, interpenetrate one another, explain one another, and a
picture of one is inextricably involved with a picture of the
other. I am, at this moment while I write, a man of today and
not yesterday: but yesterday and today are as one: there is an
unbroken progression: the I changes as I live it. How meaningless, how positively lying must be a record of the past, unless the
recorder is revealed for what he is at the very moment of recording! And there's something further: the past isn't stable, an
object: the past changes—doesn't merely seem to change, really
changes—as the continuing liver reflects on it. Anyhow, I can't
suppress the present me, and have no wish to. A critic, who,
to judge from letters I have received from people who understand me, must be more insensitive than most, said something
like this: that when I am afraid I may be boring my readers
with some lengthy discussion I interrupt it with "delightful irre-
levances" about the weather or my garden or a concert or whatnot. Can't he see, hasn't he the heart or spirit to see, that there's
nothing calculated about those bits in italics? That I *have* to put
them in, because it's the present I who's writing, and when I
feel an overwhelming sense of joy at some beauty that has come

to uplift me, or an overwhelming sense of wrong at some inhumanity I've just read about in the papers, I have to get them down? No doubt I could have produced a better work of art by suppressing them: but it's life that I'm after, not art: life turbulent and serene, life as prodigal of misery as of joy, and life, above all, unexpected.

(As a matter of fact, it's only in the narrower literary sense that the thing is formless: it has taken on, of its own volition, the pattern of a highly contrapuntal concerto. Recurrent subjects, development passages, major and minor episodes, cadenzas, anticipations and echoes—you will find them all in their places. *Tim I* is only the first movement.)

I read last night, in the *Times*, Mr Churchill's account of what happened on October 3rd when our bomb was set off in the Monte Bello islands—I've already alluded to the preliminary broadcast. The weapon, he said, was placed in H.M.S. Plym, a frigate of 1450 tons which was anchored off the islands. The ship was vaporised. A great steel ship, immeasurably tougher than the flesh and blood of human beings, was vaporised. When the flash burst through Plym the temperature was nearly a million degrees. "Normal blood temperature is 98·2-5 degrees —many of us go higher than that (Laughter) . . ." Instruments were set up to record the effect of contamination, blast, heat flash, gamma ray flash, "and other factors of interest". Gamma ray flash, you may know, rots the marrow of people who survive an atomic explosion, so that they gradually die in misery. "Thousands of tons of water and of mud and rock from the sea bottom were thrown many thousands of feet into the air and a high tidal wave was caused . . . Apart from some local rats which were killed (Laughter)" . . . and so on. "All those concerned in the production of the first British atomic bomb are to be warmly congratulated on the successful occurrence of an historic episode." Not a word, as I said at the time of the wireless announcement, about the horror and shame of being involved, however necessarily, as Mr Churchill no doubt thinks, in such detestable wickedness. There is also a leading article on the subject in the *Times*: "Dr Penney and his scientists have passed their Monte Bello test with full honours. Though the glory attaches itself to the Government of the day, a lion's share of the compliments has been earned by Mr Attlee and his colleagues who planned and nurtured British atomic energy research . . .

Britain has proved that she can make atomic bombs. It has been a costly demonstration. Now that two members of the North Atlantic Treaty Organisation possess this power, it will be helpful to examine in due course the advantages and disadvantages of integrating or rationalising the United States and British atomic programmes . . . It will be useful if parties and individuals try to clear their own minds about the general shape which British atomic development should now adopt, both before and during a partnership with the United States. How big a reserve of atomic bombs, for example, should the Minister of Defence require for his arsenal? If this is a strategic weapon better left to the immense productive capacity of our ally, is there a need for intensive effort in the field of tactical atomic missiles for the Army outside as well as inside N.A.T.O.'s boundaries? . . . The vast sums of money which will have to be spent in the next ten years should . . . be related to separate military, industrial and medical programmes. Most people will feel, on reflection, that this country will be wise to concentrate from now onwards on the second and third at the expense of the first. The Atlantic Alliance can make this possible if used for this proper purpose." Again, as with Mr Churchill, not a word of shame or horror or regret. The whole thing, with its "glory", is taken for granted. All that need concern us is money—the division of expense.

A critic in the Literary Supplement of that same *Times*, reviewing *Tim I*, rebuked me for too much emotion and too little thought. "If only," he said, "Mr Gollancz would write less like a prophet, and more like a philosopher calmly contemplating the stars!" I like calmly contemplating the stars: I do it almost every evening of my life. But there's something else to be about when the most respectable organs of public opinion can think of glory and expense, and these alone, as they contemplate the imminent vaporising of our enemies and perhaps of the world; and if a distinction is to be drawn, in a matter like this, between the heart and the head—and the distinction is a false one—then give me the heart. So I shall continue to prophesy.

And now at last we can get on to the jam, namely Repton.

PART II

CHAPTER IV

REPTON

How perfect a morning, how exactly the right sort of morning (Friday, October 31st, to give it its place in the procession of days), for embarking on a description of my Repton experience! The night was cold, flooded by a moon almost round, full of stars: and somewhere about four, in dressing-gown and great-coat, I went out and contemplated them—not to please the critic of the *Times Literary Supplement* or even myself, but because I could no more help doing so than I could help . . . stopping to listen on a walk, as suddenly I caught the sound of a song in some remote habitation, and wondered, is it this?, is it that?, humming it sketchily in unison, almost knowing it, but unable to give it a name. That country of my garden, so vast, was a single living thing: surrounded by its aspiring trees, it had come into its own while all men slept—save only myself, who had been allowed, for a moment, to share its blessedness. A breeze as of the sea was in my nostrils, and the soughing of it in my ears: yet a calm, a stillness of the kind that the Greeks called γαλήνη, held everything. My own heart aspired with the trees, in tranquillity and thankfulness.

And now after breakfast there is one of those suns, extra liquid and large in revenge for the moon, that you get only at this time of year, and only after a very cold night. Clouds of purple trail or mass over a sky of light blue; and there cannot be a single shade of brown—greeny-brown, yellowish-brown, golden-brown, and so on and so on with every enriching qualification you can think of—that isn't somewhere apparent between my garden and the hillocks beyond. It's a sight you could see nowhere but in England: and Repton, as I shall be telling you, was England regained for me.

Let me briefly recall the larger outlines of the whole lengthy enterprise to which, for close on two years now, I have found myself committed. Sitting at my fireside on that January morning, back in 1951, and writing almost at random—telling

you of Italy as I looked at Ruth's paintings, and of music as my
eye wandered on to Kapp's lithograph of Schnabel—I was
quickly led back to the second of my *anni mirabiles*; to my joy
nearly ten years earlier, in 1942. Thence I jumped backwards
again to the first of my *anni mirabiles*: to my joy at Repton. I
described, you will remember, how I had made two discoveries
there: that the boys were good, and that their goodness was
blocked in the civic and international spheres by their prejudice
and ignorance. To explain the effect of this discovery—
what I had done about it at Repton, and how it had determined my whole future life—I had to explain what sort of
person I was: so I went back to 1899, and then worked forward
to Oxford, where I broke off.

"I shall begin the next instalment," I wrote at the end of
Tim I, "with . . . the second Repton chapter, which, with
1933, 1938, and 1943, is central to the whole design. [I didn't,
but we have come to it now.] I shall describe in some detail
the experiment in political education which David Somervell
and I carried out there, and how in that dawn the place
blossomed like a rose, and David and I blossomed with it: and
how it became inevitable from this time that, as I could no
longer teach, I should become a publisher. Then, when I come
to 1919 . . ." So let me get down to it.

§ 1

I fell in love with the place immediately, as I had fallen in
love, three and a half years before, with Oxford. Many things
combined to make me do so.

Oxford had won me with a threefold allurement: she was
England, she was youngness, and she was friendship. And she
was these three, not as separate phenomena, but as a unity in
which the elements were all mixed up, in which each had its
own special nature because the others, really, had that nature
too. The essence was shared. Everything gave and received. You
could not have said at one moment "This Oxford is youngness",
and at another "This Oxford is England"; you would have
had to say, always: "Oxford, eternally, is youngness-friendship-
England."

And I had lost all this in the meantime—from the ending of

Oxford to the beginning of Repton. I know now that I was myself much to blame for my reaction to the majority of my fellow-officers and for their reaction to me: here was the clash with my father all over again, and if you haven't already learned, from my account of it, that to enter into the hearts and minds of those we may differ from is the beginning of wisdom, which is another name for charity, then nothing I can say now, by way of any further expression of remorse, will help you to learn it. I was eager and naïf: they were jaded and bored, or so it seemed to me. I thrilled to the heat of the sun and the freshness of dew: they thrilled, I thought, to nothing. I hated poverty, and the poverty, above all, that reeked everywhere around us in Northumberland: they struck me as hating the poor, or at least as being terrified of any betterment in working-class conditions that might jeopardise their own. I loved music: they liked musical comedy. My feminism involved an attitude of sexual reverence for women, and I loathed dirty stories (I like them now, if they're not scatological, though my reverence, if more earthy, is unimpaired): they were men of the world. In sum, I reacted to the majority of my fellow-officers very much as a few of my critics have reacted to me—with a mixture of hostility and contempt: and they in their turn very properly dubbed me a prig.

I mustn't blacken myself unnecessarily. I loved the better and hated the worse, which is the proper procedure: but being without charity for those who exhibited, in my view, the worse, my attitude to them was evil. I acted amiss, in the words of Dionysius, from a longing for the good. Or, to put it from a slightly different angle, moral eagerness, divorced from charity, seduced me into judgment of persons: while all the time, at the very heart of my eagerness, was a knowledge, even surer than in the old Elgin Avenue days, that any judgment of persons is opposed to morality. And the interesting and familiar paradox is this: that what I judged most in others, as a result of my eagerness, was the fact that these others judged others themselves. Whether I judged rightly or wrongly is irrelevant. While I absurdly oversimplified and generalised, I think that on the whole I judged rightly. Papageno and X would of course say the same about their judgment of me.

The good I longed for and didn't find in Northumberland can best be indicated by some verses I wrote, in the form of a sonnet, while still at Repton. I called it *Valete*, and was saying good-bye with it, not to my life there, but to the boys as they left for the army in occasional batches. I ought to hesitate, I suppose, about recording an emotion that many who read me will consider naïf; but as I feel just the same more than thirty years later I shall proceed:

> I have found great beauty in the heart of boys.
>   For friendship they have shown their souls to me
> Trembling at touch of those immortal joys
>   That speak to man of his divinity.
> One was a poet; in another's eyes
>   The trouble lurked from which clear wisdom springs—
> A poignant brooding over mysteries,
>   A high desire to learn the truth of things.
> And all were young. Dear God, who made the earth
>   For joy of April and awakening,
>   I, that have loved them, pray that you may mould
>   And make them great. Save them from growing old:
>   Give them a noble happiness, and bring
> Their splendid treasure to a perfect birth.

I had felt shut out, then, at Cambois, from youngness and friendship: for, so far as the friendship is concerned, I naturally failed to receive what I refused to give. And I hungered for it, desperately: day after day, as I thought of Ralph Rooper, and of my walks across the quad at hazy sunrise from his sitter to my own, the line he loved so, by Masefield, would return to me:—"O Time, bring back those midnights and those friends." That year in Northumberland is the only period of my life when I've felt a continuous loneliness: other, I mean, than the ultimate loneliness that is the lot of every creature as such, and will remain so until "the restoration of all things".

My sense of losing England, up at Cambois, was a little more complex. Largely, as I have explained, this England of mine— not the England I had taken for granted when a child and a boy, but the England that had become my mistress as I wandered round New College garden in the sunshine of 1914— was indistinguishable from youngness and friendship; and to lose these was to lose England too. But something in a sense more precise, something physical or so to say geographical, was also involved. Coming to me in the Garden by the old city wall

and on the banks of the Cher, my love had been a love of green
freshness, of cool waters, of willows in the breeze, of small
landscapes and everything gentle. There is beautiful country
in Northumberland too, I believe, but I didn't see it then, and
have never taken the opportunity of seeing it since; what I did
see was stoniness, and a huddle of grimy brickwork in black
mining villages, and a sort of desolation. And my heart was
sick with regret.

(To jump forward eighteen years from those days, it was
something more than accident, I think, that made me hit
upon Berkshire, and this part of Berkshire in particular, when
I decided, a day or two after Hitler had come to power, to buy
a house in the country. This must be the gentlest, or you might
almost say the most unsensational, part of all England. It lacks
the exuberance of Sussex and the grandeur of the Lakes and the
quiet loveliness of the Cotswolds and so on; it lacks anything
distinctive at all: it is just England. And it is very near Oxford.

I must tell you of something charming that happened this
summer. Madeleine and Edmond Fleg, who hadn't been to
England since the thirties, were in London for a week or so; and
Madeleine spent some hours here at Brimpton while Edmond
was at a conference. Back in Paris, she wrote us a letter with
the following postscript: "*Quel merveilleux souvenir, la maison
fleurie!*" Can you imagine how pleased I was?)

England was restored to me at that very first moment of my
arrival at Repton, when, after changing at Derby and getting
out at the little local station, I walked a mile to the Chapel,
turned left under the Arch, and wheeled sharp to the Priory
and Hall for an interview with Fisher, the Head. Here was
Oxford once more: not like Oxford to the smallest degree in
any single particular, but like Oxford in everything. I see it
now as a doll's-house of a place, gleaming, fresh, meticulously
fashioned, all just so; and Oxford too, you may remember, I
have likened to a miniature jewel. But it's not a question in this
case, as with Oxford, of a transformation wrought by memory:
for I saw it just like this as I walked past the Spire on that cold
shiny morning thirty-six years ago. The school bookshop, near
the Cross, seemed particularly childlike: and when nowadays,
once or twice a year perhaps, we get an order for some books on
its order-form, the whole village, and the larger landscape beyond, come flashing into view. But my memories of the Cross

have been spoiled. I was drinking one night with Jack Stratton
—a beefy housemaster, rich in the face, whom I'd grown very
fond of; as he had of me, which shows largeness, for he was very
much the traditional Englishman, and must have hated the
pedagogic escapades that I was turning the place upside down
with. We liked one another, I suppose, because both of us liked
jollity. One vac, I remember, he had fixed up to meet me in
town, so that we could give a joint dinner to two of his favourite
pupils. But kidney trouble detained him, and he sent me a fiver
instead.

Well, on the evening in question—it was the last day of term,
and school had already broken up—he was telling me, and one
or two others, about a book he kept locked in a drawer: English,
it appeared, but of Parisian origin. I was shocked, but curious;
the others were curious, but not shocked. He was about to produce it—fortunately he hadn't done so already—when Fisher
irrupted (though the word's a bit noisy for Fisher) piloting a
boy by the ear. He, Fisher, had been walking abroad, and had
discovered this urchin, a scrubby little Strattonite, putting a
jerry on the Cross. "Cane him," said Fisher. "All right, presently," replied Stratton. "Here and now," insisted Fisher.

Stratton, who felt it improper, I think, to perform in so public
a manner, began arguing that he had no jurisdiction: term was
over, he pointed out, so the boy, who was leaving, had officially
left. Could a host beat a temporary sojourner? Fisher laughed
him out of court, with that white throaty chuckle I had often
remarked in him: "Cane him," he repeated. So Jack tried another manœuvre: "I haven't got a cane," he said. "Then find
Alan Ayling," replied Fisher (Alan Ayling was head of the
House). "He'll give you one."

The game was up; and Stratton, with insolent slowness, fumbled about between the wall and a bookcase and produced in
the end what the boys called a bum-stick. "How many?" he
asked. "Nine," replied Fisher. So the boy was made to clutch at
his ankles, and I remember how his intake of breath became
sharper and sharper as each stroke found its mark. He shuffled
out when it was over, and so, if less literally, did Fisher. The rest
of us, forgetting the *curiosum*, discussed corporal punishment till
far into the night. I haven't the faintest idea whether the boy
was much hurt, physically or psychologically: but the scene
was a filthy and degrading one. The beating of schoolboys is

different from the lashing of criminals only in degree, and from capital punishment only in degree and in its lack of finality: and a Christian civilisation would have nothing to do with any one of them. The Philistine will jeer and be hearty about it: but ignore him: for atom bombs aren't a matter for jest, and there's contagion in retaliatory violence, whatever the degree of it. Abolish it in one of its aspects, and you're helping to abolish it in all.

I see at this very moment in the papers that three "natives" (i.e. inhabitants) of Africa have been sentenced by the British authorities to twenty-four strokes of the lash, as well as to two years' hard labour, for assaulting another "native" whom they suspected of giving information to the police about terrorist activities. A lashing with twenty-four strokes is an extreme form of torture: and they did it, "the authorities", in our name.

Why I found Repton so English on that earliest impression—physically English, I mean, with an Englishness of parkland and mead, of green lanes and little streets and mossy walls and mellow buildings—I cannot begin to explain; for the school and the village, which were all I then saw, were really, for the critical eye, nothing at all out of the common. Nor can I explain my immediate comparison—in essence, not in detail—with Oxford. Perhaps, within the context of a time and an eternity we can never understand, I was living at that second in what was so soon to follow: in a fellowship of young and thrusting minds, with the freshness of quiet country just beyond us. Anyhow I have been telling you, without a trace of romanticising in retrospect, exactly what I did feel; and the Englishness—I am still referring to mere geography—became more and more vivid to my consciousness day by day and term by term. As to the youngness and the friendship—those other elements lately lost and now recovered—they require no explanation, though I shall have a great deal to say of them presently. And you will readily understand, too, how everything came together—or not everything, for the intellectual and spiritual eagerness, which was itself almost everything, couldn't specifically be there—but how everything else came together in one place and at one season: in the Paddock, at cricket, on high summer afternoons.

There is nothing in all the world like public-school cricket, except Eights Week at Oxford, and nothing like the Paddock at Repton, where they played it.

The Paddock is a cricket-field (as you've gathered) at the back of the Priory: it merges into a buttercup meadow, and flows on, watered by streams, to the sky. Hitherward rises a slope; and on it I would lie through those long afternoons in the glare of the sun, with the click of the ball in my ears, and a company of friends by my side, and the smell of the grass in my nostrils, and the yellow and green out beyond. I was thinking in the garden this August of what I'd write about Repton, just before we went off to Edinburgh; and as the corn came alight with the sun I fell to wondering which was best—this, or the Paddock and water-meadow, or Oxford in 1914.

I became a devotee of cricket, which I had always enjoyed in an ignorant sort of way, though the last time I'd played it had been with girls at the Maida Vale High School. (I would always rush out, I remember, at the hard rubber ball, however wide it might pitch on the off, and make a swipe at it to leg.) Now I became quite learned. I mugged up one or two textbooks, and got tips from the bloods, whom strangely I was on very good terms with: not that all the chief experts were bloods, for R. L. Holdsworth, and a few other of my cleverish pupils, were in the eleven. Before an important house-match, and most of all before a match, on the home ground, against Uppingham or Marlborough or whatever other school it might be, I felt a devastating anxiety about the weather: the same that I had felt, but the other way round, all those many years before, when as a boy of nine or ten I had examined the sky for cats and dogs or the pavement for ice, in the hope that, if things were bad enough, synagogue would be washed out. But now if things were good enough—if the day dawned bright and clear, but not dangerously so—I had received, I felt, a special benediction.

Repton will always mean for me, above everything, the Paddock in summer. Much else was of greater importance: but in terms, not of struggle and of helping seedlings to grow and of making a better world and of the joy that these efforts brought with them, but of a carefree and innocent happiness, the Paddock is my Repton. I had two summers there, and each had its own special quality: the first was dawn and the second was day —a day breathlessly awaited by someone who knew, as he had not known before, what it was going to be like. The third, I am

A PUBLIC SCHOOL LOOKS AT THE WORLD.

BENN LEVY'S DRAWING

sure, would have surpassed both the others; and the thought that came into my head when I knew I could never return— though more serious ones rapidly followed—was "No summer, no Paddock, no cricket." The boys, knowing what I felt, gave me a water-colour drawing of the spot, by Maurice Clark, the art-master, who had been my neighbour. But I liked, even more, another present they gave me: all five issues of "The Pubber", which you'll hear about presently, and some manuscript essays for the sixth (that would never appear): plus a drawing by Benn Levy, the future dramatist: the whole bound, by Sangorski I think, into a volume of black morocco, with my nose, heavily gilt, on the back of it.

§ 2

I have said nothing so far, except by implication, of how the specifically public-school atmosphere of Repton impinged on me, or of how, as familiarity grew, I looked at such places in general. As familiarity grew—that is important: for I must write hereabouts in a jumble, telling you now of a quick first impression, and now of the theories, more considered and formal, that I was slowly evolving as the moments went by. And sometimes, I am sure, I shall fail to distinguish the one from the other.

You may be surprised, then, when I say that for all my passionate liberalism and hatred of class distinctions, and in spite, or more truly because, of the radical socialism that was already thrusting up in me, I felt no sort of desire to abolish the public schools, or even to dilute them, at that stage of their development—democratise them, as it was called, for such schemes were already in the offing—with a decoction of the unprivileged working class. I felt the opposite. The whole thing, you must understand, had come utterly fresh to me: in my own school, St Paul's, I had caught none of the public-school atmosphere —a day-school, *ipso facto*, can never have it. And whatever may have been the prejudices I brought with me to Repton—I suppose, though memory fails me, they were pretty strong—I was no sooner there than a delight in the place had got hold of me: a delight over and above the delights I have already described. For in this little grouping of boys (to say nothing

of the masters) that lived together and worked together and
played together, I found a young university.

In spite of all the evil mixed up with their good—and it was
their good quite as much as their evil that was to set me on my
revolutionary path—I saw the British public schools, increasingly during the progress of our adventure, as among the
few remaining strongholds of an older, a truly liberal, dis-
interestedness in that age of increasing commercialism; and
what I wanted was, not to abolish these strongholds, but to
save what was left of their liberalism from the decay that was
destroying it and even converting it into its opposite, and so to
release the original impulse for a fruitful expression in modern
conditions. As for "democratisation", this seemed to me bogus:
with the public-school ethos as it was, all you would do, if you
were to insert a thin layer of working-class boys into a community so different in its manner of living, would be to sharpen
the sense of class contrasts and intensify the friction. All such
schemes, I thought, were objectively machiavellian. The real
necessity was, not any sort of dilution, but such a new educational technique as would transform the public schools (while
doing a great deal more to them besides) into engines for
abolishing the class structure of society altogether, with its
division into rich and poor, cultured and uncultured, gentlemen and—whatever you might like to call them.

Now I am dangerously anticipating here, for I may be
suggesting that I set out, almost as soon as I arrived at the
place, to turn it into a hotbed of revolutionary socialism. This
is not so, as you will learn: our aim, David's and mine, was not
to turn it into a hotbed of anything—except of an informed
understanding, a humane tolerance, and a liberal attitude of
mind. As part and parcel of this liberalising process—as mere
part and parcel, you might say—the boys could be relied upon,
we felt, to play their part, later on, in transforming what had
struck them as bad about our present arrangements: and if the
structure of society, among other things, should turn out to
have struck them as bad when they had come to review it
with fresh and open minds, then they could be relied upon to
change that too: though a demonstration of what this structure
must mean, or of what their pedagogue, rather, might believe
it must mean, could be an element, and a vital one, in the
liberalising process itself. If, towards the end of our time, the

intention and the practice . . . But I must not anticipate still further.

The public schools, you must realise, were already in a state of transition at the time of our adventure: and my fear was that the direction they might take would be quite the worst possible. What, I asked myself, should be the aim of a genuine education-ist? Surely to elicit and reinforce that love of beauty and truth, and that selfless desire to do what is good for its own sake, which are latent, however varyingly, in most young minds, but get buried so deep under mountains of rubbish—not always, but as often as not—that they never see the light. (And this would still be a part of my answer, though not the whole of it.) The old classical curriculum, I felt, had at any rate stemmed from an understanding, however partial, of what education ought to mean: narrow though it often was, and quite unsuit-able for perhaps the majority of temperaments, it did aim, nevertheless, at imparting a love of great literature, and a knowledge, with no ulterior motive behind it, of two remark-able civilisations. Its intention had been liberal and humane; and if it had significantly failed, that was because the intention had become atrophied.

For what had the Renaissance scholars and schoolmasters really meant by their "Classics", and what had they sought to get out of it? The home of the movement was the city-state of fourteenth- and fifteenth-century Italy. These cities had achieved a virtual independence, and their very existence and their whole organisation were a standing protest against the theocratic and feudal ideas on which mediaevalism was based. In classical Greece they discovered a far-away world that had apparently been all they themselves would have wished to be. Men read and taught Greek so that they and their pupils might become, not just scholars, but "Grecians": Pericles, Plato and Phidias were studied, not merely as masters of an old world, but as models for a new. And so Renaissance "Classics" was fundamentally, in the broad sense, political.

But the new Greece was as transitory as the old. Philip of Hapsburg and his father played the part of extinguisher far more completely than Philip of Macedon and his son. For an imitation never has quite the vitality of its model. Meanwhile "Greece crossed the Alps", and entered larger and less intense societies to which the real life of ancient Athens was far more remote. The new learning ceased to be "political" and became antiquarian and, in the narrowest sense, literary. Politics moved into other channels—Calvinism, Jesuitism, Oceanic trade. But the schoolmaster had got hold of his text-books, and stuck to them. The classics of a nineteenth-century schoolroom stand in outline already before us: the minute examination of traditional texts, selected for style rather than for matter, the cult of composition, and a mess of historical superficialities, pitchforked into a perfunctory hour.

Still, the intention had been a noble one. But what was to be said of the curriculum by which classics, it appeared, might soon be superseded? For just about the time of my Repton adventure a considerable agitation was springing up in favour of a "practical" education, by which was meant, not education at all, but a rule-of-thumb training in the arts of "efficiency" and "success". Men who, one suspected, had never read a word of Goethe or listened to a note of Beethoven were hot in denunciation of German "materialism"; and meanwhile they were writing to the newspapers, and urging that "public-school education should in future be based on such subjects as would fit the schoolboy to function efficiently whether in science, commerce, or the forces of the Crown". The phrase is from a letter to the *Times*, signed by a number of bigwigs; and I remember very vividly indeed my sense of outrage as I read it. Murder—the murder of eager young spirits, the aborting of a million potentialities—this is what they proposed; and the anger that still occasionally sweeps over me (though not with the old wildness), despite all efforts to get rid of it, comes rising once more in my gullet as I contemplate this—the word fits exactly—this wickedness. It was not merely a question of the three occupations that were exclusively selected: soldiering— and you know what I thought about that: commerce—and you know what I thought about that: science—well, my feelings about that were ambivalent, and still are; it was not merely a question, either, of art, music, literature, philosophy, theology, history and a hundred other humanities being contemptuously ruled out as the stuff for a desirable career; it was a question, more broadly, of spitting on that reverence for personality, and of young personality in particular, which dare not straight- jacket what was meant to be free. "The wonderful efficiency of the Germans, both in science and languages," the letter

continued, "points to the fact that their schools and universities answer these two vital requirements better than we do."
By science they meant science in the service of commerce and
war, by languages they meant, not literature, but "modern
languages" in the mean little sense, languages studied banausic-
ally for their "practical" usefulness. *Kultur* was the devil at one
moment: at the next, we were told we must worship it.

If I wanted to preserve the public schools, this was precisely
because they had other things to think about than science,
commerce and the forces of the Crown; if I wanted to
change them, my desire was to make them more liberal, not
more commercial or militarist; and if I thought classics no
longer ideal, nevertheless "better a thousand times the study of
Homer," as I wrote at the time, "even if it involves hours of
tedious prosing about the digamma and vowel gradations, than
a steady pressure towards shorthand and book-keeping."

These sketchy remarks about the value of public schools, and
about classics, education for commerce, and the rest, may seem
to have at most an autobiographical interest, with little if any
bearing on the problems of today; for 1916 was not 1952 (to
say nothing of the year, whichever it may be, when you
will be old enough to read what I'm writing), and even then,
even in 1916, the public schools formed a numerically insigni-
ficant section of a vast educational system. But I am sure that
such a conclusion would be false. When the necessary adjustments have been made, and my own errors corrected, these
remarks are every bit as relevant to the contemporary situation
as to the days when I was teaching. I shall say more of this later:
take the foregoing, meanwhile, as a prelude to the topic—I
must get on with it now—of "political education" at Repton.

§ 3

This developed gradually, by way of Latin Prose and
Plato . . .

My interview with Fisher had gone smoothly—more
smoothly, perhaps, than it ought. We began by discussing my
salary, though discussing isn't the word, nor is salary: for the
current rate of pay for a schoolmaster was by no means sensational, except for a man at the top, and even the current one

wasn't for me. I thought the reason for my abasement rather
odd: I hadn't a degree, Fisher explained (you'll remember that,
owing to the war, I'd left Oxford prematurely), so I mustn't
expect the full figure. And yet—I should be teaching classics,
he presently told me, to the top form but one (and should be
doing so later, it turned out, to the candidates for University
Scholarships in the top form of all); and in *that* subject, anyhow,
I'd completed my course and got a first—indeed, a good first, a
specially good one. But I didn't demur to my two-pound-ten
a week, or whatever it was—"with nothing found". My ideas
were very small, and for a long time remained so (I remember
wondering, in the year of my marriage, whether perhaps by
the time I was forty I could aim at five hundred a year); and
the joy I was feeling already in the prospect ahead of me made
money irrelevant. I can sympathise, too, with Geoffrey Fisher,
if not wholeheartedly: as first and foremost a brilliant executive
(a far better one, for what this is worth, than the saintly Temple,
who had preceded him), he was doing a business man's job,
and doing it with remarkable efficiency, for the institution he
served.

That was really all. He gave me a little more detail about my
work—essays as well as Latin with the Lower Sixth, and both
with IV²b in addition: begged me to return as soon as possible,
as he was "doing three men's work in one" (I was to fix myself
up in London, before beginning the job properly): and after
shoving some Latin proses into my hand, with instructions to
correct them in the meantime, excused himself on the plea that
he must shave before interviewing a parent.

I returned after nightfall on the Sunday, and was driven to
my rooms. The landlady, Mrs Maddox, bade me welcome: a
parched little woman, always harassed, whose husband, I
believe, had died of drink. I see her, in retrospect, as a bit of
wire touched with vinegar. She must have been lonely (there
were no other lodgers), for she gossiped, that first night, a full
hour: and the picture that she painted of my colleagues was
not, on the whole, an attractive one. But some, she thought,
were better than others, notably Fisher himself.

"Have you seen the Headmaster?" she asked me. "Not a
bad man, though he *has* raised himself from nothing."

She was lacking, however, in any great enthusiasm for human
nature as such; and her tribute, even to Fisher, would still

have been tempered, I think, had she known to what a height he would come. I ought to add that she was invariably kind to me.

She broke off at last, went away, and returned with my supper. Now you know how pernickety I am about food, and how terrified that I may have to swallow even a morsel that repels me. I was as happy as could be, when at Oxford, with a banana and bar of chocolate for lunch (I could often afford nothing else) and could be as happy today; but when I'm faced with a dish that looks nasty, or is of dubious contents, I recoil in disgust or apprehension. And there was Mrs Maddox advancing, with a smile on her face and a tray in her hands: and she was advancing very slowly; and she was holding the tray well aloft, in a manner almost hieratical; and the smile didn't somehow seem intended for *me*.

When she'd got to the table and lowered the tray I saw that it carried two objects: a cinder that had once been a steak, and something nondescript, greasy and dark. The smile was still there as she placed the two dishes in front of me, and it suddenly looked sinister: I thought for a moment of poison, though why on earth she should contemplate murdering me—so soon, after all—I really couldn't imagine. But thenceforth, to the day of my departure, I was always a little afraid of her.

I managed the steak: but what was I to do with the pudding, if pudding it was? I couldn't leave it untouched on the plate, because I didn't want to make her *m'vahyish*:* "never make anyone *m'vahyish*, particularly a *goy*"† was one of my father's more attractive imperatives, and I had always done my best to obey it: without, however, making any distinction in the matter between *goyim* and Jews—not from a lack of reverence for *goyim* (some of my best friends are *goyim*) but because to do so, I thought, would smell a bit of racial bias in reverse, like philosemitism. But if I couldn't leave the thing on my plate, I couldn't eat it either. There might be suet in it, or even, God forbid, *chazar*.‡ I began getting into the sort of panic, with a touch of masochism in it, I'd sometimes experienced at exams—the sensation that while time slipped away, and would slip away with ever slippier slippiness till it slipped to the end, the moment would never arrive when I'd be able to "do" the first question. Then my eye fell on a broad shallow

* blush with shame † gentile ‡ pig

box, beneath a book-case (bamboo) that commanded the
door. Anxiously watching the latter I got hold of the box,
uncovered it, tipped the pudding in, covered it up again, and
returned it, big with pudding, to its place: in the hope of
doing away with it somehow when everything was quiet.
I was only just in time, for Mrs Maddox almost immediately
reappeared for another hour's chat . . .

I woke up early next morning, and went at once to the
window for a view of my surroundings. We were at the top of a
gentle slope; and "The Pastures", which stretched beyond,
was what I should have called in my boyhood a "countryfied"
cul-de-sac, with conventional red-brick villas on one side and
tennis-courts on the other. When I tell you what an effect the
scene had on me you must remember, little Timothy, that I was
younger than my years—as I still am, now and again, and as I
hope you will always be; for I was back in the wondering
infancy when nothing had seemed commonplace, but everything marvellous and rare. So it was paradise I was looking at.
The month was March, and the year already fresh with a
foretaste of spring: and everything—place, season and I—
seemed at one with the boys I was soon to be meeting and
knowing—that very morning, in an hour!

I dressed and went down, looking forward to breakfast and
pipe (breakfast has always been my favourite meal, and even
nowadays I invariably look forward to it); but as I opened the
sitting-room door I suddenly remembered. Bemused by gossip
with Mrs Maddox after supper I had forgotten to remove the
pudding. I looked with a gasp at the book-case: the box had
gone. Had the contents been found? Or would they moulder
in the box, wherever she'd put it, till the smell . . . ? And
then . . . ? I was never to know; but if sinister had been the
word for that smile on the evening before, it was now, at every
subsequent supper-time, to look definitely, albeit patiently,
murderous. Imagine the Mona Lisa much withered, and as
Bosch might have painted her, and you get the idea. And once
or twice she held the tray extra high, and then I'd see her as a
dwarf executioner, bringing the head to Salome—not that her
dishes gave me sexual satisfaction, quite the reverse. Poor Mrs
Miggs, as we used to call her! If she had really discovered the
pudding, the something extra in her smile may have been
nervousness, all mixed up with her pride as a cook.

I put on a gown, a B.A.'s, when I'd finished breakfast, and hurried off to the Arch; for Fisher had told me to meet him there, so that he could show me my classroom. I wasn't entitled to the gown, as you know; but had been ordered to wear it (by somebody or other, I suppose, on my previous visit), perhaps with the idea that a graduate's dignity might compensate for the absence of a graduate's cash. As to my hurry, I remembered what the little man had told me about three men's work in one, and wasn't anxious to keep him waiting; but I could have taken my time, for he turned up, according to my watch, a good eleven minutes late—with little tufts of cotton-wool at various points on his chin. It seemed early to be interviewing a parent.

I ought to apologise, I suppose, for "the little man". It slipped out; for that's how, in those distant and unregenerate days, I invariably thought of him, not knowing that he'd be an Archbishop. My reverence for the young was at that time unbounded, my reverence for the old non-existent: today my sympathies are far wider, but I still have some difficulty, and now and again have to pull myself up, about particular personalities among the old.

This morning, Fisher told me, I was to take the Lower Sixth in Latin Prose: that's why he'd palmed off on me, I now realised, that parcel of compositions at our earlier interview. But I hadn't the faintest intention of "giving them back", because (a) they were stale, and (b) I hadn't corrected them anyhow. So I announced that I'd give a lecture instead—on "The Comedy and Drama of Latin Prose". The boys clearly thought me *meshuggah*; but my father had thought it (and said it) so often that I took it for granted. I was tremendously excited. The place had already gone to my head; and now to that climate of enchantment was added a delight in exposition—in exposition for its own sake, in *showing* people things, in coming out with the truth as I saw it. I was born as a schoolmaster during the course of that happy tirade; and a schoolmaster I have remained ever since, though in a number of disguises.

The stir of expectation with which an *ita*, nicely set in its place, can anticipate an *ut*: the sense of quiet that pervades a man's being when he tucks away a *me* between a *haec* and a *causa*: the pompous glories of a well marshalled triplicate—this, and a great deal more, was the splendour I sang of (sometimes literally), with appropriate manual illustrations. (I don't suppose you'll understand any of this. The point is: Latin Prose—Ciceronian—is highly rhetorical, with all manner of sly tricks to improve the rhythmic flow, point the drama, and so on. Parts of this letter are written Ciceronianly.) The place was soon in an uproar, and the man underneath, I learned afterwards, complained to Fisher about it. "Tucking away" was particularly popular: the boys would signal to one another by knocking on their desks, and then play-act the gesture of picking up a pebble with finger and thumb and gingerly depositing it elsewhere. We ended with a triplicate from Cicero, roared in chorus.

An odd way of teaching, you may think. But remember this: that to educate—the very word is derived from a Latin compound for drawing *out* or leading *forth*—is to stimulate the process of self-education. Anything an outsider can do is the merest of preliminaries. You have to give another's spirit or mind a little material to work on: he alone can do the rest: but he'll never begin working at all unless the material you give him, and the process of working on it, seem worthy of the trouble involved. To interest, to inspire—this, in education, is the crucial beginning. Later, you can give him guidance—but always with caution—out of the stores of your experience: you can supply new material, or show him (which is better) where to find it himself: but this is your limit.

It was as a high adventure that I presented the job of living to the schoolboys at Repton. It might be the comedy of it that was high, as with the niceties of Cicero, and then the classroom was noisy with laughter; or the accent might be spiritual, as with Plato, and then the place became a shrine; or, when politics were afoot—but I'll come to that later. And yet the words "I presented" are wrong. I wasn't *doing* something to the boys, *giving* them something of set purpose; taking no thought, I was growing and learning in their company—I was living and sharing, and soon they were sharing with me. Indeed, if I must talk about giving, then I'm sure, as I look back, that my debt to the boys was far greater than theirs was to me—and this was considerable.

Are you still in two minds about such methods, particularly when applied to Latin Prose? If so, let me tell you something. The proof of a pudding is in the eating, tasteless though the

simile may seem to you in view of the Maddox affair. Well, the
Auk, my predecessor with the Sixth, had more knowledge of
classics in one little lobe of his brain than I in my whole cere-
bellum; and yet my record of University scholarships was better
than his—better, if I remember rightly, by a hundred per cent.
But it may have been a question of double one or two, for the
standard at Repton wasn't Pauline.

At the end of that first "hour" with the Sixth (any session,
whatever its length, was an "hour") I was bordering on the
state called by Nietzsche Dionysian. I have by me a sonnet
written some time in 1916, after a session of the little play-
reading society I shall tell you about presently: and there, expressed in language of course immeasurably less radiant than
his, you find a hint of Nietzsche's thought and emotion:

"I was drunk all night with longing. Joy had broken
    The bonds that keep men lonely, and each drew
Close to the other. The great words were spoken.
    Then in that theatre our spirits grew
Until the walls had vanished, and the rain
    Fell, and the sky broke over us; and we
Were standing in a vast and windy plain,
    Battling the storm, a giant company.
And all the day that followed, in a swoon
    Of urgent happiness my spirit strode
        Up, to the height we know of. And the day went,
        And the night came in glory. Well content,
    I walked towards morning down the Hartshorne road,
Lulled by the beauty of the April moon."

I have the whim, while I'm about it, to reproduce another of
the verses I was pouring out at this time. You will remember
from *Timothy* what I described there as the joy in communion,
or the communion in joy, that I had experienced since early
childhood. At Repton, new elements enhanced it. Till then, for
all my friendships, human beings hadn't been much in the picture, or not to my awareness: the communion, the sense of
merging, had been with the smell of the grass and the heat of
the sun and the feel of the rain: with all natural phenomena,
and with the spirit behind them and in them. My friendships
had been a matter of contact, often of the closest contact, but

F

not of merging and being lost. And now it was in and through the boys, above all, that I met the unity.

This was the first new element in my joy. The second argued an interchange with the life of the universe even more mutual than in boyhood. Then, there had indeed been mutuality; but, if giving had been in question, I should have said that it was nature that gave and I that received. But now I gave too: not consciously, but by way of accepted experience—of an experience that had insensibly become part of me. And it was not only I that gave—everyone gave: or everyone who loved the sum of things.

Here is the sonnet I want to reproduce. I have had to reconstruct it from memory, for it was thrown away, years ago, with masses of other impedimenta. The key words are "strengthened by our love":

"Not many weeks have passed, since on Crewe's Pond
    I skated, happy to be one of you;
[?The rime] was all about us, and beyond
    Tall delicate poplars, pale against the blue.
And now already birds are at their singing,
    Already the first shy spirit is in the air
That, strengthened by our love, will soon be bringing
    Colour and form and fragrance everywhere:
Until at last, in the midsummer weather,
    On the paddock slope, scarce breathing, we shall lie,
And gaze across the meadowland together,
    Where buttercups flow onward to the sky;
And our hearts will go in search, we know not whither,
    Of the hidden loveliness that cannot die."

Having tasted the delight of that preliminary meeting with the Sixth I was eager for more: but found to my dismay, when I consulted my diary as the session broke up, that I wasn't "in" again till after lunch. But there was still Chapel, which always followed first lesson, except on Sundays. So I went there with the boys I'd just been ragging with, and slipped quietly into a pew at the back.

How shall I explain what it meant to me, this ugly yellow building that spoils the charm of Hall Orchard? It became the centre of my life from that moment, more so even than the Paddock, for its meaning didn't depend on the weather. It was the first school chapel I had ever known, and almost the first one of any kind, for I had rarely been to service at New College. The hymns, sung with exaggerated brio by fresh young voices in unison, moved me deeply. Pernickety as I was about music in general, the quality of these hymn tunes was irrelevant: indeed I couldn't distinguish between good and bad, and still can't. I loved, most of all, "Matins in Australia" at Evensong. "The su-un that bi-ids us re-est is wáking/our bréthren ne-eath the Wéstern sky"—this was the origin of the nickname. And even nowadays, when I want to sing a sort of prayer in the garden at Brimpton or by the window at Ladbroke Grove, the words are always the words of *Hallel* in Hebrew—"Oh give thanks unto the Lord, for he is good, for his mercy endureth for ever"—but the melody is always the melody of Matins in Australia. I suppose I like, at such moments, to recall Repton.

I hadn't prayed often up till then, in the sense of presenting a petition: but I did pray in Chapel that morning: and what I prayed for was that I might become like the boys, and might be worthy of them. And I am ashamed neither of the prayer nor of recalling it. I know, of course, that I over-generalised—exaggerated, in the case of some of them, their purity of heart. But youth, when all is said, is holy ground: the spiritual body of young people has not yet, for the most part, put on corruption, or not so much of it but that sympathy and understanding can effect a cure: and ("mock on, mock on, Voltaire, Rousseau!") this will continue to be my creed. Cosh boys? They are half my point. Even the best of material—it's one of the burdens of this letter—can be ruined by an evil environment. But not often, if ever, irretrievably.

I was already wondering, before Chapel was over, whether I could hope, as time went on, to turn my room at the Pastures into a sort of Oxford study, where the older boys and I might sit and argue over tea. After all, there was little between us in point of age. The thing seemed feasible: it might happen, I thought, in a term or so. It was to happen much sooner.

November 18th

Cosh boys! Yesterday afternoon, as I was having a cup of tea, they brought me my Evening Standard; and there, splashed across the front page in enormous letters, was the headline 'I WAS OUT TO KILL. BROTHER GOT 12 YEARS—I HAD SO MUCH HATE INSIDE ME. I SHOT POLICEMAN WITH MY 45.' In a couple of columns underneath, and eight further on, the terrible story was described— terrible and pitiful and mad. Craig, a boy of sixteen, was on his preliminary trial at Croydon for murdering a policeman. He had been seen on the roof of a warehouse with another lad called Bentley, and, when police officers arrived and collared Bentley, Craig went berserk. Crying "Come on, coppers," he shot an officer dead and wounded a second: then, his gun empty, he shouted "Give my love to —" (a girl's name) and dived head foremost on to the pavement twenty-two feet below. Now he lay on a stretcher in court, with his eyes closed, silent: his spine had been fractured.

The police told what had occurred at the hospital. These are some of the things Craig had said: "I wish I was ——— dead. I hope I killed the ——— lot." (The dashes aren't mine, they're the news- paper's: so ready, as they all are, to spill out oceans of violence, so proper about sex, and the good earthy word that describes it.) "You are coppers. The other one is dead with a hole in his head. I am all right. All you ——— should be dead." And then the phrase from the headline: "If I hadn't cut a bit off the barrel of my gun I would probably have killed a lot more policemen. That night I was out to kill because I had so much hate inside me for what they had done to my brother. I shot the policeman in the head with my ·45. If it had been a ·22 he might not have died." When they searched him at the hospital they had found a sheath knife in his belt.

*   *   *

I can't get the boy out of my head—not that I want to. I broke off writing to go and hear Beethoven played by the Vienna Philharmonic at the Albert Hall. Contrasts—these are what appal me so: they are like wounds with which life gapes wide open. So many contrasts! The Pastoral Symphony, paradise—a paradise of innocence and simplicity recreated in sound by a man of thirty-seven: and Craig, who might have been like you, Timothy, if circumstances had been different, spoiled at sixteen. And another contrast: I sitting there, listening to the ripple and flow of it; and he lying in bed somewhere else, thinking God knows what. If only one could annihilate distance, if only one could be with him, really be with him, spiritually as well as physically! And a third contrast: the comfort of that pillow for his head as he lay in court on a stretcher, and the drugs they had been giving him to ease his pain, and all the care, all the loving care one must say, they had been devoting for days, and would devote for many more, to bring about his recovery: this on the one hand, and on the other the dire panoply and cold accent of justice, and what the boy, those long hours, must have been feeling, and what he had done, and what was in store for him. And the cry of love to his girl in the midst of murder and attempted suicide. Gaping wounds—and only one way to heal them: only one way to reunite, to make life whole.

I called the story pitiful, and I was referring of course to Craig. Those unhappy people who think and feel by rote will ask me, what about Miles, the policeman Craig shot? Haven't I pity for him? Yes, I have great pity for him. But can't a man have enough pity in him to pity both?

There's more in the papers this morning to fill one with horror and shame. The flagellomaniacs must be feeling proud, though I'm sure there's still enough decency about to nullify, in the long run, their propaganda. "Town demands the cat": "They say flog": "Bring back the lash"—these are some of the headlines I've read on my way to the office. At a Wimbledon meeting dissentients were howled down; and a single word, in enormous letters, caught my eye on the poster of a weekly with millions of readers—"FLOGGING". Why can't they be honest about it, and say "Bring back torture"? Because they dare not: because they must pay lip-service to Christianity. But I repeat and repeat again that the cat o' nine tails is torture, and I challenge anyone to deny it. In terms of the pain involved—the subject is so disgusting that one can hardly go on with it—there is little difference, for the time being, between lashing a man and flaying him: the two processes, indeed, are not dissimilar. And pain apart, what is the object, or if you like the result, of a lashing? Degradation: and to degrade still more thoroughly a man already steeped in degradation is the meanest, wickedest, stupidest thing I ever heard of. If you're going to make anything out of him, for the good of his own soul and of the society he menaces (and will continue to menace if he emerges from prison unchanged, not to say worsened), your object above all must be to give him, or give him back, self-respect.

A paragraph has just appeared in the papers about the flogging of a prisoner at Dartmoor. He was given twelve strokes of the cat, and "the doctor and Governor were present. The man was medically examined after each stroke." You understand *why? His heart may give out, you may kill him: and while torture is O.K., murder isn't. So you flay and examine, you flay and examine, you flay and examine . . . up to ten, up to eleven, up to twelve. God in heaven, can we ever feel clean again?*

And there's something else in the papers. A month or so after the explosion of our own atom bomb, the Americans, it is announced, have exploded a hydrogen one, in the Pacific. Ours vaporised a ship: theirs has vaporised an island. A single hydrogen bomb, dropped on London, would annihilate the capital, and spread destruction as far as Oxford and Cambridge, Brighton and Chatham.

All these things, Timothy—the hydrogen bomb, Craig ("I had so much hate in me for what they did to my brother"), and "bring back the lash"—are connected. You might think, to read of them, that Christ had never lived, never died on the Cross. Can't you almost physically see the process happening, see it with your eyes— these people, mixtures as we all are but like kittens still blind, bringing more darkness into the world, adding a darkness from within them to the darkness already there, till all is dark: instead of letting the light from within them so shine in the darkness that the darkness, I was going to say is routed by the dawn, but no, becomes dawn? For darkness and light, as I've tried to show so often in this letter, are, at any rate over a wide area, in some sense interchangeable: at the very heart of that darkness, as the meaning of that darkness, in the guise of that darkness, is light potential. And in spiritual matters homoeopathy doesn't work.

You will hardly believe me when I tell you that the Wimbledon meeting was called by a vicar. What we want here in England is a Kierkegaard. I spent last night, nearly the whole of it, reading "Attack on 'Christendom'" from cover to cover. I append a salutary brief selection:

"For what is either/or, if I am to say it, who surely must know? Either/or is the word before which the folding doors fly open and the ideals appear—O blissful sight! Either/or is the token which ensures entrance into the unconditional—God be praised! Yea, either/or is the key to heaven! On the other hand, what is, was, and continues to be man's misfortune? It is this 'to a certain degree,' the invention of Satan or of paltriness or of cowardly shrewdness, which being applied to Christianity (by a preposterous miracle, or with miraculous preposterousness) transforms it into twaddle! No: Either/or! And as it is on the stage, that however tenderly the

actor and actress embrace one another and caress one another, this remains nevertheless only a theatrical union, a theatre-marriage; so also in relation to the unconditional all this thing of 'to a certain degree' is theatrical, it grasps an illusion; only either/or is the embrace which grasps the unconditional . . .

"*The Biblical interpretation of mediocrity goes on interpreting and interpreting Christ's words until it gets out of them its own trivial meaning—and then, after having removed all difficulties, it is tranquillised, and appeals confidently to Christ's words!*

"*It quite escapes the attention of mediocrity that hereby it generates a new difficulty, surely the most comical difficulty it is possible to imagine, that God should let himself be b o r n, that the Truth should have come into the world . . . in order to make trivial remarks. And likewise the new difficulty as to how one is to explain that Christ could be crucified. For it is not usual in this world of triviality to apply the penalty of death for making trivial remarks, so that the crucifixion of Christ becomes both inexplicable and comical, since it is comical to be crucified because one has made trivial remarks . . .*

"*The Christianity of the New Testament simply does not exist. Here there is nothing to reform; what has to be done is to throw light upon a criminal offence against Christianity, prolonged through centuries, perpetrated by millions (more or less guiltily), whereby they have . . . succeeded in making Christianity exactly the opposite of what it is in the New Testament . . .*

"*We have, if you will, a complete crew of bishops, deans and priests; learned men, eminently learned, talented, gifted, humanly well-meaning; they all declaim—doing it well, very well, eminently well, or tolerably well, or badly—but not one of them is in the character of the Christianity of the New Testament. But if such is the case, the existence of this Christian crew is so very far from being, Christianly considered, advantageous to Christianity that it is far rather a peril, because it is so infinitely likely to give rise to a false impression and the false inference that when we have such a complete crew we must of course have Christianity, too . . .*

"*In the magnificent cathedral the Honourable and Right Reverend Geheime-General-Ober-Hof-Prädikant, the elect favourite of the fashionable world, appears before an elect company and preaches w i t h e m o t i o n upon the text he himself elected: 'God hath elected the base things of the world, and the things that are despised'—and nobody laughs.*"

§ 4

A couple of nights after my first chapel I made a friend on
the staff: and he was to turn out the best I was to have there.
I had just hidden some food behind the books in the bamboo
book-case—this, I hoped, would prove safer than the box—
when a man turned up from three doors off, and asked me to
come round and meet his wife. This was Allan Gorringe. He
plays a minor part in my story: if he had played a major one—
if David and I had been wise enough to ensure that he did so—
the story might have been different.

Allan was the gentlest man I have ever known, with looks to
match: his eyes were stage-blue. He lacked passion and drive,
and could never have *done* anything: indeed a critic, if he had
had one, might have called him a bit feeble. But he hadn't, for
everybody loved him. He taught schoolmasters' English (or
perhaps geography or elementary French or something) to
nondescripts: but the thing he was actually there for was to
coach the eleven, for though of wretched physique and often
ill—he died of pneumonia a month or so after I'd left—his
cricket was superb. He voted Liberal. Middle-of-the-road,
rather womanish—this was Allan.

His lady was neither. How she delighted me that first evening, and the long tale of evenings to come—the sparkling,
staccato, incisive, overflowing and extravagant Moë! And
what a name—even Una and Joy, those other names of beauty
I had loved as a child (and, by transference, the girls who bore
them), seemed no better, as rivals to it, than Jemima or Flo.
And how she talked! I talk adequately myself, but she talked
more. Yet what I liked most of all about Moë was neither the
coloratura of her talk nor the melisma of her name, but her
gift for home-making. She had the power—Sheila Hodges has
it too—of making a room delightful at little expense: a print
here, a plate there, a bit of low lighting somewhere else, and the
thing is done. The Gorringes' villa, for all the time I was at
Repton, was home to me.

The first few moments of our intercourse, however, were a
bit awkward. They asked me what I thought about the war.
I imagined they meant, how did I think it was "going". Now
you know what a fool I am about war: I simply don't understand it. But I wanted to play up: so I took a shot at it with

"Oh I don't know: I suppose we're holding them", praying that if this was nonsense it might sound like a joke: and added, with that pensive inflection people adopt on such occasions, something about "two years more". Whereupon "I," said Moë Gorringe, in an accent that combined extreme determination with a sort of contemptuous offhandedness, "am a pacifist." And a socialist too, it turned out: not a middle-of-the-road one, either. Also a feminist, militant. Yes, I had come home.

We were just getting into our stride when Euphemia Heppel turned up. This was the widow of a master who had recently been killed in the war: as radical as Moë, it appeared, and devoted to Allan, she had decided to stay on and keep in touch with things. She quickly got us off politics and on to scandal. (Take village scandal, literary-clique scandal, smoking-room-in-the-House scandal: combine them: result, minor-public-school scandal.) This meant little to me, for I had still to meet my colleagues. But I was interested in her estimate of Fisher: "Bone lazy," she remarked, "never does a stroke of work, while poor Allan has to kill himself." The truth, I found out later, lay a third of the way, in Fisher's favour, between Heppie's opinion of Fisher and Fisher's opinion of himself—his three men's work in one. He did one man's work in one.

I learned, for the rest, that the staff was a morass of high Toryism, as indeed I had expected: that the wives were even worse than the husbands: and that you couldn't have a decent conversation with a single woman in the place, except of course Moë. I left with instructions to make things hum, to put a bit of pep into things, and to turn things upside down.

The Heppel had whetted my curiosity about my colleagues, so next morning, immediately after first lesson, I looked in on the diminutive common-room before going to chapel. It was empty when I got there, but next minute a very neat little man, all cleanliness and starch and with no angles to him, came hobbling in. His face, I conjectured, had been drawn with some care in the first instance, but had got rubbed out a bit. He made a shuffling little run for the table, seized a copy of the *Times*, and held it close to his nose: and immediately piped out, not to me but to another individual who'd come in on his heels, "Nothing about the advance." His voice might have been Caffarelli's—not however for the same reason. Then with a fury that gainsaid the amiable blandness of his face, "Thank heaven," he shrilled *fortissimo*—I thought of those divas who sing sharp, carried away by their passion, on a note that's too high for them, and then suddenly break—"we're giving the devils no quarter now." Arrival number two—a fine bulldog of a man with a drum-and-drumstick arrangement in his larynx—took him up immediately. "It's our solemn duty, mah dear chap," he replied, whacking away at every word with his drumstick, "to instil into the boys such a hatred of the Hun that for the rest of their lives they'll never speak to one again." Meanwhile a third man had arrived, had gone straight to the fire, and had begun hopping about there. He wasn't scrubbed, like number one: he wore clothes (with a subfusk waistcoat, once scarlet) as ill-kept as my own: a mouse might have emerged any moment from his iron-grey hair: and he kept muttering in that high nasal accent that is so very close to Oxford, "Very vrarm today, very vrarm today." The point was, it was specially cold.

(You may wonder how I can remember all these details, and may even suspect me of inventing them. No. I kept a diary during my first two or three terms at Repton, but then unfortunately dropped it; and it has survived. This is almost the only document I have for the whole of this letter; for though I've been a great collector, as you know, I've never hoarded anything much by way of written or printed personalia. I am very ungollanczish in this respect. My late Uncle Hermann, the knighted Rabbi, published a whole thick quarto volume of some two hundred and fifty pages—the cloth elaborately gilt (with *Labor Omnia Vincit* under a coat of arms), and the paper of a quality now obsolete—bearing, for main title, this very word Personalia: the sub-title explaining it as "the story of a professional man's career told in certificates, testimonials, congratulatory messages letters and telegrams, reports and presentations, etcetera." This is a book we love reading aloud in our family circle. Sir Hermann's tenacity over a period of more than six full decades, his power of arrangement, and his attention to detail, are positively formicid. The first entry dates from 1862: " 'The Children's Picture Book' is presented to HERMANN GOLLANCZ, of the 7th Class, being the Third Prize for general proficiency." The last exhibit—a trifle out of chronological order, for good artistic reasons—is of "the Armorial Bearings according to Warrant granted on July 7, 1925, to Sir Hermann

Gollancz and his descendents." In between comes a series of
congratulatory messages on the occasion of the author's knight-
hood, some of them quite brief, such as "Bravo!!! Well done,
Sir Hermann." Mindful, in this case as always, of academic
dignity, my uncle published the book—for private circulation,
naturally—through the Oxford University Press.)

I took the opportunity, on my way to Chapel, of finding out
from Allan Gorringe who these men were. The spick-and-span
one was Shearme, a housemaster of some importance who took
the Classical Middle Fifth. The nasal one was Topham: he ran
the Army Class. They called him Tip, schoolboy for top, and
alternatively Bim, schoolboy for bottom—the latter, I understood, because there had previously been a master called
Bottom, who had left; so that Tip had to function for both.
The boys assured me, when I pressed them, that his name had
truly and honestly been Bottom: not Winterbotham or Rams-
botham or Shufflebotham or anything qualified like that, but
plain Bottom.

The third man, the bulldog, was Pruke.

By the time I had got hold of this information we had arrived
at Chapel porch, where the staff had a habit of congregating
while their pupils filed by: this was a sort of parade, and each
boy, as he noticed a master, would raise a brief and lackadaisical
finger a couple of inches towards the brim of his straw. A lot of
my colleagues were gathered there, but two stood out—or rather
one stood, the other leaned. The first was Harry ("Jugs")
Vassall, who had once captained England at Rugger, and was
now a housemaster and the school bursar. He looked like a hip-
popotamus erect, in magnificent shape; his shout was gargantuan, Polyphemous, like a tornado; even louder than his shout
was his laugh; and he laughed incessantly, and at everything.
He laughed when an urchin with a pram, whom he'd stopped
in the village to ask him his name, replied Smith: "that's|not|
much|of a name," he bellowed, with a great whacking laugh
for each word. He laughed when he broke it to a colleague that
a favourite boy had been killed. He is the only human being
I have ever come across with absolutely no sense of humour.

The man that he was now cannonading was also a hippo-
potamus, but differently hippopotoman: with not so much
height to him, and greater breadth: and in less remarkable condition. His name was Pat Exham. He had the habit of falling

asleep in the middle of a sentence. He was asleep now, leaning against a fence.

Very vivid in my mind is this first meeting with my colleagues, but vivider far is the first Sunday I had some boys up to tea. A sort of partisanship, for boys against masters, was already beginning to get hold of me from the moment of that exchange between Pruke and Jacky Shearme: and it mingled with, and in a way coloured, a happy love for the boys (not specific, for this boy or that, but generalised, for the whole body of boyhood and of this boyhood in particular) that was bringing a fresh beauty and warmth into every moment of my living. On the one hand I saw generous youth, with its life stretching far into the distance, to be made a lovely thing of: on the other, something dried up, effete, now already bidding fair to corrupt it. To be blunt: I was disloyal to my colleagues, or rather to some of them, in word and in thought. More and more, as time went on—but a day was to come when I'd pull up—I took part with my pupils in criticising and making fun of them: for I saw them as living examples of what ought, in my opinion, to be avoided. They specialised in hatred of "the enemy": they were out of sympathy with the working class: their minds were closed: they felt by rote: and they had lost the early freshness and enthusiasm, the joy in living and sense of adventure, that we ought ever to keep undimmed. All this, I still think, was true of some of them, though not (and I never thought it) of all, nor of as many as I supposed. But I made two grave errors: carried away by my passion for springtime, and what may come of it if it remains unimpaired, I took to criticising with the boys, not only, as was right, what these men stood for, but the men themselves: I judged them as persons: and I judged uncharitably. It was the old Elgin Avenue story, the old Northumberland story, all over again: I was committing the very fault I blamed others for, and, to that extent, was invalidating what I preached with such vigour. If I had been wiser, if, I dare to say—Back to Methuselah!—I had been my present age, I could have done all I had to do honestly, I could have taken what they said as examples, and still have avoided my error: I could have made an effort on my own side (however little I might have succeeded, and this would have been irrelevant, in producing one on theirs) to prevent the battle of ideas from becoming a battle of persons. But I failed to do so.

I am sorry about it, but less sorry than about some other mistakes in my life: or rather I forgive myself for it more easily. Disloyalty is the wretchedest of sins, whatever its motive or origin: but there is disloyalty and disloyalty: there is a disloyalty that springs from personal considerations, and there is a disloyalty, the better sort of disloyalty if one may venture to call it such, that is like the reverse of a medal, the obverse of which is a loyalty. Mine, I hope, was the better sort. My disloyalty to some of my colleagues was occasioned, in the weakness of human nature and the hot-headedness of youth, by the passion of my loyalty to the boys: to what they were, to what they might become.

There is another question I cannot avoid, that of homosexuality. Was there a tinge of it in my love of the boys? Nothing could have been further at the time from my consciousness; but I must say, on reflection, that I think there probably was. This time, however, I am not sorry about it at all. Who knows where body ends and spirit begins? Who knows what physical basis there may be for every spiritual experience? I loved the boys, that's all I reck of: and my love of them, and of the love I saw in them and through them, must surely be called spiritual. If my body played its part, what of that? Didn't God make the body? And if naturally, spontaneously, unconsciously the body played its part, then nothing unnatural can have been involved. I am even inclined to ask myself whether a happily married man, sexually satisfied, can ever be a really great schoolmaster. I am not at all sure that the sexual urge, transmuted into a desire for giving life, spiritual life, life as such, more abundantly to others, may not in truth be the final incentive that prompts to great teaching—or great teaching, anyhow, of the young, not for the Schools, but, by communication, for integral living.

However this may be, it was something far more than mere pleasure I would feel as I walked to my classroom. I didn't mind very much what I was going to teach, whether the rudiments of Latin grammar with the Middle Fourth or Livy and English with the Lower Sixth: no—it was the idea of being there in the same room with them, of winning contact with their spiritual and bodily presence, that made me so happy and o'erbrimmed me with such joy. When I wasn't actually "in" I should have been miserable, but for the thought of what was coming; and often in a blank period I would go down to the Arch and nod

casually to a group of boys changing classrooms, or wander
about in the Paddock so as to feel myself surrounded by the
atmosphere I loved. And yet it seems a long time, as I look
back, before I selected anyone in particular from the crowd
with the idea of getting to know him more intimately. As a
matter of fact it was only three weeks.

This boy, Leslie Jaques, was the son of a Leicestershire clergyman: but with his finely chiselled features, high complexion and
black curly hair he looked as Greek as your grandmother (see
Timothy, page 118) in the days of her young womanhood—
though not so beautiful: or like an unimportant bust by a minor
Praxiteles, coloured in ebony and red. He was round about
seventeen, I imagine, when I got to know him: the mean age of
my friends, at any given moment, must have been that or a bit
less, for they did their first military training in the Repton
O.T.C. and left with commissions at eighteen or so. Leslie's
looks, as you will have gathered, pleased me greatly: but what
made me want to know him, far more, was a certain loneliness
that seemed to encompass him, and to express itself particularly
in his smile, for all his popularity with boys and masters alike:
that loneliness you often feel in young people (who have their
immortal longings) and that makes you gentle in their presence.
So I asked him up to tea, and told him to bring along George
Hirst, who went about with him a lot, and was, I gathered, a
fine cricketer: I thought, indeed, at first that George Hirst was
not his name but his nickname.

I have an impression of strangeness, almost of mystery, as I
think of that first tea-party. I was a bit shy, and they, of course,
didn't quite know what to make of me. There was none of the
taking-it-for-granted, the free and easy atmosphere, the boisterous horseplay that was to characterise these parties later on:
and yet I ask myself, mayn't there have been something even
better—a feeling of reverence in face of what was coming but
still unknown? We sat in deep armchairs round the fire, with
plates of food—far too many of them—at our feet: and talked
of nothing in particular. I remember an argument about
whether New College or Magdalen had gone head of the river
in the year so and so: I was very dogmatic about it (and, as I
found out afterwards, wrong), because I didn't like to show myself ignorant of anything to do with Oxford. For the rest, they
made fun of the staff, and told me all the hallowed stories; and

I gave them, in return, quite a passable imitation of Pruke. I had taken a first step down that particular *descensus Averni*.

So the term passed happily away, with my tea-parties growing bigger and my visits to the common-room rarer. It was only as we were about to break up that I met, at last, David Somervell, with whom my life was so soon to be linked. He looked a bit odd, and will forgive me for saying it: since there is nobody in the world, as he knows, that I either like more or respect more. (And I, anyhow, must have looked even odder.) He is so tall that when he dossed down in London with us, many years after our marriage, we had to lengthen his bed with a chair; and my first quick impression, on that earlier occasion, was of grey flannel bags clinging tightly to precarious clothes-pegs, and of immensely thick glasses, rimmed with metal, gleaming high above a crumpled soft collar. I was a bit frightened when he accosted me, for Pruke, whom I'd passed the time of day with, had specifically warned me against him. Still, I nerved myself to listen. "Ah—er—Gollancz," he began, his left hand high aloft and all aflutter, as if patting an invisible giant on the head, "I hear that—you're not too comfortable with Mrs Maddox. Parez, you know, who lives with me, is leaving in a term or two; so I thought, as you might say, that—you might like to come and take his place." Then suddenly jumping to C *in alt* or thereabouts, "I imagine," he proceeded, "that we should—ah—get on extraordinarily well together, as you might say." At "extraordinarily well" he did a downward glissando, still flapping away with his hand: and the impression his whole performance produced in me was one of benignity superimposed on condescension. Even so, I hesitated a moment, for somehow I already rather liked him; but, mindful of Pruke's warning ("Avoid that fellow Somervell like poison"), I feebly excused myself. I was soon to regret it; but he didn't seem in the slightest put out, and talked affably on as we meandered towards Chapel. I shall say more of him later, but this at once: I was right about the benignity, but utterly wrong about the condescension; and if indubitably great as a teacher, he was not, in my opinion, without greatness as a man. But why do I speak of him in the past? He is happily still flourishing.

Pruke and Flannery, an O.T.C. bigwig, were at the porch when we got there; and as we stopped, a little beyond them, before entering, I caught a fragment of their conversation:

"I don't like our Jew," remarked Flannery.

Waves of laughter came flooding from Pruke, full of that bonhomie, a bit conspiratorial, that made him so human. "Ah, mah dear fellow," he got out on the tide of it, "ahbsolutely lahmentable!" Then, as if bored with the subject and in contemptuous dismissal: "The fellow's pahlpably not a gentleman." I couldn't have understood, at the time, how right he was, for he was using the term in its technical meaning, and I knew nothing of any of that: so I felt rather hurt.

§ 5

Away with Flannerism! Away with Prukery! We have arrived at my first summer term.

You already know something about it, for I was unwilling, when I started this chapter, to keep cricket and the Paddock inside me till I should be able to get them out in due order. But while cricket and the Paddock do still remain the essence of that term for me—I see it as a freshness of green and white in a haze of heat and sunshine, with the goddess of youth hovering over—it is crucial for my story in another way too, and a far more important one.

Before the term was half spent I was keeping open house. Innumerable people of all ages, not only my own pupils—I don't know how many there really were, but they seem innumerable in retrospect—would drop in at odd moments to have a chat or to borrow a book: for I made them as free of my library as of my talk and my time, and felt great happiness in doing so. On Saturday and Sunday afternoons the three or four chairs of my earlier tea-parties had become a great circle round the biscuits and cake; and our little play-reading society, established almost as soon as we got back and confined at first to my own form, the Lower Sixth, was now well under way. What memories I have of it! A leading figure was Jaques, who read women's parts beautifully, and, better than any, that of the Countess Kathleen. Then there was Ross, square, uncouth, with flashing eyes and beetling forehead: roughly mannered, torrential: passionately loyal to right as he saw it, and a dynamo, it was later to turn out, not only of intellectual energy, but of a sort of strong and solid goodness. And there were Orreys and Aynsworth: dear old booming Bob Orreys, flashily handsome, a man of the world; and Cherry Aynsworth, quavery, minor and affectionate. We read "The Doctor's Dilemma" that term, with Bob Orreys as Cutler Walpole, Ross as Ridgeon, and Jaques as Jennifer: "The Charity that Began at Home", run away with by Bob Orreys as General Bonsor or General Bonsor as Bob Orreys: and "The Showing Up of Blanco Posnet", with a bevy of youngsters for crowd— and quite the liveliest one imaginable. A few months later, when politics had got going, we read "A Modern Symposium": Ross wanted the Anarchist and I did too, so he had to fall back on Disraeli.

It was after one of these play-readings in the summer of 1916 that the thing happened. We had just finished tea and were on the move when Ross, in some connection I don't recall, began thundering against Ireland. The Irish were grotesquely incapable (his vocabulary, now I come to think of it, was almost identical with mine) of governing themselves: so why on earth didn't we shoot some of them, like Cromwell had? My blood was up immediately. I told him not to talk like a prejudiced fool: I asked him what the hell *he* could know about? Had he studied the question? Had it ever occurred to him that to stigmatise people as incapable of anything at all till you'd given them the chance of doing it was quite half-witted? Somebody or other had said, rightly or wrongly, that self-government, however inefficient, was a damn sight better than good government: did he know that? Had he ever considered what it'd feel like to be unable, no matter how much you wanted, to run your own bloody show in your own bloody way? Had he taken any stock of the fact that oppression, even if imaginary, embittered people? Had he, had he, I insisted: had he done any of these things, thought about any of these things, weighed up and balanced any of these things? No, he managed to get out, he supposed he hadn't. Then why on earth, I continued, should a schoolboy of sixteen or whatever he was, utterly ignorant of it all as he himself now admitted, calmly line himself up against people who only wanted what he wanted? Don't take my word for it, I added; but for heaven's sake study a question before pontificating about it.

In boomed Bob Orreys, with hack "points" culled from partisan text-books: he was a history specialist, and spoke as the scribes. Cherry Aynsworth, when he could get a word in between Orreys and me—Ross was silent—twittered about patriotism and the duty of all good Englishmen to stand by their country: and interjected an attack on the poor, who had somehow cropped up—I had referred, I suppose, to the Irish peasantry. Then, when we were all exhausted, Bobby Johnstone chipped in. He was younger than the rest, still wore bum-freezers, looked like a Renaissance *putto*, and invariably talked in an accent of slow wonder, at once emphatic and soft: his voice, if it had been his face, could have been called starry-eyed. "I *say*," he almost whispered, even more wonderingly than usual, "isn't all that *radical*, what you're saying? The radicals are *bloody* people. They ruin the country, and teach the working class to put on airs." I was flabbergasted. Here was a set of boys, nearly all of whom I knew to be decent and generous, even perhaps great-hearted; and yet not one of them, to judge from their talk, had the smallest degree of sympathy with people less well-off than themselves, or any stomach for an argument that ran counter to their prejudices. They had simply accepted like a flock of sheep what had been fed to them; and what had been fed to them was poison.

When they had gone, and I was lonely again, I thought about it all. Were they to go on like this, I asked myself, for the rest of their lives? Was so much precious stuff to be wasted, stuff that might alter the world? Cherry imagined that if people were poor (and a high percentage of the working class lived appallingly, even by present standards, in the England of that time) then the fault was almost certainly theirs: was a boy whom I knew to be sensitive, indeed exceptionally so, if nothing remarkable for brains or force of character, to grow up with such a notion irremovably fixed in his head? I couldn't bear the idea; so there and then, without reflecting on consequences, I took my decision. I would talk politics to these boys, and to any others I could get hold of, day in and day out: I would talk politics round the tea-table, politics in the classroom, politics on the Paddock. Or perhaps I did reflect, for a moment or two, on the consequences; for I must have realised, even then, that the course I proposed to embark on would make me exceedingly unpopular with the housemasters. But if this did cross my mind I must have dismissed it at once. What could I care? Let the consequences be what they might, I should be watching the boys realise, as I knew in their young largeness they *must* realise, that humanity was calling them to its service. What joy could be greater?

I was quite clear, from the beginning, as to what I meant by politics. I meant τὰ πολιτικά, the affairs of the city: I was using the word in its Greek sense, and indeed a far wider one. I wanted the boys to be citizens—not mere citizens of their country but citizens of the world: and not mere citizens of the world either, but citizens, over and above that, of the city of God. This is why, at the very outset, philosophy and religion were inextricably mixed up with the politics I saw myself teaching: and remained so to the end—not only of my Repton adventure but of the Left Book Club and of everything else in my life to this moment of living: and will remain so to the real end, if there is a real end, to the end for me I mean of life itself. But I put it feebly, for religion was not just mixed up with what I intended by politics, it was their essence. Nor, even then, did I think of politics in education as merely, or exclusively, a matter of *what* you taught, though for a long time this loomed largest: I thought of it, also, as a matter of *how* you taught—of how you taught anything. There was almost nothing, I already realised, that you couldn't teach politically, which is also to say religiously.

I hadn't read Marcus Aurelius at the time—might have avoided some of my errors if I had: but there is a passage in his Reflections that could have been inscribed over the doorposts of my classroom, as a sort of introit to the chalkings that were soon to appear on its walls:

"All that is in tune with thee, O Universe, is in tune with me! Nothing that is in due time for thee is too early or too late for me! All that thy seasons bring, O Nature, is fruit for me! All things come from thee, subsist in thee, go back to thee! There is one who says *Dear City of Cecrops*! Wilt thou not say *O dear City of Zeus*?"

I didn't, for all this, carry politics into class with me that summer. I wasn't sure enough yet of my ground, so stuck to Livy and Vergil and the humours of Latin Prose. But outside—at the Pastures, or watching cricket, or on walks, across a field of white clover and down an avenue of elms, towards the Dove country—we talked of little else. Ireland had

long since been dropped: the theme was poverty. But another
rivalled it. Horrified as I had been by the boys' attitude to
those still commonly described, even then, as the lower orders,
I was now as horrified, and perhaps more so, by what they
thought and what they said about the prime enemy of the day,
which was Germany: and by their whole wretched view, if you
could call it a view, of current history and international
relations. Here they were, going out to be wounded or killed,
and to wound and kill others: and yet none of them had the
foggiest idea of what, in terms of historical perspective and a
mature understanding, the catastrophe was about. (And don't
imagine for a moment, my dear Timothy, that this is nothing
but a lot of dead wood, without relevance for today: things
have changed a lot, improved a bit, doubtless—and also deter-
iorated a bit—but by and large, so far as the masses are concerned, ignorance and prejudice and over-simplification, on
the level of international affairs, are currently appalling. I shall
return to the topic later, when summing up.) You might have
imagined, to hear them talk, that the Assyrian had come down
like a wolf on the fold: that Europe and the world, save only
Germany, had been pacific for millennia: that the Germans,
innately evil, had never ceased to aggress: and that England,
since time immemorial, had been a fountain of international
benevolence. By the same token, they had one solitary idea of
what to *do* about things in the immediate future and when the
fighting was over: crush the Hun, and keep him crushed. I
don't want to be absolute about it, for there must have been
boys, from liberal homes, with saner attitudes, and I was even
to know a few later: also a sport here or there, or a rebel from
his environment; but I found none of them in my first little
group, and, from what I learned afterwards, I am sure that
my picture is faithful.

Most of the boys, of course, had read some history, but only
snippets of it: rarely anything except English history, distorted
by nationalism: and not even English history of a time sufficiently recent to impinge on the boy as having anything to do
with himself or the world that he lived in. There was a sort of
hiatus between what you mugged up at school and the actualities of daily existence. Foreign history, world history—they
knew nothing of it. This didn't apply, I imagine, to the history
specialists, for David Somervell, who taught them, was a

ranging historian if there ever was one, and Bob Orreys may
have been singular: but they were a small number anyhow,
and couldn't modify, to any significant degree, the prevalent
atmosphere. As for economics and their tie-up with international affairs—how the race to grab markets, for instance,
had occasioned, or at any rate influenced, some of the major
events of the century—well, anything of the kind was so
unheard of as even remotely connected with a schoolboy's
curriculum that I'm stupid to mention it. You will readily
understand, therefore, why world history, and economics too
—for the reason just mentioned, as well as for many others—
began nagging at me, during these preliminary meditations,
for a prominent place in my forthcoming programme.

Of the original crowd, Amyas Ross "came round" first:
came round, I mean, not to my own solution of these domestic
and international problems, for this wasn't at all my idea
(or wasn't, anyhow, then—nor was ever, in my best moments,
my main one), but to a recognition that they existed, that they
had to be faced, and that the solutions his friends took for
granted, in so far as they envisaged any need for solutions of
any kind, were grotesquely inadequate. He saw it all one
afternoon as we strolled round the Paddock—saw the beastliness
of poverty and war with such a sudden and almost intolerable
insight as I had experienced myself, so many years earlier,
first in the Elgin Avenue drawing-room and then on the train
from Westbourne Park: I could feel the thing happening in
him as if it were happening in me: and I knew at this moment
not only that he would give himself, for the rest of his school-
days, to a keen and independent examination of things as they
were and of schemes for improving them, but that such an
overflow of radiance would proceed from him as would light
into mental activity, and into spiritual activity too, almost
everyone round him. And this is what happened. Ross was the
Repton gadfly, or, better, the Repton saint—a matter-of-fact
and rather crude sort of saint: he did not really sting into life,
he was so full of life that others got a share of it. What mightn't
he have done later? But he died young, from self-neglect.

Meantime Cherry was getting uncomfortable. The idea of
poverty distressed him: surely everyone ought to be happy,
and how could people be happy in slums? Something, he
agreed, must be done about it, and done about it, even, by

him. But he didn't like equality either, in fact he hated the very thought of it: squire and villager, master and man, with benevolence at the top and deferential courtesy at the bottom—this is what he found irresistible; and he feared that, unless we were careful, equality might be the outcome of our meddle-someness. Bobby Johnstone was as bothered, but, that term, went no further. Such misery, of course, *couldn't* be right: but—then tell me, he continued with lingering emphasis, as if the categories he named one by one were cumulative examples of a miracle, are my parents—and brothers—and sisters—and cousins—and uncles—and aunts, none of whom agree with you, all grossly immoral? Orreys blustered, and Jaques was silent.

Ross's "conversion" marks a day that stands out in my mind for two other events, one of them social and the other culinary. The social event was this: I chatted for the first time with Hayward, solidest of the housemasters, with the possible exception of Jugs. I was watching a semi-final in the house-matches—Hayward's v. the Priory—after leaving Amyas, and found myself sitting, I can't imagine how or why, between Hayward himself and his wife, with the gallant London in attendance. Tall, parchmenty, Hayward was a gentleman: charming, in a spare sort of way: and a medium Tory. He didn't exactly *talk* to me; but he put in, every now and again, a "Yes, yes", by way, not of signifying assent, but of refusing to commit himself. His wife, celebrated far beyond Repton for the witchery of her smile, smiled bewitchingly; but when Barnes, one of the Hayward slow bowlers, took his third or fourth wicket, she leant across me and spoke. "Henwy," she said, "Barnes is doing wonderfully: if he takes another wicket do forgive him his beating." Hayward smiled wanly. "No, no, my dear," he replied, "I can't do that. He thoroughly deserves it. He's been cribbing, the silly young fool. Such a thing rarely happens at Repton." "Still," I was beginning, when I was interrupted by Jugs, who was watching from a mile or so off. He laughed, and his laugh was like the synchronised splutter of a million machine-guns. On and on it went cracking—across the Paddock, up to heaven, down to earth, back and forth, back and forth: and a term, you thought, would never be put to the rumour of that vast cachinnation. The Priory batsman had hit a four.

Meanwhile Bim, in a curious hat, had strolled over and joined us. Tapping a Haywardite on the shoulder, "A pity you haven't got a chance," he remarked. "But of course you're a vrotten side, a vrotten side." I glanced at the board. Hayward's had made a hundred and five: the Priory, in spite of that batsman, were forty-three for eight wickets.

But I want to tell you, in particular, about London. He was a gentleman: charming, in a charming sort of way: and a High Tory. He visited a good deal in the neighbourhood, and this may have been relevant (some thought yes, some thought no) for the upshot of the whole affair: his dalliance with literature, anyhow—he had shown it already by assisting at our play-readings—was indubitably relevant. You will presently see why.

When I got home from the match—this is the culinary incident—I expected to find a few boys there. I found something different. At the doorway to my room stood Mrs Maddox, looking stilly inside: and as I looked in my turn, coming up from behind her, I saw the cat at a nauseating mess that lay half on a sheet of oily newspaper and half on a rug. I knew immediately what it was. At breakfast that morning, something in the nature of a roast herring had appeared on my plate: and had gone the way of previous *nefanda*, behind the books in the bamboo book-case. I had forgotten that cats have a keen sense of smell. We said nothing, Mrs Maddox or I: silently, she gave me another chance, and I was grateful for it. But the book-case was done with for ever. I was lucky enough to find a convenient substi-tute: to wit a little market-garden, deserted, at the foot of the Pastures. Thither I would creep at dead of night, and do what I had to.

This was the only untoward incident in a summer of political talk and growing friendships. I became more and more dis-turbed, it is true, by the attitude of self-righteous contempt I could feel developing in me towards Shearme: this isn't the way, I kept thinking, you ought to practise what you preach, but somehow I couldn't help myself. Judging, as of course I shouldn't have done, from his public face only, or from glimpses I got of it, I could find nothing in that hobbling little figure but the three emotions he specialised in: hatred of the Hun, fear of the radicals, and distrust of the working class. His opinion of me was no better than mine was of him; and on top of every-thing else I seemed to frighten him out of his wits, for when I

appeared in the common-room he would lower his voice as if
terrified I should overhear him. Once, to make certain I did, I
stood listening on the threshold. Two words, endlessly piped in
his alto, were all I could make out: "Shoot 'em, shoot 'em, shoot
'em".

As summer wore steadily on, I felt increasing unhappiness at
the prospect of a desolate interlude between this term and next.
Not a single opportunity did I miss of being with my friends
during the remainder of that July: not a walk, not a service in
Chapel, not an hour on the Paddock. And when the end had
really come, and the photograph of our little play-reading group
had been taken in the porch, and they had said good-bye, I sat
down and began wondering what it would feel like—this is
exactly how I thought of it—to see nothing really alive all those
miserable weeks. Couldn't I prolong things a bit? Then I had
an idea. Off I ran down the cinder-path to Stratton's, and
shouted up to Cherry. "What time are you going?" I asked.
"Six o'clock tomorrow morning? Well, I'll tell you what. Col-
lect a few Strattonites I know, and call for me, the whole lot of
you, as early as you like. We'll go in to Derby and breakfast
together." I had the feeling that, if only for a few hours, I had
got the better of fate.

§ 6

It was at Stratford-on-Avon, where I was spending a part of
my holiday, that I got Fisher's letter. "I must write a line to
you," it ran, "to pull you up in the path you are pursuing before
it is too late." Friendliness between masters and boys was, of
course, all to the good; but there was a certain line that should
not be passed, and a certain dignity and reserve that every
master should maintain. I had not maintained it; and he
wanted to save me from finding out for myself that such a
course of action did not pay. I had to realise that there were
two distinct classes in a Public School—the teachers and the
taught; classes having constant relations with one another, no
doubt, but distinct and separate none the less. The "popular"
master was suspect, and rightly so, by his colleagues and the
more thoughtful among the boys. "If I did not think that parts
of your work have been valuable, I should not have troubled
to write to you. Yours sincerely, G. F. Fisher."

I was horribly upset, and kept re-reading the letter. In the mixture of emotions that assailed me anxiety was predominant. There is anxiety and anxiety. There is anxiety about something definite, such as I feel, in a mild and self-mocking sort of way, while I write this very passage; for the snow is descending, fog threatens, we are already in December, and I fear, with the half of my mind that isn't concentrated on Fisher, that those huge Christmas sales of our favourite books, and particularly of *Timothy*, may be ruined: and this would be doubly disastrous, because the Shaw-Patrick Campbell correspondence has flopped unaccountably—or not really unaccountably: a lot of people love getting their own back on a Socrates like Shaw, once he's dead—and, if things don't look up, we shall lose many thousands of pounds on it. That sort of anxiety is always manageable, even when it's serious, even when it's agonising, even when it's about the misfortune or death of a person you specially love: because it's sane, it isn't neurotic, it's something you can get your teeth into. But the other kind of anxiety—that's something else again. It's vague, it's about nothing, it's about everything. It comes welling up inside you from the fastness where it lurked, towards some object—any object, no matter what object, now this object, now that object—it can attach itself to: anon it's like a flame that flickers low, anon it's like a nerve the dentist jabs at: and always, whether virulent or mild—so mild maybe for hours or days on end that you might think it to have vanished, but you don't, and there's the rub—it poisons every moment, every phase of your existence. Guilt, insecurity, terror of the unknown—all characterise it: and all are mere variants of an identical faithlessness, and spring from an identical error. Get rid of the error, and you get rid of anxiety too.

For it is only when *you* desire things for *yourself* as if it *mattered* whether you had them or not: it is only when *you*, in isolation from the whole, want to get or keep *property* in bits of the whole: it is only when *you*, instead of giving yourself to the whole, feel *attachment* to this property in those bits of the whole, that anxiety can exist. So forget yourself, go out, become unattached: think and feel, I am nothing: think and feel, And yet if lost I am everything: and trust God: and say with Léon Bloy, All that happens is divine. And where, pray, is that great phantom, anxiety, now? Nowhere. It must attach itself to something, to some object of desire in the person, if it is to have any existence: or rather, there must be objects in the person it can attach itself to: but there are no such objects now: the whole person is unattached: so it can attach itself to nothing: so it cannot exist. More: as one now sees, it never has existed; it has always been a myth.

But the whole thing, you may object, is a vicious circle. You cannot get rid of the anxiety until you have got rid of the self-involvement: all right: but how can you get rid of the self-involvement until you have got rid of the anxiety? If you are anxious because you are self-involved, you are also self-involved because you are anxious. So what's the good of telling a man to get rid of self-involvement while anxiety is still lurking in him? The anxiety prevents him from doing so. The very essence of anxiety is that it is always there, when there is self-involvement: just as the very essence of self-involvement is to produce anxiety. So, wretched men that we are, how can we deliver ourselves from the body of this complex?

I can only tell you that we can: that, the anxiety notwithstanding, a change can take place in us that so weakens self-involvement as to weaken, *pro tanto*, anxiety too: and may even abolish both. I cannot tell you *how* this happens: you must discover it for yourself. Theologians speak of grace: and grace is only another word for something free in the universe, something outside vicious circles, that is always breaking in and repairing disunity between the whole and its parts. Only, grace must be wooed—it *can* be wooed, in spite of anxiety. And there's no substitute for it. I've tried all the tricks, and they haven't worked. But grace, which isn't a trick but a getting into touch with reality—grace has worked, even with such an instrument as me to play its tunes on: so that I, who have had long stretches of indeterminate anxiety, sometimes agonising, at various periods of my life, have all but entirely—perhaps I must wait a bit before saying entirely—got rid of it now. Or maybe even in that form the affirmative is too unqualified: so let me say, rather, that when I do get anxiety nowadays, anxiety of the sort we're discussing, it rarely lasts more than a few minutes; I practise my technique on it (and the essence of that technique is that it isn't a technique and isn't mine) and hey presto! the thing's a myth.

But it wasn't a myth when I got Fisher's letter; and it fastened, of course, on the word "suspect". What did he mean,

suspect? Suspect of what? Of "playing for popularity"? Of deliberately "sucking up" to the boys, with the motive—but what
motive?—with the motive maybe of personal advancement? The
idea was too loathsome: I had given to the boys, with utter
spontaneity, the affection, as spontaneous, I had felt for them.
Then another interpretation, even more detestable, came thrusting its fist at me. Could he be hinting at homosexuality? I dismissed it as fantastic, and was right, I discovered afterwards, in
doing so. I had returned to my earlier suspicion, when this, all
at once, meant nothing either; for the words "suspect *by the more
thoughtful among the boys*" were now all that mattered. Had I been
wrong about them? About their feelings for me? Did they go
away and make fun of me behind my back? Did they come to
the Pastures for the sake of their stomachs and nothing else?
Well, perhaps they did: perhaps I had made the most absolute
fool of myself. If so, I had better not return; all my happiness
would be gone, and to become a hack schoolmaster—for, if I
obeyed Fisher, that was all I could look forward to—seemed
unthinkable. Meanwhile, his letter required answering. I wrote
at length: and I asked, what had he implied by the word suspect? I waited a fortnight for his answer, and the mouse, when
it came, was ridiculous. "I refuse to write long letters," he said,
"from the tops of Welsh mountains. I will give you two instances
of what I mean. You had some boys up to dinner last term, and
borrowed the prefects' room gramophone to amuse them with.
You also went with a lot of boys to Derby on the last morning,
and gave them a feed there. This sort of thing will never do.
Yours sincerely, G. F. Fisher."

So that was that. I was no longer anxious: I was angry. I
hadn't, in fact, "given" the boys anything: we had simply had
breakfast together, and each had paid for his own. Trivialities,
however, apart, could a couple of sentences be considered adequate, even from the tops of Welsh mountains? And why, anyhow, letters at all? If the matter was so serious, oughtn't he to have
taken the opportunity, while term was still on, of talking things
over face to face? I was to find later on, nearly a couple of years
later on, that Fisher, by reason of temperament, preferred letters
to interviews, and brevity to length. I preferred interviews, and
length.

Anyhow, I bothered about "suspect" no longer. It all boiled
down, I now told myself, to a difference of opinion, as wide as

the heavens, about human relationships: about what they ought to be in general, and about what they ought to be in particular —in particular, for present purposes, as between master and boy. And now I'm going to drop the past tense, with enormous relief, and speak in the present: for being, as you know, very old-fashioned about such matters, I think in 1952, and shall probably think on my deathbed, exactly as I thought in 1916.

"Classes", "distinct and separate", "dignity", "reserve"—I reject them all utterly, in respect of any possible application of them to any human relations whatever. We don't want reserve: we want giving: we don't want dignity for the self: we want respect for the other: we don't want distinction and separation: we want unity: we don't want classes: we want free and equal individuals. I don't care a tittle who the people may be that are involved in the relationship: parents and children, husbands and wives, lovers and mistresses, young and old, rich and poor, black and white, "masters" and "men", clevers and stupids, schoolmasters and schoolboys—it makes not an atom of difference. Here is the root of the matter: *de hoc res agitur*. A hierarchical conception of human society is not only detestable to anyone with the breath of freedom in his nostrils (and everyone has it really, though many don't know that they have—even psychopaths have it, for they are desperately seeking to breathe with it through the very medium of their distortions), but involves a sort of lie: for only God ought to be thought of as presiding over human society, and there are no classes, only individuals, no distinctions, only creatures, no dignities or reserves, only nakedness, before the throne of his glory. Or, to put it in another way, a hierarchical conception of society is blasphemous, because God is the only hierarch. It is fashionable nowadays, this hierarchical conception, I know: all the more reason for fighting it.

Since "distinct and separate classes", "dignity and reserve", "lines you mustn't cross" are to be abjured in all human relations, then they are to be abjured, as a matter of course, in the relation between master and boy. But there is more to it than that. If there is one single sphere in which they are more ruinous than in any other, it is the sphere of education. To communicate—that is the prime essence, the ultimate meaning, of the whole educational process, as properly understood: to communicate, not dry facts or routine information (though these, in a workaday world, must play their part, and may

serve, over and above that, the major purpose) but wisdom
about living. And how can you communicate, pray, from
behind the barrier of a separate class? Or from behind a
boundary you must never cross? Naked contact between soul
and soul—this is the bourn. You must give yourself utterly—but
then, what has become of your reserve? And in utter humility
—but then, are you dignified? And that business of "teachers"
and "taught"—"there are two distinct classes: the teachers and
the taught"—how insensitive it is, how arrogant, how mechanical, how contrary to what, when there is a genuine "teacher"
about, is really seen to be happening! For in true education
there are no teachers and no taught. There is an interchange:
the master learns as he teaches, the pupil teaches as he learns.
Both give, and both receive. The master gives his wisdom, the
boy gives his freshness: and they react on one another, this
wisdom and this freshness, and transform one another. Something new and precious, precious for both of them, has been
struck out, has come into their lives, as a result of their intercourse: and has come into the world.

True dignity, of course, is always there, when there is real
education—but not the sort of dignity that Fisher had in mind.
Reverence given and received, equally given and received, that
is what I call dignity: and if the master reverences his pupil,
then the pupil, ninety-nine times out of a hundred, will reverence his master. This reverence, given by the younger and
fresher as a result of receiving it, confers leadership on the
older and wiser: and it is the only sort of leadership worth
bothering about. You lead, in education, not by virtue of
belonging to a class, nor by virtue of any barrier or reserve,
but by virtue of the wisdom—and the love—that you reveal.

This is what I think now, and this is what I thought then;
and I decided, accordingly, not to change my line of action by
an iota. But that's not quite accurate: in one respect I did
decide to change it. As you are aware, I had freely criticised a
few of my colleagues in those talks with the boys (though not
ill-naturedly, except maybe in Jacky's case) and had felt guilty
about it. I suspected, and later knew, that they were as critical
of me, and as openly; but as I hated tit-for-tatism anyhow this
was irrelevant. Now it could never have entered my head that
criticism of a master with a boy was in any way worse, or better
either, than criticism of a boy with a master: but my own acts

were all that concerned me: and there was this to be said about it. A "class" situation existed—the situation that Fisher had not merely recognised, but demanded; and, given this situation, my criticism involved a certain element of partisanship that I couldn't help feeling—but knew I ought to show, in the interests of harmony, as little as possible. I was being negative instead of positive. Given the same situation, there was something a bit clandestine about my behaviour, which I couldn't justify by my knowledge of a similar clandestinity against me. So I resolved to amend. I knew it wouldn't be easy, for the canvassing of pedagogic peculiarities is common form among schoolboys, and I wasn't going to be stand-offish; but I'd try. I did not wholly succeed.

§ 7

It was immediately school got back, at a masters' meeting, that I witnessed at its most impressive the clear-headedness, the grasp of detail, and the ability to mug up a boring subject that would have made Geoffrey Fisher so admirable a civil servant or business executive. He was already under way when I arrived, and the room was crowded: so crowded that I began to imagine that some of the servants had turned up, for I couldn't believe that the staff was so numerous. I started by identifying the easy ones: kept them fixed in my mind as my eye darted to others: and found, in the end, that I could name almost everyone. Many of them, being a bit uniform, had impinged on me, I suppose, as alternatives.

I had slipped in quietly, and taken a seat next to Burd, or the Auk. This was a magnificent specimen of the humanist, in appearance and otherwise. Flowing hair was drawn back from a broad forehead, chiselled closely with narrow lines; and an Italian nose, of rare delicacy and strength, jutted out underneath. His eyes were kind, his whole look one of noble austerity: and this was enhanced by two great grooves that sprang from higher than usual and ran down either cheek. His clothes were old and shabby: one of the sides of his glasses had gone, and been replaced by a curled pipe-cleaner: but the flat Balfour collar, and the dim purple tie that descended from it, gave the whole an effect of distinction. As he sat there, bending over his

Plato and oblivious of the proceedings, I felt a mixture of liking and awe for him. He was indeed a great scholar; and a fine 'cellist, too. (So I was told, for I never heard him play. He must have specialised in Vivaldi or Scarlatti, if they wrote for the 'cello.) He had been at Repton a long time. He had taken the Upper Sixth, or, the boys said, the Upper Sixth had taken him, for close on twenty years.

Fisher was explaining *à merveille* an elaborate scheme of marks by which the Cattley shield was to be awarded. Cattley was a famous and, rumour had it, ferocious ex-housemaster who, from the fastness of an Oxfordshire vicarage, had conceived the idea of presenting this annual namesake to the House that came out top for intellectual distinction. A prodigality of "rewards" had long been characteristic of the place: "copies" for a decent exercise; "distinction cards" for inability to get a prize—or not quite that, but you will understand what I mean; and "recommendations" for minor proficiency in a particular subject—they were always flying about and settling down on somebody. These were now to be carefully graded and translated into marks; and the result would be Cattley for a year. Fisher was half-way through when Pat Exham, who had been slumbering in a corner, woke up with a cry.

"Headmashter," he said, breathing heavily and labouring at his articulation, "I think that Jonesh ought to have a move. He's one of the shlackesht shwinesh in Europe; but he'sh been in my form for two yearsh, and he's only jusht below the linesh."

Jacky Shearme wasn't having any of this. "He can't come up to me, headmaster," he piped out. "I've got eighteen as it is, and that's all I can manage." "Welsh," said Pat, labouring away at it now still more heavily, "welsh . . . the boysh" . . . his head fell forward; he slept.

The interruption had jolted Burd, who must have caught a few stray passages in Fisher's discourse. "What are distinction cards?" he asked me, not at all as a judge might have asked "Who is Charlie Chaplin?", but with a genuine desire for information. I told him. "Ah," he said, "I think it unlikely that I shall ever give one." He then returned to his Plato.

Fisher, rapidly in his stride again, had soon wound up with a masterly recapitulation; but as he paused and wiped the moisture from his chin, a new voice—sweetly modulated, lingering—came from somewhere behind me. I looked round,

and saw London. "Headmaster," he said, with the air of an
Anatol paying compliments to a *süsses mädel*, "*would* you mind
going over that just once more?"

So the capital points were rehearsed: the question of "re-
moves" was disposed of: and I was just about to leave with the
rest when the headmaster beckoned me. I braced myself,
imagining that dignity, reserve, and the class structure of
public-school society were to be dealt with more fully. But no—
indeed, in a sense, on the contrary. I was promoted, Fisher told
me, to the Upper Sixth, and was to start with them at once. It
did cross my mind that, on this point at any rate, a short note
would have been in order; but I contented myself with mur-
muring that it was a pity I hadn't known in advance, as I had
spent a good slice of my holiday sweating away at my work for
the Lower Sixth. But Fisher seemed unimpressed. "Good for
you!" he ejaculated, laughed his little laugh, and passed on.

Meanwhile Pruke had been hanging about, with the obvious
intention of "buttonholing" me; and we walked down the
village together. "Well, mah dear fellow," he began, as he took
me by the arm with great friendliness, "what do you think
of him? Perfectly sickening such a man should be here. The
fellow's pahlpably incompetent. I wouldn't mind so much if he
were a gentleman. That's the trouble—no class, no breeding.
Oh, mah dear fellow, let's shut up. I'm sick of the man."

I was quite ready to shut up, as I hadn't the faintest idea
who "the man" was, and thought it best not to enquire.
(Hardly Fisher, I thought: who, if not perhaps porphyro-
genitus, came of thoroughly "good stock"). So I asked what
sort of holidays he'd had.

"The weather at the end was ahbsolutely lahmentable,
and I was stuck in this place the whole time. If we could
only get rid of that fellow Asquith I should feel a good deal
happier."

"Who would you put in his place?"

"Milner. He's the only fellow capable of running a war like
this. There's a lot of prejudice against him. But he's a democrat,
mah dear fellow, a sincere democrat. Or I wouldn't mind
L.G. What we want is a *strong* man."

"It depends on what you mean by strong."

"I know you're keen on social reform and all that. Well, I'm
a bit of a syndicalist myself. But there must be no weaken-

ing, ahbsolutely no weakening. We've got to *crush* Prussian militarism."

At this moment, by a lucky chance, David Somervell suddenly popped out from an alley-way, and saved me from the necessity of demurring—not so much to the statement itself as to its implication. "Ah, Gollancz," he said, with that condescending curve in his voice—or pseudo-condescending, as I've explained—"so here you are! Good." He was in a hurry, and passed on. Pruke fell silent, and remained so till we had got to the foot of the Pastures, where he would be leaving me. Then, with a fascinating laugh in which reservations about Somervell were nicely set off against respect for my own powers of insight, "Congratulations, mah dear fellow," he said, "you've been spoken to by Lord God Almighty."

Now don't get all this wrong: it is vital that you shouldn't, because, since I must inevitably figure as my own hero in this record, Pruke, who was my chief opponent, will tend, no less inevitably, to assume the character of villain. The truth about him, I think, was this. A critical element was strong in his make-up (as it was in mine), but so was a groping for affection; and this emerged as a desire, a very human desire, to stand well, be in cahoots you might say, with his companion of the moment. Thus: when he was discussing my own case with Flannery, I was palpably not a gentleman—and indeed I palpably wasn't; but when he was discussing "the man's" case with me, you might have thought, all at once, that my forbears had come over with the Conqueror, instead of from Poland in the eighteen hundreds.

(People are very odd about gentlemen. Ralph Straus, for example, would often eulogise someone—sincerely—for the length of a whole meal, and then add, with the air of a *cognoscente* giving the word to another *cognoscente*, "He's not a gentleman, of course." Ralph, who was charming and lovable, and liked everybody—except people who wrote his name with two s's—had other peculiarities of a similar kind. Once, after a discussion on anti-semitism in which he hadn't quite agreed with me, he leant forward and whispered conspiratorially, "I shouldn't like you to think that I'm biased: between you and me, I have a little Jewish blood in me myself." I was reminded of what had passed, so they said, between a convert to Catholicism and the Pope. The convert, looking over his

G

shoulder, had remarked *sotto voce* "I must tell you in confidence that I'm a Jew." The Pope, looking over his shoulder,
had replied *sotto voce* "I must tell you in confidence that I'm
a Catholic." And this reminds me of another good story about
the Pope and a Jew . . . or perhaps it's too irrelevant. A pity:
I've been wanting to tell it you for a long time.)

Pruke, I was saying, groped for affection. His capacity for it
was manifest in his relation to his son Paul—one of unusual
tenderness and devotion. The boy, gentle and winning, had
contracted some form of paralysis, I think infantile; and this,
without in any way crippling him, had diminished, for the time
being, his power of continuous effort. But he was of great
natural ability; and his father, who had ambitions for his
future, had managed, on a wretched schoolmaster's salary,
to send him to Harrow, and further intended him for Oxford.
It must have been soon after the exchange just recorded that
Pruke told me all this, and asked me if I would help the boy,
when our times could be dovetailed, with a little extra tuition
in Latin. I of course happily agreed; and our sessions, which
never failed to give me pleasure, were uninterrupted, if I
remember rightly, by the development of the row between
father and coach. We both regarded them, I think, as above
the battle.

There's much else that, looking back, I discover as likeable
about Pruke. His reach was considerable, and that's something
—that's a lot. He would have wished, I think, to be an
"intellectual", and though of good average brains, and highly
efficient, in his own line, as a schoolmaster—appropriately, he
took the Army Class, with Bim—knew he wasn't one. This
may explain his attitude to Somervell. I am reminded of a
similar case within my experience as a publisher. There is
a born writer of powerful intellect who, being nevertheless
anything but a "highbrow", is self-consciously aware of the
fact: and will often attack "The New Statesman"—for being
"highbrow". He imagines that they despise him. I was lunch-
ing with Kingsley Martin last week, and was amused to
discover that he had the greatest admiration for my friend:
who'll be delighted when I tell him so.

Then there was *odium politicum*, such as I had felt, the other
way round, for Jacky Shearme. As I explained in my previous
volume, the clash between Toryism, the real old privileged

Toryism making its last decisive stand, and radicalism, with the socialist viper in its womb, had been, up till 1914, of a violence nowadays hardly intelligible; a violence covered, during the succeeding few years, by "national unity", but always near the surface none the less. And I was a radical —a ruinous draught in a hot-bed of Toryism; and any liberals already there were becoming the more radical for my presence. As to the war issue itself, which was the crucial one, a "crush the Hun" attitude—with everything it implied in terms, first, of how the fight should be waged, second, of how and when it should be ended (or rather shouldn't be ended), and, third, of what should follow it by way of international settle-ment—was as typical of various layers in the England of that day as a "crush communism everywhere" attitude is typical of similar layers in the America of this. People honestly considered it all—the radicalism as well as the war issue—a matter of life and death: I mean they felt moral about it, on the "wrong" side as well as on the "right". I say so much, because I do not believe, as a few others did, that Pruke was actuated by venom.

I was looking last night through a drawer containing the "personalia" of a whole fifty years. It was crammed to the brim with "letters messages and telegrams" (one of them: FISHER WORSE THAN NORTHCLIFFE AWFUL SHAME) sent me, after I'd been sacked, by a curious assortment of boys, including toughs and oppositionists. There, to my delight, I found something from Pruke. I must have sent him an olive-branch, and this was his reply: "Thank you very much for your kind letter. I think I can say quite honestly I bear no enmity. What I did I could not help doing. It's all part of this ghastly war. Best of luck." (There was a typical postscript: "Paul has started his career in town. He is very contented, but I am fearful that his physical strength is not yet up to it.") I am persuaded that the "honestly" was exact.

So bear all this in mind while you are reading what follows, for I must tell my story, more or less, in black and white, and with a sense of the drama I feel in it: I cannot be forever inter-larding qualifications, or constructing apologias *pro vita Prukeana*. And that "goes for" everybody else I may have criticised, or may criticise henceforward, during the course of this narrative —with a single exception: which I shall discuss later on in some detail. It goes, most of all, for Jacky Shearme. We had no serious intercourse: we nodded, we said "Fine day!", we passed on. So I knew nothing about him, except his politics, which were lamentable; and though I can imagine no more dangerous influence for developing minds, I have the idea that, apart from this, he was honest and dutiful, if neither coruscating nor tempestuous. But I didn't go into all that. I disliked his opinions, and accordingly, alas!, disliked him.

I don't think I ever really disliked Pruke, and I don't think he ever really disliked me, though we infuriated one another. He was the sort of man, I occasionally felt, whom I should like to drink champagne with. As a matter of fact I did drink champagne with him, spiritually (the actual beverage was lemonade), on the very day of the conversation I've described. I got a note from him a few hours later, asking me to a party that evening. Of course I accepted. We played patience, double-demon, coon-can, up-Jenkins, and cork-snatching. It was an agreeable evening, if rather long.

§ 8

I was so eager next morning to make a start with the Upper Sixth that our room was still empty when I got there. As the boys began arriving, I noticed with pleasure that three of my particular friends, two of them major ones—Amyas Ross and Cherry Aynsworth—had shared my move-up: Leslie was to follow later. Of the other nine or ten, three were leaving at Christmas: the remainder, or some of them, will appear shortly.

This was scholarship term for about half the Upper Sixth: people sat at the end of it for Oxford or Cambridge, and then, whether successful or not, stayed on till the summer. So I had a pretty free hand: provided only I did my best to get them scholarships I could do it more or less as I liked—though the Auk, whom of course I'd consulted, had underlined the importance of "pure" classics. I felt unable to agree with him, even on pot-hunting considerations: since the boys' safest bet, I considered, anyhow at Oxford, would be to show themselves, not for the failures at Porsonism they so hideously looked like being, but for embryo Erasmuses. I accordingly went my own way. Latin prose, to be sure, remained a wonderful business. Whole

long sessions would flow away in sheer delight, as we jested of
ampullae and *meiosis*; and sometimes, if we were composing viva
voce, and two of us, at the identical moment, had spotted a niche
for some special desideratum—an *illi quidem*, perhaps, or a plain
quid?—one or other of us would bring it out, after a struggle for
priority, in a quiver of intellectual mirth. Not that many of the
boys were as good at the game as they might have been, for in
classical scholarship they shone but poorly. Ross was by a long
chalk the worst: his proses were like porridge with lumps in it,
or like a greasy suet pudding with a mass of unsuitable plums
sticking out from every inch of its surface. Nooky was best. This
was an Armenian, with the eyes of a mongol and the nose of a
boxer. In all that company of my intimate friends he alone, I
used to think, was moved to spiritual and intellectual agony by
the awareness that war could exist: the others were moved to
passion, not agony. He got a scholarship, but never took it, for
he was killed. His real name was Manoukian. Innes wasn't
bad, either: a little poet of a fellow, ugly and unpopular, who
stammered, didn't shave, played cricket (and any other game)
abominably, and knew more about "English" than all the rest
of the class put together. He was killed in the war, like Manoukian. He left me a little manuscript notebook, filled, in an exquisite hand, with his sonnets and poems. I found it in that
drawer the other day, side by side with Pruke's letter.

But it was when I started my great series of lectures (I apologise for the 'great', it slipped out, for this is how I thought of
them) that I realised, as I hadn't realised before—not fully, not
even during talks on the Paddock or round the fire in my room
—what stuff the boys were made of. We tackled many subjects
that term—the history of Greek literature, the meaning of Greek
drama, and so on: but most successful of all, far and away, was
the course on Greek philosophy and religion. I knew little of the
topic myself, though I had the necessary background: but my
ignorance, I couldn't help feeling, might turn out an advantage.
Learning and teaching simultaneously, shouldn't I be back in—
shouldn't I be automatically communicating—the wonder of
new experience that must have blessed, in that springtime, those
pioneers? And there was something else—something I mentioned before, when I spoke of Fisher's letter. Shouldn't I be
learning from the boys I met livingly quite as much as from the
textbooks I studied? Wouldn't *they* be teaching *me*—teaching me

to be a philosopher, teaching me to be religious—as *I* taught *them*? The event proved me right on both counts.

How shall I convey to you, my dear Timothy, something of the atmosphere in that bare Repton classroom on the day, which I shall always remember, when we arrived at the philosophy and religion of primitive Greece? Directly I had got going I knew that the battle was won. Preliminary shufflings as the hour neared its end, covert glances at wrist-watch or clock—no occasion to fear such things now. We were discovering the universe, the universe we lived in, the universe we were part of: we were trying to understand how these people had explained it, explained the universe and ourselves.

We would continue long after the hour, canvassing this point or that; and when at last we had to go, for fear of infuriating some master with whom the form was overdue, I at least would be heady with that elation I have experienced so often in boyhood after living a bit of life to the full. I would have the impulse to run home rather than walk, so difficult I found it to curb my emotion; and when I got there I would stride up and down, unable to sit quiet at the table and prepare for another instalment. It became our habit to go into school for daily prep., though the boys should have been at their Houses—for we grudged every moment: and if this wasn't enough, as it frequently wasn't, we would adjourn to the Pastures . . . And then a day arrived that ἐθρίγκωσεν the whole course of lectures, put the coping stone on it: the day we found ourselves at Plato, and took off our shoes before advancing to the Theory of Ideas . . .

Plato, I understand, is outmoded, particularly at Oxford, where they frown on metaphysics. Well, I am not a philosopher. But one thing I do know. Platonic metaphysics, however fantastic their detail and however untenable, in the light of modern knowledge, for contemporary minds, express a passion, as splendid as any that has ever blazed in human hearts, to reveal the quintessence of morality, namely the absoluteness of good: or I should say, rather, half its quintessence: the other half being, that God is love. And I know something else. Platonism, properly taught, can make a boy free of that fair country of religion better even than the religion of religions that far surpasses it: for it comes to him fresh and enthralling, and neither ruined by conventional acceptance nor distorted by misinterpretation. But when I say it makes him free I mean *begins* to make him free, I mean waters the seed, helps it grow: Socrates, ultimately, is no substitute for Christ.

I took immense pains with my lectures on Plato. Normally, I hate even a postcard of notes when I'm talking in public: I like to say anything that may come into my head when I'm up on my feet. But I composed and wrote out every word of those lectures, and went so far as to have them typed; and two out of the six have survived—the introductory one, and the one on education—in that same crowded drawer with the boys' letters and the little manuscript notebook and the Prukeanum. I wish the one on Ideas had survived too: I should have liked to read now what I thought about them then.

I want to reproduce, without quotation marks, something of what I said to those schoolboys nearly forty years ago, as if I were back there and you were one of them, Timothy. You may be surprised at the amount of Masefield I quote. The reason is: there was quite a vogue for him then, and even people who didn't care much for poetry made an exception in his case, and read him eagerly. *The Everlasting Mercy*, a few years earlier, had sold like a Daphne du Maurier.

I said, then, something like this:

Plato excites us, above all, by his intellectual passion. Today, only a few care to search after truth; the majority are content to go about their business, without concern for the why or the wherefor. Even among those who live a life you could call intellectual, it is rare to find anyone who brings to his normal round the devoted urgency of a lover, or of a man who has given himself to the service of some great cause. Thought has become the province of professors; and the majority of professors lead what others regard as the dullest of lives. But to Plato thought was urgent, the most urgent by far of all human activities; he longed to understand things, to know *why* they are *as* they are, and to discover for himself, by means of the reason he thought divine, the ultimate right and the ultimate wrong. Life, he knew, was good; but how make good use of it, how be worthy of it—and of oneself—unless one discover something fixed, some abiding

principle, that will explain all apparent contradictions, and guide
one through the maze, and lead one in the end to real happiness?
It was with the search for something fixed, something absolute,
that Plato fell in love; and so he fell in love with thought as its
instrument. 'Fell in love' is just: he rejoiced, like an ἐραστής,
in intellectual effort.

We may find it difficult to understand what a life such as this
must have meant to him. But as we come upon certain passages
in his dialogues he catches us up, and for a moment we are with
him. Nobody at all sensitive to literature could read the close
of the "Symposium" without being thrilled by the glory of intellectual effort. The argument on love is over; some of the
company have gone home, some have fallen asleep in their
places; but when Aristidemus wakes up ἀλεκτρυόνων ᾀδόντων
—at cock-crow—he finds three of them still at it, discussing, for
a change of topic, tragedy and comedy. Soon, only Socrates
is left; he goes away to the Lyceum and bathes, and after
spending the day as usual εἰς ἑσπέραν οἴκοι ἀναπαύεσθαι.

It is perhaps at the University that one comes nearest to feeling what Plato felt: not in the lecture-room or examination
schools, but at one of those casual symposia at which men talk
together till sunrise—and then bathe and have breakfast and
are ready for the day. And some, long after they have left, can
still recapture the old exhilaration:

"O Time, bring back those midnights and those friends,
    Those glittering moments that a spirit lends,
    That all may be imagined from the flash,
    The cloud-hid god-game through the lightning gash,
    Those hours of stricken sparks from which men took
    Light to send out to men in song or book.
    Those friends who heard St Pancras's bells strike two
    Yet stayed until the barber's cockerel crew,
    Talking of noble styles, the Frenchman's best,
    The thoughts beyond great poems not expressed,
    The glory of mood where human frailty failed,
    The forts of human light not yet assailed,
    Till the dim room had mind, and seemed to brood,
    Binding our wills to mental brotherhood,
    Till we became a college, and each night
    Was discipline and manhood and delight,

Till our farewells, and winding down the stairs
At each grey dawn had meaning that Time spares,
That we, so linked, should roam the whole world round
Teaching the ways our brooding minds had found,
Making that room our Chapter, our one mind,
Where all that this world soiled should be refined."

"Till we became a college" . . . Plato, like Masefield, understood that, though thought is an intensely personal thing, it
can attain its full spendour only when "stricken" by the
clash of several minds. Plato is above all human. He hated
shams and hypocrisy, and the sloth in our brains that would
let others do our thinking for us; but we never feel he hated
the shammers and hypocrites. That is why he is so dramatic,
for drama is the social form of art. I could go on for ever
giving examples of his sympathy. You find it at the very
beginning of the "Republic". Socrates has come to see the
festival, with its crowd and its procession of Thracians and
natives. Later, he visits Cephalus, and begins a discussion on
old age; and presently the host, "leaving the argument to his
heir", departs to the sacrifice "with a smile". Plato's sympathy
with serene old age; his delight in the vivacity of youth, which
has caused amusement to Cephalus; the kindliness of his whole
outlook: all these are wonderfully expressed by the single word
γέλασας, "with a smile". And when Thrasymachus, the coarse
boor, comes rushing into the argument like a wild animal, we
feel that Plato drew his portrait with a twinkle in his eye, and
with a sort of affection.

But if you would know the supreme expression of this sympathy you must read the "Symposium". The discussion on
love has reached its climax with the finest passage, perhaps,
in all prose literature; for Socrates has been describing how
the initiate rises from the love of one beautiful body to the love
of many, and from the love of outward forms to the love of
ideas, until at last he has a vision of absolute Beauty, undifferentiated and eternal. As we hear him we hold our breath,
straining to catch a glimpse of that passionless Beauty in whose
very presence he himself must have lived. And then, breaking
in on the silence—suddenly a knocking at the door; the noise
of revellers; and Alcibiades, with ivy and violets on his head
and a flute-girl at his side, asking the banqueters whether

they will allow a very drunk man to share their wine. The effect of this scene is indescribable. The glow of the great words is still on us; and in a flash we understand that life in all its aspects is good, and we love Alcibiades and the jolliness of things no less than we love Socrates and αὐτὸ τὸ καλόν.

We learn from this passage that the great principle Plato sought for is not only perfect Truth, but also perfect Beauty. That is to say, Plato is a poet as well as a philosopher. The poet is a man who, seeing something ineffable behind the things of this world, and seeing it as beauty, makes an effort to express it in words: in words that, even as they come, make the vision itself a little clearer to himself and to others. The vision is largely seen, as it were, by means of the expression. And while the philosopher in Plato sought for the ultimate meaning of existence, the poet in him saw hints of that meaning in the phenomena of this world, and tried to body forth the beauty that he saw:

> "Or does sweet Beauty dwell in lovely things
>   Scattering the holy hintings of her name
>   In women, in dear friends, in flowers, in springs,
>   In the brook's voice, for us to catch the same?"

Masefield shows us, in another sonnet, how it happened that the greatest of Greek philosophers was also among the greatest of Greek poets:

> "Even after all these years there comes the dream
>   Of lovelier life than this in some new earth,
>   In the full summer of that unearthly gleam
>   Which lights the spirit when the brain gives birth;
>   Of a perfected I, in happy hours,
>   Treading above the sea that trembles there,
>   A path through thickets of immortal flowers
>   That only grow where sorrows never were;
>   And, at a turn, of coming face to face
>   With Beauty's self, that Beauty I have sought
>   In women's hearts, in friends, in many a place,
>   In barren hours passed at grips with thought,
>   Beauty of woman, comrade, earth and sea,
>   *Incarnate thought** come face to face with me."

* My italics

Nor have we done when we have described the object of
Plato's search as perfect Beauty; it was also, in a sense, God. It
does not matter very much for our purpose whether Plato
actually identified God with the Idea of the Good; the question
is one on which scholars differ, and will no doubt always differ.
But he certainly uses language about the journey and its goal
that we must describe as in the deepest sense religious. Plato
was something more than a philosopher contemplating truth
and a poet entranced with beauty; he was also a mystic in
search of communion. "These are the lesser mysteries of love,"
says Diotima (she is speaking of the earlier stages of the lover's
progress), "into which even you, Socrates, may enter; to the
greater and more hidden ones—τὰ τέλεα καὶ ἐποπτικά—
which are the crown of these, and to which, if you pursue them
in a right spirit, they will lead, I know not whether you will be
able to attain." Thus pure thought, in its consummation,
becomes identified, not only with the poet's insight, but with
religious rapture: that rapture by which, leaping the gulf, men
have united with the object of their worship. In Aeschylus, for
all his piety, we find no trace of what we nowadays understand
as religious experience: in Plato we begin to feel its presence,
just as we begin to feel in him, for all the differences, an
approach to Christian ethics and a foreshadowing of Christian
morality.

The passionate seeker after truth: the lover of humanity: the
poet: the mystic—all these can express what they will through
the medium of a style that is as flexible as it is harmonious.
Sometimes you find a lightness and vivacity, with a rapid
implication here, a hint of laughter there, that remind us of
"the Frenchman's best"; and sometimes the argument unfolds
in language bare and exact, with no superfluous word to
obscure the logic. And then, in delightful contrast but without
any harshness of transition, comes a wealth of vivid imagery
paralleled, within the limits of my reading, by but few other
writers of prose. Metaphor, simile, myth—he is an adept at
them all. But it is in the passages I have described as religious
that he is seen at his greatest. Here there is an ardour, a white
intensity of passion, that seems to kindle us from the page;
yet no violence is done to the fabric, and the form becomes
all the more just as the emotion grows deeper.

In Plato we see the culmination of the Greek genius. For

passion and serenity were one to him; and we feel in our lesser
way, as we read him, the breathless quiet of joy.

That is what I said, more or less, by way of introducing Plato
to the Upper Sixth. And here is something of what I said about
his views on education:

The most important passage for our purpose is the one that
immediately follows the famous allegory in Book VII of the
"Republic", where men are compared to prisoners in a cave
who, chained up with their backs to the light, can see nothing
but shadows on a wall. I will quote the passage in full:

"But then, if I am right, certain professors of education must
be wrong when they say that they can put a knowledge into the
soul which was not there before, like sight into blind eyes.
They undoubtedly say this, he replied.
Whereas, our argument shows that the power and capacity
of learning exists in the soul already; and that just as the eye was
unable to turn from darkness to light without the whole body, so
too the instrument of knowledge can only by the movement of
the whole soul be turned from the world of becoming [i.e. this
world of ever-changing phenomena] into that of being [i.e. the
eternal world of unchangeable reality], and learn by degrees to
endure the sight of being, and of the brightest and best of being,
or, in other words, of the good.
Very true.
And must there not be some art which will effect conversion
in the easiest and quickest manner; not implanting the faculty
of sight, for that exists already, but has been turned in the wrong
direction, and is looking away from the truth?
Yes, he said, such an art may be presumed.
And whereas the other so-called virtues of the soul seem to be
akin to bodily qualities, for even when they are not originally
innate they can be implanted later by habit and exercise, the
virtue of wisdom more than anything else contains a divine
element which always remains, and by this conversion is ren-
dered useful and profitable; or on the other hand, hurtful and
useless. Did you never observe the narrow intelligence flashing
from the keen eye of a clever rogue—how eager he is, how

clearly his paltry soul sees the way to his end; he is the reverse
of blind, but his keen eyesight is forced into the service of evil,
and he is mischievous in proportion to his cleverness?

Very true, he said.

But if there had been a circumcision of such natures in the
days of their youth; and had they been severed from those
sensual pleasures, such as eating and drinking, which, like
leaden weights, were attached to them at their birth, and which
drag them down and turn the vision of their souls upon the
things that are below—if, I say, they had been released from
these impediments and turned in the opposite direction, the
very same faculty in them would have seen the truth as keenly
as they see what their eyes are turned to now.

Very likely."

Plato doubtless had in view here his famous doctrine of
ἀνάμνησις or remembrance, which derives from Orphic mysti-
cism. The soul, he thought, has had a previous existence, and
known reality in it; so to gain wisdom in this life means, not
acquiring new knowledge, but remembering what was formerly
known but has since been forgotten. If by 'knowledge' we understand a knowledge of phenomena, the doctrine, I think, cannot
be maintained: if on the other hand we mean the power of
interpreting phenomena correctly, the power, that is, of forming
right notions, it is of real value and significance.

But the great ideas of Plato stand or fall without this doctrine.
What are these ideas? First, the aim of education is not to incul-
cate—to fill a vessel so far empty: but to 'convert'—to turn the
soul round, that our eyes may see the light. How is this conversion achieved? Elsewhere, Plato lays stress on the importance of
environment—on the need for habituating the young soul, by
means of good music and noble literature, to an atmosphere of
beauty and truth. He even goes so far as to prohibit, in the
Utopia he envisages, any but the simplest of harmonies, on the
ground that the hearing in childhood of complex and excitable
music may damage the character. It is plain that such methods
will not take us very far. Everyone will have his own ideas about
beauty and truth; and if we habituate a young mind to what *we*
may think beauty and truth, and to that alone, we are in effect
inculcating. Plato is happier in the passage before us. Conversion, he tells us, is to be achieved by a process of liberation. The

teacher's business is to release his pupils' souls from every manner of impediment; and when this has been done, their eyes will be directed, not to the things below, but to the things above.

But how do we know that this will indeed be the result? Why should the liberation of a soul imply its conversion to the highest rather than the lowest? The answer is: by reason of its nature. God the Creator, Plato tells us in an allegory, fashioned a world-soul or "created god", which thereupon fashioned the lower element in our souls. But there is also a higher element in them —the element of *nous* or reason—which stems directly from the Creator, and so is in kinship with the good. If once we can free *nous* from everything that fetters it to earth, it will seek union with the highest.

I believe that Plato's answer is the true one: that the souls of men and women are divine: and that a teacher does his pupils the best service when he helps them struggle free. Nowadays we answer differently. A child, we think, is something to be tamed; and we do our utmost, not to loosen his bonds, but to tighten them. Obedience, we are forever telling him, is the noblest of virtues: and we punish him if he revolts by some barbarous or idiotic device, for we regard his independence, not as a proof that he welcomes his birthright, but as a sort of insult to ourselves. You see the result in a world of masters and slaves, of greed and stupidity, of bloodshed and strife— and yet a world, for all that, in which decency, nobility even, are always breaking through.

If education should aim at freeing humanity, what are the bonds, then, from which we must free it? Among other things, from intellectual lethargy. No schoolmaster has begun to succeed until he has created such an atmosphere of inquiry that the acceptance of ready-made opinions would seem an intolerable indignity to every member of his class. Yet if we substitute the spirit of enquiry for the spirit of acquiescence we shall end, I may be told, by producing a nation of cynics. Nothing could be further from the truth. Most young people, given freedom of choice, instinctively choose the best—*if things have not gone too far wrong with them*. They are terribly important, those last few words. For vital as it is to banish sloth from the intellect, it is as vital, and perhaps more so, to free the soul from 'those sensual pleasures, which, like leaden weights, were attached to him at his birth, and which drag him down and turn the vision of his

soul upon the things that are below'. There is only one way in
which an older man can help a younger so to free himself;
and that is by fostering his sense of joy. Such a sense is latent, at
some stage of their development, in almost every boy and girl;
there can be few who cannot look back on moments

>   "when all the glittering earth
> Was heaven itself, when drunkards in the street
> Were like mazed kings shaking at giving birth
> To acts of war that sickle men like wheat;
> When the white clover opened Paradise
> And God lived in a cottage up the brook . . ."

But the schoolmaster, alas!, may find himself too late for this
work of liberation.

By remodelling education so as to make it a means for releas-
ing all those stores of spiritual and intellectual energy that lie
hid in a child, we shall be doing more than we could ever do
otherwise to render manifest that men and women are truly
created in the image of God. I know of no argument by which
to refute those who differ from me: who hold that evil, if freedom abounds, will triumph over good. One can be guided only
by one's faith, by the knowledge of the beauty of one's own life
in its happiest moments, and by one's joy in the nobilities that
mankind at its best has achieved.

If you have followed my argument, you will understand [I
was thinking of Fisher's letter] why the teacher should feel reverence for his pupil, instead of claiming respect. He himself
may be able to catch a glimpse of the good; how can he tell but
that the child, with a soul freer than his own, may be able, in
maturity, to contemplate the full splendour of the vision?

>   "If I could get within this changing I,
> This ever altering thing which yet persists,
> Keeping the features it is reckoned by,
> While each component atom breaks or twists,
> If, wandering past strange groups of shifting forms,
> Cells at their hidden marvels hard at work,
> Pale from much toil, or red from sudden storms,
> I might attain to where the Rulers lurk.
> If, pressing past the guards in those grey gates,
> The brain's most folded, intertwisted shell,

I might attain to that which alters fates,
The King, the supreme self, the Master Cell;
Then, on Man's earthly peak, I might behold
The unearthly self beyond, unguessed, untold."

Friday, December 12th, 1952

"But O! Iago . . ." Bentley and Craig, whose preliminary appearance at the Croydon Magistrates' Court I mentioned the other day, have been before Lord Goddard at the Old Bailey; and yesterday morning they were found guilty and sentenced. Their fate was announced by the Evening Standard in two perfectly balanced headlines about an inch and a half high:

CRAIG TO BE HELD
—BENTLEY TO HANG

Contrasts again—contrasts and fragmentation! Those boys, at that moment, in hell: and I in my office, just ready, when they brought me the paper, for my afternoon nap: and the man at his type-book in Fleet Street with a nice little problem to solve, namely, the obvious key-word being HANG (HANG: wait for three weeks, then have your neck broken), how balance it with a pithy equivalent for "being detained at Her Majesty's pleasure"?—ah! HELD does it perfectly: four letters, like HANG. Contrasts and fragmentation. But until each of us suffers with all the others who suffer, in however feeble an imitation of Christ, we shall never heal these wounds.

Craig, you will remember, is sixteen. Bentley is nineteen—just old enough, under the law, to be killed.

There is a terrible lot to be said about Craig, about his past and his future; and I have done little, these last twenty-four hours, but pray that I may find, as I know I shall not, the words to say it in. He had been brought up, through no fault of his own, in an atmosphere of guns and shooting; and if you tell me that guns and shooting are not necessarily mixed up with violence, and that you can take an innocent pleasure in expert marksmanship as such, I say yes to the second half of that sentence and bloody rot to the first. Whatever the incidentals, the purpose of a gun is to give power, material power: and in the last resort the ultimate power, the power to kill. But a desire for power, and for the means of achieving it, is Satan in our hearts—Christ knew this in the wilderness: and God in our

hearts? a desire for the opposite, a desire to be in charity with everyone. I passed a gunsmith's the other day; and I thought that, if there
is indeed a hell, then that icy, spiritless, mineral array of dead
weapons, some of them beautifully damascened—can you understand, Timothy, how much more dreadful this makes them, how
much more evocative of compassion for misguided human longings?
—I thought that, if there is indeed a hell, this was hell before my
eyes. And if such things are corrupting to anyone, what are we to
say about how they may affect a young boy—with the good in him,
his sense of adventure, waiting to receive its direction, fair or foul?

Here is a bit of the cross-examination last week. Mr Parris,
Craig's counsel, was putting questions to the boy's father:

Mr Parris said to him: "I believe that during the 1914–18 war
you served with distinction in the Army? You were a captain, were
you not?"

Mr Craig: "I was." He agreed that since then he had always
taken a great interest in firearms and that between the wars he had
a Colt revolver at home.

Mr Parris: "The boy says he remembers at the age of six or
seven being allowed to play with that revolver. . . . From an early
age he had taken a great interest in firearms?"—"He did indeed."

Mr Parris: "You encouraged the family to take an interest in
shooting as you yourself were a very good marksman?"

Mr Craig: "Well, I did teach my elder boys to shoot well at
target practice with airguns and air pistols, but not with revolvers."

Mr Parris: "Did you know it was his ambition in life to be a
gunsmith?"—"Yes, but we did not take that seriously because we
did not think it was the correct calling for him to follow."

And here is what the boy said himself:

I first saw a gun when I was about seven. It was my father's.
The first gun of any sort I had was a cap and ball pistol. I was 11,
and the gun was about 150 years old.

Since I was 11 I have had a lot of guns, about 40 or 50 of them.

How did you get them?—I swopped them and bought them off
boys at school.

Why did you do that?—I used to like them.

Did you ever take them to school?—I took them all in turn.

Why?—To show the boys.

Why?—To make myself look big.

Were there any other boys at school with guns?—Yes, about five,
maybe more.

Did you swop them with one another?—Yes.

Did you ever make a gun for yourself?—Yes, I made two ·22s.

How did your interest in weapons arise?—My father.

What was your interest in them?—I liked to find out how they worked.

Had you ever fired them?—I fired some of them, I didn't fire all of them.

Did you go with your father to a shooting range?—Yes.

After you left school and were going to work did you take a gun with you?—I took a gun to work nearly every day.

Did you have a weapon which had the barrel sawn off?—Yes.

Why was that?—To make it easier to carry.

Why did you take guns to work?—It made me feel big.

Bear in mind that "It made me feel big" and consider, meanwhile, something else. The boy was still in his swaddling-clothes, or their modern equivalent, when the second world war was upon him. Hatred and violence—that was the enveloping atmosphere of his formative years. And now don't talk to me, for God's sake, about the Germans. I know all about the Germans: I know that Hitler was a volcano of hatred, that he incinerated millions, that he gassed millions more. But what has that got to do with it, at any rate for people who attempt, however feebly, to follow Christ? It is a question of ourselves, of the hatred and violence on our own side. Not that I am concerned here to rub in the pacifist moral, particularly since, at the time, I was havering about pacifism myself. I am not concerned even to ask, as well I might, what we did, granted the limits of our non-pacifist assumption, to keep decency alive. Night after night came that terrible voice from the wireless—such a tonnage of incendiaries dropped here, such a tonnage of high explosive dropped there: so many Germans, that is to say, made live torches of, so many children and babies crushed or mangled. And where, publicly or privately, were the accents of sorrow or remorse? Where the pleas, whether from churchmen or others, for assuagement of hatred? Why, the very man who is writing this now, and who cares little, in his arrogance, about what other people think, didn't dare, when it came to it, to say that we should try to love Hitler instead of hating him: he preferred in his cowardice to water it down, that simplest and most fundamental of Christian truths, and to talk, as he told you before, not about love but about mere pity—for fear of making the climate too hot for him. All this, I shall be told, was inevitable: you must keep up morale, and if but once you inject even the tiniest *globule of Christianity into the veins of a war you have lost it already. So be it: draw your own conclusion. None of that, however, is in point. The point is an undeniable fact, a fact that stands as undeniable whatever you may think about its desirability or its inevitability or your own responsibility for it or other people's responsibility for it and so on and so on for ever and ever. The point is this. Hatred and violence, for six long years, were not merely taken for granted over a huge area of daily consciousness, they were sanctified: and will anybody but a madman be surprised if a percentage of young people, some of them handicapped in the matter of gentleness already, learned the lesson too well? Christopher Craig has done a terrible wrong to one of his fellow human beings: but society, before that, had done a terrible wrong to Christopher Craig.*

And what happened when the war was over, and Craig was now nine? The violence that had been encouraged against the Germans and the Japanese, and had become second nature in so many—think back to what I told you about the training of commandos—began to explode in the face of our own society. How possibly could it be otherwise? Everybody learns from his own case, if he isn't blind about himself, how precariously human beings are balanced: there is good, there is that misdirection of good men call evil, in each one of us: and if day after day, month after month, year after year, a young man's highest duty is to maximise the evil—to kick a German in the balls as agonisingly as possible, or to break his neck with the most expert of blows in unarmed combat—is it anything but craziness to imagine that when suddenly, at a given moment, you say "be gentle and good from now onwards" he will automatically obey you? Once let the devil into a man, and you must be prepared for the possibility that the devil will remain in him longer, and possess him more completely, than you may have bargained for. Hence the proliferation of pistols and shotguns and daggers and sandbags and knuckledusters with spikes on them: hence that whole Satanic armoury in the towns and villages, no longer of Europe, but of England.

This was the atmosphere that surrounded Christopher Craig as he approached adolescence. And now there is something else to be said, and I don't know how to say it with the charity that, in this case too, nevertheless, I suppose, one must strive for. The miasma of evil has been deliberately thickened, deliberately loaded with still more poison, by that most detestable of modern institutions, the popular press: I say deliberately and I say further with the vilest of motives, namely to increase profit. For years now, with one or two decent exceptions, the million-circulation newspapers have gone all out to titillate those sadistic and lascivious instincts that lie dormant in almost everyone; for this is the way, they think rightly or wrongly, to get more readers and down their rivals. There are things of good repute in this world: simple decencies, almost commonplace heroisms, lives devoted to the service of others. To read of them can uplift people's hearts, can make us sweeter and gentler. But you will find little or nothing about them in the popular press, for they are not considered "news"; you will find everything, on the other hand, and more than everything, about disaster and violence and infidelity and villainies. Do you doubt what I say? Well, here are the headlines—but a l l the headlines, every one of them, big and small, with none omitted—on the front page of an evening newspaper of December the third nineteen hundred and fifty-two. "Lord Goddard: 'two young ruffians' need beating"; "Woman put locks on her door; she is ordered back to her husband"; "Man jailed for 12 years"; "Lady Dunne fined: race day driving summons"; "11 Czech leaders hanged"; "Film bombs fall in lane"; "Police raid Mau Mau—Kill 7"; "24 children; father owes £2"; "War Office cut staff" (small paragraph at bottom of page); "Watch and pray—Vicar's advice" (ditto—about stealing at a Church sale of work); and "Weather—bright periods". What a filthy exhibition of paganism, what a pandering to everything beastly and sniggering, that disgusting selection!

There are no lengths, literally no lengths at all, to which these people will not go. Tube stations and underground lavatories and public hoardings were plastered over, during the war, with government warnings about the effects of venereal disease; similar advertisements were carried by the popular prints; and you might find, in one or two of the worst of them, such a rash of pornography on the very same page as might have been specially designed to send impressionable adolescents to the nearest bordello.

I tell you this, Timothy. There was an invisible defendant in the dock with Craig and Bentley last week: the press that had done its utmost to help corrupt them.

And another invisible defendant was there too, I mean the cinema. How often, when I have chanced to see a film, or I ought to say an American one, any time since the end of the war, have I been compelled to shut my eyes and stop my ears in a sick spasm of disgust and despair at the brutalities being shown on the screen or being yelled on the sound-track! Shooting, torturing, killing: cracks at a man's head with naked fist: hands pinned to a table with bayonets: galley-slaves being lashed—these are some of the horrors I have caught a first glimpse of; and once or twice when I have happened to drop in at one of those syndicated houses that pepper the suburbs, I have assisted at something beastlier still—at the encouraging shouts of little boys, mingled with laughter, as they egged on the gunman, or perhaps the moll, of their choice. This sort of thing was Craig's diet. He went to the cinema three or four times a week: always, it appears, to gangster films—"because he liked them" (I shall come to that presently). On the very night of the murder—just before he committed it—he had taken his girl to see a thing called *My Death is a Mockery*. "As he sat among respectable Sunday night picture-goers he saw enacted the underworld story of a husband and his wife who turned to smuggling when their business faced bankruptcy. The film goes on to tell of a fight in a ship between the husband and an-other smuggler. Police attack the ship. One man, a Frenchman, panics and fires. [Whether Craig panicked nobody knows: he cer-tainly fired.] The owner of the ship kills the Frenchman and throws him overboard. He is caught and hanged." Now I ask you, who is guiltier: the boy who wallows in such a muck-bath, or the tycoons who, to line their own pockets, give him the muck-bath to wallow in?

The gutter-press, the gangster film—such are the ubiquitous influ-ences to which twentieth-century youth is submitted. When they mimic, these wretched victims of our culture, what they read in the one and what they see in the other, shall we cure them of their hurts, shall we change them into citizens and gentlemen, by whipping the skin off their backs with a cat o' nine tails?

But only half the pitiful story has been told. Craig was un-doubtedly subnormal. According to his father, he was outwardly gentle; according to his headmaster, he showed no anti-social tend-encies at school, and "presented no special problems other than his low standard of attainment". He was even a model of the con-venient submissiveness that stupid pedagogues find so attractive, little understanding, if they think about such matters at all, that it may point to a fatal unfreedom; for "he showed no resentment towards corporal punishment" (corporal punishment for someone like him! They should have avoided it like the devil incarnate, which is what in fact it is) "and was perfectly amenable to school discipline". Unfreedom—that is the word. All the time, below the surface, there was a disastrous obstruction in his make-up: the fountain of his humanity was estopped, and Christopher Craig *couldn't freely develop into Christopher Craig. That he could never learn to read properly, and could hardly write at all—by the time he was sixteen all he could manage was that other phenomenon of contemporary culture, "little comics", though he could follow Enid Blyton read aloud—that he could never learn to read properly must be seen as but a localised symptom of something that inhibited the development of his whole nature. But it had a dreadful consequence: his mates, knowing his defect, "took the mickey out of" Craig at his place of employment—they taunted and made a mock of him. I do not blame them. They were products, like Craig himself, of modern paganism: they lacked imaginative sympathy, they had not learned the law of love. And so the all but inevitable happened—I say all but inevitable, for it need not have happened if his case had been correctly diagnosed and the true remedy applied. Sense of inferiority produced smouldering resentment and both of them merged into a sick passion—to express, no matter how, what was thrusting for expression. At any cost, he must "feel big". So he increasingly played with the guns he had anyhow grown familiar with: he showed them off to the mates who made a butt of him: he identified himself with celluloid toughs. Then his brother got twelve years, and his hate burst its bounds. The end was murder.*

I look into my heart: I think back over the sixty long years of my varicoloured life: I remember the base impulse that moved me here, the little indication of a lurking evil that so terrified me there: I reflect on the counterbalancing good in me that was certainly no gift of my own, and on the heritage that allowed it to come through: and I say, with such a freshness of discovery that you might think no human being had ever said it before, "There, but for the grace of God, go I".

Lord Goddard does not say or think likewise. There is a state of experience, Timothy, be it in time or be it in an unknown dimension, that we symbolise as undergoing judgment at the judgment-seat of God. Lord Goddard will come to that experience, as we all shall; and he will have to answer, as we all shall, each in his own case, for every act and every thought and every emotion that has had a place in his life. What he said and how he acted on December the eleventh in the year of our Lord nineteen hundred and fifty-two will be included in the count. I may not sit in judgment on him myself, much as I am tempted to do so: the prerogative is God's: but if God finds him guilty, I cannot help feeling, he will get more gentleness than he gave.

Yet if I may not sit in judgment on Lord Goddard, I may at any rate say this: that, in my opinion, he acted amiss. I do not refer to his performance of a Judge's function, to his administration of the law: even to mention its scrupulous fairness would be impertinent. I refer to something quite different. These were his words as he finished with Craig:

"I can only sentence you to be detained until Her Majesty's pleasure be known.

"I shall tell the Secretary of State when forwarding the recommendation to mercy in Bentley's case that in my opinion you are one of the most dangerous young criminals that have ever stood in that dock. Never have you expressed a word of sorrow or remorse for what you have done . . .

"It is quite obvious that the people of this country will not be safe if you are out of prison. I shall recommend that you be kept in confinement."

A newspaper account continues as follows:

"Immediately after the formal words of the sentence, Lord Goddard, in a harsh voice, rapped out the order to the warders: 'Take him down'."

Before Lord Goddard's judgment-seat was a naked human soul. A boy of no more than sixteen had committed a terrible crime, and was being sentenced to a terrible fate. Was harshness in order? Was contempt? Wouldn't humility have been better—the humility any wise man must feel in the presence of the mystery of suffering and sin? And shouldn't there have been respect too—yes, respect, for Craig was also a person, was also fashioned, like Lord Goddard, after the likeness of God? Then: "It is quite obvious that the people of this country will not be safe if you are out of prison." Two separate implications are clear: first, that if Lord Goddard had his way this boy of sixteen would be kept in prison for life; and, secondly, that repentance is inconceivable. But is repentance ever inconceivable? Dare anyone suggest it? "And when he cometh home, he calleth together his friends and neighbours, saying unto them, Rejoice with me; for I have found my sheep which was lost. I say unto you, that likewise joy shall be in heaven over one sinner that repenteth, more than over ninety and nine just persons, which need no repentance."

As touching repentance, there is one phrase that seems to me more terrible than any other in that whole speech of condemnation: "Never have you expressed a word of sorrow or remorse for what you have done". For surely I am doing Lord Goddard no injustice when I read it as implying that the less repentance Craig shows, the more harshness and contempt should be accorded him. I take the opposite view. The less repentance he shows, the more love should be accorded him: for the boy, unrepentant, is void of love: love is the gateway to repentance: and the surest way of evoking love in another is to give it him. Is it nonsensical, in such a case, this talk of love? No, my Lord Goddard. There is one human being, at least, who loves the boy: there is one human being, at least, who would do anything in the world to help Christopher Craig become Christopher Craig.

So let us turn from the wretched past to the future. That Craig must be kept in confinement till his spiritual fabric is repaired—so much is obvious. The public safety demands it. But what sort of confinement?—that is the question. Despite reforms here and there, despite a slow movement in public opinion, despite the efforts of a few devoted men and women, governors and wardens and suchlike, to serve humanity, our prisons, by and large, still remain what they have continuously been since revengefulness and cruelty invented them —hideous landmarks of our paganism, very symbols of our unregenerate hostility to Christ. Their evil can be expressed in six short words: there is no love in them. They should be "vales of soul-making"—but what are they? Dead wastes of frozen matter, spiritless enclosures for an army of the damned. Everything about them is military: everything about them should be humane. How dreadful to think that a man in prison is no longer a man but a cipher: no longer Paul, no longer even Jones, but 10560! For it is in prison above all that a man should be Paul: there, above all, his quintessence, his uniqueness, what makes him Paul and no one else, must be released from the corruption that has spoiled it, and helped to come through in all its fruitfulness for himself and mankind. Coldness, impersonality, harsh commands, sullen obedience—these are the very last things required: living contact is required, the awakening of spirit by spirit. A prison is icy and static: it should be warm with a climate for growth.

And if there is no love in prisons, the cause is clear. Very few really believe in the ethics of Christ when the testing-point comes: when the sense of personal outrage is so great that hatred and revengefulness rise instinctively. But the testing-point is everything. Not to believe in Christian ethics, not to follow Christian ethics, at the testing-point is not to believe in them, not to follow them, at all. Well, little though I may follow them often, as I know very well, I do believe in them truly. I believe that every human soul is worth saving, infinitely worth saving; and that the human contribution towards saving it is to sympathise—which means suffer with— and love.

More and more, as I said at the beginning of this volume, I see our attitude to crime and punishment as the point on which every- thing turns: as more fundamental, even, than our attitude to wealth and poverty, to war and peace. For here at last is revealed, quite naked, the quality of our relation to our neighbour, and through him to God.

*   *   *

It is Monday morning, I am back in the office, and I have just read the above to Sheila Hodges. "Yes," she replied, "but . . . oh, I don't know. Lord Goddard is a product of the environment every bit as much as Craig is. So is Craig's father; so are newspaper proprietors and cinema magnates and journalists and so on; so are you and I. So where can there ever be a start when everyone's in- volved in this mess, and everyone affects everyone else?" Well, of course Tiny is quite right about Lord Goddard and the rest of us. Everyone has to fight his own temptations—or to stand ready, rather, for the grace that will help him transform them—and chief among mine, as you know, is to be out of charity, not with murderers or thieves——

> *"Having been tenant long to a rich Lord,*
> *Not thriving, I resolvèd to be bold,*
> *And make a suit unto him, to afford*
> *A new small-rented lease, and cancel th'old.*
> *In heaven at his manor I him sought:*
> *They told me there, that he was lately gone*
> *About some land, which he had dearly bought*
> *Long since on earth, to take possession.*
> *I straight return'd, and knowing his great birth*
> *Sought him accordingly in great resorts;*
> *In cities, theatres, gardens, parks, and courts:*
> *At length I heard a ragged noise and mirth*
> *Of thieves and murderers: there I him espied,*
> *Who straight 'Your suit is granted', said, and died."*

——but with judges and newspaper tycoons and people generally in George Herbert's "great resorts". I do try my best, wretched best

though it may be, to avoid this old error: or rather, I try when I re-member to: and I did remember to (with perhaps a fractional measure of success) in the case of Lord Goddard this last week-end, while forgetting completely in that of newspapers and films. And now already, as a result of Tiny's goodness, I feel rather more Christian about everyone concerned, and would even like to resay, with greater sympathy and less self-righteousness, some of the things that cried out to be said. But I shall leave well alone; for it is part of my autobiographical purpose, at the contemporary level, to express day by day what I feel at the moment of writing—and later on, if I repent, to say so.

As to Tiny's "where can there ever be a start when everyone's involved in the mess, and everyone affects everyone else?" the answer is "don't calculate". The upshot, in time or eternity, is out of our hands. We know that, involved though we are, we can make a start, under grace, any moment and every moment ourselves. Nothing else should concern us. "This only is charity," says John Donne, "to do all, all that we can."

*   *   *

A week has gone by, and I've written nothing—quite unable to get on with Repton, though I had been looking forward to a long spell at home from Friday till the Monday after Christmas, with only a day at the office to interrupt it. Repton seems impossibly re-mote, with so much suffering and folly (which is of course a form of suffering) dumbly crying out for something to be done about it. The News Chronicle has been conducting a Gallup Poll on the question "What method do you think is best for dealing with persons commit-ting crimes of violence?", and the result is reported in the headline "2 out of 3 say thrash them"—with 2 out of 3, also, in favour of the cat o' nine tails rather than the birch. Mr Lewis Waddilove, a British Quaker, has been touring South Korea with an American colleague, and has issued an account of what he saw there. Sixty thousand children are separated from their parents, about half of them being in some kind of orphanage, and the rest at large. Among them are bad cases of starvation. (Try for a moment, Timothy or anyone else who may be reading this, to get behind that figure of 60,000 and those bare statements "at large" and "starvation", and imagine any single child you know, your own perhaps, wandering about hungry, hungry to the point of starvation, and alone.) Then, the sick. In several hospitals, Mr Waddilove found, there was no one to look after the patients. Refugees numbered two and a half million, of whom a quarter of a million were in desperate need. There they are, all about in the world, each in his separate place—the people with starved bodies in Korea, the people with warped minds in Great Britain: and one is a bit of them, as one sits here in a Berkshire village—and what can one do about it?

Or again: Mr R. A. Butler, the Chancellor of the Exchequer, has been making a speech. Next year, he said, talking to a body of business men, we must export more. "Competition is growing; from Germany and Japan it is getting fierce, and the more desirable the market the more salesmen from these and other countries shall we encounter there." An increase of some twenty per cent, he insisted, must be their aim. His hearers pressed for "incentives to exporters, particularly by taxation relief", and discussed "the psychological problem of bringing it home to people"—the "people" being work-people, and the "it" being that their own standard of living depended on their working harder.

The dreadful thing is this: if one says, a few days before Christmas, that Christ died on Golgotha expressly to save us from such wickedness and folly, and to show us a better way, one is considered cracked. But isn't it the plain truth? And don't we fail to realise it only because we carelessly go on with a stereotyped, hack sort of thinking, and concentrate all our attention on those fragments of reality, ourselves and our nation—people who happen to be living together in a particular place—and forget the whole? Compete to the death against people who live somewhere else, so that we may be happier, "better off", anything you like—isn't that what Mr Butler demands? And doesn't Christ demand the opposite? There are no British or Germans for Christ: there are only children of his father. Or, if you think this sentimental, though God knows why, say then that what the world is crying out for is not fiercer competition in export markets, but unification—unification for the benefit, never mind birthplace or colour or nation or race or religion, of everyone's body and soul. They are amazing, some of these churchmen: they spend hours trying to convince you that Christ's body was rapt from the tomb, but begin babbling of "practicalities" the moment you mention what brought Him there: namely His insistence on the kingship, over pagan "practicalities", of righteousness and love.

And I saw, last week, the sister of a psychopath—certified as such by several doctors, including one in high favour with the Home

Office—who had been sentenced to three years' imprisonment for passing stumer cheques, and got two more, on appeal, from a Judge who doesn't believe in psychopathy; and I talked, last week, to a charming young girl almost mad with irrational fears—clearly traceable, in part, to a mistaken upbringing; and I heard two Christians, last week, neither of them merely nominal ones, defending our imposition of collective punishment in Kenya as "realistic" and "expedient"—collective punishment, that meanest of outrages, not only against the New Covenant, but against the Old one too.

What, then, does one do about it all? I have had a curious feeling this last couple of days, as I have sat lazily reading with a quarter of my mind—a feeling that I find it almost impossible to express in language. If, I have been feeling—if apart from anything specific one may do, such as getting up a fund for Korean refugees, or visiting prisoners, or writing to the Press, or writing this letter—if, over and above things like that, one quietly longs enough, or, better, waits enough, to become "one flesh" with all suffering humanity, then perhaps . . . no, I do not quite mean what I was going to say . . . is it rather, maybe, that this is a way, or the only way, of praying, and that all prayers are answered? I do not know: but I have the desire, which brings a sort of confidence with it, to lie expectantly fallow, not so much to the thought, as to the fact, of other people's suffering. And there is another curious thing: that now, almost as if a duty had been done, I can go on with Repton. Et si verba tandem quamvis mediocria in ima nocte inveni, tibi sit gloria omnis, nomen ineffabile.

§ 9

It was not till my course of lectures on Greek philosophy was well under way that I got going with the most insistent job of all: that of discussing, by way of regular classroom "work" after those preliminary skirmishes outside, the whole universe of contemporary affairs. I doubt whether it was either chance or exactly design that led me, eager though I was, to delay a bit. I seem to have felt instinctively, rather, that the ground must be first broken up: that the gem must be shown in its setting: that eagerness to think in general must come earlier than thought about particulars: that the instinct for righteousness must be aroused before you gave it some material to work on: and that I must safeguard the boys at the outset from becoming, in the long run, as much echoes of me as they had been echoes of their environment—this is why I was so insistent, then as always, on the obligation to think independently.

Still, I had to make a start. How? I decided, in the end, on something pretty humdrum: I would set poverty, that old Pastures gadfly, as the subject for an ordinary school essay, and see what they made of it.

They made worse of it, even, than I'd expected. Ross, of course, was all right, if as lumpy in English as in Latin (but what matter, in this context? *Le style, ce n'est pas l'homme*): and Cherry, whom I'd been hammering away at for weeks—ever since that preliminary "go" at the Pastures—showed traces of thought, though not too many, I was glad to see, of mine. (Glad, and sorry of course too.) But the rest! I had been prepared for a certain amount of ignorance and complacency, but not for quite as much as I got. Cuddyfoot—one of those dull, heavy martyrs to duty that suggest married love with the light out—reiterated, with the conscientious severity of a schoolmaster fiddling with his cane, that the poor, one and all, had made their own beds of poverty, and must accordingly lie on them; and Osserton, an amiable ass who wore enormous round glasses on a pink lunar face, made a few brief remarks on the beauties of alms-giving. Innes was poetic and spiritual: there were worse things than poverty, it wasn't money that counted, and the poor, anyhow, weren't as poor as they made out. What appalled me, in case after case, was the horrible stagnancy these essays revealed; there had been no stirring of the waters, no worried attempt to arrive at bedrock. I fairly let myself go when I gave the things back. I immediately got into conflict with Cuddyfoot.

"Have you really *thought* about it?" I asked him.

"I think so, sir," he replied. (He always meticulously called me "sir", and we were never to achieve any contact.)

"Well, my dear fellow, your essay shows no sign of it, I can assure you. You talk the most awful drivel. You keep saying that poverty is the fault of the poor, but make no effort to prove it. *Can* you prove it?"

"Well—I don't know. But we pamper them too much. It's drink that does the harm."

"You're making a sweeping statement about a vast numbe of people. Have you taken any trouble to get information? D you know any *facts*? Any figures?"

"No—I can't say I do."

"Then why on earth do you make statements you can' prove?"

"I wrote what I thought. And I still think it's true."

Here Ross came tearing in, like a bloodhound that's scentec its quarry: "But you've just admitted," he cried—and ther hung about him the overpowering excitement people exhibi at football matches—"that you don't know anything abou it."

"I meant I didn't know anything special. What do *you* know about it? Do *you* know anything special?"

"That's got nothing on earth to do with it. We're discussing *now* whether you're entitled to make the statements you make in your essay. I agree with V.G. that you're not."

"Still," said Aynsworth tremulously, "I don't believe in socialism. Men weren't intended to be equal."

"And who told you that that's what socialism means?" I asked him. "Not that we were talking about socialism, any how."

"What *does* socialism mean?" drawled Holdsworth.

I must write a few sentences about Holdsworth, for he wa one of the four (with Jim Harford, Leslie Jaques and Amya Ross) who were to be in the vanguard of our struggle agains Persia, though only Amyas remained long enough to lead th stand at Thermopylae. He was a stylist, a man of grace: superb for these qualities, as a batsman, and getting by for them, bu no more, intellectually: the sort of classic that eventually scrapes through with an exhibition at Worcester or Jesus. Slow in movement and speech—though he could easily have wor the mile had he wanted to, and I believe, now I come to think of it, actually did; smilingly hooded in look; as handsome a Jaques, but more—I was going to say, surreptitiously: he hac less passion in him than Harford or Ross, and a touch, even, o scepticism. Though a leader of what we called "the movement" he never gave himself to it with quite the ultimate surrende of those other two: by reason, however, not of the tiniest dis loyalty, but partly of the hovering scepticism aforesaid, anc partly of earlier affiliations never abandoned. We became grea friends: I still have the scrap of paper, with "Good-bye, V.G. 'Sworth" on it, that he dropped in my letter-box just before leaving for the front, weeks after I'd been sacked.

David Somervell, in a privately circulated *libellum*, has described that first trio of leaders, Harford, Leslie and 'Sworth —Ross succeeded them when they left two terms later—in language I couldn't better. "All three were boys," he wrote, "with a natural charm that disarmed hostility. Good looks, good breeding, gentleness and courtesy were the very essence of them. Holdsworth had many points of sympathy with his housemaster, Hayward, and, as he told me afterwards, had 'never dared to introduce him to the *Nation*'. Jim Harford met the cold and cynical irony of —— with unwearying forbearance. There was indeed about all these boys, but most particularly about Jim Harford, a serene elevation of character, amounting to a kind of saintliness (for saintliness as distinct from virtue is commoner in youth than in maturity, as both Plato and Words-worth observed), that coloured the whole movement." Yes, saintliness: I have already used the term, you may remember, when speaking about Ross.

Within minutes of Holdsworth's question "What *does* socialism mean?" the whole place was in an uproar. Everybody was talking at once. Cuddyfoot and Ross were arguing furiously at one end of the room, 'Sworth and Harford more quietly at the other. I couldn't catch what they were saying in that din, but Jim was obviously putting a case with conviction and brio. It was the first time I had ever seen him animated. He had sat there, more often than not, looking sour and almost twisted, as if buried beyond recall in a truly terrifying introspection (he had been tormented, I learned afterwards, by just such an agony of conflict as I had experienced myself at adolescence and later: for those two elements were unusually strong in him that derive from a common source but often clash in emergence, desire for goodness on the one hand and responsiveness of sensual make-up on the other). But now he was smiling, and what had seemed twisted before suddenly straightened into serenity—and, I thought as I met his glance, into hope. Holdsworth must have been tardy in seizing the points of Jim's argument: there were worried wrinkles on his forehead, and I could see from his expression that he was drawling worse than usual.

I was determined at this stage to break in, so I shouted at the top of my voice "You really must stop; stop, stop." The din subsided immediately; but Ross, turning round for a moment from his parley with Cuddyfoot, cried out with a life-and-death sort of urgency I always found irresistible "Do *please* let me go on; I'm converting him!" Then Jim gave such a chuckle of sheer joy that I wondered how I could ever have thought him twisted.

I had got so excited myself that I could hardly keep quiet: but I let Ross have his say. He was on his feet now, leaning against the hot-water pipes over by the window and half-turned towards Cuddyfoot. He talked very deliberately and very emphatically, saying every now and again, in an imploring tone of voice, "Don't you *see*, my dear fellow? Surely you *must* see?" As he worked himself up to a climax his forehead seemed to broaden and grow lower, his eyes to sink in still more deeply behind that overhanging mass, and his mouth, always unshapely, to become gigantic: hideously ugly he looked, and quite noble.

When he had finished, after I suppose a full quarter of an hour, I took over from him. They wanted to know what socialism *meant*? All right: never mind for the moment whether it was folly or heavenly wisdom, this is what it meant. Poverty, it said—not destitution, but the ordinary poverty of the ordinary working man—was definitely part of our whole social system: it might be a good thing or it might be a bad thing, but so long as industry was run as at present a class of people would always exist who, in comparison with ourselves and those like us, must be called poverty-stricken. A particular individual might have sunk into poverty through some fault of his own: another might have raised himself by luck or his own exertions to comfort or wealth. But, individuals apart, the class remained: and would inevitably remain until we made a fundamental alteration in our whole way of running things.

Then I begged them to try and put themselves in these other people's shoes: to imagine themselves turning a handle from morning till night, with neither money nor leisure to engage in the hundred-and-one activities, jolly or serious, that made our own life so attractive. Of course we might find, on examination, that a class of some such kind must exist in the nature of things: that any change would be a change for the worse in this best of all possible worlds. Many reasonable people thought so. Or we might find that there was a better way out than the one socialism proposed—and that I'd explain in some detail another time. But could we, dared we as decent human beings, condemn great masses of the human race to such misery without at any rate investigating the matter?

But I begged them, most of all, to remember what I'd said, in that lecture on the Cave, about thinking independently. Each of us had been given a brain so that each of us might furnish a tittle to the grand alphabet of truth; and if we simply accepted the ideas that our parents had held before us, or that the majority held now, or that our form-master was expounding at this moment, we were neglecting an instrument that had been entrusted to our care for the good of humanity. Education didn't mean the "getting up" of a lot of mouldy texts: it meant the free development of everybody's personality for the benefit of everybody else's.

As I spoke I could see them responding, each in his own special way. Ross could hardly keep still: he saw everything so clearly that he wanted to get on with it at once, and to turn the monologue into a duet. Jim was smiling serenely; the wrinkles multiplied on Holdsworth's forehead, but when I had finished he drawled out a "yes". Cuddyfoot alone seemed unaffected. Standing still in that moment of quiet—I had been pacing up and down—I felt more deeply than ever before how very generous these boys were. What I had taken for vicious snobbism in their essays was but thoughtlessness; they were reaching out, nearly all, for the good, and it was only because they were ignorant of undeniable facts, and hadn't learned how to think, that their "good" was so questionable. For instance: Their ambient climate had been such as to imbue them with the idea that socialism was vile: they hated vileness: so they hated socialism. Well, my job was to give them facts and make them think: and then what a crowd they would be!

All this was, of course, far too simple. But, call me Rousseauite if you will, or anything even nastier you can think up, I am still persuaded that my theory and practice were fundamentally sound.

Uproar was just beginning again when the wretched bell

H

clanged a change-over. "It's perfectly sickening," I said.
"Directly one gets going one has to stop. Who are you going
to now?"

"The old Auk," replied Jim, with a chuckle like the one he'd
greeted Ross with. Burd, now doing classics and English with
the Lower Sixth, still took history with the Upper.

"Balls about Theodoric," added Holdsworth. "We've been
doing Theodoric ever since I came into the form. He takes a
term over a year."

"I say," interjected Amyas, turning round towards Holdsworth, "d'you know? He caught Bobby Johnstone writing
letters the other day. He said it was the greatest blow he'd ever
had."

"Yes, isn't it marvellous? Nobody's done anything else with
him for years."

I began a rather feeble remonstrance. After all, Burd was an
awfully decent old thing—now wasn't he?—and quite the most
elegant classicist, except Gilbert Murray, I'd ever come across.
It was a beastly shame to rag him. But Amyas ruined the effect
of my sermon by exploding with laughter, and bellowing out,
in his rough, forthright manner, "My dear man, don't be
absurd; you're getting pompous!" This was more than I could
bear; so I desisted, and went home.

Thus began, in October 1916, the second or classroom phase
of our "movement" at Repton. Political and sociological dis-
cussions were soon competing with my lectures on Plato for
tops, as the boys called it, in their franchise: and before long
had won hands down. Conservatism, Liberalism, Socialism,
the League of Nations, Liberty of Opinion, Censorships,
Imperialism, the White Man's Burden, Hypocrisy, Patriotism,
Internationalism—these were the subjects we canvassed, day
after day and from a dozen points of view ("dozen" is the
word: there were a dozen in class); and I wish I could give
you an almost visual impression, to match my own, of what,
in that atmosphere of passionate sincerity and fierce argu-
mentativeness on the boys' side and of elation on mine,
seemed indeed to be unrolling before my eyes. These boys were
beginning to think: and their intellectual life, as a result, was
developing with the joyful inevitability of physical life in the
world's springtime. Freshly, spontaneously, without a trace of
affectation or self-consciousness, they were leaping to en-

compass those great principles that they recognised as akin to their own nature; and I have seen boy after boy, as he realised, for example, the meaning of liberty, and got a first rapid glimpse of the wide country this realisation opens up, experiencing an upsurge of happiness comparable only to the catch of breath with which we look on a beautiful vista, or hear tell of fair heroisms and generosities. A miracle was happening, only it wasn't a miracle, all men having the spark: average school-boys were rediscovering for themselves, centuries later and far from Greece or Judaea, the simplicities taught by Plato and Christ.

The purpose of education, by the same token, became an increasingly favourite topic: Livy was forgotten, and those parts of the Republic that illumine educational problems, and that had already been touched upon briefly, took up a lot of our attention. The Cave was very popular, and presently appeared, in coloured chalks, on the wall. Indeed Plato and Catullus were the only Greeks or Romans we thought worth bothering about the latter part of this term. I made a feint at getting them to read a remote moth-eaten comedy by Plautus, but they refused to prepare it, and I didn't blame them. They got their scholarships, as I've mentioned, all the same.

It was now too, I think, that the craze for τόποι* sprang up. They are as difficult for me to explain, away from that atmosphere, as "the stunts" will be later. τόπος, or in Latin *locus*, means literally "place", but is used in rhetoric to signify "commonplace": a stock passage, general idea or hack argument, applicable to many different subjects, that the orator can always turn on at a suitable moment. Well, our τόποι (which started, I suppose, as τόποι proper—during our hilarious Latin Prose sessions) eased the labour, not of rhetoric, but of social enquiry. They were rather like Wagnerian leitmotivs, reinforcing, or binding together, the multiple fabric of the political drama we were living, and giving it unity. Wotan's Spear or Siegfried's Sword would leap in, confident and irresistible: or Valhallah would flood our room with its solemnity: or a phrase from the Spring Song, echoing through, would remind us of Siegmund and Sieglinde. The "Duty of Independent Thought" τόπος, to be fanciful about it, was Siegfried's Sword: the "Kingdom of Heaven on Earth" τόπος, Valhalla: and the "Common

* tŏpoi

Humanity" or "Universal Sympathy" τόπος Siegmund's and
Sieglinde's *Lenzlied*. The fag end of the term I'm talking about,
and the whole of the following one, were dominated by the "common humanity" τόπος. The τόποι were sometimes unspoken,
but present in our consciousness just the same: were sometimes
enunciated by me: more frequently, were launched into a discussion by one or several of the boys. There was often a conflict
of opinion, and rich argument, as to whether some particular
τόπος was appropriate or not. A boy, say, would defend British
rule in India on the ground that, while he believed in the
"self-government" τόπος, you could hardly apply it to coloured
men: whereupon someone would cry out "common humanity
τόπος": but another would object, because—well, because you
couldn't apply the "common humanity" τόπος, as between
white men and coloured men, any more than you could apply
the self-government one. Then the argument would begin, and
dart about across the whole surface of the globe and up to
heaven.

My own favourite τόπος, and I think Amyas's too, was the
"right of everyone to free development" τόπος. But nobody
was more adroit at the manipulation of τόποι as a whole, or
at finding happy but unexpected places for this one or that,
than 'Sworth.

(The τόποι might almost have been given numbers to ensure
brevity, as jokes are, according to Max Schuster, at sessions
of the Gag-writers' Association of Hollywood. When the port
has been brought on (or if not port, the equivalent) at the
annual banquets of this body, it is customary for the members to
rise one by one, and say "Number 7" or "Number 101" or any
other sort of number that may appeal to the individual's fancy:
everybody immediately translates in his head, and laughter
ensues. A candidate for membership is given a list of these
numbers, and an exposé of their meanings: and when everyone else has performed he has to rise and do likewise—and
is duly elected. Such a candidate recently rose and said
"Number 66": but there was dead silence. He turned to the
Chairman, and asked "Why hasn't anybody laughed? Haven't
I done what you said?" "Yes," replied the Chairman, "but
you told it so badly.")

As each new τόπος established itself it was chalked on
the wall: at first to left or right of the Cave, and later, when

these spaces got full up, in any odd corner we could find.
Of course, everybody didn't have to believe in a τόπος for it
to be considered chalkable: that would have contravened the
"duty of independent thought" τόπος: to be chalkable, rather,
it must have established itself, not in the sense of being accepted
by everyone, but in the sense of being thought worthy by
everyone of serious consideration. When the Auk took over
again, after I'd been sacked, one of the first things he did was
to abolish Cave and τόποι by whitewash: I was upset about
this: I thought it a poor return for my attempt, however feeble,
to save him from the inconvenience of being ragged. But then
he probably didn't know about that.

I have always liked chalking things on walls, and I sometimes
wonder what the psycho-analysts would make of it. My room
at Henrietta Street is decorated in this way with all sorts of
devices, though pictures of Moses, in various states and situa-
tions, predominate. I don't know whether or not I shall tell
you about Moses. Probably not: but, if I decide to, I shall wait
till I'm dealing with 1919, for it was then that he started—on a
beam up in Camden Hill Square: now, Peter Ibbetsonishly,
he's many billions of years old. Anyhow, you can see him
whenever you like in the Henrietta Street office, scootering,
gondoling or flying:

Moses plain

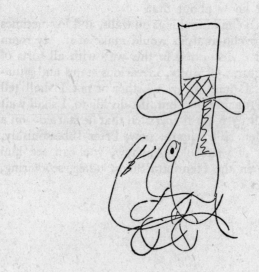

Moses tipsy

Moses in his little smoking-jacket

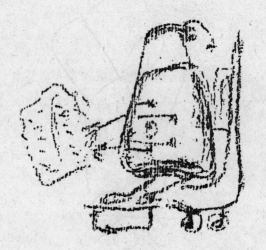

Moses natty for Christmas

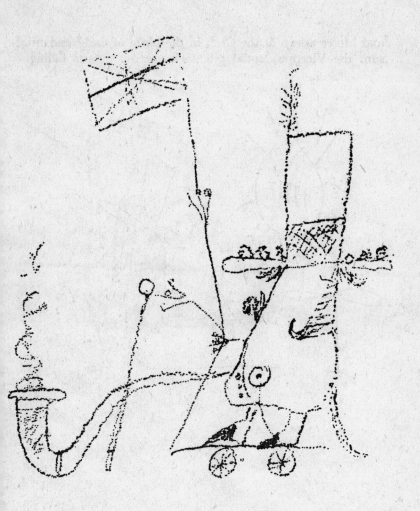

and Moses asleep at the Club in the blaze of the Presidential
sun: the Vicepresidential pitchfork nearby: manna falling

. . . and minor members of American firms, who've never visited me before, often turn up and beg for an interview, though I deduce pretty soon it's the Colonel they're so anxious to see. For they gaze about vaguely: at the dust and the good plain furniture and the holes in my carpet—but particularly at Moses: and when I enquire what I may be permitted to do for them they mutter something about "having been advised to see your room" and then hurriedly excuse themselves. Occasionally, as they say good-bye, they mention Dickens. (Martin Secker's office, it occurs to me, must have been rather like mine: he was much irritated by the success of *Jew Süss*, which obliged him to put in a telephone.) These last few months, however, they've been wasting their time; for recently, when I was in America, the staff did an Auk on me, from motives of hygiene and antisepsis. A lot of precious personalia have gone for ever, but Moses is reappearing in considerable numbers.

But I'd better stop now about Moses and get back to my lambs, otherwise the critics, who'll unfortunately have to see this, will accuse me of being garrulous. (And why write a letter at all if you're not going to be garrulous? That's the whole point of one. What some of these voters—have you ever read Gwyn Thomas?—don't seem able to get into their heads is that this really *is* a letter.) Not that I have very much more to tell you about classroom proceedings in the autumn of 1916. One discussion, though, stands out in my memory with peculiar sharpness. It arose from an essay on the following theme:

"If (a) you knew, beyond question, that the universe was coming to an end tomorrow morning: (b) you also knew, beyond question, that nothing would follow—no hereafter for anybody or anything: (c) you could do something tonight that you'd always thought wrong—lie, for instance: (d) you would make your own life more pleasurable by doing it, and nobody else's less pleasurable—would you do it or not?"

This is the best subject I know for getting down to ethical bedrock. Fisher, however, thought otherwise: he was quite angry with me, I learned afterwards, for casting doubt, by the mere hypothesis of everything ending and no hereafter, on a fundamental of Christianity. To do so, of course, was half the point, or one of the innumerable points. Was the sanction of morality the existence of God? Was it personal survival? Was it both? Was morality, on the other hand, sanctionless—αὐτὸ καθ᾽ αὑτό? Or was the hypothesis essentially unthinkable, and the whole enquiry quite meaningless? These were some of the questions that arose; and the boys revealed willy nilly, by the way they answered them, not merely the size of their brains but the essence of their characters. Punishments and rewards, I was happy to note—in the hypothetically abolished hereafter—didn't figure at all prominently in these essays: so I was confirmed in my estimate of young human nature: and the boys, or the majority of them, showed themselves far better moralists than the Prince, or local Emperor, of a great Church who unburdened himself in my presence a few months ago. I had told him I didn't believe in Hell. "Extraordinary!" he exclaimed. "But don't you try to behave decently?" I assured him I did my best. "It beats me!" he replied (though a Prince, he had a happy common touch in his talk). "If I didn't believe in Hell I should go on the razzle!" I expounded, the same evening, a Cabbalistic doctrine to the effect that God has placed a particle of the Godhead in every human soul. "I think that man Gollancz must be cracked," he told a friend of mine later. "He talks about God cutting himself up into little bits!"

§ 10

All this time I was getting to know David Somervell. There was something casual, almost taken for granted, about the way in which our acquaintance became friendship: as if we knew it must happen, and didn't mind how or when. What made me go round, I think, more and more often to his long, low, cretonne-armchaired, dimly-lighted, rather Oxfordish room that autumn, taking time off from the Gorringes, was that he played the piano—with delightful badness: for amateur music-making in the home, if it's bad enough but not too bad, can indeed be more delightful, for a certain mood, than the finest concert-hall performances imaginable. The reason, I suppose, is that the king has taken his crown off, and sits talking familiary like one of ourselves. I had an example of amateur delightfulness this spring. I must have heard *Fidelio* a couple of dozen times

during the last half-century, and every now and again, as on
that occasion in Paris I told you of, the performance has been
superb. Lotte Lehmann, Richard Mayr, Tauber, the Vienna
Philharmonic Orchestra—could I hope for anything like it
again? Well, not far from here, at a little place on the other side
of the Bath road called Hermitage, there is a music-camp, where
amateurs, with a sprinkling of professionals, foregather for the
various holidays and live in tents round a barn: the barn being
for their music-making. They must have been going a full
quarter of a century, but had never attempted an opera till
they decided, this spring, to put on *Fidelio*. They turned the barn
into a tiny theatre, holding about a hundred: they engaged a
professional singer: for the rest, they made do with their own
resources. The performance wasn't up to much, really, and one
could have picked a hundred holes in it if one had started being
critical: but as I sat in the same room there with Marcellina
and Jaquino and Leonora and Florestan, as I watched the
prisoners fumbling their way about almost on top of me, I was
moved by an emotion so nearly intolerable that I began to
doubt whether I could see the thing through. It was as if one
were suddenly all mixed up with fidelity and freedom and
hope, and not merely watching symbols of them from the
outside.

David's piano-playing didn't give me that sort of emotion,
but it pleased me greatly. He made no fuss about his deficien-
cies, of which he was well aware, but simply played when I
asked him to: just as now and again, to help a colleague, he
would do Latin with a class that knew a lot more about it than
he did. For Lord God Almighty was humble: not Uriah
Eepishly, nor yet from blindness to his own qualities, but in
the sense of taking himself, rough and smooth, for what he was.
The smooth far outweighed the rough. He had it in him, I
suspect, to be as great a historian as anyone of his time, but
though he has written a number of books, one at least of them
remarkable, he has never won fame, except perhaps for his
abridgment of Toynbee. Fame, popular or professional, is a
matter of touch and go, as I know very well from my experience
as a publisher: time and again I have seen it won by a series of
lucky chances, time and again I have seen it fail to be won
because the chances haven't materialised. The idea that
everyone's quality must be recognised sooner or later seems to

me nonsensical: but I can't prove it, for if I tried to by producing exhibits I should be making them famous, and so belying myself. David, anyhow, deliberately forfeited any chances that might have come his way; for he was a historian second and a schoolmaster first—a man dedicated utterly, but without bother or self-consciousness, to the vocation of schoolmastering.

He had deep stores of affection, particularly for the young; and a certain plainness and lack of exuberance withal, in style of living and writing and thinking, that made him as good a complement, or foil, as you could imagine to an *exalté* like me. Looking back, I feel great gratitude for the way he coped with, or rather maybe just accepted, my idiosyncrasies. Temperamentally, after all, we were at opposite ends of the pole. I must have jarred on him often: but never once did he express the smallest irritation, either to me personally or, I am certain, to others, about anything, however unsympathetic, I said or did. His loyalty indeed was flawless—and so was his courage: I had nothing to lose by my doggedness but he had almost everything, for, round about thirty at the time, he was jeopardising an assured status in the only profession he cared for. And yet he never faltered: if I cannot pretend that he was more tenacious than I was, he was certainly not less so. But did he quite realise, I once or twice asked myself, what he was at—in respect, I mean, not of jeopardising his position (he would never have considered this), but of turning the place upside down? Did he look upon it all, in his plain way, as rather more ordinary than it was? I occasionally thought that a certain innocence, a certain taking of the right thing for granted, misled him a little here. And yet—his worldly wisdom was a good deal greater than mine.

David was thoroughly alive to current happenings in the Upper Sixth, for he had an excellent nose; and one night, towards the end of that preludial autumn, we fell to discussing matters seriously. While keeping the thing going in the Upper Sixth just as it was, couldn't we, we asked ourselves, broaden it and carry it a stage further? The existing procedure had serious limitations. There was that wretched bell, for instance, which not only decapitated an argument at the end of every hour, but had cramped and hurried us all from the outset. One wanted more space to manoeuvre in. Then, why only the Upper Sixth? Why not everybody old enough to get some value out of the proceedings? And there was the question of formality, continuity, all the rest of it. A boisterous go-as-you-please, a gusty wind that sent cobwebs aflying, was the essence of that Upper Sixth climate. This was all very well, indeed as good as it could be: and yet wasn't there room, also, for something a little more like, not perhaps an Oxford lecture-room, but say rather the best sort of contact of an undergraduate with his tutor? And finally, what about personnel? I also was all very well, and perhaps as good as I could be: but there was David; there was Allan Gorringe; perhaps there were others who could take a hand. Let us have as much variety as possible, at the emitting as well as at the receiving end. It was not good, in anybody's interest, for Gollancz to be alone.

So we thought up the Civics class. Now don't let there be any mistake about what "Civics" meant. There had been a Civics class at Clifton at least ten years before, and the thing was currently common in America. But Civics had always meant, so far as I am aware, the study of various *institutions* and the like—cabinet government, local government, parliamentary procedure, revenue and taxation, administration and justice, a little elementary law, and so on. Knowledge of such matters is of course very valuable, and the ordinary boy's ignorance of them is, or was, grotesque. But we hadn't this sort of thing in mind at all, or not anyhow for the period of breaking up the ground: later on, when the boys were afire, they would have the *sitzfleisch* (a mixed metaphor, I suppose) to tackle (another one) such banausic necessities. But meanwhile other issues were far more important, namely the great ideas, the great movements that were battling everywhere around: imperialism of this sort and that; militarism and a League of Nations; capitalism and socialism; competition and co-operation; etcetera. They were more important for two reasons. They were more important in their own right: these, and not those, would shape the future of the world. And they were more important educationally: they would engage the citadel of a boy's being, strike him as akin and immediate, in a way those others never could, and arouse that enthusiasm for knowledge, that passion for finding reasonable answers to ultimate questions, which is more precious even, in the case of anyone still growing, than

knowledge itself. Most crucial of all: immanent always as the
real substance, or vital content, of the argument would be the
summa summarum, religion, morality, ethics. So it was on topics
such as these that we would concentrate, dealing with them
sometimes in the abstract, and sometimes by way of concrete
example from contemporary affairs; but we should also find a
place, we envisaged, for such a survey of current events, or
particularly important ones—a survey direct and for its own
sake—as would marshal all available facts, relate them to one
another, and thus expose history in the making. For the rest,
we would be as reverential to these young minds as we "knew
how": we wouldn't conceal our own opinions, but would be
as scrupulous and sympathetic as possible in the exposition
of conflicting ones: and if we should overweight the balance,
as well we might, other influences would restore it—with a
vengeance.

Such was to be the substance of the Civics class, as we
planned it that evening in Somervell's room. The right
manner, the best way of running it, seemed equally clear. We
wanted no jamboree, no dropping in and out. The class should
be voluntary; but once a boy had sent his name up (and been
accepted) he should be obliged to attend for at least a whole
term. Leisure would have to be sacrificed, for we should choose
a half-holiday for the weekly session; and the boys should sit,
not in armchairs by a fire, but at desks in a classroom. They
must take the thing seriously, or not at all.

We went down to see Fisher. David was bland, I was
eloquent. Quite a series of interviews followed. In the end, just
as Christmas was looming, Fisher laughingly agreed.

CHAPTER V

REPTON (CONTINUED)

§1

IF YOU ARE TO understand how our drama developed from the beginning of 1917, when the Civics class came into being after the Christmas holidays, to the spring of 1918, when I was sacked, I must write you a little history (world history—not Repton history) of those months. You may be tempted to skip it: if you do, what comes later really will be unintelligible to you. Besides, there is an eternal lesson in these events.

This, then, was a time of peril for England, in the immediate military sense, of a sort more desperate than any that had faced her since Germany had been halted in 1914. The year 1916 had closed in gloom for the Entente. The simultaneous offensive on all fronts, planned a year before, had misfired, the French army was at a low ebb and the Russian still lower, and the Somme had failed to produce visible results in any way proportional to its cost. But all this was but a prelude to the disasters of 1917—Ypres, Passchendaele, the submarines.

Ypres. We attacked in July; and when, three months later, our offensive ended at Passchendaele, we were no nearer our objective, or very little, of driving the Germans from their submarine bases in Belgium. Our casualties numbered four hundred thousand; and great companies of men, already mutilated and dying, were literally drowned in the mud.

As to the submarines, they cost us nearly a million tons of shipping in April alone: sixty per cent of this was British: and it was clear that such a ratio of loss must ultimately starve us into surrender. We had food, at one moment, for no more than six weeks.

By the beginning of 1918 the submarine menace had been checked, though not ended; but owing to Russia's elimination, a diffusion of effort, and our vast casualties, the numerical balance, formerly in our favour, had now been reversed. America, however, was on the move: for Germany, it was that

spring or never: so she launched, late in March, a stupendous
and final offensive. We were now very close to defeat, and
it was while we were poised on its razor-edge that I left
Repton.

Keep in mind, then, two crucial facts about the year and
four months I shall be dealing with in this chapter: the slaughter
was—as I've told you; and we were at grips with defeat.
Keep in mind, too, something else, something that bears on my
own thought and action. We had established a close blockade
of the Central Powers; and by 1918 three quarters of a million
Germans—German civilians, I mean, women and children
and the old and the ailing, not soldiers—were dead as a result
of it, for rations had dropped to a third of what was needed for
health. Eighty per cent of public schoolchildren were suffering
from rickets, and mortality from tuberculosis in Prussia was
two and a half times as high as in 1914. They were burying the
dead in mass-graves, for lack of wood: they were wrapping the
infants in newspaper, for lack of cotton. If Englishmen were
dreadfully anxious, Germans were in despair.

And now consider the peace aspect of the war, as we can
call it for short.

Two conflicts were rapidly developing during the period in
question: first, between the "settlement by negotiation" men
and the "knock-out-blow" men; and, second, between the
League of Nations men and the Catoites—the advocates of a
Carthaginian peace. These conflicts were proceeding, in greater
or lesser degree, in most of the belligerent countries, if not in
all: and of course they largely coincided. But not, as we shall
see, wholly. Let us take them in order—"settlement by negotiation" first.

(I) In December 1916, just before our period opens, Woodrow Wilson, on his re-election to the Presidency of the United
States, had offered mediation to the belligerents, inviting them
to state their conditions of peace. Germany, who, a few days
before, had addressed a note to the neutrals announcing "propositions" for a permanent ending of European strife (she may
have wanted to treat while she felt strong enough to dictate
terms), proposed, in reply, direct negotiation between the
belligerents in a neutral country. The Allies denounced this
proposal as a manoeuvre to sow discord among them: declared
that to sit down with an undefeated Germany in total ignorance

of her "propositions" would be "placing their heads in a noose": and demanded, first, expiation for war-crimes and indemnity for destruction to the full, and, second, reduction of German territory—as well as dismemberment of Austria by the liberation of Czechs, Serbs and the rest. Wilson next invited Germany to define more exactly her conditions of peace; and was now informed that his proposed mediation could not be accepted, on the ground that to do so might give the impression that her previous offer had been inspired by fear. Wilson, however, continued to work for a settlement by negotiation: said in January 1917 that "only a peace between equals could endure": and begged Bernstorff, the German Ambassador, to get a statement of peace terms communicated to Washington, so that a conference might again be proposed. But nothing came of this, for Germany had now decided to stake everything on an unrestricted U-boat campaign, and thought she could win in five months. Her decision was communicated to Wilson, who declared war on April 6th.

Charles, who had succeeded Francis Joseph as Emperor of Austria and saw a threat to the Austrian monarchy in Allied appeals to Czechs and Slavs, now took a hand at settlement by negotiation. He proposed that Germany should cede Alsace to France and receive Poland in compensation: Austria to indemnify herself in Rumania. This didn't suit the military commanders in Berlin, who wanted, on the contrary, to deprive France of the Briey mines and to force Belgium into a military and economic union with Germany. Charles, nevertheless, sent an autograph letter to Poincaré on May 24th, expressing his willingness to support "the just claims of France to Alsace-Lorraine": to work for the re-establishment of Belgium and Serbia as sovereign States: to grant Belgium an indemnity: and to give Serbia an outlet on the Adriatic. The Allies merely observed that no mention had been made of more territory for Italy.

The Russian Revolution broke out in March; and the Bolsheviks, who were not included in the Provisional Government, proclaimed that Russia sought no gains from the war and was ready to conclude peace on the basis of "no annexations and no indemnities". The phrase thundered through the world. Next, a Dutchman proposed that socialists from the various countries should meet at Stockholm, for the purpose

of compelling the belligerents to clarify their war-aims. Arthur
Henderson, leader of the Labour Party and a member of the
War Cabinet, supported this proposal, and so, overwhelmingly,
did European socialists; but the Allied Governments, at a
meeting on May 28th, rejected the whole idea of it, and refused
passports to British and French delegates.

Things were now becoming desperate for Germany; and in
July 1917 a motion was passed in the Reichstag demanding
peace by negotiation, without territorial acquisitions or financial or economic restraints. The resolution emphasised, however, Germany's determination to fight on for so long as "the
enemy Governments threatened her with conquest and oppression." Bethmann, attacked by the majority, resigned, and
Michaelis, who succeeded him, accepted the resolution "as I
understand it"—a qualification that might mean anything.

The Pope now took a hand, begging the belligerents to
negotiate on the basis of arbitration, reparation, reciprocal
restitution, and freedom of the seas. The Allies as a body sent
no reply. Wilson refused. As for Britain—she could enter into a
parley, she stated, only after an unequivocal declaration that
Belgium would be restored. Germany demanded that Belgium
should grant her the right to undertake commercial ventures,
and should preserve the separation of Flanders. So the papal
initiative came to nothing.

The New Year of 1918 was now approaching; and the conflict—between the "peace by negotiation" men and the "knock-
out-blow" men—became sharper. In Germany, Hertling,
pacific leader of the Bavarian Catholics, had been appointed
Chancellor, but was powerless against Tirpitz and Ludendorff.
In France Clemenceau, becoming President of the Council, had
exclaimed "*La guerre, rien que la guerre*" in the Chamber. But in
England there was a startling development. Lord Lansdowne
—ex-Secretary of State for War, ex-Foreign Secretary, ex-leader
of the Tories in the House of Lords, ex-member of Mr. Asquith's
War Cabinet—published a letter in the highly bourgeois *Daily
Telegraph* (the *Times* having refused it) that suddenly crystal-
lised things out. Warning everyone that a prolongation of the
war would mean ruin for the whole civilised world, he called
for a precise and detailed statement of Allied peace-terms. His
vision extended, perhaps, a little further than 1919.

(II) I want to break in now, as at December 1917, on this

account of the one conflict, and, going back a bit, to consider
the other: namely, that between the League of Nations men
and the Catoites.

The idea of obviating war by some mechanism of international government had long been in the air, and even on
paper, when Woodrow Wilson, in that same message of
December 18th 1916, expressed the hope that a League of
Nations might be instituted as part of a durable peace-settle-
ment. The thing was now, not merely in pamphlets and books,
but on the agenda: and the peace aspect of the war, during the
whole period I am discussing, was everywhere dominated by it.
I said earlier, you will recollect, that the two conflicts "partly
coincided, but not wholly". They ought to have wholly
coincided. One of the roots of the matter is to be found in those
words of Woodrow Wilson—"only a peace between equals
can endure". If you refuse to negotiate at any stage of the
conflict, if you insist on imposing terms after a knock-out,
it is fantastic to imagine that, whatever you may have said
in advance, your League, when you get it, can be anything
more than an instrument, initially at least, for preserving the
new *status quo*: a *status quo* which, having been imposed after
a knock-out, will be resented, if for that alone, by your late
enemies. And though your League may contain provisions for
the peaceful settlement of disputes, the very honeycombing of
the *status quo* with the potentiality of such disputes, owing to the
imposition of peace-terms that will necessarily have impinged as
unjust, will mean that, if and when your late enemies have come
in, you will have a territory for demands and refusals—for internal manoeuvring, for the formation of new alignments—instead
of an orderly instrument for adapting present arrangements to
changing circumstances. The thing has been poisoned from the
start. There's nothing genuinely new about it—it's simply a
new form of power politics. For it to be genuinely new a new
spirit must have been there in advance—the settlement coincid-
ent with the formation of your League must have been, as far
as possible, an agreed one.

All this was thoroughly understood by the out and out anti-
Leaguers. They wanted neither League nor settlement by
agreement. They thought both unpatriotic—the first, as putting
tabs on their country, the second, as depriving their country
of some of the power it might win. By the same token, there was

the question of security: put their trust in new-fangled inanities, instead of powder and shot? Their Catoism was consistent—in respect of the war, in respect of the settlement, in respect of the League: crush the Hun was their motto, and when you've crushed him keep him crushed. *Mutatis*, in the various countries, *mutandis*.

But there were Catoites of a sort who were also Leaguers of a sort. They wanted a Carthaginian peace—very much so; but then the League wasn't a bad idea either. Lloyd George was typical of the half-and-halfers. It was Lloyd George who, replying to Woodrow Wilson in January 1917, expressed himself as a devotee of the new concept: and it was Lloyd George who, when all was over, said to Riddell "The truth is, we have got our way. We have got most of the things we set out to get. . . . The German navy has been handed over, the German merchant shipping has been handed over, and the German colonies have been given up. One of our chief trade competitors has been most seriously crippled, and our Allies are about to become her biggest creditors. This is no small achievement." No small achievement indeed: out of it came the whips of Dachau and the gas-chambers of Buchenwald. Not that Lloyd George was a real *jusqu'auboutiste*, any more than he was a real anti-Leaguer (or pro-Leaguer): you might have called him, oxymoronly, a moderate *jusqu'auboutiste*. Woodrow Wilson, on the other hand, cared for nothing but the League; and Clemenceau, that grim old Hebrew prophet with no atom of Christianity about him—his defence of Dreyfus had been a matter of justice, not of love—cared for nothing but finishing the Boches.

How shall I give you any idea of the passionate hopes that were centred on the League of Nations? We were young then: I don't mean only those of us who were young in age—I mean the world was young, blessedly young in such matters. There was no touch, among real League men, of the shoulder-shrugging or outright cynicism with which the concept of Uno was approached towards the end of the second world war. The power of veto is like a great angry sun that illumines the difference. People were saying, when the plans for Uno were drawn up, that here at last was something sound and realistic: if it didn't go as far as the League, it would do more. We should have scorned such a pettifogging mentality in 1917. We wanted a new start, we wanted the spring: and the very essence of that spring was to be the substitution of majority decisions for the international anarchy in which your own "vital interests" were always sacred. The idea of the League was a moral, a religious idea. We believed that nations could learn to live in community, as individuals had been learning; and faced with the mud of Passchendaele, and German starvation, and all the hatred and lying that so appalled us, we were determined to get on with the job. It wasn't the old "soundness" and "realism" in a prettified form we were after: it was goodness. You must get that clearly in your head, if you are to understand anything of what follows.

(III) I have spoken of two conflicts, but there were really three. Self-determination—the principle that no people should be under a rule that it thinks of as alien—was another of the great ideas that dominated this period; and the third conflict was not so much between those who proclaimed a belief in it and those who didn't—for almost everyone proclaimed a belief in it—as between those who did really believe in it, and would have wished to apply it whatever their own "vital interests", and those who took it up as a catchword, with the idea of applying it rigorously when it suited their purpose, and not at all when it didn't. I cannot discuss here whether self-determination, in all cases, is quite as progressive as some people thought: suffice it to say that genuine self-determinationists were inspired by a truly freedom-loving and internationalist spirit, whereas nothing at all was to be said for the bogus or unilateral ones. The "no annexations" men, too, were on the side of the angels —except when, facing defeat, they were suddenly anxious to avoid annexations in their own disfavour.

(IV) These several conflicts came rapidly to a head in the early months of 1918.

The Governmental exchanges can be quickly recorded. Lloyd George said on January 5th that England would support France to the death in its demand for a "reconsideration of the great wrong of 1871", and outlined three indispensable conditions for peace: restoration of the sanctity of treaties; a territorial re-arrangement of Europe, based on the right of self-determination; and the establishment of an international organisation to limit the burden of armaments and lessen the probability of war.

Three days later President Wilson, in a speech to Congress, expounded his Fourteen Points. Apart from territorial questions, these demanded (a) open diplomacy, (b) freedom of the seas, (c) removal of economic barriers, (d) reduction of armaments, (e) colonial adjustments, with native interests as one of the criteria, and (f) a League of Nations.

Germany, replying to Lloyd George, declared that in view of the military situation she was not in a position to negotiate on the bases laid down by him, and demanded their revision: letting it be clearly understood that any bargaining on Alsace-Lorraine would be wholly inacceptable. Germany and Austria jointly, replying to Wilson, approved of his theoretical clauses (a League of Nations etcetera), but refused to consider the independence of Belgium, the cession of Alsace-Lorraine, or the restoration of Poland. Austria, in particular, saw ruin for her monarchy in any recognition of the right of her subject nationalities to autonomous development.

Whereupon representatives of England, France and Italy, meeting at Versailles on February 4th, issued a very short statement. After full consideration of the recent utterances of enemy statesmen, they said, they could see no approximation in these to the moderate conditions suggested by the Allies. "Accordingly, we must fight on until such time as our military pressure shall produce a change of temper in the enemy Governments and peoples."

The gulf seemed unbridgeable; if you looked a little closer, however, the picture was rather different. There were "peace strikes" in Austria and Germany: a split was obviously developing between the Austrian and German governments: and British Labour had issued a statement considerably less intransigeant than Lloyd George's—suggesting, among other things, that a plebiscite should be held, under the auspices of the League of Nations, to decide the future of Alsace-Lorraine. There was clearly a strong body of opinion on both sides—nobody could say how strong—in favour of at any rate preparing the ground for a peace by negotiation, instead of relying on a knock-out blow.

Many Englishmen, in these circumstances, considered the beam in their own eyes instead of the mote in their enemies': and could not fail to observe that, while Wilson breathed a far more liberal spirit than Lloyd George, both, when they

came down to particular cases, imposed all "sacrifices" on the
enemy.

But they observed something else. Lloyd George, in his
speech of January 5th, had been strong on self-determination;
and though Wilson had not been so explicit in the Fourteen
Points, he was to declare, in his "Four Principles" speech of
February 11th, that (1) each part of the final settlement must
be based upon the essential justice of that particular case and
upon such adjustments as were likeliest to bring permanent
peace; (2) peoples and provinces were not to be bartered about
from sovereignty to sovereignty as if they were pawns in a
game; (3) territorial settlements must be made for the benefit
of the populations concerned, and not as a part of any mere
adjustment or compromise of claims among rival States; and
(4) all well-defined national aspirations should be accorded the
utmost satisfaction consistent with permanent peace. That is
what he said, and nothing could have been plainer. But—the
Bolsheviks, meanwhile, had seized power: and one of the first
things they had done was to ransack the Petrograd archives,
uncover the secret treaties that had put on record what the
Allies were promising one another in the event of victory, and
publish them.

There was nothing specially frightful, I suppose, about these
treaties, given the ordinary power-political assumptions that
ruled on both sides; and it might be pleaded, in the case of the
Italian one, that Italy's co-operation may have impinged on
our statesmen as the alternative to defeat. So I will merely
record the head-on clash now revealed: between highfalutin
blather about self-determination on the one hand, and those
concrete arrangements on the other which the Allies, all
except America,* had long been bound by, which everybody,
including Germany and Austria, now at any rate knew they
were bound by, and which they showed no intention at the
moment, for all their profession of principles wholly inconsistent with such rapacity, of denouncing or even modifying.
To take two cases only, France was to get, not only the Alsace-
Lorraine publicly specified by Lloyd George, but all territory
—German territory—west of the Rhine; and Italy, under the
Treaty of London that had bribed her in as our ally, could
demand that 229,261 Austrians, 1,528,958 Jugoslavs, and a

* She had been a neutral at the time

number of Greeks should be transferred to her sovereignty.

You will readily understand, therefore, that many in England, not to speak of Italy and France, were gravely disquieted by the abrupt announcement at Versailles, which signified the triumph of *jusqu'auboutisme* and dealt a blow, as they thought, to their hopes for a real League of Nations. Though they differed about details, they agreed on three basic necessities. They wanted a clear statement that the desiderata proclaimed by Wilson in his Four Principles had superseded the secret treaties: they wanted to encourage the "peace strikers", and other pacific elements in Germany and Austria, by disclaiming any desire for a punitive settlement: and they wanted to keep the door open, whatever the military situation, for *pourparlers*. So might the impending slaughter be staved off—slaughter in which, as it turned out, the British casualties alone were to number more than 300,000: so might the sort of settlement be avoided likely to produce, in due course, a second and even wickeder conflict. You will readily understand, also, that passions were strong on both sides: and when you realise further that these were months of utmost peril for the British army—a peril, I say with respect, that intensified "normal" patriotism—you will have understood already, perhaps, why the Easter term of 1918 was almost inevitably to be my last.

§ 2

"The sun was warm, the sky was clear, the waves were dancing fast and bright" on the Repton political-education front from January 1917, when the Civics class came into being after the Christmas holiday, till some point in the following autumn. Or that's what it seemed like.

We announced the class, and invited applications for membership, directly school reassembled. Thirty-eight applied, and of these we rejected half a dozen on the score of age. Then we got going.

I opened with a couple of introductory lectures. The first was bare and factual: it did little more than run over, in a programmatic sort of way, the main topics, at home and abroad, we should be dealing with subsequently. The second was a bit richer: I let myself go (but quite restrainedly) about the general

principles, freedom and fellowship, that ought to guide us, I
suggested, in the work of national and international reconstruction. Parliamentary reform, the position of women, and the
future of the Empire took up the remainder of our time, with
several lectures for each topic. There's no record, in the book
we afterwards wrote about it all, of who talked about what:
but I've little doubt that the Empire was David's job, and
the women mine. Parliamentary reform could have been
either's.

Pretty pallid, you may think, this initial programme, and so
it certainly was in comparison with the ones that succeeded it.
But the boys wouldn't have agreed; for the wind of intellectual
excitement, previously cabined in the Upper Sixth, had begun
to blow about now and fill (driving sweet buds like flocks to
feed in air) with living hues and odours plain and hill. And not
the plain and hill of Repton only; for one or two other schools,
notably Eton, rapidly followed our lead and established Civics
classes.

I have drawn on Shelley for an image; and now others come
hithering and dithering before my eyes, as with Matins in
Australia echoing faintly around me I live again, eager for
you to share it, Timothy, that transformation of 1917. I think
first of a desert suddenly blossoming with roses: but—a desert,
when before I was even thought of so many young things had
been about? No description could be more faithless. Moreover, it might mislead you; for few of those blossoms, to be
honest, were of the sort you would think good enough for exhibiting (to say nothing about prizes), and there were tracts,
even tracts very close to the sun—to David Somervell and me,
to Jim Harford and Amyas Ross—that remained barren, anyhow visibly. So forget about deserts and rose-gardens, and recall
Die Meistersinger, Act II:

The old watchman has sounded his horn as the clocks have
struck ten: fires and lights have been put out: and you are
lulled, in that Nuremberg alley, by the light of the moon, and
the scent of the elder (*Wie duftet . . . !*), and the calm of the midsummer eve. And then Beckmesser turns up, and starts cater-
wauling: Sachs replies with his hammer: Beckmesser caterwauls
worse, Sachs redoubles his hammer-blows: the neighbours,
more and more of them, open their windows and peep out:
young David rushes in, cudgels Beckmesser: other apprentices

follow, then the neighbours, the journeymen, the *Meister* themselves: and such a riot develops, such a wildness of vituperation
and fisticuffs, that if you didn't really care much for music you'd
stuff up your ears. *Wahn, Wahn!* Out crashes the orchestra,
with Beckmesser's idiocy dominating it: no longer can Sachs's
wisdom echo through, or the lovers' happiness, or the sweet
melody of the midsummer night . . . When the noise is at its
climax the doddering *Nachtwächter* reappears, and blows his
horn again: and in a trice there is nothing but the light of
the moon, and the scent of the elder, and the peace of *Johannis-
Nacht*.

What started it all?

> *"Gott weiss, wie das geschah?*
> *Ein Kobold half wohl da!*
> *Ein Glühwurm fand sein Weibchen nicht;*
> *der hat den Schaden angericht'.—*
> *Der Flieder war's:—Johannis-Nacht . . .*
> *Nun aber kam Johannis-Tag*

> "God knows how this befell!
> 'Twas like some impish spell!
> Some glow-worm could not find his mate;
> 'Twas he aroused this wrath and hate . . .
> The elder's charm . . . Midsummer eve . . .
> But now has dawned Midsummer day!"

Of course the parallel isn't exact. I am to be equated, I suppose,
with Hans Sachs, and Pruke (to be uncivil about him) with
Beckmesser; but my wisdom wasn't equal to Sachs's, and it
was I, and not Pruke, who took the initiative. Moreover, there
wasn't that much wrath and hate: you were aware for many
months, by and large, of nothing but a sort of generalised
vivacity, with no division, or at any rate no obvious one, into
two hostile parties: and if fisticuffs will have to be mentioned,
as I'm sorry to say that they will, this will be only once, near
the end. As for the *Kobold*, it had nothing to do with glow-
worms—political education did the trick; and I should hesitate

to describe Geoffrey Fisher, who ended it all, as a doddering old watchman. But the succession of tempi, the general atmosphere: the concern, the aliveness, an aliveness, in our case, of intellect and spirit—identical!

I have said that "the sun was warm, the sky was clear", etcetera, during the first nine months or so of the Civics class, adding, however, "or that is what it seemed like". There was no overt hostility from any member of the staff except Pruke, and even his was not *very* overt. The housemasters, marrow of Repton's bone, appeared either indifferent or delighted. Harry Vassall—that term, I remember, he visited a wealthy old recluse in the neighbourhood, who had invented a delicate piece of mechanism for weighing the earth: Harry laughed, and the machine was broken—Harry Vassall, I was going to say, almost exploded with enthusiasm. "It's about the best thing that's happened since I came here," he told David that January, and was even anxious to campaign for recruits, if we had wanted him to, which we didn't. Vassall was our barometer: take a look at him, and you knew the weather. Now weather, of course, changes—that's almost what it's there for. When things were blowing up to a climax, a year or so later, it was Vassall who threatened to sack a boy for reading "The Nation"; and when everything was over, shortly afterwards, it was Vassall who purged the library of an *opusculum* by G. D. H. Cole. Nobody else went quite so crackers as this. Is it possible that so vast a physique and so unfailing a heartiness concealed a tendency to trim? May the glare of self-confidence that ever bronzed his magnificent visage have been coupled with a certain insufficiency of moral stamina? A critic or two thought so.

(And yet I mustn't be unfair to old Jugs, for he was a really big man in his way, and perhaps the greatest of all Repton "characters". For heaven knows how long he had been warp of the place's web: headmasters had come and gone, but Vassall had gone on for ever, holding each one's hand in turn. Withal, he was unfailingly kind-hearted. And perhaps I'm wrong about his sense of humour: the gargantuanly large and the microscopically small are alike invisible.)

Quite as cordial, to begin with, was Hayward, if less rumbustiously so; and this was important, for he typified the general body of housemasters, in a way Vassall didn't. Indeed the only dark horse in that stable was Jacky Shearme—not that horse is the word for him.

So everything went swimmingly—but there must have been perilous currents below from the very moment we started. People like Hayward, to say nothing of Vassall, can have approved of our experiment for one reason only: because they didn't understand what it meant, or rather imagined that it meant what it didn't. They thought, I imagine, in terms of old-fashioned "civics" when they bothered to think at all: took it for granted, I mean, that parish pumps, proportional representation and, as a possible extravagance, the reform of the House of Lords would be the fuel we should stoke up our fires with. And there was always Pruke (whom I find myself liking better and better as I proceed with this narrative). He hated the thing from its outset, as of course you'd imagine, and set himself to smash it: the reason being, in my opinion, that he understood what was afoot—a general process of liberalisation—far better than most of his colleagues did. I needn't bother you with the details—and I'm in no position to criticise, anyhow, for I, after all, had been imitating him to my friends. And if he lampooned us in the Army Class, I'm in no position to complain of that either.

Apart from all this, I had made myself pretty unpopular, as you are already aware—I mean long before the Civics class started—with a section of the staff: for I had gone about all over the place since the day of my arrival talking liberalism, votes for women and so on, and they were mostly Tories and masculinists. In addition, as you also know, my general attitude had been pro-boy and anti-master; and even a general attitude of that kind very quickly gets about. Not that I hadn't friends on the staff—I had quite a number; but the boys so delighted me, I so instinctively gave all my care and devotion to what I thought to be their interests, that I had little time for really nursing my friendships with any of my colleagues, except, of course, David and Allan. This was tactically as well as spiritually a mistake, and if I hadn't committed it the outcome might conceivably have been different. Old London and I, for example, were long on excellent terms; and though he could never have been an ally he might very well have continued benevolent, instead of becoming, as things blew up, one of our

bitterest enemies. Jack Stratton, too, whom I was to grow so
fond of a good deal later, ought to have been in our confidence
from the start: he, also, could never have been an ally (for he
didn't care a damn about politics) but might easily, loving the
boys as he did and in his fondness for David and me, have
exercised a moderating influence on both sides. Then there
was Balmers. This was Henry Balmforth—Mr BAHMforth as
Vassall used to bellow—who came to Repton on some date
I don't remember in 1917. He was a quiet little parson, as
good a Christian as you could find, and wholeheartedly with
David and me; and we ought to have brought him in far more
actively than we did, though he helped us a lot during later
developments and wrote me a beautiful letter after I'd been
sacked, full of Greek and charming compliments. It comforted
me, in those dark days, almost as much as the ones that poured
in from my boys. It also shamed me a bit: partly for its
generosity—I was already becoming aware of the spiritual
weaknesses, to say nothing of the tactical blunders, which, I
reflected, might have been responsible in high measure for
the catastrophe; and partly because he had inserted accents
on his Greek, and had got them correct. I have always been
weak on Greek accents: when I embellished *Tim I* with a
quotation from Theocritus Gilbert Murray accented it for me.

But the biggest of our failures was Honk: namely Hooton,
the social-credit man. He interlarded his conversation with
"honk, honk": that's why they called him Honk. But his honk
wasn't the honk of a motor-horn: it was more like a muffled
ejaculation trying to escape from a thermos. He was some sort
of scientist—attracted, I dare say, to social credit for the reason
that it turns on a formula, just as many (many scientists, I
mean) are attracted to Marxism for the reason that it does
likewise: his outlook was thoroughly liberal in the broader
sense, and if he concerned himself with poverty, as his own
special pigeon, rather than with war, he abominated both.
He was "our man", of course: but remained oddly detached,
partly, I think, from an understandable prudence—a poor
schoolmaster, with family responsibilities, has his job to consider—and partly, or mainly, because he doubted the value of
"politics" as an instrument of education. (His predilection for
science no doubt came in here.) We ought to have made efforts
to convert him: we didn't bother to. So while he collaborated

in the Civics on one early occasion, he was never the ally he might have been.

Thus we went on our way—blithely, self-confidently: caught up by the exhilaration of the moment, never stopping to plan or manoeuvre.

Meanwhile affairs in the Upper Sixth, that Easter term, were becoming more and more delightfully *scherzando*. New τόποι were flying about, and jostling for a place with the old; and scholarships now in our rear, some of them almost literally— not that, to be honest, they had ever really bothered us much— we could at last ease the reins off our "politics" and give them their head. I recollect, as the main feature of that period, a comparative survey, very disputatious, of ethical systems: with a majority, at a summing-up, in unqualified favour of the Christian one, and a minority opting for Stoicism. It was early in the same crowded term that I happened to imitate, one morning, Arthur Playfair and Nelson Keys: and a lot stemmed from this: for the enterprise caught on, we began thinking what fun it would be to go and hear them together in London, and soon, as successive holidays arrived, we were adopting certain houses of light entertainment as a movable club, and dining with one another, when money afforded, in state. I may as well, while I'm about it, pursue that topic to its end, running ahead a bit, and then returning . . .

Let me first give you the atmosphere. I can't do better than reproduce, from the *Encyclopaedia Britannica*, a passage headed "1917". The writer is R. H. Gretton:

"With no illusions left on the nature of the war, the country entered on 1917. It was a strange year. Towns, at first because of air-raids, and later also for the saving of coal, were in complete darkness at night. Food, without actual rationing as yet, was often short, and, with the increase of Government control of supplies and prices, was no longer freely obtainable; restaurant meals were definitely restricted. Alcoholic liquors had been largely given up . . . and were, in any case, becoming very expensive. . . . Yet there was much spending of money, and much rather fevered gaiety. This was partly because the enormous Government requirements had vastly increased the currency and spread money all over the country in high factory pay, military pay, camp and equipment contracts; partly because of the feeling that all the hard work justified the turn to what distraction was possible. A grimmer phase of the same feeling permitted any extravagance to the armies, to the men back from France or on their way there, hung about with the bewildering mass of trench equipment—gas-masks, entrenching tools, weapons, food-tins, packs—half buried in coats and mufflers, the strange, heroic, infinitely patient figures which poured out of or into the leave-trains at Victoria station. So in a tragic England there was dining and dancing and theatre-going as never before. It was only too easy to feel that no one could count on life; the hour must be taken as it came . . ."

The picture is exact: see it as a background to what follows. As the months went by, more and more of our lot were "on their way there". Nooky went first: loathing bloodshed, he wanted to get on with it, and disappeared from Repton, unnecessarily, a month or two before the end of the summer term of 1917. He was presently killed: I don't know why, but I think of his ugly squashed nose even oftener than of my dead Oxford friends, of Bernard Strauss and Ralph Rooper. The original triumvirate—Jim, Leslie and 'Sworth—followed him a few weeks later, and had left England within the year. There was always somebody you were saying good-bye to.

So, in that climate, we loved going to "shows" out of term-time: we kept together like this. Present would be, on a normal occasion, a few still at school but shortly leaving, and perhaps a couple up from camp: a round half-dozen in all. We never went to concerts or plays, always to revues: I can't explain why—if you've got anything of the atmosphere you'll understand why. And the shows that we went to were always the same shows, till one or other of them came off: we got to know them by heart, and would have thought it a kind of treason to chop and change. There was the Palace, with Arthur Playfair and Nelson Keyes—Arthur Playfair had a pun that delighted us, something about clap 'em and Balham: there was "Bubbly": there was "Gin and Bitters": there was "Yes, Uncle"—with a chorus that I think of as the opposite number to Matins in Australia, earth over against heaven:

"Think of mé-e when the flags are—flýing
And you hear them—crýing
'There they go!'
Think of mé-e when the drums are—beáting
And you hear them—greéting
Every boy they know!"

. . . but "Bubbly" was the thing. "Bubbly" was intimate: we would sit in the front row, a bit tight (we were a bit tight quite often, but harmlessly), and the stage and ourselves would be one, and both would be Repton. It was for the last night of "Bubbly", at the end of April or beginning of May 1918—term had ended, Jim and 'Sworth were just off to the front, and I was booked, without knowing it, for the sack—that we staged our final dinner: third in the series, if I remember correctly, and far the best.

We would be about a dozen for these special occasions. We wore white ties: we made speeches, drank toasts: we were ritual, within war-time restrictions, about the food and the wine. (I hadn't got to the point, at this stage, of feeling a clash between my pleasure in such traditional pomposities and my hatred of a system that produced the social cleavage they symbolised: and indeed Moses, even nowadays, as you will have noticed, normally travels by scooter, but wears a top hat. Not that levels of income were much in point then: I was earning considerably less than a better-paid worker.) We were also very gay: we would rehearse silly jokes (revue τόποι) and sometimes burst into song—"When the m-moon shines", or "Widows are wonderful", or "And if I tóld them, that I was waiting for the bús, they wouldn't beliéve me, they wouldn't beliéve me". But below the gaiety, below the festive masquerade, our talk was serious. Concern for the world, and for the "movement" that was trying to change it, was the *basso continuo*. And good-fellowship sanctified our frivolities: by reason of it, we were living, in and through these frivolities, a sort of "spirituality of material things" τόπος.

We were specially happy at that last dinner, and specially concerned. We could not bear to break up: so we met again next day for lunch.

You may wonder how I managed all these gaieties on a salary so diminutive. Well, somehow or other I did, for I never ran

into debt. We were Dutchmen—each paid for his own: the
pound went much farther in those days than it does now: Mrs
Miggs charged me practically nothing—fifteen shillings a week
or so—for my lodgings and food: and I spent little, on ordinary
occasions, in London. Porridge, bars of chocolate (at a penny
a time), bread and jam and bananas were the staple of my diet,
fortified, every now and again, by a feast in Soho: this, at
such delightful establishments as the *Petit Riche* or *Moulin d'Or*,
would set me back half a crown: and I shared rooms with
Ralph Rooper and Adrian Boult—behind that strange sightless
courtyard in Oxford Street—which cost us, complete with the
prettiest of housemaids and a valet called Alfred, only sixty
pounds a year for the three, or twenty pounds each. Many of
the boys were in the habit of using them—our rooms and the
valet—when passing through London. Wooden cut-outs of
Pavlova and Mordkin, of Nijinsky and Bolm, pirouetted or
mimed on a mantelpiece. The address, for purposes of a plaque,
was 36A Dryden Chambers . . .

And now I must get back to my more or less orderly narrative
of what happened at Repton during the earlier part of 1917.

Jan. 28th, 9.15 a.m.
*A quarter of an hour ago Derek Bentley was killed. They had
given him food, pinioned him, and made him walk to the gallows:
then they deliberately broke his neck.*

*When Blake was trying to draw something once, a phantasm of
Lillith kept coming before his eyes, and he had to get rid of her by
drawing her first. Bentley is before my eyes—and has been so all
night: but I couldn't write about him then, for I had other fish to
fry: I can do so now, because mercifully it is all over.*

*Bentley, you may remember, was Craig's companion. He had
been in custody a quarter of an hour when the constable was killed.
But it was alleged that, at some point or other, he had cried "Give
it to him, Chris"; and this legally constituted murder. He has been
described by a Member of Parliament as "a three-quarter-witted
boy of nineteen".*

There are two things I want to say:

*(1) The case for not deliberately killing him, as he has just been
deliberately killed—after being kept waiting "three clear Sundays"
and all last night, while most of us were carelessly asleep—by no*

means rests, at any rate primarily, on a possible unsoundness in the jury's verdict. It rests on this: that to submit any human being, whether guilty or innocent, to that mental and physical torment is to deny God and outrage Christ. "And the King shall answer and say unto them, Verily I say unto you, Inasmuch as ye have done it unto one of the least of these my brethren, ye have done it unto me." Isn't Christ brother to all men? Isn't Bentley, then, brother to Christ? One of the least of his brethren, perhaps—but "one of the least" is the whole point of Christ's saying. Whenever people make a man suffer as they have made Bentley suffer, Christ is crucified; and the veil of the temple was as surely rent in London this morning as it was rent in Jerusalem that first Easter.

What Bentley had himself done to others, what sort of boy he was, this is totally irrelevant for Christian ethics. More: its irrelevance is the very core of those ethics.

(2) A popular sheet, one of the few you could call reputable, wrote as follows last Sunday when demanding a reprieve: "This newspaper has no sympathy for the weak and stupid Bentley." They relied, they said, on something quite different: "He had a fair trial and was sentenced according to the law. But is it fair that he should hang when his leader and accomplice avoids the final penalty of the law?" The implication is: if his leader and accomplice had been old enough to hang, then Bentley would have properly hung too.

No sympathy for the weak and stupid Bentley! Then we are to have sympathy—with whom? With the strong and the wise? But sympathy means to suffer—to suffer with: to share, by an act of imaginative fellowship, not the serenity of the righteous, but the misery of the erring. To live in others—particularly those that seem wickeder (the presumption!) than ourselves; not to judge—particularly those we think worthy of judgment; to love our neighbours—particularly those we find it irksome to love: that also is the core of Christian ethics. And my point is this: that paper was lying. They did sympathise—you can be sure of it, you could smell it in the whole article—with the weak and stupid Bentley; but they had to deny it . . . because . . . it wasn't a thing that they felt they could say. They dared not say it. For here is the truth: the overwhelming majority of journalists, of politicians, yes, and of churchmen, simply take it for granted that the English are pagans, and that if you want to get anything done you must avoid all suspicion of having "fallen", however lightly, for the Sermon on the Mount. So they pay tribute, not to the balm of Nazareth, but to the iron of Rome; and by assuming that we are wholly unregenerate they are helping to make us so. They toughen the whole atmosphere. A battle is always proceeding, at any rate in most of us, between paganism and Christianity: they give comfort to the paganism.

If only they would be braver! If only they would dare to be publicly decent! If only they would make the appeal that so many await! For their estimate of England is false, and I call in evidence the public reaction to this present iniquity. I never remember such an outcry against an execution: an evening paper has reported, for instance, that of the letters that have come pouring into its offices six to one have been for mercy. This is due, people say, to Bentley's age, to the comparison with Craig, and to the fact that he didn't personally kill anyone. No. Circumstances such as those have merely actualised, in a large section of our people, a conviction long latent: that capital punishment, whatever the circumstances, is a barbarity that darkens the world. Many of them don't realise what is at the root of their own reaction: don't appreciate, I mean, that while seeming to be outraged by a case so exceptional, and only by this, they have really been influenced by considerations far wider. The exceptionality of the case, as it were, has given a buried feeling about every *case its chance to get through. Bentley's youth has, I am sure, moved them most; and they might quickly understand, if their leaders would make the suggestion—or rather a knowledge of it, already lurking, might quickly come into their consciousness— that age, like innocence or guilt, is irrelevant. Suffering is suffering, whatever the age; cruelty is cruelty, against whomever committed; and if it is monstrous that a boy of nineteen should be treated as Derek Bentley has been treated, it is equally monstrous that a man of fifty should be treated so. And what can God reck of age? We are all, in his sight, but as babes yet unborn.*

§ 3

Just before the Easter holidays of 1917 a bit of thistledown, delightful to look at, came scurrying into view: and revealed that gusts from the Civics class, now firmly established as an area of high disturbance, were freshening up, even at this early stage, the circumambient weather. There was a Debating Society at Repton, with two chambers: a Commons for the hitherto dumb, and a Lords for the already vocal. A boy opened his

lips in the Commons, and next session he was automatically
a Lord. So a Lord, by and large, would be a man of intellectual brio, as well as probably a greybeard; whereas the Commons reflected instinctive opinion—there were things you took
for granted as a right-minded Englishman, and you voted
accordingly. The chambers sat together, but divided separately.
Well, they debated, that evening, the dismemberment of Germany (dismemberment was the actual word: "In the opinion of
this House, Germany should be dismembered at the conclusion
of hostilities"): and though the Commons were almost unani-
mously in favour the Lords were against, if by the slenderest of
majorities. A year earlier almost everyone, in Lords as well as
Commons, would have been in favour; a year later, when we
debated the disfranchisement of conscientious objectors—I say
we, because a sextet of masters . . . but I must keep that in
store for you.

The Easter holidays ended, my term of terms began: the
summer term of 1917. The sun was perpetually at its zenith: I
might have been translated to the empyrean. Cricket was the
setting—cricket on the Paddock, cricket away: and if I savoured
it more keenly now than ever, this was because, as a *cognoscento*,
I had been looking forward to it for months, whereas previously
I hadn't known what I was in for. Twice I went to Uppingham
with the eleven, twice I sat there while they played, twice I returned with them; and I was as happy, every minute of the
time, as when, a decade earlier, I had raced to Covent Garden
of a glaring afternoon, or examined wayside flints for fossil
sponges.

Political education, too, was in a way at its zenith that term,
even though the Amyas "stunts", most remarkable of all Repton activities, were still to come; for with the exception of a
public row with Pruke, due, as I now realise, to my own folly,
no sound of the imminent thunder reached our ears. In the
Upper Sixth, a set of talks on the theory of money created quite
a furore: largely, I think, because . . . because I was nothing of
an economist, the topic fascinated me, I was forever getting it
up, I was forever letting it go, I was getting it up all over again
now for the purpose of these talks, the glow of rediscovery was
on me, and my hearers glowed accordingly. (It wouldn't be a

bad idea, by the way, for schoolmasters to be prohibited from
teaching anything but their hobbies, so that a classic might deal
with physics or a historian with geology. Mistakes in teaching
don't matter: what matters is prosing away at a thing you know
so well that it bores you, a thing devoid for you now of all
mystery.) As for the Civics class, we couldn't accommodate all
the applicants; and this was the more remarkable, because it
was summer, the evenings were beautiful, and you could stroll
by the Steinyard, or take a walk across the fields towards Mel-
bourne, instead of sitting in a stuffy classroom. David lectured
on Trades Unionism; Honk on Individualism and Co-operation;
I on the Organisation of Peace and a League of Nations—and
Pruke on Conservatism.

We had been true to our intention of trying to broaden our
basis, and had tackled Pruke, as a leading conservative, directly
school reassembled. We offered him a free hand: he could
choose his own subject, and speak to the length he preferred
(the number of lectures on any one topic varied, in our normal
practice, from two to four). He accepted with apparent enthusiasm, but seemed to cool off a bit later; and when the lectures
were finally delivered—all sorts of curious obstacles had intervened, for which, he appeared to think, we were responsible,
though honestly he was doing us an injustice—they failed to
impress. The fact is, Pruke was no fool. There he stood, facing
boys that he looked on as "ours", with ourselves, David and me,
hovering round—we had had the stupidity, and I must confess
the bad taste, to turn up: we always attended, whoever the
speaker, for the Civics were in our charge: but we ought to have
made an exception, and let him get on with it alone—there he
stood, then, *in partibus infidelium*: and he was determined to fall
into no traps. Did we expect the blare of trumpets, the beat of
drums? Were we waiting for a superb dithyramb in honour of
Empire? Well, he would disappoint us: he would attempt something moderate, unemotional, closely reasoned. But breadth
and vigour were precisely what he specialised in: intricate argumentation, unfortunately, was precisely what he didn't. So he
stumbled, he halted: a Caruso, you might have said, teaching
counterpoint, when all you wanted was to hear his high C's.
Seven words, with an occasional variation, appeared to make
up the bulk of his discourse: "Let m' put it in another way".
But this may have been an aural illusion.

Now I had a dreadful characteristic in those days, a characteristic, I am sorry to say, that I have never entirely got rid of. I couldn't control my facial expression: worse, I didn't want to. If anybody said something stupid (in my opinion), or wrongheaded, or base, my features would signal accordingly. There was something rather good about this, but a lot very bad. I couldn't bear to leave error unchallenged: and this was good. Equally, I was incapable, not indeed of knowing (for that everybody ought to know it was one of my own major tenets), but of remembering at the moment when such knowledge might be useful, that error in Victor Gollancz's sight might not always be error in God's: and I was incapable, also, of remembering at similar moments that there is such a thing as courtesy. So when, towards the climax of Pruke's discourse, I thought I detected—on top of everything else!—an undistributed middle, or a *petitio principii*, or something of the sort, my expression said "blithering idiot!". David saw: the boys saw: Pruke saw, and saw that the others saw. He turned on me in fury, which was natural; and for two or three minutes we snarled at one another, to the delight, I remember, of Ross, and the gentle amusement, with a touch of cynicism in it, of Holdsworth: and to my own present shame and remorse. We calmed down after a bit, and he got on with his peroration: but a collaboration that couldn't have succeeded anyhow had become doubly impossible.

And now for the crucial event of a term chock-a-block with events—crucial not only in itself, but in what it would lead to: the foundation of the Pubber.

The Pubber! "What a shame!" said a boy who had never contributed, after it had been suppressed. "It was all so extraordinarily romantic!" Romantic is the word; and that is why, when anybody who was there falls to gossiping about these *praeterita*, he always begins with the Pubber.

Repton, of course, like every other school, had its official magazine, called the Reptonian: the usual parish affair, with lists of academic and athletic distinctions, an occasional letter from some distinguished O.R., and maybe a potted sermon: printed, you can be sure (though I don't remember), on that smooth shiny paper known as "imitation art". There had also been a sheet called *The Scorpion*, given to lampooning, in the

manner of a gossip-man on a Sunday newspaper, boys and
masters alike. This had been suppressed, as it doubtless deserved,
round about the Easter of 1917; and now Jim Harford, in a
preliminary discussion with David and me, put up the idea of
a successor. Why not start a serious journal, he asked, on the
lines of the *Spectator* or *Nation*, to canalise the political waters
that were swirling into spate? Nothing could have pleased us
better. So the project was referred to Fisher, and he laughingly
agreed.

Jim was editor, with a committee of five: Manoukian, Benn
Levy, Raynermiddlethorpe, David and me. Raynermiddlethorpe, whom you haven't encountered yet, was a Jekyll and
Hyde man: Dr Jekyll was a dreamy violinist, Mr Hyde had
directed *The Scorpion*. His department in the new enterprise
was "space"; and whether by dint of his genius, or in an access
of local patriotism—not only at Repton, but at Derby on the
one side and Burton on the other—every inch had been booked
within a week. Bill Peach, the village "*Cab* Proprietor, of over
30 years' standing", was there, and I could never understand
why the word "Cab" was so heavily underlined in issue after
issue, nor indeed why the word "standing" had been chosen; so
was Melen the baker, and Mrs Patterson the draper and grocer,
and Taylor, her "high-class" rival (but only on the grocery
side), and Astle the coal merchant, and W. S. Matthews, "*THE*
recognised Umbrella Hospital". (It has suddenly occurred to
me that a proliferation of 6-point underlines commonly observ-
able in my advertisements may be a throw-back to the Pubber.)
The Midland Drapery Co. came in from Derby, with a full page
for its 38 departments, ranging from millinery and ribbons,
through crewel work and baby linen, to curtains and bedsteads;
so, with modester spaces but quite as effectively, did the Union
of London and Smiths Bank (incorporating Samuel Smith and
Co. of Derby), Pullen's, where you could not only buy furniture
but also sell or exchange it, and Mrs Turner, official "Hair-
dresser to the School". From Burton-on-Trent, Horne Thompson & Co. promised pianos, and Ellis and Son complete outfits
of tailoring. Raynermiddlethorpe, if he wasn't a genius, then
certainly knew a lot about these people they'd have preferred
that he shouldn't have known.

David and I were on the committee in two capacities. We
advised—and we really did only advise, never interfered; and

we were responsible, with any help the boys might give us, for the "Notes" (on current events) that came at the beginning of each issue—and displayed, as an outside critic observed, a "restrained strength even more remarkable in boys than the qualities of the other parts of the paper". I should add that there were to be two issues each term: that the price was sixpence: and that "any profits made on the sale of this paper will form the nucleus of a fund for the purpose of founding an annual school prize for an Essay on a subject of current political importance". But I've forgotten to explain why we called it the Pubber. This was an abbreviation of its official cognomen: "A Public School Looks at the World".

I spent some happy hours last night reading the first couple of issues—those of June and July 1917; and I want to withdraw everything I said about the blossoms at Repton not being worthy of exhibition. They strike me now, these first issues (and the following ones were even better), as an astonishing performance; and I shall hurry through their contents with you.

The introductory editorial, doubtless written by Harford, must be quoted in full, as it sets out, with sobriety and exactitude, what the paper was there for:

"There are some people who know all about trains. They can tell you at a glance whether an engine is a six-coupler or a 462 or an Atlantic compound. A slight rumble is heard, and they tell you that a goods-train with fourteen sepia-toned bullocks in the last truck but one is coming along. Moreover, they know all the working parts of the engine, and could describe accurately a coupling-rod or a slide-valve or a super-heater. To such people travelling is a joy—they know how and why the 'wheels go round', and thus thoroughly enjoy a period of time which for the uninitiated is a succession of boredom, putting banana-skins under the seat, and looking out of the window. To drive the engine itself would be to them the ideal of bliss.

"Still, the fact remains that they do not drive the engine, and their knowledge is of no solid use either to them or their fellow-passengers. Now, this world may conceivably be likened to a gigantic slow-moving railway train—yet with a difference. In old days, it is true, the world was driven by the engine-driver and his assistants, the stoker and the guard. In other words, Governments were despotisms, and the citizens or travellers had no say in the matter one way or another. They might get up the subject for fun, so to speak, as one might get up slide-valves, but there was an end of it. They were passengers. However, in the year 1649 the passengers cut off the engine-driver's head, and slowly but surely took the running of the train into their own hands. As things stand, there are, or ought to be, no more passengers; for we are all responsible for the running of the train.

"Everyone must ask himself what part he is going to play in the great journey. Is he going to be a mere 'passenger'—the very word has come to have a contemptuous significance—and shuffle his feet and gaze languidly out of the window? If so, definitely he will be bored. This paper is founded in the belief that the people who get the most joy and interest out of life are those who know how the wheels go round, the great wheels of life that revolve slowly but surely, and that the best life and the most interesting life is led by those who do their part in controlling the motive power. It is in the belief that the study of politics (which in our sense includes every branch of corporate life from Church to Trade Union) so far from being the dull and heavy thing it is too often supposed to be is the most absorbing study in the world, that this paper has been set on foot: with the object of presenting in an elementary, and we hope not uninteresting, way some of the main features of the problems of contemporary social and political life."

This was plain-sailing stuff—just the sort of simple statement required: other articles were more exciting. I pick out, in particular, Amyas on Psychology and Politics, Nooky on Revolution, Jim Harford on the Future of Democracy, and somebody or other who signs himself Y (I can't imagine who this can have been—no name I remember began with a Y) on Sin.

Amyas, in an essay of some fifteen hundred words, pleads for the application of psychology to politics. Man is a creature of emotion rather than of intellect; but the average citizen does not realise what a slave he has become to emotional impulses, while the political cliques, who *do* realise this, have so used it as almost to ruin democracy. At the time of an election many voters are influenced, not by careful thought, but by the unconscious assimilation of catchy posters, the headlines in party papers and pamphlets, and the excitement of polling day. Between elections, the situation is similar: men and women, on the average, swim with their stream, for thinking is a process to be avoided, and party catchwords, appealing to the emotional side of human nature, are the real attraction. Of those who think carefully about politics, very few would pretend that they agreed absolutely with the views of any party of the time.

"It is certainly deplorable that so few should think seriously about State affairs, but is it possible to remedy this evil? The answer which is on the tip of every tongue is 'Education'. But unfortunately all processes of education at present in use are either technical or ethical. If political education exists on an appreciable scale . . . it consists in the rousing of vulgar and sensational emotions, entirely removed from serious thought, such as those produced by saluting the flag, or else a one-sided insistence on certain political tenets. Those who are well educated according to present standards are quite as liable to those pitfalls as their less fortunate brothers. The sort of education really needed is the creation of a new habit in the brain, which shall affect and displace all other habits. This is the habit of mental curiosity—of testing all motives before they are discharged into action. Intellect alone cannot do this, since the emotional nature of man is too strong. But an intellectual habit raises the process into the ranks of 'Emotion'. The good citizen has the hardest of all tasks—that of keeping his mind perpetually open, of never allowing the brain to get into a groove, which it will do permanently by the time he is twenty-five unless he prevents it."

The politician is then similarly dealt with, and the essay concludes with a plea for specific reforms, legal and educational. "Unless they are carried out in some measure after the end of the war, we had better dispossess ourselves of any desire for democracy and return to some other form of government."

Jim Harford, equally concerned about democracy, finds that the current system of parliamentary representation has failed to secure, in an adequate measure, government of the people, by the people, for the people; and quotes H. G. Wells (his influence at this time was tremendous: Amyas quotes him too) to the effect that "in Great Britain we do not have elections any more, we have rejections", and that, through the mysterious workings of the party organisations, the harrassed voter is reduced to "a ridiculous selection between undesirable alternatives". If England is to become a true democracy, a better system of representation is the prerequisite. P.R. and votes for women are obvious reforms: but parliamentary procedure is also in need of an overhaul—in matters of foreign policy, for instance, the French committee system might be adopted.

But this is only a beginning: the economic sphere must be examined. The fact that England is not really governed by the voice of the people is shown by the conditions of working-class life. Misery, distrust, ignorance, poverty exist and thrive among the working classes—nine-tenths of the population: and this proves the failure of present-day democracy. Nor can Parliament, even a Parliament with high working-class representation, solve the problem alone: the working class must itself take a hand in its own sphere. Our first duty to the nation, then, is to secure the democratisation of industry, government of Labour, by Labour, for Labour. Autocracy is justifiable only as a temporary expedient among backward races. Labour is no longer a backward race—in its ranks are found men of the highest intellectual capacity, who could assume command in their own world if the system allowed it. We must give them the opportunity of solving industrial problems for themselves and their comrades.

"Lastly, and most important of all, we must by educational legislation extend the field of personal competition. The cause of the present division of our society into classes is not the presence so much as the absence of competition. The greatest social hostility exists not within but between the classes, not between people who can compete but between those who cannot. The best work must be done by the best people. At the present moment a large number of professions are reserved for public school and University men, while the public schools and Universities are to all intents and purposes closed to all except the sons of those who are at present in those professions. Thus we have created an aristocracy of birth and wealth, totally opposed to the spirit of democracy. There must be an open road for talent, an aristocracy of intellect, will, and determination, and to secure this there must be 'a broad highway from the elementary schools to the Universities', as the

new Minister of Education has put it. We must spare no pains
or money to make education from the bottom to the top available to every single member of the community. And lest this
newly-created class of intellectual workers with one accord
'down tools' and demand a human being's job, industry must
be made a profession as interesting and as remunerative as any
other. Labour must come to be regarded, not as a field for
exploitation by the capitalist, but as a highly essential part in
the organisation of any community. The workers must control
their own conditions of work, and must be offered as great a
share of the good things of life as anybody else in the land. The
biggest task before democracy is the discovery of an industrial
system which will satisfy these requirements, and our part in
that task is to ensure, first, that those whom the question most
nearly concerns may have every freedom to develop the system
themselves; and, secondly, that by our sympathy and our
purses we may pave the way for the development in them of
that social interest and intellectual vitality to stimulate which
must be the aim of every true democracy."

Nooky on Revolution—a really brilliant, tightly packed
affair of some three thousand words, showing remarkable grip
and considerable erudition—is more difficult to summarise.
Discussing revolution as such—as a phenomenon exhibiting
many similar features in its various instances—he considers the
psychological reactions and material conditions that tend to
produce it, the stages that mark its progress, the activity at
particular moments of the several classes and types, and its
wickednesses and nobilities. While believing that revolution
may be the only way to make people realise a new possibility
of life, so tenacious is the hold on them of past traditions, he
nevertheless ends with an interrogation mark: "How then is
revolution justified if it is exposed to so many dangers on the
way, the results of ignorance, passion and vice; if its failure
merely strengthens autocracy or sets up a more complete
tyranny than before? Did the French Revolution succeed? Did
the uprisings of 1848? Will Russia emerge triumphant? Such is
the riddle of the sphinx."

But what I like most of all in these Pubbers is the essay
on Sin. The writer starts by assuming "a great lonely God"
who is possessed of a primal instinct, creativeness, and who to

realise himself, to complete his being, creates man, and earth, the scene of his activities: because, being lonely and loving, he thinks that he will enjoy his creation, and that we shall, too. Now, love of a person carries with it two separate desires: a desire for the loved one's happiness, and a desire for his love. Somehow or other the two became inextricably connected, and that was, as it were, the state of mind of the Creator. He wanted us to be happy and he wanted us to love him, and the two became inseparably joined—only by loving him were we to be happy, and only by being happy were we to love him.

Then, after touching on the problem of evil, the writer puts this question: "What is perfect happiness, and how can we prove it to be such? Has everyone the same standard of happiness?"—and proceeds as follows:

"Broadly speaking, I think it is true to say there is a definite state of happiness which everyone who has experienced it would pronounce to be ideal. Give anyone a week to find out whom they thought to be the happiest people of their acquaintance, and I think it would invariably be found that the people finally indicated would be on the one hand the unselfish, on the other those who appreciated the beauty of nature and the treasures of art, who had cultivated the life of the mind, who had a sense of history, and who, with an ever-deepening wonder and delight at the mystery of the universe, were roaming in the regions traversed before them by all the great minds of the past —the happiest being those who combined unselfishness with love of beauty and knowledge. On close observation those who were first thought to be happiest (probably the most prosperous) would be found to be only rather jolly on occasion, and rather hard, distrait, and anxious the rest of the time. Those who kept up the most continuous level of happiness would probably be found to be those who were unselfish, cared for books, and enjoyed the arts.

"Harmony, then, or human perfection, is the perfect synthesis of love and knowledge. Sin is the opposite of these, namely, selfishness and blindness of soul, which shatter this harmony; and they are 'sinful' because they cause unhappiness. Selfishness implies the absence of happiness rather than the causing of its opposite, but that is just as much a sin. In the same way, the man whose soul is blind is not fulfilling God's purpose, since he is not getting a creative and active interest out of life, and, therefore, he is sinning.

"But, it may be said, it is perfectly easy to conceive of a man who is all-loving and by human standards practically all-knowing, and who is yet unhappy. Christ has been termed the Man of Sorrows. To this it must be replied that in the present state of the world perfect happiness is impossible, since love causes us to sorrow for the unhappiness in the world. But at the same time we must assert that the life of love and knowledge is the happiest possible, and that the growth of the possibility of perfect happiness proceeds hand in hand with our efforts towards progress.

"Finally, it may be objected that to take happiness as the ultimate aim of all action is fundamentally immoral. So it would be if happiness consisted in lying on one's back and listening to music and eating fruit all day. But the happiness that man is to seek is an active, a creative, a vigorous, a splendid thing. It must be perpetual struggle and effort, perpetual love and work for others. It must imply, not merely enjoyment of one's own happiness, but a constant rejoicing in that of other people. The harmony of life is not the harmony of the placid sky, but the perfect blending of a thousand sounds and colours and thoughts, and when this is achieved earth will be changed to heaven, and the will of man will be merged in the will of God."

Admirable. I might almost have written it myself. But I suddenly remember Cherry Aynsworth did.

The other "middles" in these two issues are of slighter, but still of considerable, interest. Nooky, with vestigial patriotism, takes the stand for Irredentist Armenia, and scores an effective series of points against people who forget to remember the rights of small nations when it suits them to do so. Holdsworth is a bit heavy about Taste—which I shouldn't have expected: Levy quite the opposite about No Annexations—which I should. A few outsiders provide ballast (unnecessarily—the feature was dropped): including the late William Temple, whose career so closely paralleled Geoffrey Fisher's, if in two points only: for both were Headmasters of Repton, and Temple was, Fisher is, Archbishop of Canterbury. His article, with its plea for

humanism in education ("entry into the great world of history,
literature, science, and art is the real emancipation of the
soul") as against submission to Chambers of Commerce ("whose
interest in education is almost entirely concerned with efficiency
of production"), would bear reprinting. So, for the matter of
that, would Geoffrey Fisher's Commemoration Sermon, which
was splashed in the July issue; he might have been lecturing
to the Civics class, or writing an editorial for the Pubber, when
he used these noble phrases:

"In the world is to dawn a new era of a league of nations,
banded together by community of interests and ideals, no longer
in the collision of rivalry and distrust, but in the unity of co-
operation and sympathy, based on the liberty and justice which
are the watchwords of democracy. And in this nation is to come
a new life. The grim horrors of poverty and squalid homes, of
selfish competition and bitter industrial strife, are to be banished
by a new citizenship, in which sympathy displaces self-seeking;
in which true education drives out the sins and evils of ignorance
and small-mindedness; in which public life is governed by Christian principles directly applied. Class will understand class; employer will work with employé; man shall greet man as his
brother."

There remain poems, the usual reviews, and "a list of books
we recommend for the study of contemporary affairs"—its
twenty-one items carefully balanced, with Belloc's *General Sketch
of the European War*, John Buchan's *History of the War* and Lord
Hamilton's *The First Seven Divisions* under "The Military Situation"; Brailsford's *A League of Nations*, Leonard Woolf's *International Government* and E. D. Morel's *Africa and the Peace of Europe*
under "The International Situation"; and books by Milner,
Bertrand Russell and Lionel Curtis under "Reconstruction".
Finally—the Notes on Current Events, supplied, as I've told
you, by David and me. I want to say something about these,
in view of the upshot.

They start in both issues, and were to start in all subsequent
ones, with a survey of the military situation, unimpeachably
"patriotic" in tone: full of Hindenburg lines, Siegfried lines,
Oppy lines, unparalleled magnitudes of concentration, inevitable counter-attacks, threatened pivots, "the almost startling
completeness of the British success at Messines", and so on. The

course of the Russian Revolution is carefully and, on the whole, objectively traced, with some bias, however, in favour of "the great body of Moderates, led by Kerensky; they are uncompromising socialists and anti-imperialists, who look to a just and early ending of the war, but will have no truck with the kind of separate peace that would be nothing but a victory for German autocracy." The Irish Convention, and its suggested personnel, are warmly welcomed, Sinn Fein being instructed, however, to modify its intransigeance; while further afield "the wind-up of the work of the Imperial War Cabinet, and still more, perhaps, the excellent speeches of General Smuts, have served to make 'imperial consciousness' more vivid than ever before. The question is—what next?" The Committee stage of the Reform Bill (which was to enact woman's suffrage) is described—with hearty approval on the whole, but a sentence or two of mild regret at the defeat of Proportional Representation; and the munition strikes are cautiously dealt with—"a sound judgment, in possession of all the facts, might or might not give a verdict against the strikers. But, as we do *not* know all, or even many, of the facts, the following points, as making in the opposite direction to our natural prejudices, might be borne in mind . . ." Etcetera, etcetera.

Prudent, middle-of-the-road stuff, all this: neither bolshevism nor pacifism.

The Pubber was not the only development that term. We took in hand a remodelling of the curriculum.

I have mentioned, so far, only my own forms—the Classical Sixths, Lower and Upper: for these, as inheritors of the Renaissance tradition, were as authentically *the* Sixth at Repton as Classics and Greats had been for centuries (I suppose—I haven't verified it) *the* Schools at Oxford. But there was also the Modern Sixth: there were History Specialists: and there were seniors who "did", more or less exclusively, Science and Mathematics. (I have omitted the Army Class, for somehow or other it escaped our attention.) Now we wanted the boys to develop, not merely into classics or historians, scientists or mathematicians, but into citizens and, above all, into men; and what sort of education was it, we asked ourselves, that left some of them as hazy as I was about the physical structure of the universe, others deaf to the rumour of those temporal happenings that had fashioned the modern world, and all utterly ignorant of how nation did business with nation, or of what happened behind the scenes when you wrote a cheque? We had the Civics class, now, and that was something, but besides being voluntary it was harnessed to politics in the narrower sense: and our classroom innovations had been haphazard, and impaired by our ignorance of a lot that demanded inclusion. Surely a place ought to be found in the regular curriculum for subjects that concerned every single human being as such?

If we were to pull off anything of the kind it would mean juggling with half a dozen time-tables. I wasn't a good juggler: David was: and Fisher could juggle like a Cinquevalli. So, when we took our proposition down to him and again he agreed, he set to work on David's draft; and before term had ended a sizable hole had been made in the programmes of all concerned—scientists, classicists, mathematicians, etcetera—and filled with Modern History (two hours), Outlines of World History (one hour), General Principles of Science (one hour), and Political Science and Economics (three hours): seven hours in all out of a total, I suppose, of about thirty. The scheme was to come, and duly came, into operation at the beginning of the Christmas term.

Two other subjects ought to have been included, but either we had funked putting them up or Fisher had vetoed them. The first was Comparative Religion. "Some people indulge in quarrels," wrote Ramakrishna, "saying 'One cannot attain anything unless one worships our Krishna', or 'Nothing can be gained without the worship of Kali, our Divine Mother', or 'One cannot be saved without accepting the Christian religion'. This is pure dogmatism. The dogmatist says 'My religion alone is true, and the religions of others are false'. This is a bad attitude. God can be reached by different paths." How often, for a good fifty years now, has that thought, you would think so elementary, come leaping into my mind! And the irrationality, not to say the blasphemy and pride, reprehended by Ramakrishna —you see more of it, with the proliferation of neo-orthodoxies, every moment that passes. I quoted earlier a reputable publication on "the vague sublimities of Eastern thought": as if anything were more remarkable in that thought than the precise distinctions, the subtle discriminations and the refined analyses that characterise it. Aldous Huxley has only to open his lips about the Divine Ground for people who prefer the concept "God" to make a mock of him. Even within Christendom itself you find a similar aberration: Protestants hate Catholics—religiously, of course I mean, if the adverb is in order, not personally—and Catholics dismiss Protestants, in a mood of sorrowing wonder that men can be so blind, as without lot in the divine conspiracy that they themselves—*selbstverständlich!*—are party to. Indeed, they seem further from one another, some of these warring Christian sects, than from those outside the pale, just as an independent left-winger, particularly an extreme one, is more hateful to Moscow than a Tory; and to sympathise with another's position, in the climate of religious as of political exclusiveness, is to commit the heresy of "objectivism". Your own group is in the know: all the rest—other Christians, Mohammedans, Buddhists—know nothing. I am reminded of a conversation I had, just as Dunkirk was falling, with a man of renown and integrity whom I greatly admire—a Christian, a socialist and a Member of Parliament. "WHAT GOD IS CONSIDERING," he suddenly told me in the middle of lunch, "IS THE FOLLOWING: are we good enough for him to save? If he concludes in the affirmative, he will not allow Germany to overrun us; if, on the other hand, he concludes in the negative . . ." I do not suggest that my friend, who is a bit prone to exaltations, should be considered at all typical; but is the difference so great, after all, between a man who imagines he knows what the Deity is "considering", and a Church that lays claim to a permanent monopoly of spiritual truth? However certain we may be of our own certainties, and I am averagely certain of mine, we ought to realise, at any rate on reflection, that other certainties exist under Heaven, and that God, who gives an exclusivity of his confidence to no creature or group, can alone judge between them. The whole business is stupid and arrogant—an outrage to the divine majesty; and religion, that impulse for union with the principle of unity, ends, by a hideous paradox, in the fostering of divisions. If people could only learn in their youth that the very search after God, a common search, proves men brothers, and that the particular form it may have taken, here or there or wherever, largely derives from historical accident, things might be happier.

The other subject we should have liked to include was—I don't know what to call it: say the history of Christian achievement. I can best explain what I mean by quoting from a little record we wrote, *Political Education at a Public School*, while our experiment was still in being. "If school 'Divinity' is in its present sad state," we remarked, "we must blame, not the Classical tradition, but the Protestant one. When Northern Europe broke the fetters of priestcraft, it set up the Bible in place of the Church as the source of infallible authority. Much was gained; but much was lost. For a Church can live, and grow better, just as it can grow worse; but the Bible is finished and complete. For school purposes, 'Divinity' and 'Bible-work' have come to be almost interchangeable terms. Now the latest book of the New Testament was written about the end of the first century A.D., and the limitation of 'Divinity' to the study of these books, whether in themselves or in commentaries or in paraphrases, carries with it the inevitable assumption that God's work among men either ceased abruptly about 100 A.D., or entered at that date upon a new and infinitely less important phase. In the Bible the works of God are plain for all to see; the simpler the intelligence, the plainer they seem. But now 'God moves in a mysterious way', and for the plain man that is usually equivalent to saying that he does not move at all. The problem of miracles reveals our difficulty in an acute form. Our Protestant tradition accepts as a whole the Biblical miracles and rejects as a whole all reputed miracles of later date. In face of this, no amount of teaching to the contrary will convince the ordinary boy that in the Bible we have a picture of how God works in the world today. To him the whole thing is irrelevant, and a religion based on the Bible alone is a religion out of touch with the modern world.

"Of course the Bible must have a very important place in the new 'Divinity' teaching as we conceive it. But room must be left for other and more modern things, for 'the growth of Christianity and its influence on the world'. What we want is not so much the history of the Church as an institution, for as an institution it has seldom been Christian. We are thinking of Christianity as an idea, constantly assaulting the mind of man through the ages and engendering in him an explosive and rebellious energy that has refashioned society here or there for the time. Take, for instance, the Evangelical Movement. Here was a body of men, the early friends of Wesley, living in the cold daylight of Walpole's England, who yet knew the spiritual glories and terrors of the disciples of the first century. But that is the least important part of the matter. Out of these ecstasies grew and broadened a movement that first created the modern conception of the devoted parish priest; and finally, rising to national politics, abolished the slave trade and started factory reform. This is clearly only one among many possible subjects. The Franciscan movement might be treated in the same way. But it is still more important that 'Divinity' should come down to our own time . . .

"A common objection to suggestions of this sort is that they are dangerous; they will shake the boys' faith. But what faith shall we be shaking? Is it a lively and an active faith, taking Christ as the pattern for mankind, and judging every problem of school life by the standard of his gospel? Such a faith need not fear any such teaching as is here suggested. It will not be shaken but confirmed. What will be shaken, and one hopes fatally shaken, is the lazy inconsistency of the conventional attitude of mind that pays a lip-service to Christianity and ignores it in every moment of life . . ." A bit clumsy, that last sentence; but the root of the matter is in it.

So with the revised curriculum through (apart from these minor exceptions), the term ended, for me, in a mood of quiet exaltation. Everything was going so wonderfully! I had a vision of innumerable Pubbers, of a Civics class everywhere, of curricula increasingly humane: of an England saved by schoolboys from poverty and an earth purged in classrooms of war. But I was sorrowful, too, at the thought that Jim Harford and Holdsworth, and so many others, would be leaving for ever. Most schoolmasters, I suspect, or at any rate most sensitive ones, are saddened by the feeling of self-division, of losing a precious part of one's own person, that I experienced then. No longer to participate in the development from seedling to plant, from bud to flower! There are few lonelinesses like it.

§ 4

The Christmas term of 1917 was the beginning of the end. It was also the beginning of the Amyas era, for he had been left,

REPTON PRIORY AND CHURCH, LATE 18TH CENTURY

by Jim's departure, in a position of undisputed moral leadership. Above all, it was glorified by "the stunts"; and these
I shall describe straight away and with exceptional pleasure,
leaving catastrophe till later.

What "the stunts" meant was this: political education,
which had started at the river-mouth, was moving upstream
and beginning to freshen the headwaters. (In plain English,
the younger and even the youngest boys were becoming
affected.) This was Amyas' work. Now in charge of his House,
Vassall's Priory, he began testing the notion that politics, in
our sense of the word, could be the medium for such a joyful
endeavour, co-operative and unrestrained, as had long been
the mark, in theory and sometimes in practice, of school
athletics. He envisaged a House as a vigorous and genial
community, in which all, young and old, would partner one
another as equals (with fagging reduced to a minimum, and
the prefect system unobtrusive) for the purpose of keeping
abreast with what was happening outside. David and I had
nothing whatever to do with it: not only the idea, but all the
practical details, came from Amyas and the little band of
devotees that gathered round him. I am happy to take credit,
with David, for the original movement, but only Amyas could
have produced its fine flower.

A political society came first. Its twenty-five members, well
over half the House, undertook to "gut" between them all the
leading English newspapers, with a few French ones thrown
in. They sat in conclave every Sunday; the most important
events of the week were considered in turn, and the members
put forward, one by one, such opinions on the topic in question
as they had severally culled from the organs entrusted to them.
These opinions were compared and debated: a brief synopsis
was drawn up, with the topic above and typical newspaper
extracts below: then somebody typed it out and pinned it up
as "the news of the week". This was no affair of intellectuals
—consider the numbers involved—but a piece of genuine
democracy. And the House, bear in mind, was quite an ordinary one, if not more so. But the results were not ordinary. Some
of the middle-form boys, it appeared, were showing remarkable
improvement in "English". A master, for instance, who had
been in the habit, once a term, of setting "anything you
please" as the essay topic, with a couple of pages in large

handwriting as the usual result, found himself called upon, in the middle of all this, to correct an affair of more than three thousand words and much scrupulous argumentation on "The Planning of National Guilds". Priggish? Nonsense: alive. The Priory of Amyas and his friends, at the zenith of their activities, could have been likened, by anybody in the know, to one of those urgently pioneering *Kibbutzim* of the first generation: in which, after a day in the fields, they would sit through the night turning Shakespeare into Hebrew.

Other developments rapidly followed. A modest but useful idea was the question board, on which a boy could raise difficulties that had occurred to him during the course of his reading. Next, the Library got a coat of new paint: a political section was started, in which books about the Greeks and Mill's *Liberty* jostled Brailsford and Bertrand Russell. But you will get no idea of "the stunts" if you imagine that politics, in the narrower sense, marked the limit of these activities. Important new books of every kind were reviewed by volunteers in a folio, which anyone could examine. Rubbishy novels of a past generation disappeared from people's shelves: modern plays, modern poetry took their place. But though the drift was towards Masefield and Flecker and Rupert Brooke and A. E. and John Galsworthy and the like, older books were not neglected: long before catastrophe intervened the great poets, the great dramatists, were arriving . . .

Music came next. Gramophone recitals started up, with a double set of programmes: one for popular music, namely bad, and one for classical, including romantic, namely good. But Gresham's Law didn't operate: the good drove out the bad. So much so, that House piano recitals were presently under way . . .

Last came (and last did go, for the matter of that) what might, I suppose, be called Ruskinism. Public-school studies, in the Repton of that era, were hideous places. A movement developed for beautifying them: it began with "Japanese" lampshades, moved upwards through pretty curtains and decorative tablecloths, and ended with Medici prints. Long before catastrophe intervened (to repeat a phrase—as you might fiddle with a tooth that was hurting you) hardly a room but had its Medici; and collections of Medici postcards were common as well.

All this cost money; but they found it with a zeal that even Ross could hardly credit, when he recalled that, only a few months before, "Old Baboon had cared for nothing but the tuck shop".

And now wavelets were rippling out in ever widening circles. Tentatively, reluctantly—the narrower patriotisms always dread the cry of copy-cat—other Houses got going. The thing might even, in the long run, have infected Jacky Shearme's. But catastrophe intervened.

There are parallels, probably, to the Priory Transformation Scene, but I can't think of any. Klingsor's Magic Garden isn't in it.

I want to emphasise here that all these movements, and not only the Political Society, were genuine House movements. Had they been the work of a little cultured coterie there would be nothing specially remarkable about them. The miracle lay in this—and I may call it a miracle, because people who didn't assist at it are inclined to believe it never happened: the boy in the street was caught up. But an aspect of the affair more noteworthy, perhaps, than any other has still to be mentioned.

"I don't see any connexion between politics and purity," remarked dear old Applebotham (who makes a solitary appearance here) to Allan Gorringe one day, when they were discussing Priory doings in the common-room. "It's all nonsense to me, what you're saying. But I wouldn't deny that something funny seems to have happened to the Vassall boys." Their funniness was their "purity", which had been becoming a by-word.

There was as much schoolboy immorality at Repton as at other comparable establishments, and as much at the Priory, until Amyas took over, as at other Repton Houses. I use the word immorality by way of shorthand: I mean the various sexual practices, solitary and mutual, that every schoolmaster knows about, including those which, in my opinion, are more or less harmless as well as those which are not. But I confine myself, in what follows, to the obviously harmful ones, such as excessive masturbation.

Now in many public schools of my day there was an atmosphere, on the boys' side, of tolerance towards these practices: accompanied by constant discussion, sometimes open, sometimes secret, which encouraged and often actually suggested them. The House prefects, it is true, usually made an effort at suppression; but since, on the one hand, they had "been as bad as any" in their day and everyone knew it, and since, on the other, these were practices, they pretended, that "nobody with an atom of decency in him could possibly be guilty of", the very partial success of their endeavours derived mainly from the fear they inspired.

The common method of dealing with the evil was a system of "talks" by heads of Houses and housemasters. These followed a stereotyped plan: they would be either religious, with references to the temple of the body, or medical, with warnings of imminent doom: or perhaps both. The medical variety, by and large, either terrified a boy (and so might easily drive him back, in his despair, to the very thing he had been warned against) or cut a minimum of ice, if any—what nonsense, all that stuff about the ruin of his cricket or football, when he knew very well, if the sermoniser didn't, that old so-and-so, who had brought off that marvellous century and saved the school's onions, was an adept at vice! As for the other variety: school religion, dogmatic and unspeculative, could rarely make an appeal at all strong enough to counterbalance an overwhelming fascination; and if the sermon should be accompanied by exhortations to pray it might positively make things worse— for to get into the habit of praying against the onslaught of temptation means to get into the habit of thinking about it, and to get into the habit of thinking about it means to grow self-conscious, to succumb. Not but that a sense of Christ's presence can do a lot to help a boy in his struggles, if he's religiously mature: the trouble is that most boys aren't.

I do not suggest that conversations between master and boy were always useless. Indeed, while in one way there was far too much talk on the subject in another way there was far too little. What was wanted, I felt, was a relationship between master and boy, created by frank intercourse on other topics, such as would naturally bring the boy to the master for aid in these difficulties, with the sure knowledge that the latter, instead of lecturing him, would speak as one who had faced similar difficulties in his own boyhood, and would be anxious only to help and explain.

When the verbal appeal failed, boys were commonly beaten . . .

Now it was actually the problem of schoolboy "vice" that set Amyas on his course at the Priory. For the first fortnight of his headship he followed the old method: he examined suspicious cases, discovered a few he had failed to suspect, and even, I am sorry to say, did some "bumming". Then he abandoned probe and cane for good and all; got the boys down to "politics"; and won the trick, if not also—for the future guards its secrets—the game and rubber.

What happened was this: they had found a new interest in life, the Harry Vassall boys—and more than a new interest, a new joy. As day succeeded day, they felt powers they had never suspected awaken within them. Members of a small community engaged in absorbing activities—of a club, you might say, for the pursuit of romantic adventure—they had lost that sense of boredom, that feeling of "nothing on earth to do or think about", which had been, to so great a degree, at the root of their difficulties. Their natures were developing harmoniously: sex was finding its place. Call the process, if you like, sublimation.

This interest, this joy in life, had been touched off by "politics". The subject was the boys' own nature, the nature of each as a member of the human race and a part of the universe; and hardly one of them but found, in some corner or tract of this marvellous territory, the inspiration to vital work and decent living. They started reading widely, as we have seen: a hundred topics held their attention: poetry, plays, good literature of every kind—all were reached from the one starting point. Within a very few months the sex problem had become, as much as it ever can become, especially in the case of young people, a thing of the past.

I don't want to claim too much. My direct experience amounts only to this: that a remarkable head of a particular House, in a single public school, was enabled to achieve, by the methods in question, an uplifting of the entire moral tone that may well have been unique in school history. You may think a certain discount appropriate, for the reason that these experiments were new. This was a company of pioneers, with the enthusiasm characteristic of pioneering: they felt that they were making history, and whether you admire them or whether you laugh at them making history they were in their own little cosmos. It is possible that so much spiritual energy might have slackened a bit when the thing had become normal.

I am persuaded, however, of this: the lines the Priory achievement were based on are the lines we must generally follow, if we are to win a reasonable measure of success—no more can be expected—when attempting to grapple, whether in boarding schools or day schools or no schools at all but the world outside, with the sexual problems of boyhood. A Vassalite remarked once to David, apropos of his part in the stunts, "You see, it's the only thing I've ever found to do here really on my own." It was, in fact, his one adventure. That last word gives the clue. Boys must have their adventures, and the only adventures that can compete with the absorbing one of an indulgent sexuality are adventures that make the latter appear sordid and mean in comparison. I do not for a moment suggest that "political" education can alone do the trick—my reasons for preferring it to any other lie quite outside such considerations; but whatever sort of training we may give a boy—and it will differ in different cases—it must be such as to engage him as wholeheartedly as those Reptonians were engaged.

§ 5

I must return now from the Priory sideshow to the main entertainment; and I would ask you to recall, in its rough outlines, the little history I attempted of events during 1917, on the war and peace fronts alike. You will remember—critical military situation, moves for the clarification of war aims, and so on.

The Pubber of November 1917—the one that started the row—strikes me, on a rapid survey, as surpassing its predecessors in grip and interest. Amyas, now editor, contributes a deeply religious essay on "The Best Life"—odd, that they should have called him a Bolshevik!—which sums up as follows:

"The ideal life is not possible for man alone. For God is the Ideal Life, and man, to realise it, must be swallowed up in God's personality. To him who has thought till now that human love is an end in itself, to the atheist who deceived himself, to the man who imagined he could live by intellect alone, the old words come back with all their pristine force and clearness: 'You must hate father and mother if you will follow me'."

Innes sends some verses, and so do I; correspondence appears for the first time: David commends my book, "The Making of Women", and I commend his, "A Companion to the Golden Treasury": and the Civics class time-table announces Gorringe as lecturing on "Liberalism", David on "Modern Ireland" and "The Present Position of Trades Unions", and me on "Modern Russia", "Alsace-Lorraine", and "Method in Social Enquiry".

Nothing explosive in all this. The bombshells were as follows:

Cherry Aynsworth—he was coming on now, as you will have gathered, with remarkable rapidity—had written about patriotism. He concluded as follows:

"Such is patriotism based on competition: it forgets love in hate. True patriotism should look within. It should be, first, a love of all the individuals who are our compatriots. True patriotism would abolish poverty. It would spend less time watching the dockyards of its neighbours, and more time in investigating its own slums. It would spend less time abusing Lord Haldane because he admires the German schools where he was educated, and more time seeking to improve its own educational system. It would spend less time in making England invincible in arms, and more time in seeking the principles of universal peace. A dangerous folly, the reader may say, in such a wicked world as ours. Well, so long as we live in a wicked world, we must, no doubt, take the necessary precautions against the wickedness of our neighbours. But so long as we do *nothing* but take precautions, so long as we assume the wickedness as part of the eternal order of things, so long will our 'patriotism' remain that of the ape and the tiger.

"For the noblest form of patriotism is love of humanity, and there is plainly no room for the competitive instinct here. We must learn to think not so much in terms of nations and races as in terms of humanity. People think of the world as a place of many races, all of whose members are, by chance, human beings. They should think of it as a great company of human beings, divided by chance into many races. Just as every man can only find his true self by merging himself in his nation, so each nation can only find its true goal in the service of the world, that whole of which it is a part, and to which all its service is due."

The sort of service that Nooky, very soon after, would be giving his life for.

And then there was Amyas. He couldn't leave well alone and be content with his stuff about God: he must needs supplement it with actualities.

He wrote a second article, called "The Policy of 'State Your Terms'." He had beaten Lansdowne to the post by a head.

And now the cloak and dagger stuff begins. Somebody puts up the Ox (an athlete, and rather a friend of mine; universally popular for his kindness, but not intelligent) to write a letter to the Reptonian. He duly writes it: he complains of the "cosmopolitan influence" (=me) that is vitiating the "healthy patriotism" of the school. You might think from "healthy patriotism" that it's Cherry they're shooting at. But this is not so. That indeed has been the original intention; but then Fisher, all at once, is overheard to remark that Cherry's pieties could very properly have been delivered from the Repton pulpit; so the guns are trained on Amyas instead.

Now "The Reptonian" has a censor: and the censor is David: and David understands the law of libel, besides being a friend of mine, and involved a bit personally, anyhow. He can't pass the letter; but instead of destroying it he interviews the Ox, appeals to his better nature, and suggests a conference. The conference meets: Pruke, the Ox, the Head Prefect (most gracious of neutrals), Amyas, David and I. The upshot is this: we shall print at the front of the Pubber, in every subsequent issue, the legend "Nothing that appears in this paper is to be taken as expressing the opinion of the school as a whole". All that night, as I toss in a stupefied doze, the phrase goes ringing through my head: *Nothing* that *appears* in this *paper* is to be *taken* as *expressing* the *opinion* of the *school* as a *whole*. *Nothing* that *appears* in this *paper* . . . Da capo.

And now we make a blunder, trivial in itself but rather serious in its effect on the alignment of forces. We are still on excellent terms with old London; and knowing his patriotic soul to have been shocked by all those heresies in the Pubber, and misled by our passion for equity, we suggest a collusive correspondence. He shall write a letter of protest: we shall publish it, with **our** reply. But one thing, alas! we have forgotten: his devotion to literature. Six long pages turn up, full of stormy Ciceronian rhetoric: excellently done in its way, but with so many "plums" in it—"poisonous weeds of pacifism" and the like—as to be unsuitable, on the whole, for publication. We detect in it, too, the innuendo that Amyas is a potential shirker; and we are to learn, in confirmation of our insight, that somebody or other has reported to London that somebody or other has heard Amyas asseverate "I'm not going to take a commission"—and indeed Amyas *has* asseverated it: adding, however, "I'm going to enlist". Now what are we to do? We can't reject the thing, as we have asked for it. So we proceed, I am afraid, as follows: we elaborate a screed that at once answers and parodies the original, following the latter point by point and employing the same vehement rhetoric—I am pretty good myself at Ciceronian plums. Our hope, of course, is that the Headmaster will censor both letters when the paper comes to pass through his hands: and this he duly does. Then, with misplaced candour, we show our reply to London. Henceforth, he is with the opposition; and this, in view of his county connections, is rather serious.

It looked, at first sight, as if the December Pubber, which followed hard on the heels of the November one, the one with the offending articles in it, would put everything right. Amyas was at his best in a moderate but uncompromising editorial, headed "The Paper and its Critics". I must print quite a chunk of it.

After making a little light hay of the "Nothing in this paper" business ("Is it supposed that the Manchester Guardian represents the politics of all Manchester?") Amyas proceeds:

"But a second and much graver charge has been made, namely, that our policy is opposed to the vigorous prosecution of the war—a charge which, if it were true, would have justified, as it would undoubtedly have caused, our suppression by the school authorities . . . Let us state the foundations of our policy in the plainest possible terms.

"Our policy with regard to the war is: win it. We stand for all the great ideals for which England first entered it, and for which thousands voluntarily enlisted and went to their death:

an unselfish patriotism, the rights of small nations, the maintenance of international law and justice, and the erection of a new Europe based on mutual goodwill. We stand for those ideals with all the more insistence today because we believe that, in the terrible strain on nerves and temper which the length of the war involves, those ideals are apt to be dimmed and forgotten. We insist on the fact that this is a war of liberation from an old and evil order; and if we preach the necessity of a new order that will be the antithesis of Prussianism rather than one based on hatred of the Prussians, we do so in the name, not only of wisdom, but of patriotism itself.

"An editorial in our last issue strongly supported the policy of 'State your Terms'. Why? Because we see in this policy the surest means not only of reinforcing that passion for righteous battle which was so splendid a feature of the early days of the war, but also of bringing both a speedier and a healthier conclusion to a conflict that becomes a sin when it is protracted a day longer than the interests of humanity demand. We believe that the sort of peace for which the Allied peoples are fighting is a peace that will usher in an era of goodwill, instead of a time of hostile preparations, issuing in a war far more horrible than this. And we know that deliberate misrepresentation of the real desires of the Allies is being used in Germany to stiffen the backs of the people with the idea that they are fighting a war for very existence, and so to stop the growth of a democratic movement. Therefore we desire that the terms of the Allies should be stated —not in vague phrases, such as 'restitution, reparation, and guarantees', which can always be misinterpreted, but in actual territorial readjustments, in proposals for economic settlement, and in schemes for a League of Nations. 'State your terms' in accordance with the ideas of all the noblest spirits who are fighting—and then fight on for the victory that will secure them. If the enemy accepts them tomorrow, so much the better— blood and hate are saved: if they will not accept them for six years—well so be it. We, at any rate, shall not flinch."

Precisely. And then, turning on a few pages, people must have rubbed their eyes; for the Headmaster himself had weighed in— and tacitly exonerated the Policy of State your Terms article: which had said in November, with but trivial variations, what "The Paper and its Critics" said now. "Sir," wrote Geoffrey

Fisher, "it is perhaps desirable that I should state in your columns that I have censored three letters sent to you by correspondents, of which two severely criticised, the third warmly commended, this paper. I censored the three impartially because I thought that the chief cause of adverse criticism and the necessity of commendation to balance it were removed by your editorial, and that anything likely to perpetuate an undesirable controversy should not appear in your columns simultaneously with that which is designed, and, in my opinion, well designed, to remove all cause for it. No one will suppose that I agree with all your views: with some I violently disagree. But the impartial reader of your editorial will not fail to note how closely you anticipate the spirit and even some of the details of President Wilson's speech to Congress on December 4th last. Yours faithfully, G. F. Fisher."

So I felt, as we broke up for the Christmas holidays, like a cat that suddenly finds it hasn't been run over after all.

§ 6

I ought to say something, before describing the end, on what you might call the other side—in defence, I mean, of those who fought us.

A little under the impact of the developing opposition at Repton, but far more in the context of the battle beyond—the battle of ideas and emotions that was raging with increasing intensity during the latter half of 1917—our own work had been undergoing a change. I can perhaps best put the difference like this. During the first two or three terms of our experiment we had been anxious to expound, almost in the abstract—using current events rather by way of illustration—certain ideas, unfamiliar to the overwhelming majority of Reptonians, that seemed valuable to us; but now we were more like leaders of an urgent army, fighting for a particular application of those ideas in an immediate and critical engagement. We were as eager as ever that the boys should think their own thoughts; but with numbers overwhelmingly on the side of what was now the opposition (for battle had been joined willy nilly), our passion for independence of thought, in alliance with our eagerness to keep the flag flying, was becoming, not so much swallowed up

K

in, as fused with and indistinguishable from, partisanship. So
what had started as a school of politics was ending as a school of
liberalism. Those last four words ought to tease you: I shall
return to them.

Beyond the Paddock, let me remind you, lies a buttercup
meadow, watered, especially in the more boisterous months, by
a stream called the Steinyard, or Stinker. If this was an opera in
the manner of the *Ring*, and I was writing a prelude to Act III,
I should whip it up, after a lot of low rumbles on the timpani
and a squeak or two on the piccolos, to a blaring announcement
of the *Stinker-Motif*. An enormous bang on the bass drum would
follow.

You know about the Debating Society. Well, a week or so
after we'd got back it announced the topic for debate a fortnight thence: namely, "That this House deplores the disfranchisement of conscientious objectors." The Representation of
the People Act of 1918 (disfranchising, for a period of five years
from the end of hostilities, any C.O. who refused to do the
war-work allotted him) had outraged liberal opinion; and I use
liberal in the broadest sense, for Lord Hugh Cecil had been a
violent oppositionist. The issue was almost symbolic: people on
the one side saw disfranchisement as making a mock of the
ideals we were fighting for, people on the other saw any attack
on it as an insult to the men who were risking their lives at the
gravest crisis of the war. So tempers were exacerbated; and the
cleavage of opinion in the country as a whole gaped as widely
at Repton as anywhere. The opposing armies got in training for
battle, and it was seen, when the day duly dawned, that a trio
of masters had emerged on either side to reinforce their juniors.
Our lot consisted of Allan, either Balmers or Honk (I'm not
sure which), and myself: David abstained, for he deplored the
whole business. I don't remember their lot. Meanwhile a little
gang of roughs, a physical force party, had been drilled by
some stalwart or other in the camp of the patriots. I don't
believe it was Pruke.

The course of the debate can be easily guessed. Every speaker
on the liberal side dissociated himself from C.O. opinions and
based himself on freedom of conscience, every oppositionist
treated the motion as one in favour of pacifism. And a Prukite

master, a dimmish clergyman of a few months' standing—I
have suddenly remembered him as one of the three senior
Midianites, and even remember what he looked like—suggested
the horsepond as a suitable place for his opponents.

The result was a triumph for liberalism. We won, in the
Upper House, by a majority of fifteen to eight, more or less as
we'd expected: but when the Lower House divided, against
a continuo of that eager susurration typical of crises at Westminster, and the tellers announced the result, people could
hardly believe their ears. Hordes of fags had been impressed
by powerful Prukites to turn up (for the first time in their lives)
and vote patriotic; but a third of them, in a House of unprecedented size, had plucked up courage to disobey orders
and vote liberal.

Next morning, about noon, a boy of some little seniority
who had spoken in favour of the motion (and developed, I am
sorry to say, into a Tory politician, as a result, you may think,
of his sufferings at this season) was chucked in the Stinker.
Not only Pruke, but even Hayward, openly applauded. And
some of the little rebels were grossly bullied.

So *Die Meistersinger*, Act II, had reached its climax, and the
gentle hamlet re-echoed to the plonk of bodies in water and the
thwack of blows on boys' bottoms. Physical violence, it is true,
had long been the recognised method for settling conflicts of
another kind: but never before had the itch that provoked it
been ideological.

Recourse was had, at this point, to the Ober-Burgermeister.
A group of pacifyers proposed to interview Fisher, and tell him
he mustn't tolerate such hooliganism. It was to consist, according to original intention, of Allan, Balmers and Honk, plus a
kindly individual whose name I've forgotten; neither David
nor I was to be included. Now this didn't suit us at all, for we
feared the upshot: the easiest way, in our absence, of satisfying
the peaceable and orderly would be to suppress political
education altogether. David eventually got himself on, with
the utmost difficulty: I didn't, for they thought me too fiery. So
when it came to it there were really two deputations, neither
of them quite trusting the other: Honk, Balmers and X were
for peace at any price, David and Allan for a peace that didn't
fling into the toilet-pan the objects we'd been fighting for. I
awaited the result with Moë Gorringe; she was looking more

him "unacceptable", for he believes that ye should resist not evil, but that whosoever should smite thee on thy right cheek, to him thou shouldst turn the other one also. The vicar appealed to his Bishop: who supported the church council, explaining that for a man of such views to officiate at the parish in question, which had particular occasion, it turned out, for disagreeing with Christ, would be the equivalent of a teetotaler evangelising at Burton-on-Trent—as indeed it would; but why then, if you don't want to evangelise, wear a dog-collar? So the vicar appealed to the Archbishop. The Archbishop's reply, through his chaplain, is published in today's papers: he "does not wish to make any comment on the situation that has arisen."

§ 7

Three days—but three days—before the beginning of the summer term I received Fisher's letter. By an attractive piece of irony I was on the point of setting out for Chelsea barracks, where I was taking a holiday course for the purpose of improving my O.T.C. work. The letter simply informed me that I should not be returning, and that all our experiments would be stopped.

I have a curious idiosyncrasy, as I think I mentioned in *Tim I*, or maybe in the earlier pages of this instalment—or rather did have until, quite a long time ago now, I learned to accept instead of fearing. My idiosyncrasy was this: I would worry myself sick over impending catastrophes, vague or defined, but when the thing actually happened I wouldn't mind a bit. (Or perhaps the syncrasis wasn't idio: King David, I seem to remember, had it too.) Now of course I had been feeling anxious, all holidays, about the future at Repton, and had done an awful lot of pacing up and down, considering various possibilities and ticking them off, one by one, on the fingers of both hands; but anything so dreadful as being *sacked*, as being banished for ever from the place of my loves and my desires, had never entered my head. For a second, if as long, I was stunned; I should have seen agony and horror in my eyes, if I could have looked at myself. And then it was all over. I felt peaceful, lighthearted, even gay: *le roi était mort: vive le roi!* I would help them to carry on at Repton as best I could: I would keep in touch with them all, with the people who'd gone and with the people who remained: and I'd try to do again, in some new way or other, what I'd attempted, with a high measure of success, during this last couple of years. It was the "high measure of success", I think, that gave me such a feeling of happiness even in the moment of catastrophe. In that same moment—I remember quite clearly—I passed my blunders in review: but a consciousness of achievement predominated. And in that same moment, also, my future course was set. I recognised that schoolmastering was closed to me, except at schools of a type—"experimental" or "freak"—that appealed to the logical processes of my brain, but not to the affections of my heart; and I decided then and there that I would somehow or other slide into "political" publishing, with the reservation that, at the age of forty-five, I would enter national politics. If I chose forty-five, this was partly because, as I calculated, I ought to have achieved a financial competence by then, and should be able to act independently and according to conscience—without danger, that is, of having to follow any particular course of action at any moment of my political career, for fear of jeopardising my livelihood; and partly because I should be dividing the best years of my life between the activities that appealed to me most, in roughly equal proportions. Throughout the twenties and early thirties I adhered to this intention of entering politics at forty-five; but (a) my relevant birthday occurred at the time of Munich, when, what with the Left Book Club and my other activities, I thought I could do better outside, and (b) publishing had so got into my bones, any sort of publishing but political publishing in particular, that to abandon it would have been unthinkable.

Meanwhile, Fisher's letter had to be dealt with. I sent him a telegram in reply. I don't remember what I said, except that I begged, or more probably demanded, an immediate interview in London. So he turned up next morning at Dryders.

I am as vague about that interview as about the wording of my telegram. I remember that he was embarrassed, and that I was gay. I remember feeling that I rather liked him. I remember two, but only two, of his sentences: "I have supported you consistently for a year and a half" and "David Somervell is the most obstinate man I've ever had to deal with". But I was able to construct, from his remarks at that manufacture of such weapons for the purpose of domestic explosion. They were scrutinising the Pubber, moreover, with microscopic care; and suddenly, at the bottom of the very last page of the very last issue and in a type you could hardly read, which itself looked suspicious, they came across the words "Published by the Repton School Book Shop, Ltd., and Henderson and Sons, 44 Charing Cross Road, W.C.2." They made enquiries: they were told by their expert in such matters that Henderson and the Bomb Shop were one: and the fat was in the fire.

For this was by no means the first they had heard of the Pubber—else they wouldn't have been scrutinising it. There was a master at Repton (he hasn't figured here yet) who really *was* of "cosmopolitan" origin, and therefore exceptionally patriotic; and a relative of his, it emerged, had some professional association with the War Office. Letters had passed to and fro, and the War Office, given a sight of them, had concluded, quite naturally, not only that Repton was a hotbed of pacifism, but that the entire neighbourhood, from Derby to Burton-on-Trent and between the other two points of the compass, was aware of it. And bits of the neighbourhood may really have been aware of it to their own satisfaction, for through certain of the housemasters, and the parents of a few boys, rumours were circulating in Society. The extent of these rumours, however, was grossly exaggerated: people believed what they wanted to believe when they talked of the school being in danger of emptying, for next term it was fuller than ever.

But the War Office decided to act. How precisely it acted I don't know: it threatened, some thought, to disqualify the Repton O.T.C., and refuse a commission to any member of it, unless I was sacked. But its action, whatever it may have been, decided Fisher in his turn: unless what really decided him was the attitude of the compact majority of housemasters, and above all of Hayward and Jugs.

An amusing sequel to the War Office business occurred several years later. I suddenly got a letter from the Board of Education, asking me to prepare them a paper on the Repton affair: they would find it, they gave me to understand, of considerable assistance in their work. But I was too busy with my young marriage, and refused.

*   *   *

I may as well round off the story, and I can do so in a few paragraphs. David's position, with me in the wilderness and our experiments kiboshed, was a very peculiar one. He might have resigned, but that seemed pointless: the boys remained, and he wanted to see what they would make of things. Fisher requested "no political discussion" whether in school or out: David refused: Fisher accepted his refusal: so David went back with a free hand. The position was impossible from the start, but David exploited it to its limits. The centre of gravity was Vassall's, with Amyas in charge and the "stunts" in full swing. David and Amyas were in close contact, and the "Nation" and "Herald", now taboo, reached the others through David. The movement, in short, had become a rebellion, though an honest and open one. Its development was almost entirely on House lines: the "stunts", as I've explained, began to spread. David, meanwhile, ran a small and unofficial sort of Civics class, Fisher tacitly consenting.

At half-term, fresh alarms from the War Office: mere gossip for the most part, but enough to precipitate a new crisis. A prefects' meeting was called. Orders were issued that all political activities in the Houses should cease instantly and entirely—a strange meeting, I was told: it lasted an hour and a half and developed into a vigorous wrangle between Fisher and Amyas, the latter supported by others. "These boys are impossible," remarked Fisher to David next morning. "They will take nothing on authority." Bless them, retrospectively. This meeting had one dramatic consequence. Amyas, after a week of feverish excitement spent largely in David's rooms, took himself off. The school was no longer any place for such as him. What a sigh of relief must have gone up at the departure of probably the most remarkable boy the school had ever produced!

David's turn came next. Fisher presented him with a pledge of silence on all political matters. David refused. What would have happened if the two of them had been left to fight it out on their own is in the order of the song the siren sang—conjectural, but no more. For Honk stepped in, and David, in place of the possible sack, agreed to withdraw "for the duration".

"Well, we've had a long fight," remarked Pruke to the Army Class, "but we've won. We've got rid of the last of the traitors." The last of the traitors would not, after all, be returning. He took a job with the Ministry of Munitions—on Mr Churchill's dislike, left me entirely—because I felt I could be with them, could see as they saw and feel as they felt, be one with them. Dislike and hatred I *know* are simply the result of being unable to do this—we feel we cannot be one with anybody who is in the least different from ourselves. And we can only make that love, that happiness possible by being ourselves—and the school *was* becoming itself . . ."

"And far more than any of your reforming theories I liked your poetic jolly view of life and the Upper VIth room, I simply love thinking of Repton and reading Catullus and the thrill of Plato and your madness and the bounding feeling of life—it was great . . ."

"It made me feel that life is very much what we like to make it, and that by individual and collective effort we can make life worth living both for ourselves and for others . . . With politics as the subject there was some inducement to work hard. No one seems to know why he toils at Greek verbs, and there is a terrifying amount of drudgery to go through before the classical 'education' begins and many, perhaps most, people never reach the required standard . . . There was such an increase of hopefulness and light-heartedness in the school, which harmonised perfectly with our serious efforts. One might be tempted to suppose that schoolboys were lighthearted enough already and that further encouragement was unnecessary. In some cases this may be so, but the lightheartedness is of the wrong sort, born of carelessness rather than hope, and is really only superficial. There are, however, many boys who get gloomy and introspective at a certain age and to them the movement was a veritable godsend. I know this. Old ——, you know I like and respect him, used to say to me 'You're too introspective and not boyish enough, you need games', and he used to say 'I don't believe in boys learning what interests them, education is to prepare them for an *un*interesting world and should accustom them to drudgery.' I remain puzzled to this day; I am told to be happy and boyish, and in the same breath to prepare for an extremely uninteresting world! And he used to say 'You read too much about these wonderful ideas of yours; you know, my boy, the world is run by humdrum people, when all is said and done.' 'Therefore be humdrum', I suppose he meant. The movement, instead of discouraging thought altogether, encouraged hopeful thought; it was active, not passive . . . I couldn't have imagined I should be interested in Greek philosophy, but now I want more; the intellectual joy I felt in it was marvellous. It was Greek without tears, I could never have got to it with my Greek . . .

"The movement did a lot for me morally. It showed me two things; it showed me what the Christian spirit was, and it showed me that it was worth having . . . I hadn't understood before how bad intolerance was. There had been an awful lot of intolerance. A new boy had to conform. If he had independent views he was cut off from his fellows, and the isolated tended to priggishness and the outsiders were left to stew in their own juice. This went on a lot in some of the Houses right up to the end of last term, but not among people who had come under the influence of the movement . . . I really did see the idea of applying Christianity to politics in one way or another, a thing which one doesn't necessarily see out in the world, where it's bad form to talk religion. I feel that once one has applied Christianity to politics and found it not as easy or as pleasant as it seemed there is no turning back; reasons which might prevent a beginning would not be enough to stop ideas in full swing, and such reasons, when they clash with Christianity, are unworthy, and generally financial . . . I wish I were a poet, for prose, and bad prose at that, will not suffice to express the overwhelming gratitude I feel."

"I am far more comfortable at this hotel after the reception camp at Blandford, though at present a dour-looking Scot is playing a number of tunes that the Salvation Army would find it hard to beat. But these hymns brought back 'Major Barbara' to my mind, and all the wonderful things of Repton.

"I cannot wait. I must have news of the place. Was it not wonderful? The atmosphere of comradeship, the wonderful feeling of vitality which was in our midst. Surely we must not be content with what happened at school, but must make the world a thing of beauty and love and life . . ."

or if occasionally perhaps there was, then only to a degree to which everyone, or almost everyone, myself certainly included, is prone. By and large, and as Pruke himself pointed out in a letter already quoted, they acted, given what they stood for, as they had to act.

(3) I am not so sure about Fisher: his case is more complex. Let me begin with a little sketch of his make-up.

I have heard him described as a Cecilian conservative. This, in my view, is incorrect. Lord Hugh Cecil was passionately opposed to the disfranchisement of conscientious objectors: Lord Robert was a passionate devotee of the League of Nations. But Fisher is passionless, at any rate in the realm of ideas. He follows Aristotle, not Plato: he believes, but with a belief itself devoid of excess, in aurea mediocritas. He distrusts sentiment, which he confuses, or is apt to confuse, with sentimentality, as so many others are: his kindliness, which no one could question, stops short, just a little, of warmth. Order, efficiency, discipline—not, however, a discipline of the sort that would strike him as harsh—these are the values that tend to frighten the more glowing ones away from his spiritual landscape. Ranks, classes and hierarchies, within reasonable limits, seem inherent, to his vision of reality, in the nature of things. And yet he is a liberal, a moderate liberal, withal. To call him intransigent, narrow-minded, would be unfair: he sees the other man's point of view. His preference, too, is against oppression, cruelty, injustice, racial discrimination, all the rest of it; but he would never really *battle* against them—battle with his whole being as Shaftesbury battled, as Wilberforce battled. He resembles, perhaps, the average foreigner's idea of the typical Englishman: or call him a Stoic, though not an Aurelian one. And then I think of him again, almost by the opposite token, as a good deal like my father, given, of course, the vast differences in background and upbringing. "I must say," he once remarked to me at some particular moment of crisis, "if it's a choice between all this turmoil and what you call deadness I prefer deadness." I am back again in Elgin Avenue and can hear my father's very tones. That sentence of Fisher's, indeed, illuminates as perhaps nothing else could the psychological conflict between us. His humour is temperate, mine sanguine; and God alone knows, little Timothy, which of them does more good (or more harm) in the world.

I must not, however, give you the idea that I found him disagreeable. The contrary is the case. With an intellect so brilliant (but never taking the jump into genius that lesser people's sometimes do) and a sense of humour so keen (but spoiled a little, I used to think, by something easy and mechanical about it) he was a delightful man to chat with, and I liked going down to the Hall for the pleasure of his company. I positively invented excuses, on occasion, for doing so. But there was always that final reserve. He never really gave himself.

Now political education can have made little appeal to such a personality as this. It meant noise, enthusiasm, difficulties, controversy; and these were repugnant to him. It also meant, as it got under way, educational results of a remarkable, and, for the Repton of those days, an altogether unprecedented kind, and he saw this as clearly as anyone; but you must remember that schoolmastering, with its struggles and strivings, was by no means his vocation, any more than priesthood is. He was called to something quite different: to the work, first and foremost, of preserving institutions, and then, should he be able, of enhancing their prosperity. If he became a schoolmaster and a priest, this is because, as a product of the rectory at Higham on the Hill, he saw the greatest ecclesiastical office as his natural goal; and schoolmastering, as well as priesthood, is one of the regular roads to it. With a different background, he could have become, quite as easily, a top civil servant or a distinguished proconsul: but always a cautious and 'safe' (albeit impeccably honourable) one, and always devoted above everything —unless 'devoted' has an atmosphere of too much strain about it—to the stability and prosperity of the institution he served.

What, in the case of Repton, did 'prosperity' mean for him? That 'numbers' should be steady: that the life of the place should be conventionally 'pure' and free from scandal: that boys and masters should carry on smoothly. And yet he gave us our chance. Why? Because he is fair and, up to a point, open-minded, and *wanted* to give us our chance. He suspected, I think, that our experiment would succeed in a humdrum sort of way; and both the success and the humdrumness would have pleased him.

But he not only gave us our chance, he supported us to all but

the very end—to a point, that is to say, when any hope of humdrumness must long since have vanished. Again, why? For three
reasons. First, he valued our energy now that it was there, even
if, on the whole, he would sooner we had never turned up with
it; for intellectual efficiency, after all, was an element, though
a minor one, in his conception of prosperity, and intellectual
efficiency was not the strong point of the staff as a whole.
Secondly he saw in us, as time went on, a formidable combination of rashness (myself) and obstinacy (David); and—well,
unless and until something really quite dreadful occurs you ride
the whirlwind. Thirdly, the thing might turn out, not indeed
the sort of success he had hoped for, the quiet, moderate sort,
but a success all the same, as bringing a balance of public credit
to his institution and incidentally to himself. (Weren't there
rumours that Eton and Harrow, right up at the top, were beginning to imitate us?) I really mean "incidentally"—I am not
being sly. Personal considerations probably moved him to an
average, a human degree, but no more.

It will be clear to you from all this that his support, though
very definite, was support with a strong reservation. A moment
might arrive when the "turmoil", a thing anyhow of excess,
would be becoming an excessive sort of turmoil: when the "prosperity" he really believed in would be facing a peril, in his
opinion, rather more serious than he had bargained for: and
when a hypothetical balance of public credit would no longer
be looming as large as an actual balance of its opposite. If such
a moment should come, his procedure would not be in doubt.
He would put an end to the whole business, which had anyhow
never engaged him in its own right. He would put an end to us
also: the experiments were ours and not his.

So he held this card up his sleeve, not improperly I think
(unless it is always improper to hold a card up your sleeve, or to
hold it up there too long), at every stage of the affair: when he
accepted the Civics class; when he accepted the Pubber; when
he gave his imprimatur to the very writings that were to aggra-
vate our offence, for he censored every word of the Pubber, as
you will doubtless recall; when he accepted the changes we had
proposed to him for the regular school curriculum, and put
them into practice as late as my last term but one; when he
repeatedly exonerated us; and when as a punishment for the
Stinker affair, in my last term of all and towards the end of it,

he did no more than interrupt, for the time being, my work with the Civics class and give Amyas a colleague, after awarding but a fifth of his censure to David and me. And then the moment arrived, and the card was played. What moment it was I cannot say: but at some point or other in that Easter vacation the War Office—on top of "solid" opinion at the school and elsewhere—finally forced a decision. He could of course have gone down to Whitehall, laughed his little laugh, called their bluff, and been away in five minutes. But political education, as I said at the start, made little appeal to him.

It was typical that he should sack me by letter: but equally typical that he should come up to Dryders in response to my telegram and let me say what I wanted, for all his formidable preoccupation with the necessary readjustments. Typical, also, that he should speak of me quite favourably when he addressed the whole school on the first day of term, and announced my dismissal. The weakness of his position seems to have struck people harshly that morning. "The Boss's speech," a boy wrote to me, "went down awfully badly. It sounded as if he didn't believe what was said about you, but hadn't the guts to face criticism in county circles."

That is—no, that isn't what I think of him: that is what I thought of him these many years ago. For I have been living in 1918: an earlier I has been painting his portrait—a highly critical young man of twenty-five, who has just been sacked. What do I really know of Geoffrey Fisher, of his character and motives? Why, I've hardly met him in the interval, though of course I've read about him in the papers. Is it a portrait of the real Archbishop, the one I've painted? I cannot say. Is it a portrait of the real Headmaster? After so many years, I cannot even say that. And there is this: as I try to leap the gulf, and to look at things, not as a boy of twenty-five, but as a man of sixty, a bit of fineness suddenly obliterates everything else: he gave us our chance, and few others would have done so. My major emotion, accordingly, is one of gratitude. I am rather surprised about this.

(4) My own case remains. What did I do well, and what did I do ill? Well, the evidence is in front of you, and you can judge for yourself. I shall give you a little fresh material, however, and make a few points myself, later on in this chapter.

February 20th, 1953
The first peach-blossom is out in the conservatory

and I've been sacked for the second time: by the Prison Commissioners this time, from the roll of prison visitors. I can't tell you why at the moment, I'm in too much of a hurry, but I'll find an opportunity before I've done.

§ 2

So I come to the two major questions: (1) Is political education desirable? (2) Is it feasible? Now I beg of you not to say, my dear Timothy, as a certain type of person always will say, that I've reversed the proper order of the questions, and that it's stupid to make a lot of palaver about the desirability of an innovation you've set your heart on, if you'll perhaps be discovering later—as we may or may not be discovering in our present example—that the thing isn't feasible anyhow. It's the other way about that's really stupid, for petty-mindedness is always stupid, and it's petty-minded to fix your eyes on practicalities and let proprieties go hang. Practicalities have got to be considered, heaven knows, but unless you are determined to consider them within the context of proprieties you blunder disastrously. The construction of Utopias is as divine an activity as artistic conception; and just as every great poem, every great painting, every great piece of music started as a Utopia, so the other sort of Utopia, if steadily pursued by a sufficient number of the faithful, will end in great living.

"There is one who says *Dear City of Cecrops!* Wilt thou not say *O dear City of Zeus?*"

And not only will Utopia be realised, in the long run, as a whole—it must be, in a form however different from our own poor imaginings, for it incarnates goodness, and goodness is ultimate reality—but one finds, if one is steadfast, that little particles of it can be realised in the short run too, can be realised, perhaps, immediately: and suddenly, as a result of the little particles so realised, the whole thing becomes more feasible.

When I ask, Is political education desirable?, this is what I mean: Should "politics" as we thought of them at Repton—including politics in the narrower sense, ethics, philosophy, history (world history in particular), economics, anthropology, comparative religion—be the staple of pre-university curricula? Not in this school or that, not in public or experimental schools merely, but throughout the whole edifice of national education? I emphasise the word "staple". I do not mean that every single young person would chiefly "learn" politics: I do not mean, either, that any single young person would be "learning", meanwhile, nothing else: I mean that politics would be taken for granted as the main element, but only the main one, in a boy's or girl's education, unless good reasons forbade. Political education, that is, would be the recognised norm of today, just as classical education was the recognised norm in the public schools of my youth. Do you remember my little excursus (though it wasn't mine at all, in point of fact, it was David's) about the *intention* of Renaissance classics? I described it as political. The new curriculum would realise that intention, under modern conditions and for the nation as a whole.

But even under the heading of desirability I must make a large assumption. I must assume that the great majority of boys and girls remain at school till eighteen or nineteen, to the ordinary leaving age, that is, of young ladies and gentlemen: whereas—in January 1951 511,000 children between the ages of 14 and 15 were still at school; but only 140,000 between 15 and 16, 66,000 between 16 and 17, 30,000 between 17 and 18, and 10,000 between 18 and 19. This is scandalous, unless you don't happen to believe in education, or at any rate school education, as of course a lot of people don't. One day we shall put such things right. And yet if in one sense the assumption is crucial, in another it can be ignored; for though you can't have *real* political education for a child leaving school round about 14 or 15 or even 16—so much of his time will have been taken up with necessary rudiments—you can still have a babyish form of it, which is something, though not much.

Very well, then:

(a) *Is political education desirable?* How can I persuade you that it is—and not merely desirable, but a matter, educationally, of life or death—if my whole long account of what happened at Repton has failed to persuade you? I can do no more than make two bold assertions, and regard them as proved if I can but meet the outstanding objections that probably stare you in the face.

My first assertion is this: As an instrument for education in education's own right—for developing a boy or girl as an individual rather than as a member of the community, though the distinction is largely a false one and its falseness is largely the root of the matter, community being the crown of individuality and individuality the substance of community so that the two are essentially one—as an instrument for education in education's own right the discipline of politics is a discipline like no other. Let a boy begin reflecting on the life of his own time and the shock of principles around him: begin examining the machinery by which his own world is moved: begin wondering about the meaning of his own existence and of existence in general—and such an impulse for inquiry has been born in him, such a passion for the spiritual and intellectual chase, as will stimulate, better than anything else could, the unfolding of his whole personality. The deepest waters are stirred, and the classroom becomes a rendezvous for happy spirits in search of adventure.

Why? Because it is the nature of a young human being *as* a young human being—growing daily in self-consciousness, but in other-consciousness too: not yet used to it all, not yet spoiled, freshness and wonder still lingering: wrapped up in himself, but with others pressing round him: linking up with those others or already linked up with them—to be enthralled by the human condition and the arcana of the universe.

Even so a young plant reaches out (and grows by doing so) to the air and the sun.

What other kind of discipline, for the generality of human beings, could ever compare with such as this, what other kind of spark could ever kindle such a flame? For the generality, be it noted; the qualification, please assume, applies to all that immediately follows, and will be considered itself in due course. What, then? Languages? Well, everyone should make a beginning, when at school, with a language or two, for humanistic, artistic, internationalist and "practical" reasons; but their study cannot engage the whole person as that of politics can, however brilliantly they may be taught, and a real mastery of them is achieved, if at all (special aptitudes apart), only when the learner has come alive enough in his total human nature to feel passionate either about literature as such or about the understanding of other peoples. Mathematics, then? Necessary, of course; but educational only in the very limited sense that they encourage care and accuracy. Classics? I have dealt with them already. As to "the elements of a commercial education" and "Army Class work", I may perhaps be excused from discussing them.

And now for the qualification. I do not say that *no* boy or girl can be fired in the manner suggested, the truly educational manner, by a study of classics or mathematics or modern languages. (I do say it about commerce and Army Class work.) Higher mathematics in particular, I imagine—I know little about them, but have always wanted to know a lot—can brim a boy as nothing else could (and a girl, too, of course: I use boy, antifeministically, throughout, to circumvent "his or her") with intellectual and spiritual energy; and though higher mathematics hardly come within the range of a schoolboy, they may perhaps cast their splendour behind them, for people of a certain temperament, to ordinary classroom preliminaries. But "for people of a certain temperament"— there's the rub. There may be people, there assuredly are people, born to be fired by mathematics or classics or modern languages, and fired uniquely: but *every* human being is born to be fired in some measure by interests proper to a human being as such. That is why—I am still speaking within the context of my first assertion (namely that as an instrument for education "in education's own right" politics are invaluable) and as if no second one were to follow—while everybody should "do" a certain modicum of mathematics and modern languages, politics should be the staple of the overwhelming majority, mathematics and so on of a picked minority.

Science and history remain—the history of "history specialists". What applies to mathematics etcetera applies to these two as well, only more so (or do I mean less so?—the minority, I mean, becomes larger). But history "on its own", even when taught by a genius like David, is less valuable for the average schoolboy than the politics that include it: its antennae are fewer, it strikes home with less profound, less immediate an impact. As to science, its general principles, as I have said— and as we were beginning to practise at Repton—should come in under the grand umbrella of a political education: but while developing a boy's accuracy and care, like mathematics, and, if the master is good enough, a scrupulous regard for verification, ordinary classroom work, which deals with matter and laws, cannot move the stiller depths of living creatures in the way that politics (by an act of union) can—those excepted, and I do not think they are many, who already feel, even in school laboratories, the presence of something numinous. If I had to choose, still within the context of my first assertion, an alternative to politics as the norm, I should put history first, science second, and the rest a long way after.

I come now to my second assertion, which is this: politics should be the staple of pre-university curricula because, apart altogether from their value as an instrument for education "in education's own right", they, and they alone, can directly lead the young towards citizenship. If you look at it afresh—we get accustomed to appalling anomalies—you will think it incredible that young people should be erupted from the matrix of their academies in the condition called at Athens "idiotic": as ἰδιῶται, that is, as "people who take no interest in politics" (for this is the meaning of idiōtai), or, if they do take an interest in them, then take it on a foundation of nothing better than a lot of ignorant prejudices. What is the world crying out for? What was it crying out for in 1918? What has it been crying out for since organised communities first appeared? Good men, of course: but men capable of applying their goodness in the national no less than the personal sphere, and in the international no less than the national. And this can be done in one way only—on the basis of knowledge: knowledge of facts; knowledge of ideas; knowledge of the motives that have moved human beings and still continue to move them, often so obscurely. Without it a man is at the mercy of any unscrupulous demagogue or shrieking newspaper, and we plunge on with increasing precipitancy from one disaster to another. What becomes of "informed public opinion"? It is as if a baby just fresh from the womb were compelled to find its own food and drink, and to talk, read and move like any adult. For be certain of this: once a man is about in the world, once affairs begin pressing upon him, once he is occupied with earning his liveli-hood and other personal involvements, the opportunity has been lost: he cannot now *begin* to "learn politics", though if enthusiasm and some little experience have been already acquired he can advance in the knowledge of them.

Even if, therefore, political education had no special value as an instrument for education "in education's own right", I should regard it as the desirable norm. But it has: and moreover —the beautiful justness!—its two values are one. Political disciplines enhance personality for the following reason: our own nature unfolds the more fully, the more fully we involve ourselves, by study and imagination, with others.

I sum up, then, like this. Politics should be the normal basic subject: it should not be exclusive for anyone: science, history or whatnot should be basic for a minority specially responsive to them: but they should learn some politics too.

So much for the desirability of a political education. Before asking "Is it feasible?" I must deal with such outstanding objections as might, if justly taken, invalidate its desirability.

The first of them will long since have occurred to you. Can politics, whether in the broader or in the narrower sense, be taught without propaganda? And isn't politics, considered as a school subject, the one above all others from which the smallest element of propaganda ought to be excluded? Now let me, before dealing with this matter in its contemporary application over the entire educational field, hark back for a moment to Repton and the average public school of my day. For the fact is this: though doubtless there were exceptions, the whole system, in one of its aspects, really amounted to a kind of propaganda—propaganda none the less effective for being covert. A boy was pitchforked into a public school with a

Masters engaged in political education who happen to be liberals can be a little less scrupulous, if I may put it so, in presenting their case for the great liberal principles—freedom of thought and discussion; the sanctity of the individual conscience; the paramount importance of moral and intellectual independence. For not only will they be creating a habit of mind that will *naturally* criticise, and so be annihilating the advantage that propaganda for particular principles and policies might otherwise give them, but, over and above that, propaganda for liberalism carries with it—this is the beauty of liberalism—the instrument for its own overthrow, for the overthrow, I mean, of liberalism itself. If the liberalism survives, it will survive on its own merits. All this, of course I know, will be a red rag to the bull of neo-authoritarianism. That's partly the point of it.

Two reflections remain. The first is obvious. An impressive example of liberalism openly practised, and in particular of tolerance and respect for other people's opinions, is worth all the propaganda for it in the world. The second is this, and it adds something important to what I said about "glow". The best of all ways to induce tolerance in a boy is to attack him in the innermost citadel of his intolerance: to put the case against convictions, above all, that he thinks nobody of any intelligence could ever challenge, and to put it at its strongest—even if you happen to share those convictions (and you must never pretend that you don't). If you win him to see the other point of view, you may have cured him of intolerance altogether; for he will have learnt how idiotic it is in his own proper person. And you can impart a glow to the presentation of that case as if that case were your own: for you are desperately concerned now, not about opinions you happen to hold or reject, but about tolerance. If I suddenly found myself teaching at one of those establishments—they exist—where almost everyone is an of-course type of socialist, I should spend a lot of my time presenting the case for enlightened self-interest. And if in another hypothetical establishment I were up against a bigoted anti-authoritarianism, I shouldn't rest until I'd said everything possible in favour of—let me say of Newman's "Apologia", which I was reading last night and found wholly antipathetic: *en belle revanche*, you will understand, for authoritarianism itself.

Now I knew all this very well at the time of our Repton adventure; most of it, in fact, is taken almost verbatim from a book, called "The School and the World", which we wrote, David and I, in the summer of 1918 and got published through Chapman and Hall. (Copying it out, with retouches here and there, has given me the pleasurable illusion of having written a lot this week-end, and despatches me to Oxford, for an amateur performance of *Fidelio*, with an easy conscience: though as a matter of fact I have written practically nothing. *Later:* the performance was really fine: but I enjoyed most of all a remark by a German I happened to overhear—"Beethoven, in my obinion, was a genius.") Whether I adequately lived up to my knowledge is for you to decide. In some respects I did: to the very end I was careful to put conflicting points of view as honestly as I could. In some respects I didn't: I was not a living example of tolerance. Still—have another look at those letters the boys sent me, and notice how a passion for tolerance, and an obviously genuine one, is precisely what marks them.

My chief sin at Repton is one you may think me a bit fantastic for describing as such, but this is not so. I have a *mana*. What is a *mana*? Dr Marett describes it in the *Encyclopaedia Britannica* as, among other things, a "wonder-working power". Some people have a *mana*, some haven't; some a weak one, some a strong. If you want an alternative to "wonder-working power", call it magnetism, or compulsiveness, or, to be plainer but even more inaccurate, just personality. Possessing it, you can make people do, within limits, and even think, within narrower limits, what you want them to do or think: or in the alternative (both cases are possible) people may react to you like that automatically, without there being any question of your "making" them—without, at any rate consciously, your willing it.

My *mana* is strong. It enables me, for instance, when taking a collection at a meeting for some "cause", to get five times as much, despite obvious handicaps, as the most beautiful woman in the world, with a voice like Emmy Destinn's and the skill of pebble-man Demosthenes but without *mana*.

There is, technically, a good *mana* and a bad *mana*. A good *mana* is linked up with religion, a bad *mana* with black magic. Licht-Alberich has a good *mana*, Schwarz-Alberich a bad one. You use a good *mana* for the glory of God, a bad one for the glory of Satan.

This distinction is a true distinction at a certain level (dear me, I'm beginning to talk like an Ouspenskyite: must I study pass when religion claims to interfere with a man's private life."

The second of the objections that could reasonably be urged against political education ties in with the first. "While a formidable strife between masters of different creeds might be engendered," wrote the *Manchester Guardian* in a review of our experiment, "it is arguable that the finest political spirit might be fostered by approaching such problems under the conditions of fairness and courtesy on which the public schools pride themselves." (I remember wondering whether a little irony was intended.) "Might be engendered": shouldn't it, the critic may ask, have been "must be engendered", or, at the very least, "will probably be engendered"? Wasn't the "formidable strife" in our own case an all but inevitable consequence of our activities? And could anything be worse for the moral (not to mention political) education of the young than the spectacle of such conflict, and, in the lamentable event, their participation in it? What do we want our fine old system to turn into—a sort of permanent bye-election?

Now to begin with: expel at once from your mind, if it's lodged there, the idea that schoolmasters, when untroubled by politics, behave in the fashion of an earlier, a prelapsarian existence—prelapsarian, unless, to be sure, the Fall itself was premundane. I have just been reading a brilliant "Life" of Hugh Walpole by my colleague, Rupert Hart-Davis, so the Walpole incunabulum, "Perrin and Traill", is very vivid in my mind at the moment. It came out just as I was leaving St Paul's (or perhaps a bit earlier), and a few readers were inclined to dismiss it as the ill-natured revenge of a clever man who had mistaken his profession. But nobody said that of G. F. Bradby's "The Lanchester Tradition", which appeared, I think, simultaneously: what they did say—what other schoolmasters said—was "how on earth does this Rugby man come to know about *us*"? And then there was Alec Waugh's "The Loom of Youth", and Arnold Lunn's "The Harrovians", and, best of the lot, Selver's emery-papered "Schooling". These records, admittedly—or most of them—date from about forty years ago; but I can find no reason for thinking that school atmospheres, in the meantime, have

vastly changed. Many schoolmasters become such not because
they are dedicated men, but *faute de mieux*: they are wretchedly
paid—always have been: financial worries may trouble the
married, unsatisfied sexuality some of the bachelors: faced with
critical young minds, they must be forever on their toes to win
respect and retain it: they run the risk of being jeered at for
their eccentricities: and when you add to all this, in the case
anyhow of boarding establishments, the petty local atmosphere,
the claustrophobia of a monasticism that no awareness of
dedication to a divine service may have endowed with a
sense of larger freedom—then you might really find it wonderful if everyone behaved like a saint. Why, I know a publishing business, a very famous one, in which the two partners,
it is said, sat for years in adjoining offices and communicated only in writing. But boys are aware of every move
in the game, hear the last syllable of gossip; and if I had to
choose, for the subject of their talk, between a row (partially,
at any rate, disinterested) about the status of conscientious
objectors, and old so and so's detestation of old so and so
"because he's stolen my scholarship work"—an actual Repton
case, this—I should plump for the former.

But for all that, and comparisons apart, later developments
at Repton were clearly undesirable. Were they also inevitable?
Or, to put it in a more useful way, would political education
engender, whatever the circumstances, or be likely to engender,
a clash between masters of the sort properly describable as
deleterious? Not at all, in my view. The evidence from Repton
is neither here nor there, or, if anywhere, then here—I mean on
my side of the fence. Of the factors most likely to produce a disastrous explosion not a single one was absent. Our experiments
took their rise at a time of great peril for England: it suddenly
mounted, this peril, more than once during the course of them:
and they inevitably centred, to a high degree, in considerations
of policy bound up with it. So nerves grew tauter and tauter,
and presently snapped. Secondly, we lacked all experience; we
had to journey, like Antarctic adventurers, without a fore-
runner to guide us. Thirdly: Pruke and I, to mention only the
two of us, were an extremely unusual collocation: both of us
remarkable, no doubt, for our qualities, but as remarkable for
the defects of them. Fourthly, Amyas, for all his genius, yoked
a bit dangerously, in point of temperament, with me. Finally,

God and their neighbour. And the best of all methods? In the very act of teaching politics, to behave politically.

I spoke just now of intellectual freedom. Everything, of course, depends on whether you believe in it or not. A lot of people don't believe in it nowadays, and naturally, by token of the very freedom they denigrate, they are entitled to their opinion. But I have been assuming a belief in it from beginning to end of my apology for political education: *some* point of departure must be accepted, and education for any type of authoritarianism seems, to my way of thinking, a fantastic contradiction in terms. So if you gird at intellectual freedom, you will dismiss this whole argument about controversy as beside the point; if on the other hand you value it, you will conclude perhaps somewhat as follows: Let everybody differ from everybody on every topic save two: the infinite possibilities of the boys he teaches, and the infinite value of freedom of thought.

There is a third and last objection to the desirability of the schemes I've been discussing, or one midway, perhaps, between objections to their desirability and objections to their feasibility. "All very well," critics may retort, "what you've been saying, but how on earth are you to find enough competent people to teach politics?" I shall pass this by for the moment, and, taking the desirability of political education as proved, go straight on to consider our second grand question, namely:

(b) *Is it feasible?* Or more fully: Is it feasible to make "politics" the normal basis of school education throughout the entire national system?

For decades, of course not: maybe not for a century, or far longer.

Apart altogether from the difficulty about the current school leaving-age (a difficulty that will be overcome), the whole trend is the other way. Education at school (I have touched on universities in my earlier volume) becomes more and more banausic. I am thinking, of course, in percentages: I mean, not that the number of children who receive what I should call a relatively humane education—adjusted upwards to cover the increase in population—is absolutely smaller than the number who received it say a hundred years ago (though even this may be true), but that the percentage of those humanely educated, out of people educated at all, is immensely lower. There is of course a good deal of gain here, as well as a good deal of loss, because the percentage of people educated at all, out of the entire population—the percentage of people who can read and write and do arithmetic and so on, whatever exactly the "so on" may mean—is also, by the same token, immensely higher: and I do not, for the time being, complain. These, one must hope, are the growing-pains of democracy. But the results, meanwhile, are appalling; and if you doubt what I say, look at the popular press, and be convinced. And matters are getting steadily worse. I think, in particular, of a Sunday newspaper, sober, informative and even idealistic until a few years ago: it has been becoming under my eyes, week by week, a medium for that species of pornography, typically English I am afraid, which saves its face by the wretched pretence of exposing immorality.

The overwhelming majority of Englishmen, "educated" just sufficiently to earn their living, to occupy a pin-hole in the industrial machine, to read the sensational and pornographic press, and to relax against the background of Light Programme inanities, go to form a huge, irresistible *Urmensch*, in and through whose mentality—think of waters in a channel— almost the whole of English life is lived sordidly, materialisti- cally, and under the dictate of self-interest. God forbid that I should appear to be criticising any particular class or any par- ticular individuals: the masses constantly show, when occasion arises, that in their private relations, and in response to an appeal that comes home to them, they can be as good, at least as good, as any possible élite. But the course of western history, with its relentless pagan drive—to material prosperity: to the annihila- tion of a boredom that ought never to exist: to speed, physical excitement, all manner of titillation: to the conquest of nature, never mind for what purpose—has resulted in this: we are but half the men we might have been if the physical advance, which I am far from decrying (for without it men remain, for the most part, near the level of beasts), had been accompanied by a spiritual one, instead of hypnotising us with its glamour and becoming, at the last, an all-in-all. The process, moreover, is accelerating.

And this increase in tempo—if you fly at the speed of a car you must fly at the speed of sound, if you fly at the speed of sound you must fly at the speed of light: an ordinary bomb is no good, it must be an atom one, an atom bomb is no good, it must be a hydrogen one—this growing preoccupation with *achievements*, material achievements, is affecting, as time goes on, even those patterns of education that used, designedly at least, to be liberal. Everywhere the tendency is to learn, not disinterestedly, but in order to "do well" or "get on".

It would be fantastic to imagine that a process so impulsive can be halted overnight, and replaced by another. I shall certainly not live to see the day when political education is established: perhaps you will not, either. Then why talk about it so much, you (or at any rate others) may ask? Because that is the way we human beings work. Wars have raged since the beginning of history: they are raging at this moment as I write: but does that absolve us for a moment from the task, not merely of advocating universal peace, but of formulating plans for its realisation? Dreams are stronger than reality; for they make, at however long last—or so we must believe, if we ask ourselves why God has allowed us to dream—a better reality.

There is nothing really far-fetched, you know, once one gets right away from contemporary pressures, about the idea of political education. "The proper study of mankind is man," wrote Alexander Pope; and all I am doing is to emend him, and say "The proper study of mankind—not solely or even mainly of adult mankind, when the opportunity has largely been lost, but of mankind while it is learning—is God, man and the universe." Is there anything extraordinary about that? Isn't it plain common sense? Or go back further, and say (as I said, let me remind you, at the very beginning of all this talk about Repton) that I am proposing to revive, in a modern setting, the Renaissance ideal of a liberal education. Of course my details may be all wrong, and I am not wedded to them; some of them, even, I may think better of before I go to press. The broad aim is all that matters.

Is nothing feasible, then, here and now? Yes, something is feasible. Any schoolmaster who agrees with what I've written can do a little experimenting on his own, so far as he is allowed; anybody, not a schoolmaster, who similarly agrees can become one. It's all nonsense, that business about an inadequate supply of suitable men: the supply is there, but most of the men, for one reason or another, never think of becoming schoolmasters.

If only they would! They could help, by a fraction however minute, to make the dream a reality.

I have never been able to understand why so many shy off from the prospect of schoolmastering, or why schoolmasters grouse so; and I am happy to remember that of those who survived from the little company of youthful leaders in my original Upper Sixth a high percentage ignored prejudice and became schoolmasters themselves. I needn't bother to describe disadvantages: I have already done so. But the compensations! I used to envisage, in my room up at the Pastures, a devoted army of young Greek warriors, who would invade the public schools and pioneer for a true education. Nor was "Greek" out of place; for there was something about the sunlit freshness of a cricket-field that recalled the April of our civilisation. Yet I would speak, not of public schools, but of any school. You live in the company of growing creatures: you find a freshness, a high-heartedness about them that renews your own springtime: and as you watch their hearts and minds, see them develop, so you hope, into makers of happiness for themselves and the world, you have the tranquil satisfaction of knowing that you may have helped them if only a little, and that a bit of you may live on, many years hence, in grown men who have realised, with your assistance, their potentiality for goodness. I have been a schoolmaster, and I tell you there is no happiness like it.

And yet the appeal should be based on something soberer than prospects of happiness. Education is the keystone of politics: the future of the world will depend on its educators. A schoolmaster will live in obscurity: he can hope for no Embassies, no Palaces of Westminster, no Whitehalls. But he might do well, before embarking on another career, to bethink himself of Banquo:

"Lesser than Macbeth, and greater.
Not so happy, yet much happier.
Thou shalt get kings, though thou be none"

INTERLUDE ABOUT PRISON COMMISSIONERS

February 28th, 1953

I promised to explain why the Prison Commissioners sacked me.

I started visiting at Wormwood Scrubs about three years ago, and did, I think, reasonably well. I visited every Friday, and my method was, not to give a miserable few minutes to each of perhaps half a dozen prisoners, but to concentrate on two or three, and eventually on one. The one in question was a delightful young man whom I shall call Ronnie Jones. Round about twenty-five, and of a parentage unknown to himself or anybody else, he had been in and out of prisons, with a preliminary canter at Borstal, for some little time. He specialised in the theft of lead.

He greeted me roughly at first, remarking that, so far as he was aware, he hadn't asked for a visitor. He allowed me, however, to sit down and have a chat; and suddenly, just as I was going, fished a box out from under his bed—he was lying in it already, at only half past six: it's more comfortable in bed than on a chair, once they've banged you down* for the night—and offered me one of those diminutive cigarettes, as precious to a prisoner as Havanas are to me, that they buy out of their shilling or so a week. So we became friends, and I always looked forward to my visits.

One week he wasn't there. He told me the following Friday that he had just finished seven days c.c.—close confinement in a punishment cell—for "swearing at an officer". On such occasions, it appears, there is a formal, cap-off sort of trial, and the warder, before sentence is promulgated, has to repeat the exact words complained of. "Filthy, they were," said Ronnie, explaining why a defence had been impossible. "You know what I mean. I shouldn't like to repeat them to you." He always took that line: treated me like a baby, and as if anxious to safeguard my innocence. He told me once that he had blued five hundred and twenty pounds, the proceeds of a robbery, in three weeks. After working it out in my head I expressed myself sceptical. He assured me he wasn't lying. "Then how did you manage it?" I asked. "In the West End," he replied. "You know what I mean," he added vaguely—this was what, in the technology of the radio, would be called his signature tune. "Restaurants and so on." "But that's nonsense," I said. "I'm much richer than you, and know all about West End restaurants; and I couldn't possibly get rid of the stuff at that rate—it

* Locked you up

*works out at nearly thirty pounds a day." "Well of course," he said,
"I had a different woman every night: special, you know what I
mean. I wouldn't like to tell you . . ." I tried to make him change
his mind, but couldn't: he was clearly determined not to sully me.
He was equally concerned for my freedom. "Peculiar places, these,"
he once remarked. "They wouldn't suit you at all. I don't advise
you to get into one." His attitude to the Scrubs was rather like that
of a man who has chosen a second-rate hotel from motives of economy
and now regrets it. I sent him a message one day postponing a particular visit. Next time I went I asked him whether he'd had it.
"Message?" he said. "They don't give messages here. Shockingly
run, this place. You'd be amazed."*

*I asked him, that Friday after his c.c., about the punishment
cell: I wondered how bad it had been. "Well, not exactly bad," he
replied, "but different, you know what I mean—not like home.
I've been in this cell for two years. I always bang it up when I go
to the shops, not like some fellows who leave theirs open. I know in
a second if anybody's been here—I don't know how I know but I
know. I don't allow it. I complain to the warders." He had a great
feeling for home, without ever having known one, and for all
familiarities. Looking at his window one evening, ablaze with the
setting sun, I asked him whether birds ever came there, and told him
about Toller's Schwalbenbuch: how day after day the same
two swallows, mates, had perched on the poet's bars, and he had
fed them, and they had become friends.*

*Ronnie got quite excited. "You know the sunrise?" he asked.
Yes, I replied, I knew the sunrise. "Well in that cell opposite,"
he said, "a bird comes every sunrise. You can put out your arm
and feed it, like this you can put out your arm. Of course, only a
sparrow." I told him I'd give a copy of the Swallow Book to
the prison library, and then he could read it. This would have
pleased Toller, who committed suicide in 1938 because he hated
fascism and feared it was going to win.*

*Ronnie was a man of great natural delicacy. "Jew" and
"Jewish" were regarded in his milieu as terms of opprobrium, as
in many other milieus; and if he ever had occasion to use them—as
when he asked me about the matsos that he had just seen arriving for Passover—he always pulled himself up at the initial "J"
and hurriedly substituted "you know what I mean."*

*I kept in touch with him, of course, after he'd come out, and was
able to be of some service to him in connection with an affair involv-*

ing bacon, which anyhow wasn't his line. He has been doing well for some time now. I ran into him the other day near the Strand, strolling—I was strolling—with Daphne du Maurier. I introduced them. He was ravished, as well he might have been.

But Ronnie isn't really the point: it's only that I enjoy celebrating him. To continue, therefore: occupied with this letter, and anxious to get on with it, I dropped my work at the Scrubs in July '51, as soon, that is, as everyone I'd been dealing with had left: my intention being (and I think I made this clear) to take it up again in a year or two. The following January I got a letter from the Commissioners, thanking me for my work and reappointing me a visitor. But this January I got a letter in the contrary sense: my name had been removed from the roll. I wrote to enquire why. If the reason, I said, was that I was cluttering things up while on the shelf, and that I should be reappointed in due course, I had nothing to complain of: if, on the other hand, it was something different, I should like to know in terms what it was. The former reason, I added, seemed improbable, in view of my reappointment the previous January, when I hadn't been visiting for six months.

"Sir," ran the reply—expressed, you will notice, in language which, if emanating from anyone but a government official, might appear a little lacking in human warmth—"I am desired by the Prison Commissioners to refer to your letter of the 4th February 1953, and to say in reply that their letter of the 20th January last was not intended to convey the impression that whilst unable to invite you to serve as a Prison Visitor during 1953 they would extend an invitation to you to serve again in a subsequent year.

"It has been their invariable practice, in agreement with the National Association of Prison Visitors, to decline to give reasons for not renewing an invitation and they regret, therefore, that they cannot offer you any further explanation."

Now what had happened, I asked myself, between the beginning of '52, when my work was considered valuable, and the beginning of '53, when it was considered the reverse: as I hadn't been doing any in the meantime? I had no need to rack my brains for the answer. It was this: I had published "Who Lie in Gaol" by Joan Henry.

This book described conditions in Holloway as a former inmate had seen them. It got a remarkable reception (being applauded by Bertrand Russell among others) and will lead, I feel certain, to vital reforms. But it annoyed, of all bodies, the Howard League for Penal Reform. Mr Benson, Member of Parliament, its Chairman, wrote a letter of furious denunciation to the Manchester Guardian, *impugning, not only Miss Henry's accuracy, but her motives. Naturally, I replied—particularly about her motives, which happened to be known to me. I ended by asking whether the Commission proposed to hide behind the skirts of the League, instead of meeting these charges themselves. Eventually, the Commissioners were "drawn"—and gave me, in my opinion, the major part of my case.*

That is all. The only possible inference is this: the Commissioners are unwilling to give the freedom of our prisons to anyone determined to speak his mind. One thing, however, I ought in fairness to add: I had used some expression—I cannot be bothered to look it up, and am quoting from memory—such as "the utter abomination of our whole penal system."

A word in conclusion. Given the utter abomination aforesaid, for which the nation, and no particular individual in any particular establishment, must be held responsible, Wormwood Scrubs, so far as I could judge, is humanely administered.

PART II (RESUMED)

CHAPTER VII

FROM REPTON TO MARRIAGE

With cricket proceeding at Repton, I spent, nevertheless, an agreeable two or three months or so in London. I
was still under military discipline, and might at any moment
be sent off, I feared, to do paper-work in a barracks or defend
an outpost of Empire; but in the meantime my old friend
Douglas Jerrold, who had been wounded at Gallipoli and was
now in the Ministry of Food, hurriedly got me a job there. I
might as well have been at the barracks: so far as the work was
concerned I had never been so bored in my life, not even at
Cambois. By a quippish piece of irony—you will certainly not
have forgotten those enormously long chapters on Jewish ortho-
doxy in my earlier volume—I was put in charge of Kosher
rationing; or not exactly put in charge—I had to juggle, following a directive, with little groups of fiddly squares on bits of
cardboard, to ensure that people forbidden bacon didn't get too
much cheese. I am exceedingly bad at puzzles, and invariably
made a mess of it; and anyhow it took no longer, spin it out as I
might, than an hour or so a day. How I loathe the Civil Service!
I was not without some trifling experience of it, for I had
volunteered, during one of my Repton holidays, to assist at the
inauguration of the Ministry of Munitions: indeed, they offered
me a permanent job there, not, I think, by reason of my efficiency, but because, when a new Ministry is founded, you must
above all "acquire staff"—any sort of staff, but as much staff as
possible. I rejected the offer, as the last few hundred pages have
made clear: I even wrote a poem about it, beginning

> "Sit here for ever, talking steel
> And helping slowly to amass
> A safe reserve of zinc and brass?"

and continuing with the question, what sort of person did they
take me for? Zinc and brass, when the Paddock was calling?
Grotesque!

Nevertheless the days, as I have said, meandered pleasantly,
for there were many diversions. I read *The Portrait of a Lady* and

The Princess Casamassima at the office, and Douglas and I, with an occasional third, would lunch delightfully, after a walk in the sunshine, at Canuto's in Baker Street or old George Stone's *Moulin d'Or*. The boys, of course, were always in and out of Dryders, my base: and twice I returned to Repton for a week-end with Moë and Allan. I found, on the second occasion, that my room at Mrs Miggs' had been padlocked, metaphorically or perhaps literally: the reason being, I understood, that a boy had been caught there, reading *Salome*.

My London idyll, or *ersatz*-idyll, was interrupted, and shortly afterwards terminated, by one of those miserable, mean-looking envelopes that would argue, if one weren't in the know, a laudable economy at Whitehall. This was from the War Office: they had the honour to inform me that I had been posted to the Manchester Regiment for the purpose of garrisoning Singapore. I moved heaven and earth to get at any rate a stay of execution, pointing out that, if I left my Kosher rationing, the entire Jewish community would be in peril: but was unsuccessful. So I made my arrangements. I bought a loathsome looking pistol at Moss Bros. (or did I have it already, from Northumberland?) and enquired about a sword. This, they told me, was unnecessary: a tropical mess kit, on the other hand, though not wholly indispensable, would be well worth my while. But I was out of funds, despite a loan (of £50) from my ultimate boss at the Ministry, Sir Stephen Tallents—whose kindness I am happy to celebrate; so I made do with a sola topee.

As the moment for departure drew near, excitement began to mount in me. I had never left England before, and now I was to see, not only bits of Europe (I hoped), but the blazing and sun-drenched and glamorous and fabled and immemorial East. I was one of a composite draft, and our first place of call was Taranto. As we journeyed down the eastern shores of Italy we might have been travelling, from our pace, through a dense English fog before fog-signals were invented. We would go clanking along for an hour, stop a day or two, appear to be starting, fail to do so, really start, and pull up with such a grinding of brakes as my dentist might have envied. As for the filthiness of the train I have no doubt there are suitable images, though I can't think of any. The lavatories—but a friend has advised me not to talk about lavatories any more, as I overdid it in *Timothy*: so I'll leave them to your imagination, and you'll require, let me tell you, an exceptionally vivid one. Yet there were compensations. One looked out of a window and, forgetting lavatories, saw paradise: and, arrived about half-way down, we stopped for two whole days at one of those innumerable little places on the Italian seaboard (there must be at least half a dozen of them) called Castellammare. I bathed: I sat in the sun: I drank vermouth at a wooden kiosk: I lay adoze under an orangey striped awning: and I fell in love with Italy. Back in the train, I wrote a chapter on Morality for *The School and the World*, which we had projected, David and I, just before my departure; and got on well with the military, as never before. They called me The Sheep; they said I looked like a sheep when I laughed.

Arrived at Taranto, I hung about there a fortnight: got my chapter off to David: and encountered Jack Haldane, going the other way—he looked ferocious as an officer in the Black Watch, and appeared to be enjoying the war: his courage, I understood, had been leonine. Then we embarked, and touched first at Port Said: where, attracted by a callipygian book-jacket, I bought a Parisian *curiosum*. I read it for a quarter of an hour. At the end of the first five minutes my eyes (to employ a euphemism) had nearly popped out of my head (to continue the euphemism): at the end of the second, they were back in their normal position: at the end of the third, they had almost disappeared behind their sockets—and I sent the thing flying, illustrations and all, from my port-hole into the sea. I was to regret this, a little, next day, and, a little less, the day after: but presently I forgot to be *troublé*. In the meantime we had entered the Canal, and were making for Suez: battened down by night, or, if we took only one night, then that night—but battened down may be a solecism: what I mean is, we had to pack ourselves, stark naked except for towels (the heat was so appalling), in the entrails of the ship, hermetically sealed to stop a glimmer of light from escaping: the idea being that the Turks, or some such people, were everywhere about, though I should have thought that if they couldn't see us they could certainly hear us. We stayed but half a day in Suez proper, and I spent most of it trying to get a postcard, for I wanted to write home: but I did not succeed: for wherever I went the word postcard was interpreted pregnantly—that is, to signify dirty postcard—and I thought that these would be unsuitable. From

Suez we moved out into some sort of desert, where we encamped for a fortnight. I am vague about the geography: I was fond of saying afterwards that I had lived in the shadow of Mount Sinai, but I may have been wanting to sound ancestral. Here, however, is a true story about my sojourn near Suez, and a charming one, I think. You may have heard that there is hardly any twilight in that part of Egypt: one minute it's blazing, the next it's black. Well, I had gone for a walk along a roughly beaten path that crossed the desert, when suddenly I couldn't see anything: nobody could have seen much, and I, perhaps because I don't like carrots, see less than most people after dark. So there I was, lost and a bit frightened: the lone and level sands stretched far away, with no feature to catch my eye, even if I could have seen it. Then suddenly I felt my hand touched, and, looking down, saw a small human shape. It was a little Arab boy, and God knows (in a special sort of way, perhaps: anyhow, let us call it a miracle) where on earth he had come from. He led me back home with a courtesy so charming that only Schubert could express it, and then disappeared—went off, that is, in an ordinary fashion.

From Suez we ran down to Aden, not, indeed, being able to run anywhere else; and, after coaling there, turned sharp left: crossed the Gulf: and entered the Arabian Sea.

We were bound for Colombo, where I was to pick up a boat for Singapore. You will never have heard of Richard Middleton, Timothy: hardly anyone seems to have heard of him, even today. He must have been writing his stories about fifty years ago, for I remember reading them at St Paul's. Several are masterpieces, and I never know which to put first; but after playing about with "The Conjuror" and "The Coffin Merchant" I usually decide for "The Ghost Ship". This is what it is about: a ghost-ship, painted black and all covered with carvings, blows one evening, during the gales of '97, into the middle of landlord's turnip-field, a little off the Portsmouth Road and half-way between Portsmouth and London. It lies hard on landlord's turnips, but eventually sails away to a noise of fiddling and with port-holes ablaze. That is about all. Well, I had the impression, in 1918, that we glided on a breath into Colombo, came to rest above her boulevard, and cast anchor in her paving-stones. We descended a rope-ladder: and there we were, just outside an hotel, where I had a tooth stopped.

Perhaps, if I must dissipate my fantasy, Colombo is built like Venice, with boulevard for Piazzetta; the boulevard is a sort of beach; and the ships ride close in to it.

So I came to the Far East; and I shall not bother you with an account of my doings there, which were quite uninteresting. Shortly after arriving at Singapore I fell sick of some stomach complaint, and went to hospital. By the January of 1919 I was back in London: before the summer was through I had got married

and was already on the outskirts of publishing; and Moses had appeared on the beam.

I shall end the main narrative here, leaving over for volume III, which will follow in about a year, the delightful preliminaries of marriage, marriage itself and its problems, my life as a publisher, and all the rest of it. But I must tie in a loose end before I've finished with the present instalment: I must trace the development of my thought on the war-and-peace question from what it was when I was teaching at Repton to what, as expressed in the opening pages of this volume, it has recently become. And that will mean, in its turn, a preliminary canter over the sunlit but occasionally tempestuous expanses of political publishing.

CHAPTER VIII

THE WAR AND PEACE QUESTION

THE "CHARGE" OF PACIFISM they brought against me at Repton was quite untrue in the sense in which they brought it. In another sense it was half true.

I can best clarify my position at that time by dealing in turn with (1) my attitude to hurting and killing (2) my attitude to war (3) my attitude to the 1914–1918 war.

(1) I have never been able to bear the idea of hurting or killing any living thing. Or perhaps I ought to say "hurting" rather than "hurting or killing"; because, though killing is loathsome to me, I have done it scores of times when something hurt has had to be put out of its agony, and would have found it as impossible not to do so as to have inflicted the original hurt. Time after time I have half-noticed a crushed worm on a London pavement and passed it by in my absorption, and then remembered it later and compulsively walked back, a mile maybe or more, to put it at peace. (And let me say in this connection that knowing very well the perils and difficulties, spiritual and other, involved, I find it almost impossible to understand how anyone can oppose euthanasia, when the sufferer desires it. The religious answer, of course, is that God alone may kill or keep alive. Yes, but we are God's instruments, and he tells us, through our consciences, what he wishes us to do. Besides, I don't find any similar objection from opponents of euthanasia when it's a question of our killing, quite on our own and without God coming into it at all, thousands or tens of thousands of our fellow human beings with napalm or atom bombs.)

My horror of hurting (and of killing, except in the circumstances mentioned) derives, I believe, from two sources. It derives, in the first place—I feel more definite about this now than when I touched on the matter in *Tim I*—from a strong, and perhaps unusually strong, element in my make-up of sado-masochism. The process is the familiar one of compensation. It derives, secondly, from "reverence for life". The first source is physical, though a groping spirituality produces the compensation: the second is wholly spiritual. Ultimately, doubtless, the dichotomy is a false one: but, at a certain stage of analysis, it has its uses.

Reverence for life, which is far commoner than people suppose, forbids us to stop the joy, spontaneity and growth in any living creature: partly because to do so would be to outrage the God that has created them, and partly (though the two are indistinguishable) because we love them ourselves.

The phrase "reverence for life" is Albert Schweitzer's. When I published "A Year of Grace" about eighteen months ago only one review annoyed me. It was by somebody or other—I forget his name—who objected to the inclusion of anything "so absurd" as the following, from Schweitzer's *Civilisation and Ethics:*

"If in summer he [the man who reverences life] is working by lamplight, he prefers to keep the window shut and breathe a stuffy atmosphere rather than see one insect after another fall with singed wings upon his table."

It is a pity that the reviewer did not take to heart a passage that almost immediately follows:

"He is not afraid of being laughed at as sentimental. It is the fate of every truth to be a subject for laughter until it is generally recognised. Once it was considered folly to assume that men of colour were really men and ought to be treated as such, but the folly has become an accepted truth. [I wonder. A South African "native" has just been awarded eight strokes of the lash and a year's hard labour. His offence was this: he had asked people to contribute half a crown a year to a fund for fighting racial oppression.] Today it is thought to be going too far to declare that constant regard for everything that lives, down to the lowest manifestations of life, is a demand made by rational ethics. The time is coming, however, when people will be astonished that mankind needed so long a time to learn to regard thoughtless injury to life as incompatible with ethics." Not that conscious ethics, really, are in question: it is a matter of how you are made, how you instinctively feel—though your feelings can become strengthened and permanent by attention or weakened and eventually non-existent by carelessness.

"The lowest manifestations of life." I feel about the almost microscopic insects that you find in the bath on a dry summer morning very much as Schweitzer feels about moths, and would think it impossible to turn on the taps and get going until the last remaining speck had been manoeuvred on to a little piece of shaving paper and deposited in safety. With that habit, a very egoistic one, of imagining myself singular, I had thought this a personal oddity until I found that many others did the same. I have, anyhow, a peculiar love of small insects, and felt happy, a few months ago, to be spending the night with a moth. I heard it fluttering about as I got into bed, after turning on my reading-lamp: it must have been resting inside, athwart the parchment. Now such creatures commonly injure or even kill themselves when a lamp is alight, by blundering against the glass; on the other hand, I wanted to read. So what was I to do? I thought of conveying it to an unoccupied room, but couldn't catch it, being *ungeschicht* in such matters; and I couldn't put it out of the window, because (a) I couldn't catch it, and (b) a rainy hurricane was blowing. So I settled down to read and see what happened. It was a wise moth, for its flutterings were circumspect; and I waved it now and then out of danger. But the sentiments of the book I was reading—the *Tao Tê Ching*—very soon made me anxious: and I turned off the light, for to practise the *Tao* was clearly far better than to study it. The flutterings stopped immediately. When I woke in the night I felt wings on my face, and was pleased. At dawn I woke again, and saw the creature asleep on a match-box. I dozed awhile in its company: had a bath: returned to dress: found it gone from the match-box: soon discovered it, very comatose, on the table: touched it gingerly: couldn't stir it: and thought it dead. But this was not so; for Ruth, to whom I mentioned the matter over our early morning tea, at once descended to my room, set it fluttering again, caught it easily, and put it out of the window (for the rain had now ceased). I felt, as it flew off, that my room had been shared by a charming companion.

Many, I imagine, feel likewise about things that grow—grow from the soil, green things, grass and flowers and such—because they are obviously beautiful and appealing (most insects are appealing, but more obscurely). When my paths have got so tussocky with weeds as to be almost indistinguishable from the lawn I tell my gardener to put down chemical: but invariably feel remorse, the sense of having committed a blasphemy, when I see a strawy nothingness where there was once the sap of life. It is the same about cutting flowers: one does it, but one is ashamed of doing it.

I went into the garden early one morning last June, very happy after a specially good night. The old border was at its best; and as I watched the flowers swaying in a gentle summer breeze—the helenium and loosestrife and coreopsis, and those clustering white things like pincushions that I don't know the name of, with a lot of casual, self-sown poppies mixed up with them—a memory came nagging at me. I searched about on my shelves when I'd gone in till I found what I wanted—from *Creative Unity* by Tagore:

"One day, in a small village in Bengal, an ascetic woman from the neighbourhood came to see me. She had the name 'Sarvakhepi' given to her by the village people, the meaning of which is 'the woman who is mad about all things'. She fixed her star-like eyes upon my face and startled me with the question, 'When are you coming to meet me underneath the trees?' Evidently she pitied me who lived (according to her) prisoned behind walls, banished away from the great meeting-place of the All, where she had her dwelling. Just at that moment my gardener came with his basket, and when the woman understood that the flowers in the vase on my table were going to be thrown away, to make place for the fresh ones, she looked pained and said to me, 'You are always engaged reading and writing, you do not see.' Then she took the discarded flowers in her palms, kissed them and touched them with her forehead, and reverently murmured to herself, 'Beloved of my heart'. I felt that this woman, in her direct vision of the infinite personality in the heart of all things, truly represented the spirit of India."

There are two sorts of person, I think, in this context, the difference being due to variations in tradition and physical make-up and the way life has treated them and the way they have treated life. For the one sort, to speak of daisies rejoicing under the risen sun is to use a metaphor: for the other, it is to state a fact.

(2) My attitude to war was a special case of my attitude to hurting and killing. Here, all my passion was concentrated—had been concentrated ever since, at the age of six, I had come upon that appalling picture—into a desire to *prevent* war. I hadn't even considered, before 1914, either (a) whether a growth of pacifism could prevent it, and, if so, whether I should declare myself a pacifist, or (b) what, if and when it came, ought to be done about it. Such questions, if they *had* occurred to me, would have seemed impossibly remote. Moved spiritually by a hatred of war, I thought, so far as its prevention was concerned, in exclusively economic and political terms.

(3) The war came. The fact that I was unfit for foreign service (though of course, had I wanted, I could have wangled myself out to the front, as a lot of other people did) enabled me to hold in suspense, a dishonest suspense, the answer to an obvious query—could I personally wound or kill? At the back of my mind, I rather think, there was more than a doubt of it. I remember the bayonet practice in the Inns of Court O.T.C. There was a row of stuffed sacks hanging horribly from an elongated gibbet, which we had to rush at and stick with our bayonets; and the sergeant-major who was training us—how well I can see him now, his face very broad and brick red, and all but expressionless—used to say as we stood to attention "Get him full in the chest with it; and give it a twist when it's in—it makes the wound worse." I could carry on at all only by making a desperate effort to think of something else, or by pretending it was a meaningless game. I spare you an examination of how far cowardice—fear, not of wounding and killing, but of being wounded and killed—entered into the matter; and I don't need to tell you that I ought to have faced the thing squarely, and that, unless my answer had been in the affirmative, I oughtn't to have been in uniform.

The personal issue apart, pacifism in general was as much outside the realm of my thinking as it had been before the outbreak of war. The thing was there, and we had to go through with it. All that concerned me, now, was that it should be ended as quickly as possible, and on terms that would stabilise peace.

Did I want, then, to *win*?

Yes.

I did not even begin to believe—I must make this clear—that

the Germans were solely responsible for the outbreak of war; I saw the roots of it as far back in history, and what had happened on that high summer day as but an episode in the universal impulse that had brought one country after another on to the stage of a power-mongering world as the aggressor of the moment. Morally, I thought, personal egoism and greed, not of Germans or Austrians but of humanity in general, was the cause of it: in the political sphere, which was merely one aspect of the moral one, it was nationalism, again not of Germans or Austrians but of every single country at some stage or other of its development, that must bear the blame. But I went further than this. I saw both the egoism and the nationalism as at once expressing themselves in, and enormously intensified by, an economic, capitalistic imperialism: or rather in a number of these imperialisms, some already on the wane and some approaching their zenith, that clashed with one another in this quarter or that as they fought, offensively or defensively, for the markets of the world. So that "justice", as between aggressors and resisters, came into the matter, neither in the larger historical perspective nor in terms of fundamental morality, but in an immediate sense only. Unless something radical was done about it, little advantage would accrue from the fighting. One nation, in the event, would go down, another would come up; but no basic change would have occurred, and the whole thing, with bigger and bigger wars in prospect, would go on as before. It would always be the same play; only the actors would be different.

(It would be irrelevant to discuss at this point the rights and wrongs of my analysis—though of course it wasn't my analysis at all, but the ordinary socialist one of my day; and in any case I have already done so in *Tim I*. But I must repeat that there was far more of truth than of falsity in it. I have already quoted Lloyd George: let me now quote President Wilson. "Is there any man or woman alive," he said in 1919, "let me say is there any child, who does not know that the seed of war in the modern world is industrial and commercial rivalry? This was an industrial and commercial war.")

Why, then, did I want to win? Because—oh, because I didn't like the idea of being conquered: because I loved England: because the war, having happened, was *there*, and you must choose between the belligerents: because I hated nationalistic war-mongering, and though there wasn't very much in all this talk about Prussian militarism—hadn't others been militarist too, and how, for the matter of that, had we built our own Empire?—still there was *something* in it, still the militarism of Germany, as Germany had developed, was almost symbolic of barking lieutenants and bullying sergeant-majors and uniforms and obedience and everything else I found loathsome or ridiculous. At its simplest: an Allied victory would give far more hope to the world than a German one.

That is how I saw things at Repton.

§ 2

The war-and-peace question was not very obtrusive during the decade that succeeded my return from Malaya. This was natural; for the twenties, if they lacked the shadowless innocence of that earlier day before a first world war had come to darken it, were nevertheless still years in which the outbreak of a second one seemed sufficiently remote. If it wasn't glad confident morning, the twilight was only beginning.

The economic crisis of 1929 brought a change. I suppose a great many people, not directly affected, were transformed by the apprehensions and uncertainties that so suddenly assailed us. I recall the case of my oldest living friend. Clever, even a bit "smart", fascinated by modernities, rather arrogant, inclined to radicalism in politics, he could have given the impression to very few of being deeply concerned, in a personal way, with the fundamentals of religion: and indeed, if the concern was there, I for one, who knew him well, was unaware of it. But the crisis was to make of him, at any rate to outward seeming, something astonishingly different. He became an *illuminato*, adept in a religious way of life somewhat esoteric in character: and, what is probably more important, he developed a gentleness, a tolerance, a humility, a quietism and a readiness for giving himself to others (not deliberately —by the mere fact of being there) such as endowed him with a quality of healing and peace. He became, in fact, a bit of a saint, and remains one. But he is still very clever and witty.

Nothing of the kind happened to me. I became the reverse of quietistic. Hatred of war came rushing up again in me with the force of something newly awakened: for though no one could say where the trouble would start or with whom, it was clear, to anyone of my political colour, that given such ubiquitous turmoil, and such growing destitution and insecurity, a clash could be avoided, if at all, only by a gargantuan effort. So I asked myself, what little could *I* do?—and answered, inevitably after my Repton experience, "You can help to enlighten people; you can show them that, if capitalism persists, this sort of crisis is inevitable, and the final result will be war." That was the beginning of my active political publishing. Novelists were already flocking to me, for I was becoming successful, and my advertising was spectacular; but it was political publishing that I thought about night and day, just as it had been political education that had captured me at Repton. The passion to make people *see* that had come blazing up, thirty years before, in the Elgin Avenue breakfast-room, was again in my vitals; and now, I thought, I could really do something about it. So I got going: I began pouring out a great mass of informative books, all with the familiar yellow covers. The most important of them, at this time, was G. D. H. Cole's "Intelligent Man's Guide through World Chaos": a vast tome, full of facts and figures, which I issued in an enormous edition at a ludicrously low price.

(And I should like to interpose this. Just as the Repton atmosphere had been covertly propagandist, so, before I started these activities, was what I may call the bookshop atmosphere of Great Britain. I do not of course mean that no leftish books were published, or even that none of them sold: I mean that such books were rare exceptions, and that ninety-nine booksellers out of a hundred quietly boycotted socialism. I remember the case of a book—and a very valuable one it was —expounding the tie-up of commerce with politics. I asked my salesman in London to make a specially good job of it. He got orders for twenty copies. I asked him, "What did the booksellers say?" "They just laughed," he replied. If the book had been written the other way about, his twenty would have been two hundred.)

There are days in a man's life when his duty seems quite beyond question, and he never stops to ask himself "Might something else be better?" This is how I felt about things then. Pacifism was asleep in me, biding its time: it could hardly have seemed relevant to what alone I regarded as actual—namely how, when every moment was precious, I might use such resources as had been granted me to prevent, or help in preventing, another war. To *prevent*—once again that was everything. The possibility of joining a pacifist movement, and working actively in it, never entered my head: if it had, I should have rejected it as a betrayal. I had other fish to fry and the frying of them absorbed my whole attention. There have been periods throughout my life when I have anxiously re-examined my ideas, and then, sometimes for months on end, have shown a painful indecision; but when I have at last made up my mind to do a thing, I go obsessively at it to the exclusion of everything else.

Then came 1933. For all that I have just written, I don't think I had ever really faced the possibility that Hitler might come to power. We had been at Salzburg for the festival, Ruth and I, the previous summer, and had idled a little at Munich (there was a delightful *Figaro* at the Residenz theatre, a place almost as exquisitely rococo as the music itself) on our way back to England. Arrived here, I found the manuscript of Edgar Mowrer's *Germany Puts the Clock Back* on my desk: I rejected it, as far-fetched and war-mongering. And yet I ought to have been convinced by what I had experienced at Munich itself. Strolling one afternoon to the *Alte Pinakothek* we had passed the Brown House. Guards, with steel helmets and bayoneted rifles, were standing on the pavement; and as we hurried away I had a feeling of naked contact with filthiness that I had never had before and have rarely had since, except when reading of executions.

But when I opened the *Times* on that January morning I didn't doubt for a moment what was coming: I knew that war, some time or other during the next ten years or so, was all but inevitable. Franci was only three or four then, and I saw very vividly the London of eleven years later; and before the month was out I had bought Brimpton. And now what I had felt to be my duty as a publisher took a new turn. Before, it had been a question of enlightening people, in a general sort of way, about the causes of war: now it was a question of preventing a war that was just round the corner. Sense of urgency gave way to maddened feverishness: no more than a split second, now, in which to pull up one's feet from the quagmire!

I must draw a distinction at this point between my attitude in the middle thirties to the hypothetical Hitlerite war and my attitude twenty years earlier to the Kaiser's actual one. Not that I took an innocent or man-in-the-street view of the second conflict any more than I had of the first. I already felt about it, before it came, much as I was to feel about it when, in 1941, I answered Lord Vansittart with *Shall our Children Live or Die?* Politically, to make another of those false distinctions, I saw it in the light of the recent economic crisis (for which the world had been to blame, not Germany alone) and of the peculiar incidence of that crisis on German economics: an incidence that had largely resulted from allied policy during the twenties, and from a panic in America which, itself the result of a maladjustment inseparable from international capitalism, had drained the German economy of credits just when they were most urgently needed. Still politically, I saw the Hitlerite menace in the light of Versailles, which was itself to be seen in the light, not only of the war it had "settled", but of a whole succession of previous ones—with now one nation guilty, in the immediate sense, and now another. (And let me interpose here that the whitewashing of Versailles at this time, by people who knew better, was a nauseating example of the *trahison des clercs*.) On the moral issue, I told myself (as I had told myself in 1914), there had hardly been a country that hadn't aggressed somewhere and somewhen if the prize had seemed big enough. As for psychology, the "German" character, in so far as it existed, was to be explained by a long series of events with which a high proportion of those then alive could have had nothing to do, and for some of which the Allies themselves bore a share of the blame. As for Hitler, he, like the rest of them, was the product of his environment; and, without going into the question of free-will and determinism, one could at any rate say that if innumerable circumstances, outside his control, had been different, he might have been different too.

The two cases, for all that, were not at all on all fours. If the possibility of the Kaiser imposing his will had seemed deplorable, the possibility of the Nazis imposing theirs was something you just couldn't contemplate: and my passion to prevent the one was far greater than could ever have been my passion to

M

prevent the other. There was an awful stench of evil about
Nazism that poisoned the world: it got into one's nostrils and
one's soul, and spread loathsomeness everywhere. I constantly
saw it—saw it physically, I mean, with my eyes—as a mass of
festering ulcers. And I still draw a rigid distinction between
fascism and Stalinist communism at its worst: I don't at all
agree, here again, with Rebecca West, who talks indifferently of
Nazi-fascism and communist-fascism. Their practice is often
identical—indeed the communist practice is sometimes worse
than the Nazi: the careless, almost contemptuous inhumanity
of a Russian slave-camp, for instance, is in a way more detestable than the deliberate ferocity of Belsen. But communists
don't think freedom intrinsically bad, and unfreedom good: or
peace intrinsically bad, and war good: or gentleness intrinsically bad, and ruthlessness good. The Nazis do or did. For
Stalinist communism is a *pessima corruptio optimi*—I persist in
regarding it as an (abominable) Christian heresy: Nazi-fascism
is a glorification of evil. And yet, talking like this even of
fascism, I must pull myself up. I must remind myself, in the
words of Dionysius the Areopagite, that "even he that desires
the basest life, yet in so far as he feels desire at all and feels
desire for life, and intends what he thinks the best kind of life,
so far participates in the Good."

Very well then: I felt passionate about checkmating Hitler.
But pacifism, genuine pacifism, previously asleep, was simultaneously beginning to stir. I began to wonder whether military
resistance—killing your enemy, hacking your enemy's guts out,
driving your enemy mad—could ever be right. If it *could* ever
be right, then it must be right when you used it, as in this case,
to prevent the enslavement, the utter degradation of mankind:
but could it? If the worst happened, if war came, shouldn't I
find myself a pacifist? Shouldn't I say, don't retaliate, don't
despitefully use them, don't wound, don't kill? And yet surely
to *prevent* a war that immediately threatened was demanded,
above everything, by my very hatred of war, my very hatred of
wounding and killing? By, I almost began to say—my very pacifism? But, with time so short, very few pacifists about anyhow,
and an utter inability to get at the German people, in a pacifist
way, across the totalitarian barrier, how could you possibly prevent Hitler from aggressing except by building, in opposition
to him, such a firm and united resistance as he wouldn't dare

to challenge? And how could you possibly get the nations to unite in such resistance unless they understood what the fascism really was that they were up against? So I concentrated on these methods of prevention—on explaining what fascism was, on work for a unified front: always with what I must call a semi-assumption at the back of my mind, that, if the prevention didn't "come off", then we must fight. I think semi-assumption is the correct word. The fact is that I never really faced the issue: or rather, I *avoided* facing it with a sort of unconscious deliberation. Throwing myself into the work of prevention by the methods explained, to the exclusion of everything else, I held in suspense, so to speak, the sufficiently obvious fact that those methods implied, given their failure to prevent war—implied in a logic that was also honour—just the violent resistance that I was on the point of repudiating: and implied, in any event, rearmament. This is the sort of muddle I was in. The best that can be said of it—and I say it with pleasure, never having been one of those who turn with fury or resentment on their previous selves, or never when reasonably sane—is that it wasn't an ignoble muddle.

I am not going here into the history of my political publishing (or of the political activity that was bound up with it) during the phase in question, for I want to deal fully with that, together with communism in general and my relation alike to communism and communists, in another volume. I need only recall now that nine considerations impelled my activity: (1) We must prevent war; (2) we could do it only by uniting as many nations as possible in opposition to Hitler; (3) in view of Germany's geographical position, if of that alone, the Soviet Union, France and Great Britain must be the core of any effective combination; (4) no such unity was conceivable unless these peoples and their regimes learned to understand one another; (5) no such unity was conceivable, either, without unity at home—a unity of all anti-fascists, from communists at one extreme to a section of conservatives at the other (I am writing in shorthand: communism and conservatism may or may not be extremes in relation to a particular set of circumstances, the essential extremes being totalitarian disrespect for personality and Christian liberalism—though that is shorthand too); (6) domestic unity was demanded, also, by the need for preventing such a triumph of indifference, or even of pro-fascism, here in Britain itself, as would encourage Hitler to strike; (7) this triumph could be further obstructed by (a) the indifferent becoming anti-fascists, and (b) anti-fascists growing keener, more active; (8) the prerequisite for such a change was a greater understanding of what fascism meant by way of internal bestiality and external aggression; and (9) to effect this understanding, an exposé of fascism must be supplemented by an exposé of its opposite— of the socialism that has for pith and marrow, or alas! (as I must now say) ought to have, the ideal of international brotherhood.

These were the ideas, then, that lay behind the foundation of the Left Book Club. "The aim of the Left Book Club is a simple one," ran its prospectus. "It is to help in the terribly urgent struggle *for* world peace and *against* fascism, by giving, to all who are willing to take part in that struggle, such knowledge as will immensely increase their efficiency." To prevent war— first and always: to do so by checkmating the country, or regime rather, that threatened it: to hinder a spread of the neurosis that informed this regime: and to use *knowledge* as the weapon—to bring hidden things to light, to expound theory, to reveal practice—it was this, and this alone, that moved me in those midthirty days when the Spanish war had just started, and fascism had made its first major bid for the conquest of the world. That we launched the Left Book Club within weeks of Franco's arrival on the mainland was by no means accidental, for the danger of a second world war had suddenly grown more imminent. But my attitude to the conflict in Spain was ambivalent. I supported the Republicans, of course: I tried to pump up enthusiasm— within myself, I mean—for the International Brigade: but my heart was cold. There was nothing in me, not a trace, of the "Thank God we can now have a smack at 'em" sort of feeling that elated so many anti-fascists in those days. I saw the dead and the dying too vividly.

I want to re-emphasise the words peace and knowledge that I used just now. The Left Book Club made many blunders. It was in its way a terrific movement, with a great surge and drive about it of a kind that makes steadiness difficult. More and more, as time went on, the immediate objective—a united front, at home and abroad, to prevent war—loomed as of an importance so overwhelming that one was trapped, or trapped oneself, into committing many sins by the way (even within the assumption on which the Left Book Club was based), if of omission, on the whole, rather than of commission. It is clear now, for instance, that the communists were far more influential in the Club than they ought to have been, if indeed this could have been avoided; and, in spite of all pressures from Club opinion, the immensely difficult problem of suppressing nothing about the Soviet Union, while avoiding all danger of hamstringing the movement—with such an objective!—or even of killing it, should somehow have been solved. (I write "suppressing nothing", for I don't at all mean that we lied, or I at any rate didn't; but there is such a thing as saying to oneself—about truth— "thou shalt not kill; but needst not strive officiously to keep alive.") Further: I personally allowed myself—to anticipate in a single sentence the full discussion I am reserving for another volume—to get into a false position, intellectually, with the communist movement itself: which I can express perhaps by saying that for about fifteen months I was as close to the communists as one hair to another and that for every minute of those months I was billions of light years away from them —as I have been all my life. But sitting here in this peaceful library, so remote from all that turmoil—with Berdyaev's "Dream and Reality" on the shelves just opposite, and Milton on my right, and the trees outside—I can say this with as clear a conscience as a man can ever have: I worked for nothing but peace, and if I now see that the total effect of our campaign was to some degree propagandist, in the bad sense, rather than enlightening—but not, I think, to a significant one, on any long view of the final effect it was to have on people: for what we did fundamentally was to shake them up and make them think, so that presently they thought for themselves and took their own course—if I now see the propaganda that marred us, I rarely saw it then (I am still speaking only of the period up to Munich), or rather the moments when I did see it were quickly lost in the flood of tidal urgency that was sweeping me, forever onward, towards the shore of my desire. Do I whitewash myself? Perhaps, or perhaps not: who am I to decide?

I want to say something else. *Within the limits of a non-pacifist view*, the Left Book Club or Popular Front tactic was the only possible one. If support had been strong enough it would probably have prevented the war: nothing else could have done so. (As for pacifism: however rapidly it had increased in many of, or all, the threatened countries, one can hardly believe either that Hitler would have been deterred by it, or that it could have become sufficiently widespread and firmly rooted during those very few short years as to issue, over a large enough area, in Gandhian resistance—not that this can make a genuine pacifist any less of a pacifist.) And it very nearly *was* strong enough. Mr Churchill's adherence might have been decisive, and there was thought to be a chance of it. I remember very vividly hanging about over a crucial week-end at a Fleet Street pub, while he seriously considered, or so it was said, putting his name to a memorial that begged for closer understanding, or a greater effort to achieve it, with the U.S.S.R. He replied, however, that anything he could do he must do in the House of Commons. Or so again it was said—the whole thing may have been a myth. For the rest, what a galaxy of speakers we had at those huge or tiny meetings that became ever more numerous as catastrophe approached! I could fill many pages of this letter with no more than a selection of their names. To mention only half a dozen or so, there were Wilfrid Roberts and Dick Acland for the Liberals: Bob Boothby for the Tories: Harry Pollitt and Palme Dutt for the Communists: Stafford Cripps, Nye Bevan, Russell Strauss and Ellen Wilkinson for Labour: Eleanor Rathbone, independent: and Harold Laski and John Strachey for the Left Book Club itself. And there was the Dean of Canterbury.

I'm going to give myself the pleasure, at this point, of attempting a little portrait of the Dean—"th' bloooody red arse of a dean", as one of the comrades, I regret to say, used to call him. I feel the urge to do so because I spent such a lot of time and thought last night over the bit about my muddle in the thirties— I was four and a half hours over a couple of pages of manuscript, which means about a page of print—that I want to refresh myself with the Dean, who requires no thought at all. Of course I can speak of him only as I knew him in those comparatively remote days, and as I have deduced him in the interval from what I happen to have heard or read: the last time I had any direct contact with him was very early in the war, when he suddenly made an unannounced visit to Brimpton, no doubt prompted by the brethren, in an effort to persuade me to associate myself with an idiotically thin communist manœuvre called "The People's Convention". Anything with "people" in it, at that time, signified communist to a *cognoscento*.

I don't know the Dean's ancient history: but he was a man, in the early nineteen-thirties, full up to the brim with (a) a passion for decent living, which he saw as demanded by his Christianity, and (b) a mania for panaceas. I'm not attacking him for the latter—at various times of my life I've had a similar mania myself, a bit modified by a hovering scepticism; and as for the former, all it meant was that his Christianity was genuine. I daresay he was a lot of other things too, indeed he certainly was, as was shortly to become apparent; but let us isolate these two leading characteristics, for a moment, from everything else in his make-up, and also from all sorts of urges which no doubt partly explained them. In other words, let us refrain from psychoanalysing him.

It is beautifully revealing that, just before I got to know him, he had been a fanatical Douglasite or social-creditor. Social credit was a panacea if there ever was one: it combined a frightening mathematical formulation, which he understood, I daresay, very much better than I did, with what was, in essence, an almost ludicrously simple contrivance for abolishing human ills: as if the world were a faulty machine, and you could get it to function by manipulating a knob or improving a lever. (The Dean, as he was fond of remarking, had been trained as an engineer.) But he grew dissatisfied with Douglasism. It was too negative for him, had too little to do with morals: he was a Christian first and an engineer second, and the Christian in him defeated the engineer. So he began looking about, and he found what he wanted in the Soviet Union. Marxist communism, also, was a panacea: hung about though it might be with a massive and intimidating paraphernalia—historical materialism, dialectics, surplus value, the freedom of necessity, and so on—yet the thing in its bareness, and considered as a device for reforming the world, was as simply mechanical a conjuring-trick as social credit itself. But, from the Dean's point of view as a Christian, his new love had this advantage over his old: he saw Russia as attempting, not merely, in a negative way, to remove a defect that made society immoral, but rather, in a positive way, to build a moral society. Thus the Christian and the engineer were reconciled.

So far, so good. But the Dean was destroyed (for if his

make-up had been only a little different he might have become a
great man) by a number of tragic defects, many of which merge
into one another. By spiritual pride: by intellectual arrogance,
coupled with a brain not of quite the first order: by vanity: by
the temptations—or rather by a lack of resistance when
assailed by the temptations—inherent in a magnificent presence: by an absence of mental scrupulosity or pernicketiness:
and, certainly not least, by his ability as an actor. What an
actor the man was! I see him, with the eye of imagination,
as conning his speeches for hours before a cheval-glass: but
when he came to deliver them they gave an irresistible impression of bubbling spontaneity. There was a little trick—I must
have assisted at it dozens of times—that he was specially fond
of and never failed to bring off. He would be describing the
spotless purity of Soviet morals ("I was walking one day down
a great broad street in Kiev: thē *boys* were walking *up* one side
of it, thē *girls*—*down* the other: there was *no* barging, *no* horseplay") and would come, in due course, to a personal experience. It-was-thís. (Something extraordinary is happening; I am
beginning to mimic his tone of voice as the sentences—my own,
not his—come to shape in my head.) He was out in Moscow
one midnight; but amazingly—what might *not* have happened
in a capitalist country?—he was sexually unmolested. But that
wasn't all. "Don't imagine," he would continue, "that I was
protected by my clerical appearance. I wasn't dressed in gaiters;
I was dressed"—and then he would hesitate: give the impression of fumbling about in an effort to make himself clear:
suddenly smile as if he had found what he wanted: point his
finger, and say: "like that charming young man in thē front
row there." The audience was always delighted—and still
more by the sequel: "But in Warsaw," he would continue, in
a tone of mingled horror and contempt, "ha! in thē very shadow
of the Cathedral I was accósted by a wóman!"

His gestures were masterly. His hands and his legs (gaitered)
were exploited to equal effect, sometimes separately and sometimes together. A delightful example of the togetherness was
the careful set-piece in which he poured scorn on the bourgeois
depreciation of Soviet technology. Some Soviet airmen had
recently done a flight from Moscow to America, an unusual
feat, it appeared, at that time. "Ha!" would say the Dean,
"they tell you in this country that thē Soviet airplanes are tied

up with bits of string. Then can they explain"—by this time he had quietly manœuvred himself to the extreme right-hand side of thē platform—"how an airplane tied up with bits of string could take off from Moscow, and then go úp" (hand straight out)—"úp"—(hand at head)—"úp" (hand near heaven) "and óver—óver—óver" (he was half-way across thē platform now) "and at last dówn—dówn—dówn" (hand back at side, body near the left-hand wings) "in Ămérica?"

His most effective use of a moving-hands-and-stationary-legs ensemble was for illustrating the contrast between capitalist and Soviet economics. "In *capitalist* countries," he would not so much say as sing, with a depreciatory trough on the "cap" of capitalist, "*wages* are going down—down—down, *prices* up—up—up" (hand at suitable positions): "in thē Soviet Union" (with a slow, wistful smile of delighted incredulity) "*wages* are going up—up—up, *prices* down—down—down." A pantomime followed that I always think of as his masterpiece. "Butter—two-thirds-of-thē-price." He raised his hand, with a rather noble deliberation, high above his head, held it there for a moment, brought it suddenly and rapidly down to the level of his nose, and then performed a sort of horizontal *vibrato* with it in the air. "Stockings—half-thē-price." His hand was raised as before, but brought down for the *vibrato*, as he stooped a bit, to his middle. "Eggs—ā-quarter-thē-price!" Crouching low, he *vibrato'd* on the floor. To compare smallish things with colossal ones, it was rather like the deaf Beethoven conducting, according to a famous description: "At the *piano* passages he sank upon his knee, at the *forte* he leaped up, so that his figure, now shrinking into that of a dwarf, disappeared under the desk, and then stretched up far above it like a giant, his hands and arms working as though, with the beginning of the music, a thousand lives had entered every member."

He had a wonderful stock peroration. The heart of it was a moving account of a play he had once seen in Moscow—quite recently in fact—called "Thē Black Boy and thē Mún-ky": the excellent burden of it being that black boys, white boys and monkeys are all equal. "And I came away from that theatre saying to myself 'This is Sunday'—and it was [I never quite understood what "and it was" added]: 'yet nowhere in Chris-tendom is so Christian a sermon being preached.'" When, after a few months of this, some busybody informed him that the

N

theatre had been closed down and the dramatist liquidated as deviationist and even counter-revolutionary, he was torn, I imagine, between loyalty to the party line and more personal considerations: for where could he find a substitute so effective? But of course loyalty won.

The applause as he resumed his seat was always deafening, and he would acknowledge it, as I have never seen anyone else do, like a prima donna. After letting it run its course for a properly adequate length of time but not a dangerous one— dying fires must be replenished—he would rise from his place in a tentative and deprecatory manner and bow charmingly from side to side. You expected to see a liveried attendant coming up with the flowers, or a lady who understood singing, or at any rate physical distinction, throwing a bouquet from a box.

The applause by members of the communist party and fellow-travellers, when they hear something they want to hear, is indeed like nothing on this earth. The reception of a Churchill as the saviour of his country is like the scratching of a cicala in comparison.

Now this sort of thing is very bad for a man with the Dean's characteristics. It goes to his head: or, to vary the metaphor, he can't bring himself to say anything or do anything that will rob him of his drug. I watched the process happening. Apart from this, he was a man specially doomed by another set of characteristics to suffer the alchemy-in-reverse that changes so many noble-hearted communists, but not by any means all, into intellectual and spiritual automata. I touched on this earlier. It is partly a question of religious loyalty: it is partly a question of such pressure—pressure by group public opinion— as only characters of exceptional moral courage can withstand: and it is partly that a human being who will adhere for more than a year or two to such a disciplined orthodoxy as that inherent in the communist movement may already (may, not must) have an element of unfreedom in him which the ortho-doxy and discipline will tend to deepen into moral serfdom. And so a moment arrives for the majority of these people (however honest they may be at one level of honesty, and they are often, at that level, quite exceptionally honest) when they simply cannot think for themselves: the party line really has become the truth for them. I recall an episode in my own office on September the so and so (I forget the exact date, though it ought to be a famous one) 1939. The day before, a communist girl—a very dear and good girl, whom I greatly loved—had upbraided me for not being pro-war enough. "Of course I know you support the war," she said, "but you don't seem as passionate about it as you used to be about the pre-war, anti-Hitlerite campaign." That night the party line changed. Next morning she came to see me again. "How *can* you support the imperialist war?" she asked. "I hadn't expected it of you." And I am quite certain that everything prior to the change of party line had completely vanished from her consciousness.

So the Dean has become what he has become. He recently returned from China, after investigating a communist charge that America had "unleashed"—this was probably the word—bacteriological warfare. I had felt, for my own part, pretty neutral about the truth of this matter. I can't for the life of me see why people who think nothing of burning the marrow out of their enemies with napalm bombs should feel so indignant at the idea that they could possibly infect them with paratyphoid, which is much less painful—and as for official denials, governments always deny everything. But I was persuaded by the Dean that there could be nothing in it. He brought back evidence that wouldn't have convinced a moron, to say nothing of an ordinary, non-communist human being with a brain the calibre of his own.

And yet I must end by saying this. Hewlett Johnson, for all that he has become, is still a great deal more religious, in the best sense, than many Churchmen far above him in the hierarchy. For he still passionately cares about *something*, which he sees, with however darkened a consciousness, as millenial: those others are mere business men and functionaries.

§ 3

I come now to Munich in this autobiography of my pacifism. What happened to me then was very simple and almost commonplace, for it must be happening all the time to people everywhere; and yet I wonder, Timothy, whether I shall find, many hours hence, that I have wretchedly failed to make you free of it. I am afraid so. But I must try my best: I must weigh anchor, and leave the shore.

May I, perhaps, in fear and trembling at my presumption, say the following? Or may I, rather, instead of saying something, ask something?

God's grace: does it sometimes operate, I wonder, by calling out, to counterbalance a particular degree of error (the error we name evil), a corresponding degree of devotion to truth—of that desire to live in harmony with τò ὄν, with the real, with God himself, which we name goodness? The words "corresponding degree" are the ones I want to stress. I mean something like this, to speak anthropomorphically, and to give the supreme example: God may think it sufficient, in an ordinary case of a man being wronged, to give him grace *not to hate* the one who wrongs him; but if the very best man in the world is to be submitted to the worst possible agony and the last degradation . . . is to be crucified . . . for being what he is, then there is only one answer—he must *love* the ones who wrong him, who crucify him: and God gives him the grace to do so. And we see, if that be true, not only why this answer and no other must proceed from the crucified one, but also why the crucified one has had to be, from the beginning, no other than the very best man in the world, or Christ: for it is only the best that can fully and finally answer the worst—can clear away every mist, so that the sun may shine forth with its splendour undimmed. And we can even see perhaps, in a glass very darkly, why his crucifiers, who are also God's children, have to be what they are and to crucify him: not that the scriptures may be fulfilled, but that the way may be shown for eliminating that separateness, involving evil or error, which is a necessary stage on the road to a unity no longer of undifferentiation but of differentiated particulars. And if Christ is indeed God himself, who is all reality, then his acceptance of crucifixion, and his response to it, must mean—still more patently than could otherwise be manifest—that enmity and hatred are non-sense.

It seems dreadful to speak of my own case after that, and I can do so at all only because I believe it to be a very common one. What happened was this. The intensification of evil in the summer and early autumn of 1938—the fact that evil, and indifference to it, were reaching out in ever widening eddies

and seeping down ever more deeply into men's souls—suddenly
spoke to me and said, as it must have spoken and said to
countless others: "Nothing in the world is strong enough to
withstand all this evil but goodness: and the essence of goodness
is to be good for the sake of goodness, and not for the sake of
withstanding the evil." Everything that had occupied me
publicly during the preceding few years, when the degree of
evil had been smaller, or my awareness of it less vivid: all my
ideas and activities and aspirations, now seemed, in a moment
—not good enough. And everything that I had *been*, privately,
all my life—this seemed something worse than not good enough,
it seemed fellow to the evil that was agonising me. I use the
distinction between "public" and "private" partly because that
is how the thing struck me, partly because it is a real distinction
(the distinction between giving alms and supporting measures
for the abolition of poverty, which remains a distinction for
all that an integrated personality, doing one, will also inevitably do the other), and partly because, not being an integrated
personality, I responded differently to what was said to me in
my public and in my private capacity—with a large element
of compromise in my public capacity, with none at all, within
the limitations of my human and personal weakness, in my
private one. And if the claim "none at all" seems too arrogant,
wait, and you will see what I mean.

So far as the public capacity was concerned, it was the Left
Book Club and the whole political activity revolving round it
that I stared at afresh. And I saw—how shall I say what I
want to?—something rather wicked about it, mixed up with a
great deal that was good: an element of Hitlerism, almost, in
reverse: a degree of contamination by this thing it was fighting, inseparable from the fact that it was *fighting* this thing
(then should one, ah! should one be *fighting*, in that sense, at
all?): some breeding of evil passions, as well as of noble ones:
and a certain encroachment of the mechanical—of the brute,
runaway quality of a vast machine—on the spiritual. And I
was both frightened and ashamed by what I saw.

I began publishing my thoughts on September 22nd, the
day of Mr Chamberlain's second visit to Herr Hitler. What I
emphasised, in an editorial written for the *Left News* while
those conversations were going on, was that, if war came, there
must be no trace of the wrong sort of war feeling—nothing but

sympathy and compassion for the people of the fascist countries: and that we must avoid above anything a struggle *à outrance* and the curse of another Versailles. But it was in "Thoughts after Munich", on October 20th, that I gave expression most fully to everything in my heart and mind that I had so far really faced. I want to print a lengthy extract from that editorial.

"The events leading up to Munich," I wrote, "Munich itself, and most of all the situation in which we find ourselves as a result of Munich, have inevitably led to a searching re-examination of policies, values and ideas. In comparatively—however comparatively—normal times one inevitably considers day by day only the necessary *application* of basic principles, which one has already firmly accepted: but those three days, September 28th, 29th and 30th—the day on which (with the knowledge we then had) world war seemed inevitable to most of us, the day on which we were awaiting a statement from Munich, and the day on which we knew that fascism at one blow had been enormously strengthened—produced, at any rate in me, something of what I imagine happens to a man on his death-bed: the most ruthless self-criticism, and a determination to achieve an honesty as great as is humanly possible. As a result, there has been a strengthening of beliefs already held, but some shifting of emphasis.

"The examination must first touch the Left Book Club itself. The Club was founded two and a half years ago with a simple aim: 'to help in the terribly urgent struggle for peace and a better social and economic order, and against fascism, by giving, to all who are willing to play their part in that struggle, such *knowledge* as will immensely increase their efficiency.' In other words the Left Book Club set out as an *educational* body—an implied result of such education being to convert thoughtless and apathetic men and women into eager, active and self-directing citizens. This weapon of education was to be used for the purpose of reaching two positive goals— the preservation of peace, and the creation of a juster social order: and one negative one—defence against fascism. I put it in that way, but it is clear that the three goals are one."

There follows a long section dealing with the growth of propaganda in the bad sense, and here there is an echo of my

Repton experience. I continued, and now the echo rings stronger:

"Let me say at once that I take my full share of responsibility for those developments in the wrong direction of which I now see a danger, and which I am terribly anxious to prevent. Passionately believing in certain ideas, I have allowed myself, I think, to become too much of a propagandist and too little of an educator. I would go further and say that my eagerness to express certain ideas has, in the rush of day-to-day work, tended to overlay what I hope I have never forgotten: namely, that only by the *clash* of ideas does a mind become truly free, and that no mind not free can have that utter conviction which will render it immune to any assault of passing circumstance. I think it right to add that in my view the publications of the Club have tended to concentrate overmuch (though by no means exclusively) on two or three points of view, and to forget that any author has a place in our ranks, provided only that his work is of value in the struggle 'for peace and a better social and economic order, and against fascism.'

"We have had, to be sure, great and genuine difficulties in this matter. To take only one example, we have published very few books by Liberals: and certainly from time to time we have made strenuous efforts to increase the number of such contributions. But I ask myself—might not we have succeeded in these efforts if we had really been determined to overcome all obstacles?

"It is by no means to be inferred that, because I have said all this, I am personally less of a socialist than I was. On the contrary, Munich has made me, if possible, more of a socialist than I was, and more anxious than ever to explain, in my own writings and through my firm's publications, the need for socialism. But, with fascism rampant, we have to fight the battle of the French Revolution all over again; and to fight it here and now is every bit as important as to work for socialism itself.

"There is another consideration—and it is by no means the least important. There is in the world today a terrible spirit of lying, and false propaganda, and violence, and unscrupulousness, and mob hysteria. These are above all the marks of fascism: and Munich has enormously strengthened their power abroad and is likely also to strengthen their power at home. It seems to me that one of the paramount necessities of our time is to preserve what is menaced by this evil. No one knows better than I how partial is our democracy, how circumscribed is our freedom. No one is more bitterly resentful than I that the freedom of the unemployed is the freedom to rot in unemployment. But for all that the spirit of our civilisation is something totally different, so far at least, from the spirit of fascism: and I believe myself that, as a result of Munich, the importance of preserving this spirit is overwhelming.

"I have often quoted at Left Book Club meetings that famous passage from *Mein Kampf* in which Herr Hitler explains the Nazi doctrine of propaganda: 'The object of propaganda is not the weighing of various points of view, but the exclusive emphasising of one. It should not aim at telling the truth, if it is favourable to the other side, nor should it present facts as they are to the people. If propaganda allows even a glimmer of justice to the other side, doubts will immediately arise as to the justice of its own cause.'

"With such methods we can have nothing to do. Not only are they *unnecessary*, because our case is a true case: I believe they are *wrong*, in that they carry within them the seeds of their own destruction. They mean death: and the human spirit craves for life.

"To be a bulwark, then, of truth and scrupulosity, of respect for other people's opinions, and of utter freedom of thought and discussion, must be one of the main tasks of the Left Book Club in the months and years to come. In this sign we shall conquer: without it, we have half lost to fascism already.

"No Left Book Club member will, I think, reply that 'the end justifies the means' . . . [For] at the present time, and in particular in the post-Munich era, when fascist ideas (which, while they spring out of the economic soil, have acquired, in my view, completely independent life of their own) are stalking through the world, the vigilant defence, moment by moment, of the values thus attacked must be in the forefront of our aims. And any employment on our side of such methods, *whatever* the purpose, would be to weaken that defence.

"I want to say one word more in this connection, and I say it with great hesitation, because it must necessarily sound pharisaical. There can be no member of the Left Book Club who hates and detests fascism more than I do: I hate it as a Jew, but I hate it, infinitely more, simply as a man, who sees everything decent and human being trampled underfoot by it. But, hating fascism, I do not hate fascists: and just because hatred, not only of ideas but of persons, is a mark of fascism, and just because fascism has been so immensely strengthened, I believe it to be necessary, if we are to fight fascism, that there should be no hatred of persons in our hearts.

"I want now to revert to the main theme of this article—the necessity for *thought* by Left Book Club members: and to speak about its bearing on the present situation, national and international.

"In the short period that has elapsed since Munich, Herr Hitler has extended and consolidated his power with almost incredible rapidity. I wish I believed that this threat of fascism to the world could be met by the simple method of pacifism. I cannot believe it—not for a moment. This article would become impossibly long if I attempted to give my reasons: but I should like to repeat here what I have said on many former occasions during the last two and a half years, namely, that progressives opposed to pacifism should feel far more closely akin to pacifists than to imperialists, however true it may be that certain immediate policies of the latter coincide with certain immediate policies of our own.

"In my view, then, it is literally a matter of life and death that in the face of the Hitlerite menace we should make ourselves strong—not so that we may defend ourselves against the world (how is such a thing even possible?) but so that we may play our just part in a recreated system of collective security. But having said this, I want to say something else that I regard as not one whit less important: and the failure to say it, which I find widespread, indicates that failure of *thought* of which I have been writing.

"If we *simply* re-arm, if we *simply* shout anti-fascist slogans, if we *simply* declaim about 'defence of the Empire', then, in Professor Tawney's fine phrase, 'Hitlerism has already conquered in our souls'. There is, in fact, a most grave and pressing danger: that, because Hitler is Hitler, we should get into the habit of regarding with equanimity a war against *him*. I don't mean that I think there is a single person in this country who at the moment, consciously or unconsciously, *desires* war: but

I do think that, not a desire, but an unconscious *acceptance*, of war may creep into some people's minds, unless they remind themselves day by day and hour by hour what war would mean. It would mean years and perhaps decades of agony and degradation and stupidity.

"I have been asked [I meant I had been asking myself]: 'Isn't your insistence on the evil and horror of war inconsistent with your plea for collective security? Collective security implies, in the last resort, readiness to go to war. Or is it all bluff? And do you intend, if your bluff is called, to run away?'

"This is a bona fide argument that requires full-length treatment, and I hope to deal with it in a later article. Suffice it to say here that I think collective security, *combined with a positive peace policy*, gives us far the biggest hope of *preventing* war: we must therefore work for it: and if war nevertheless were to come, despite collective security, it would have to be gone through with, immeasurably evil and degrading though it would be.

"You hear people say 'There are only two possibilities. One is war: the other is the creeping of fascism, without what is ordinarily called war, over a great part of the civilised world.' This is defeatism of the worst kind. We *dare* not say 'One or the other'. We *must* say 'Neither'.

"What does saying 'Neither' in practice mean?

"It means this. Side by side with the negative and sterile, though necessary, business of making ourselves militarily strong to resist fascism, we must so strengthen the positive forces working, not merely *against* fascism, but *for* the things fascism menaces, that there is an ever growing good counterpoised over against the fascist evil—a good that will increase and encroach as fascism is now encroaching, and will ultimately conquer, by peace and not by the sword.

"That is what I call a positive, a constructive peace policy: and isn't it something fine enough to claim every bit of work, every bit of devotion, every bit of optimism we can summon to the task?"

I ended by giving examples of such a policy in some detail: at home, freedom of speech, and a determined attack on the poverty and unemployment then so widespread and so visibly degrading; abroad—a great educational campaign in explana-

tion of democratic ideas: planning for abundance "by offering
to share with others the resources that are available in our vast
colonial territories" (I was quoting Stafford Cripps): and freedom for India. My concluding words expressed the hope that
we might still play our part "in saving the world from the two
scourges which I bracket together as the most terrible mankind
can know—war and fascism."

While re-reading "Thoughts After Munich" this last half
hour I have been comparing it with what I know was going
on in me about the time I was writing it; and I have done so
with a curious emotion. There are no positive, or obtrusively
conscious, dishonesties in it, I think; and the emotional balance,
throughout, is on the right side. It is clear where my heart was
—there is more real conviction in my plea for sympathy with
pacifists than in the insistence on collective security that follows
it; and I did at last face what I'd previously held in suspense—
that you couldn't say "Collective security is the only way to
prevent war" without answering the question "Yes, but what
are you going to do if it fails? Are you going to fight or not?"
But I was still dreadfully muddled, and still shirking: never
more obviously than when excusing myself from a discussion
of pacifism on the ground that space didn't permit.

What it comes to is this. The division—between the something
in my nature knowing good to be demanded unconditionally,
and the something ready to do evil that good might come of
it—was not yet healed. But I was already a stage further
towards the healing of it: and that it would eventually be
healed—that the myth would disappear in the sun of reality:
that, in the matter of peace and war, I should become, without
qualification or reservation, a pacifist—was now inevitable.
The process was not a quick one: it took from Munich to a few
months ago.

The inevitability was increased, if the solecism may be for-
given, by the change in my private life that the impact of
Munich effected. Or the development, rather than the change:
for the seed had been there from the beginning, pushing up
towards the light with a terrible amount of misdirection, but
pushing up, none the less, even in the very worst of my un-
kindnesses to my father or of my self-righteous egoisms. Does

this, I wonder, sound smug? I fear so; but I assure you I don't feel the least little bit smug, as I reflect on how little has come of it all in now pretty nearly fourteen years. And yet I am immeasurably grateful for the little that *has* come of it: and I shall proceed.

"And he said, Go forth, and stand upon the mount before the Lord. And, behold, the Lord passed by, and a great and strong wind rent the mountains, and brake in pieces the rocks before the Lord; but the Lord was not in the wind: and after the wind an earthquake; but the Lord was not in the earthquake; and after the earthquake a fire; but the Lord was not in the fire: and after the fire a still small voice. And it was so, when Elijah heard it, that he wrapped his face in his mantle, and went out, and stood in the entering in of the cave. And, behold, there came a voice unto him, and said, What doest thou here, Elijah?"

The Lord was not *in* the wind, or the earthquake, or the fire: not *in* the tempestuous political movements, which, however, properly and inevitably accompanied his passing—as did also the fascism (and now the Stalinist communism) they opposed: the Lord was *in* the still, small voice—in that smallest of all things, in that grain of sand which is also eternity, the individual human soul. And the voice said: "What doest thou here, Elijah?" What doest *thou* here, Elijah? What doest *thou* here, Victor?

I looked within. I am not going to catalogue what I found there—the faults of conduct, the weaknesses of character, the sins of commission and of omission, and the rest; for I want to avoid, if I can, being smug in reverse. Everything boiled down to selfishness or egoism in one form or another. And I knew this: if I tried to be better myself, if I tried to be, humbly and not wilfully, a channel for goodness, I should be answering evil with a directness not otherwise possible, with an absoluteness that evil itself could not sully—however minute or non-existent the temporal effect of this might be: but *unless* I tried, I should be a traitor—however passionate my loyalty to anti-fascism, or the prevention of war, or "ethical principles", or any of the rest of it. I did not fall into the error, for it is a dreadful error, of becoming quietistic, of abandoning politics and public affairs; but these took on in my mind, from that moment, a quality of relativism, of temporality, which (despite the paramount importance of never shirking temporalities in a temporal world) could be healthy and saving only if everyone engaged in them lived his own private life, every minute of the time, in a way as little out of harmony with goodness as might be possible for him. And "every individual" meant, again unless I was to be a traitor, myself. I needn't go on to point out the connection of all this with my "Thoughts After Munich", or a more general connection: namely, between the changes in me (a) as a private person, and (b) on the level of public affairs.

I can best sum up these changes by recalling a few sentences I wrote in *Tim I*, when dealing with my attitude to my father: "This is not to imply," I said, "that my embryo Christian morality was merely theoretical. The essence of it, on the contrary, was precisely that it was not theoretical. Morality, I believed, must engage a man's whole life; and in one sense it engaged the whole of mine. But not in the final sense, not in the only sense that ultimately matters. I had still to learn that what finally matters is not the *about* what but the *from* what: that an intellectual understanding of what goodness consists in, however just, and a desire for the triumph of that goodness, however genuine, and a determination to bring about that triumph, however passionate, are not yet in that order of reality where a single pure impulse lives eternally: that all battles are shadow battles except the battle a man fights in the innermost citadel of his own being: that until he has won this battle he is useless either as a sheet of glass for the flooding in of good to the universe or as a sheet of iron for the shutting out of evil: and that something must happen to him, some free acceptance of an offered grace, before this battle can be won. 'Except a man be born of water and the Spirit, he cannot enter into the Kingdom of Heaven.' This is why love is not love unless it can love, without taking thought, the unloving: this is why tolerance is not tolerance unless it can tolerate, without taking thought, intolerance. I was to learn all this, many years later, at the time of Munich. I know it now, but barely have the power to live in accordance with the knowledge; for still the old Adam is very strong within me."

I am anxious that you should draw no false conclusions from anything I have been saying during the last two hours or so, and from one phrase in particular, namely: "I responded differently to what was said to me in my public and in my private capacity —with a large element of compromise in my public capacity, with none at all, within the limitations of my human and personal weakness, in my private one." All I mean is that I faced to some extent, but not as honestly as I was able, what I was doing in my public life, but did face as honestly as I was able how I was living in my private one. Or so I think, in both cases. But, even in the latter of them, I did nothing very heroic about it. I didn't aspire to be a saint—well, I suppose I did, from time to time, but never more than half-humorously, and never with the smallest serious hope of ever becoming one. I did not give all my possessions to the poor. But I did try, in ordinary feeling and conduct, to be a little better than I had previously been; and I did try, day by day, to remember to try. I tried, that is, to be a little more generous, a little more considerate, a little more courteous, a little more loving, a little more sympathetic, a little less self-righteous, a little less hot-headed and prone to anger: and I tried, above all, so to accept the offered grace that I might become the sort of person who no longer had to try, but was better—because he was better: because he was purer in heart.

Do I need to explain why, as I said, this change in my personal life made an eventual healing of what I have called the division in me "still more inevitable"? I do not think so. Nor will you be surprised when I tell you that, by very reason of the fact that the healing was inevitable but hadn't occurred, I now redoubled my efforts on behalf of collective security and the United Front—baskets in which were all my eggs of peace. As if miraculously, war had been staved off by Munich (and my reaction to Munich was that of Léon Blum and, I imagine, a great many other politically conscious men and women—a mixture of shame and relief, with the relief predominating; how unfair we were to Neville Chamberlain!): but the danger henceforth would be more pressing than ever—it was a matter of minutes now, it was just round the corner. My doubt as to whether collective security had ever been right—my suppressed conviction that it hadn't been—with its rearmament, and its implication that if it failed to prevent a war we must fight, made its success in preventing a war—in that at least—something to be pursued with a new, a more desperate, sense of spiritual as well as physical urgency. To have staked everything on a single morally dubious throw, and to lose into the bargain—that would be intolerable.

Between Munich and the outbreak of war eleven months later, I must have spoken almost every night in cities and villages up and down the country, and sometimes in several on a single night. A sort of fever had got hold of me. I would travel by train to wherever it was, have the car sent up, and leave in it near midnight. I remember an evening when I had been speaking at Cardiff: we set off for home in dense fog with a silver frost, and, getting to Oxford about four, put up at the Mitre and slept in our clothes for an hour or two, until the fog lifted. I would normally arrive home between three and six, have a bath, get as much rest as possible, read a huge pile of newspapers, and leave for the office at a quarter past eight. When I got there I would prepare for more meetings. The biggest of the lot was at the Empress Stadium, with twenty-three thousand in the hall, and almost as many, or that's what it looked like, in the street outside. Lloyd George was the star speaker: he had joined us at a minute before midnight, won over by Stafford Cripps. The old man sat in his car till the meeting started, smoking a Havana and turning over the pages of a carefully prepared script. He received an ovation; but I had to stop him from the chair when he was only a third of the way through, for he had already much exceeded his time. He was very benevolent about this.

§ 4

There is little to say about what followed—after the outbreak of war; or little I don't wish to defer, for it belongs in another context. I was "pro-war" throughout, though I considered, but after a momentary relief at the idea of it decisively rejected, a Peace of Amiens, which Lloyd George was advocating. I went down one afternoon to visit the old man at Churt, and discussed it with him. He was miserably defeatist, not from any pacifist motives, but because he was sure we couldn't win: he had shrunk, though I still reverenced him, as Winston had grown.

Another kind of defeatism, the "revolutionary defeatism" of the communists, infuriated me. There was no more pacifism in them than in Lloyd George, though they were ready, of course, to gang up with pacifists for their very different ends (but then I had been ready, in Popular Front days, to gang up with communists for mine). And they didn't become defeatists because they were sure we couldn't win: whatever may have been in their hearts, they got to the point of behaving as if anxious that Hitler should win. Ulbricht, now a very big noise in East Germany and then an emigré in Scandinavia, wrote a terrible article in which he contrasted British imperialism unfavourably with Hitlerism; and though I can recall nothing quite as bad as that in the propaganda put out by our British communists, they seized on any point, however grotesque, that could be utilised for whitewashing Hitler and discrediting us: and if they couldn't find one they invented it. The climax of their campaign (before Hitler attacked Stalin and turned communists everywhere into German-haters) was a horribly cruel attempt to spread "alarm and despondency" in the shelters and to sabotage fire-watching. I edited a careful documentation of their goings-on, called "The Betrayal of the Left": and am very glad I did so, for the facts are now readily available, and haven't to be dug up from old files of the *Daily Worker*. A little earlier—already in 1939—I had written a pamphlet called "Where are you Going?", which was more a plea than an exposure.

But though, once the war was there, I was as anxious as anyone that we should win—or, to put it perhaps more accurately, that Hitler shouldn't—and though I was always making efforts to tie up a Government job, and volunteered for the Home Guard (but to my relief was rejected: officially on account of eyesight, really, I think, of my name, for Newbury, our local centre, and one of the pleasantest towns in all England, is a little out of touch with such matters—and I remember, apropos, that a Tory M.P., who disliked something I'd said in his constituency, expressed disgust that a refugee from Nazi oppression should be talking like that, and refused to withdraw when Eleanor Rathbone enlightened him, but retorted "Don't split hairs: what difference can it make where the fellow was born?" A charming story is told of this Member, who was gallant, as well as honourable, in House of Commons terminology. Though a man of over sixty he had never been to Europe, but was eventually persuaded to try Paris, which he'd heard rather well spoken of. Arrived at Calais, and asked by the douanier "*Avez-vous quelque chose à déclarer, monsieur?*", he looked him up and down and replied "Speak English, my man, or not at all")—I was saying, before that enormous parenthesis, that for all my orthodoxy on the war issue my heart wasn't really in the fighting, as it never has been in any sort of fighting and never could be. To mitigate evil passions, induce a measure of historical perspective, and stop people doing things they'd afterwards regret—it was this above all that concerned me: and when, about the time I was compiling "The Betrayal of the Left", Lord Vansittart got an immense sale with "Black Record", a wicked denunciation, as I thought, of the whole German people, I replied with "Shall our Children Live or Die?", which had no comparable success. My concern for appeasement (a word, like "peace" itself, that has long been demanding rehabilitation) was intensified by what we learned, towards the end of 1942, about the gas ovens and incinerators: and this final inhumanity awoke in me with still greater immediacy and inevitability the one final answer to it. I was within an inch of pacifism. Ten years later I have become one.

There must be a purpose, in God's economy, for pacifists and resisters alike, otherwise they wouldn't be here. That of pacifists, one may think, is to keep absolutes alive in a world of relativities.

Easter Day, 1953

I thought I had finished—but the garden this morning!
Every shape of every tree, every line of every plant (the
young tendrils, the buds!), every tracery, every bird-song
. . . the mist. . . . Get accustomed to being about at the
time of this theophany, little grandson, and no one will ever
have to teach you anything about love of the creator.
Your own heart will prompt you to bow the head and bend
the knee in a free man's worship.

APPENDICES

THE PÉGUY IN ENGLISH

I don't like the man who doesn't sleep, says God.
Sleep is the friend of man.
Sleep is the friend of God.
Sleep is perhaps the most beautiful thing I have created.
And I myself rested on the seventh day.
He whose heart is pure, sleeps. And he who sleeps has a pure
    heart.
That is the great secret of being as indefatigable as a child.
Of having that strength in the legs that a child has.
Those new legs, those new souls,
And to begin afresh every morning, ever new,
Like young hope, new hope . . .
He who doesn't sleep is unfaithful to Hope.
And it is the greatest infidelity.
Because it is infidelity to the greatest Faith.
Poor children, they conduct their business with wisdom during
    the day.
But when evening comes, they can't make up their minds,
They can't be resigned to trust my wisdom for the space of
    one night
With the conduct and the governing of their business.
As if I wasn't capable, if you please, of looking after it a little.
Of watching over it.
Of governing and conducting, and all that kind of stuff.
I have a great deal more business to look after, poor people,
    I govern creation, maybe that is more difficult.
You might perhaps, and no harm done, leave your business in
    my hands, O wise men.
Maybe I am just as wise as you are.
You might perhaps leave it to me for the space of a night.
While you are asleep
At last
And the next morning you might find it not too badly damaged
    perhaps . . .
Put off until tomorrow those tears which fill your eyes and
    your head,

Flooding you, rolling down your cheeks, those tears which stream down your cheeks.

Because between now and tomorrow, maybe I, God, will have passed by your way.

Human wisdom says: Woe to the man who puts off what he has to do until tomorrow.

And I say Blessed, blessed is the man who puts off what he has to do until tomorrow.

Blessed is he who puts off. That is to say Blessed is he who hopes. And who sleeps.

A NOTE ON THE PHYSICAL
RESURRECTION OF CHRIST

I want to withdraw something I said in *Tim I*. Writing about the physical Resurrection, as distinct from the spiritual Resurrection, I suggested—while apologising for any offence I might give—that "no educated man genuinely 'believes in' it now: believes in it (without mental reservations, interpretational gymnastics, or half-conscious self-deception) in the way in which he believes, say, that cruelty is vile". I am sorry I said this, for it has hurt one or two of my friends: who justly point out that I have no warrant to make assumptions like that about other people's beliefs. So I unsay it.

I still think, however, that the physical Resurrection—by which I mean the disappearance of Christ's body, in the manner called miraculous, from His tomb—cheapens, and destroys half the wonder in, the world's greatest happening. I don't suggest for a moment that such a miracle couldn't possibly have occurred: I suggest that its occurrence would have been not only meaningless, but against meaning. It would have been dishonouring to God and to man, and to the body, God's creation, and to death, his creation no less. God took on a human body—I accept, for the purpose of argument, the orthodox dogma, than which nothing, in any case, could be more beautiful: he took on human nature: but then suddenly, in his human aspect, he absolves himself, as it were, from one of the conditions of the nature he had brought into existence and has himself now assumed—the condition, I mean, that our bodies return to the dust and become one with it. The very meaning of physical death is that the body, having worked out its usefulness, is now irrelevant. On the assumption that Christ is very God, I find something infinitely moving in the idea that His body, like yours and mine, lay mouldering in a forsaken grave till it passed into earth. That the one we love best should become worms—even this would lose part of its horror (part, because of human weakness) if Christ's body did the same. Can there be anything wrong or nasty in what may happen to her, if it happened to God? For nothing wrong or nasty can happen to God, who is all beauty and all truth.

I don't think of it as a question of whether God could have achieved such a miracle, for of course he could, but of whether he would have wanted to. We read in St Matthew: "Then the devil taketh him up into the holy city, and setteth him on a pinnacle of the temple. And saith unto him, If thou be the Son of God, cast thyself down: for it is written, He shall give his angels charge concerning thee: and in their hands they shall bear thee up, lest at any time thou dash thy foot against a stone. Jesus said unto him, It is written again, Thou shalt not tempt the Lord thy God."

THE WRITER'S THANKS, ETCETERA

THE WRITER'S THANKS

THERE ARE SEVERAL people I wish to thank for helping me with this book.

First, as always, my wife.

My secretary, Queenie Smith, did a job of typing that I should have thought incredible, were it not that she specialises in the incredible.

As to Sheila Hodges, there is nothing that I can really add to what I said about her in my note of thanks at the end of *Tim I.* In spite of having to bear the burden of our publishing business more or less single-handed during my absence in America, she nevertheless found time, somehow or other, to read the galleys with the greatest care: and at once put her finger on passages that required reconsideration. I have followed her advice in all cases but one.

David Somervell was good enough to read the Repton chapters with the closest attention, and to send me three pages of notes, all interesting and many important, for my guidance.

Others to whom I owe a special debt of gratitude are Diana and John Collins, and Harold and Hilary Rubinstein.

The Repton Librarian was so very kind as not merely to lend but to give me the print reproduced opposite page 279.

ACKNOWLEDGMENTS

THE EXTRACT WITH which the book opens is taken from *Cry Korea* by R. W. Thompson, published by Messrs Macdonald. The account of the training of commandos on page 17 is from *The Anvil* of April 1949, the writer being Norman Price. (*The Anvil*, a Christian magazine edited by the Reverend Marcus Morris, has ceased publication.) Both the French and the English versions of Péguy's poem on sleep are from his *Basic Verities*, published by Messrs Routledge and Kegan Paul. Simone Weil's *Waiting on God* is also published by Messrs Routledge and Kegan Paul: the translator is Emma Craufurd. Aldous Huxley's *Grey Eminence* is published by Messrs Chatto & Windus. Kierkegaard's *Attack on 'Christendom'* is published by the Princeton University Press in the United States and the Oxford University Press here: the translator is Walter Lowrie. Tagore's *Creative Unity* is published by Messrs Macmillan. The Turgenev story on page 110 is from *Dream Tales and Prose Poems*, published by Messrs Heinemann: the translator is Constance Garnett.

I am grateful to all concerned for granting the necessary permissions.

Permission to include poems, and extracts from poems, by John Masefield has been kindly granted by the poet and The Society of Authors.

For the short section dealing with the history of 1917 and the first half of 1918 I have drawn to some extent on articles by Captain B. H. Liddell Hart and Charles Seignobos in the *Encyclopaedia Britannica*, and on Stephen King-Hall's valuable *Our Own Times*, published by Messrs Nicholson & Watson—sometimes using the writer's words: but the interpretation that I have put upon events is my sole responsibility.

The easy arrangement by E. Pauer of "Handel's Largo" is reprinted by permission of Augener Ltd.

* * *

The description of *Fidelio*, on page 31, as "the more flesh-and-blood counterpart" of *The Magic Flute* was suggested to me by a passage in Professor E. J. Dent's great study *Mozart's Operas*.

PUBLISHER'S INFORMATION

THE THIRD INSTALMENT of this letter will probably be published during the autumn of 1954, and will be called *Last Words for Timothy*.

Printed in Great Britain by
The Camelot Press Ltd., London and Southampton